THE
TRIUMPH
OF THE
WEST

DI011063

The Triumph of the West

J. M. Roberts

LITTLE, BROWN AND COMPANY • BOSTON • TORONTO

LIBRARY
ARAPAHOE COMMUNITY COLLEGE
WITHDRAWN
SOUTH SANTA FE
LITTLETON, COLORADO 80120

COPYRIGHT © 1985 BY J. M. ROBERTS

ALL RIGHTS RESERVED. NO PART OF THIS BOOK MAY BE REPRODUCED
IN ANY FORM OR BY ANY ELECTRONIC OR MECHANICAL MEANS IN-
CLUDING INFORMATION STORAGE AND RETRIEVAL SYSTEMS WITH-
OUT PERMISSION IN WRITING FROM THE PUBLISHER EXCEPT BY A
REVIEWER WHO MAY QUOTE BRIEF PASSAGES IN A REVIEW

FIRST AMERICAN EDITION

LIBRARY OF CONGRESS CATALOGING-IN-PUBLICATION DATA

ROBERTS, J. M. (JOHN MORRIS), 1928–
  THE TRIUMPH OF THE WEST.

  INCLUDES INDEX.
  1. CIVILIZATION, OCCIDENTAL.   I. TITLE.
CB245.R57   1986   909′.09821   86-4348
ISBN-0-316-74989-3

HAL

PRINTED IN THE UNITED STATES OF AMERICA

WITHDRAWN

CONTENTS

APR 14 1987

PREFACE

This book is the outcome of a series of television programmes made for the BBC. Television and the printed word are such different media that programmes cannot simply be transcribed and set out as continuous prose. What follows is a historical essay, or group of essays, built round the same central theme as the television programmes: what is the nature of the dominance which western civilisation came, in the course of time, to exercise over virtually the whole globe? How did it come about? How does it express itself today? These are questions which have fascinated me for many years, but I have in no sense studied them exhaustively. This book is more tentative: it has no pretension to dispose of any of the themes it takes up or to exhaust scholarly argument about them. I am, too, quite ready to acknowledge that specialists will find shortcomings in what I have to say. All the same, it appears to me that there is something useful to be done in setting out certain arguments which I believe must be considered if we are to understand our own world properly. So it is without an apology for its form that I offer this book to its readers; of its shortcomings within its form, of course, I am only too aware, and I can only plead that writing a book at the same time as being a vice-chancellor of a first-class university, and taking part in the making of a television series, has left me far less time than I should have wished to pursue matters upon which I have only had time to touch, to set out fully arguments I have only been able to summarise in a bald assertion, to develop implications. I can only hope that my readers will recognise that the intention of what follows in these pages is serious, however inept its execution.

This book has not reached publication without many difficulties. I must particularly thank my editor, Mrs Susan Kennedy, for her patience with a harried author, easily irritated by them. Because of the book's connexion with the series, though, this is also a fitting place to thank those who worked with me in making the films. First come the producers: Messrs Ray Sutcliffe, Derek Towers, Denis Moriarty and Miss Ann Hummel; they extended to me many personal kindnesses, much tolerance for my ignorance of their craft, and have taught me more than they could have predicted (or will believe) of their fascinating but often intractable medium. Those who saw the films will be well aware of the skill they brought to bear and I am very grateful for it. Many a time, too, I have owed much to their personal assistants for attentions to my comfort and convenience, and I am happy to be able here to thank Mss Alex Branson, Linda Dalling, Valerie Brundle and Jane Mayes. Mr Robert McNab, Miss Joy Curtis and Miss Betka Zamoyska were assiduous and resourceful research assistants; to them, too, I extend my warm thanks. Ms Elizabeth Rowell has my deep gratitude for keeping my appearance reasonably consistent over several years, no mean task. Unhappily in so big an enterprise as this series so many people were engaged in the technical work of filming, recording, editing and dubbing that I can only single out a few colleagues with whom I was most frequently working. Through Messrs John Else, Colin Waldeck and Mike Southon I hope I can thank also the other cameramen and their assistants. Messrs Doug Mawson, John Hooper and Bruce Galloway in the same way represent the sound recordists whose skills, like those of the cameramen, have contributed so much to the best use of our time. As editors, I am particularly indebted to Jeff Shaw and Stephen Evans, who have borne the heaviest burdens, but also to Keith Raven, Richard Brunskill, Julian Miller, Keith Long and their assistants. Among my BBC colleagues, though, my deepest thanks go to our Executive Producer, Mr Christopher Martin. It was he who first opened discussions about a television series, and it was under him, at long last and amid many difficulties with which he grappled tirelessly and effectively, that our schemes came to fruition. I found him the most congenial, understanding and realistic of colleagues.

It is not only to friends and colleagues in the BBC, though, that I owe my thanks. I could not have written this or taken part in the production of the series without generous backing and support from many of my colleagues in the University of Southampton. Besides recording my thanks to the University Council and its Chairman, Sir Bernard Miller, for allowing me to spend time on this project, and to successive Deputy Vice-Chancellors who have helped to make it possible, I should like to thank two other people especially — Mr Derek Schofield, Secretary and Registrar to the University, for the many practical steps he took to ease my tasks, and Miss Sheila Evans, my secretary, whose contribution to my work was indispensable and invaluable: to both of them I am profoundly grateful. I should also like to mention a special debt to Mrs Ann Crouch, who discharged rapidly and efficiently a very large and continuing task of typing.

The heaviest charge of all in many ways was nevertheless borne by my wife and children, who for four years and more have seen far less of me than they should, and have been very patient in dealing with an often distracted husband and father. They have had a hard time; I hope that they at least will feel that this book is some small justification for all I asked of them and all they gave.

INTRODUCTION

Whatever ills and uncertainties faced individuals, it seems to have been much easier to feel optimistic about society as a whole in 1900 than it is today. Whatever qualifications they made, thinking men and women in what was called the 'civilised world' could feel in those days that things were all the time getting better and that the skills and power which went with civilisation would make sure that progress continued. Problems were being solved very quickly; those which remained looked as if they too would give way to human ingenuity, perhaps before very long. Only a highly educated few felt pessimistic as they looked at the century ahead.

That confidence went with a sense of belonging to a particular civilisation, that commonly called 'European', 'western', or the civilisation of 'the West'. Its sheer energy and power excited people. Sometimes it seemed almost as if western civilisation's main characteristic was its power to create change, but its technical ingeniousness and wealth seemed to express some deeper superiority, too. Everyone knew there had been other great civilisations in the ancient past. Some of them had survived into modern times. But nineteenth-century China, say, was usually thought of as hardly more alive than was ancient Assyria by those who belonged to the 'civilised world'. That notion stood in an implicit contrast to everything else, the *un*civilised rest of the world which, above all, did not share its dynamism.

Western civilisation had come to birth and matured in Europe, before spreading across the seas to other continents settled by Europeans. By 1900, North and South America, Australia, New Zealand and South Africa were its overseas centres and strongholds. Not all of those continents and countries reached the same levels of civilised achievement in all sides of their life. But that was true in Europe, too; it was freely admitted that in some parts of Europe — Russia, for instance, or parts of the Balkans — the process of civilisation had not gone as far as it ought to have done and that you could reasonably argue about whether they ought to be regarded as 'civilised' or not. Nor was western civilisation outside Europe confined to lands settled by Europeans, for the men of the West had been for a long time civilising the whole world in their image by means other than migration. As their ideas and institutions spread round the globe, some of them were prepared to concede that there were westernised Indians, Chinese, Africans, who could be counted as 'civilised' men. In the last two or three decades of the nineteenth century, indeed, one wholly non-western country, Japan, appeared to be joining the civilised world, accepting its standards, ideas and many of its ways. Nevertheless, around 1900 most thinking people would have broadly agreed that it was only in a 'western' world, however you might precisely define it, that true civilisation was to be found.

Over eighty years later, many now find it hard to feel so sure. Far less can they take it for granted that western civilisation will go on being the main source of mankind's future progress and well-being. Some even think it may have shot its bolt. The reasons for such misgivings are patent. We have put men on the moon but cannot find a way to give all our fellow-humans enough to eat, far less a chance of running their own lives such as many of us take for granted. Huge numbers of people seem to have no share in the wealth created by science and technology, though the mirage of it is more and more tantalisingly dangled before them. Our ability to improve the lot of the poorest sometimes seems actually to be decreasing as time goes by, yet their numbers grow and grow. Within the old European heart of the western world, too, this century has turned out to be more, much more, violent than the last. Men have killed one another, on a horrific scale, in huge world wars. Though, mercifully, Great Powers have not fought one another for nearly forty years, there has been fighting — much of it wasteful and pointless — going on somewhere almost every day since 1945. Age-old hatreds and bitterness have not been exorcised; new ones have appeared. Political passion, religious bigotry, fear, ambition and envy are as destructive as ever. New creeds only gave them fresh scope. Such forces have often caused war in past centuries, and now seem more dangerous than ever. It is conceivable that if international politics are mismanaged as they have often been mismanaged in the past, nuclear and biochemical weapons may obliterate whole peoples and much of civilisation itself.

Intellectuals in western countries seem to feel such misgivings with special intensity. Even their old faith in the technological dynamic is questioned. Material progress has never been so swift, but has brought its own costs, damaging the environment and setting new problems. Not even material betterment, it turns out, is 'for free'. It may be that this is just because the scale has become so much bigger, but technical prowess no longer seems to point so obviously and unambiguously as once it did to a cheery future. Moral and political difficulties do not go away because we have better electronics or medicine: they only look more menacing as a result. Even the Russians, who (officially, at least) cling to a clear, uncomplicated faith in progress long after it has crumbled elsewhere, now seem to falter. Citizens of the great North American republic, in a more optimistic age 'the world's last, best hope', now dabble with oriental religion, mysticism and the fads of those who reject individualism. Both Soviet Russia and the United States of America are burdened by environmental problems, alcoholism, dissatisfied minorities and economically crushing armaments. Both evidently doubt their power to dominate events and grapple with a frustrating inability to impose a secure order on their international environment.

The troubling of the western psyche has been going on for decades. The rolling back of European empire and the loss of a monopoly of technological and economic power by old states is one source of dismay; it was easier for western governments to feel abreast of the game when they needed only to take their own wishes into account in running the world. Yet this is only a very small (and very recent) part of the story. More damage may well have been done to the self-confidence of the West by its horrified recognition of what it released from the cage and so narrowly escaped — the insane evils of the 'thousand-year Reich', for example. It was hard not to sense something deeply flawed in a civilisation which, while leading the world, led it almost to the extermination camps. Yet the roots of uneasiness go back further than 1939, when the Second World War began, or 1933, when Hitler came to power in Germany. Well before 1900, artists, philosophers and scientists were nibbling and hacking away at the absolute standards of the old, confident West. Its civilisation had been based on faith in the rational, objective intelligence: yet where was reason, where was the objective (let alone autonomous) intelligence after Freud? The esteem they had enjoyed had rested on enduring values: Marxists, anthropologists and racialists made short work of such things. Western civilisation had cherished a prolific artistic tradition which, however richly elaborated, looked back to classical standards and to an aesthetic which was assumed to be accessible to all men willing to learn and enjoy — but romanticism, subjectivism, surrealism, and then the simple hunt for sensation at all costs, changed all that.

It was against such a background that a German professor published a book called *The Decline of the West* just after the shattering end of the First World War. It is not surprising that it became a best-seller. Its title caught on, even if the book was not much read, a misunderstood but seemingly apt catch-phrase which registered a loss of faith in a whole culture. To talk like that, of course, is only metaphor. We ought to scrutinise any such language very hard. Yet many people would accept it, because falling back on metaphor seems to be the only way of expressing the magnitude of what has happened. Set aside the extreme pessimists and, at the very least, articulate opinion in western countries is less self-confident, less sure of its values than it would have been at the beginning of this century. Is it right to go on from this and conclude that our civilisation has, in any final sense, 'failed', or can be usefully described as in 'decline' in any but a comparative sense? These are questions still very much open to debate. Such big historical assertions almost always are. I am more inclined to reject the gloomiest verdicts and to attach more weight to what men do than to what intellectuals say. There are some arguable (and less subjective) grounds for resisting the most pessimistic conclusions. And it is worth trying to do so. Moral and aesthetic judgements about the past affect our lives now. If they are not soundly based, they can easily destroy historical perspective, and so further obscure our own predicament.

This does not mean we can smugly ignore the horrors of the past and trumpet its 'achievements'. It is a matter of trying to assess the historical effectiveness of western civilisation so as to judge correctly its sheer impact on human development. At least that should help us to understand our present world a little better. I do not think it need be taken as axiomatic that the day of western civilisation as a world-shaping force is done, or that the West can look back only on sterile triumphs. These things have to be demonstrated, not merely asserted. There are dangers in underrating the enduring difference — for both good and ill — which the West made and is still making to the world. If we make erroneous historical judgements about it, our present problems will be just a little more intractable, just a little more menacing, because our understanding of them will be distorted. A sense of the real weight of the past is the beginning of political wisdom. Our past includes a world radically reshaped by the West.

That is the West's ambiguous triumph — the difference it has made to the world. A flawed, complicated and paradoxical triumph it may have been, but it was one nonetheless. This is an attempt to explore that triumph historically and to discover a little more about ourselves in the process. It is a historical essay rather than a work of history. It is in no sense a complete account either of general history or of any particular bit of it. The full picture from which those reflexions emerge will have to be sought elsewhere. It is emphatically not an exploration made in a vainglorious, far less an aggressive spirit. Triumphs have their costs, often terrible, and they have their ironies. The Romans knew this. They would sometimes give successful generals what they called a 'triumph' to celebrate their victories. His captives in chains before him, the laurels of victory encircling his brows, his cheeks streaked with the ritual vermilion of these ceremonies, the victorious commander was hauled in procession in his chariot through the streets of Rome to the Capitol to receive the thanks of the Senate. And as the sun blazed down and the trumpets brayed and the Romans screamed their applause, the general would sometimes hear the voice of a man who stood beside him in the chariot — the voice of a slave, put there by a superstitious and cautious people to remind their soldier that he was not, after all, a god. 'Remember,' the slave would say from time to time, 'thou too art human.'

I

ONE WORLD

As an abstract idea, civilisation is not very easy to pin down, but civilisations as historical facts are easier to discuss. Even when historians disagree about how many there have been, or whether a particular candidate should be included in the list, or on many other questions, there is a list of civilisations usually accepted as such by virtually all serious students — those of ancient Mesopotamia or Egypt are on it and so are those of China, and of classical Greece and Rome, to name only some obvious instances. In naming them (or others) historians pick out major traditions within which human life went on across the centuries in ways unlike those of other traditions and often growing more unlike them as time passed. Because civilisations build up elaborate social organisation, permit massive concentrations of labour, devise writings which make the accommodation and exploitation of mental capital much easier and do many other things, they generate in time a cultural potential which cannot exist outside them. They thus make human differentiation yet more marked. Societies cradled by civilisations long continued to grow more diversified. For the whole of historical times — the era of civilisations — people have thus had a much greater chance of living lives strikingly different from those of most other human beings than had their prehistoric ancestors. It might almost be said that with civilisation appears the first chance of a human being living a truly individual life.

Yet civilisations have identities. Usually, the societies which are their subdivisions, though distinct, look similar in their institutions, both social and political. They often share some generally accepted style or technology, and always many values and beliefs. Of course, within the same civilisation people may speak different dialects and languages, worship different local gods, obey different (and competing) rulers and wear different clothes. Yet they have in common things which they do not share with people in other civilisations. Frequently, one of these is a special way of looking at authority and the cosmos. Civilisations usually express their agreement about such matters in myths or religious structures, bodies of inherited images and metaphors. Until our own day, all civilisation has had some sort of ordered religious belief at its core. Such beliefs are often among the most important ties holding them together. Shared assumptions lie at the heart of a civilisation. Consequently, the differences between civilisations are the outstanding evidence that people are capable of living in very different ways. Such differences go very deep indeed. They are not just a matter of how you dress and what you eat, but about what you think eating means, about the way you conceive the natural world about you and the stars above you, about what you owe to your rulers, your slaves and servants, your community, your family and yourself. They are about faith and myth, and faiths and myths profoundly divide and differentiate human beings.

For most of the last five thousand years there have been several distinct civilisations living in the same world but apart, side by side. Until very recent times, there was often not much interplay between many of them. Even when in direct geographical contact, or locked in open conflict, they seem always to have been separated by invisible membranes which, though permeable enough to permit some cross-fertilisation, have proved immensely tough and enduring. Civilisations have co-existed for centuries, even sharing land frontiers, but still passing little to one another which led to any essential change in either. Their own unique natures remained intact. Sometimes, of course, even the simplest communication between them was lacking and they had no chance at all of learning from one another. The civilisations of South and Central America grew, matured and decayed, untouched for centuries by anything from outside their hemisphere, and, often, by anything outside their mountain or rain-forest fastnesses. It is possible that Chinese civilisation would have had a big effect on the Incas had it reached them: but it just could not get across the Pacific to pass on what it had to offer. Even when there was some intercommunication, it did not always lead to significant exchanges. For about four hundred years, from about 200 BC to AD 200, China was ruled by the Han emperors, one or two of whom may have had some diplomatic contact with imperial Rome, but that could not be described as a significant cultural link. China and Rome never underwent any real cross-fertilisation. Nor did China pass much directly to medieval Christendom; a trickle of trade and the reports of a few travellers do not really amount to very much. The technological knowledge from China which may have been taken up by Europeans, can only have come to the west via intermediaries. To the nearby islands of Japan, on the other hand, China could deliver direct a certain view of the state and family, a calligraphy, and an ethical teaching. Thus there appeared a Japanese civilisation, clearly related to that of China (though, once established, soon distinct and assertively independent).

One way of measuring how much richer and more varied human life became as the centuries go by is provided by very simple, everyday objects. Wheelbarrows do much the same sort of job in countries all round the world.

Once we have used the word we have a fairly clear impression of what sort of tool is referred to. Yet some wheelbarrows are very unlike others. The kind of wheelbarrow the Chinese have used for thousands of years looks very different from its European equivalent. Though for many purposes mechanically more efficient (the wheel is in a different place and takes more of the load's weight off the arms of the man pushing it than does that of the European model), it remains confined to one part of the world. It is a local answer to a universal problem; the same technical job does not always have to be done in the same way. Even within a single country such as England spades come in many shapes and sizes. All spades are used for digging; but different local materials, different craft traditions and different soils have led to widely varying designs. Weapons are another kind of tool; a twelfth-century crusader's sword was quite different from that of the Saracen he fought, as an old story about Richard Lion-Heart trying to cut silk relates. The fine blade of his great opponent, Saladin, did the job much better than his heavy weapon. Both swords, though, were utterly unlike those later produced by the great sword-making artists of Japan.

Similarly, buildings have always had to do much the same jobs; they were meant to shelter, protect or impress. Architecture is the most utilitarian of all arts, yet it long varied widely from country to country and even from neighbourhood to neighbourhood. The availability of certain materials is one explanation. The presence of skills and experience is another. At that point, though, we come back to the human and traditional element, the selectivity of a particular culture. Men are not only restricted by materials; they also take account of tradition and models, whether by following or rejecting them. Salisbury Cathedral, Aurungzebe's mosque at Lahore and the Meiji shrine at Tokyo are all religious buildings, but they are utterly unlike one another except in the implicit respect their builders showed for the laws of physics. True, they are all places of public resort, but that takes us no great distance. It is not the similarities, but the differences, between what goes on in a Protestant American church, a Nigerian mosque, or a Buddhist temple which are the most important explanations of differing architectural form. Even within the limited class of Christian religious buildings, attitudes changed across the centuries so that, for instance, it has been at some times and places virtually impossible to think of building a church except in one prevailing style (say, imitation Gothic), whatever secular buildings in the same society might look like.

Clothes, too, have long shown social differences. The human body is much the same the world round, give or take a few marked differences of skin colour, stature and distribution of hair and fat. But because climate, materials and accumulated skills have long varied from place to place and from time to time, different peoples have dressed very differently. One need not go to the extremes of Eskimos and Bantu for examples; over much of China cold winters and a shortage of cheap domestic fuel led to the adoption of the padded cotton clothing which has survived into the era of central heating, while Laplanders, on the other hand, dealt with their climate by wearing the skins of animals.

For almost the whole of history, then, clothes have been signs of group membership. The barbarian dress of the first Europeans to go to Japan fascinated Japanese artists, who recorded it in the first of a long series of sketches and paintings which went on being made for three centuries or so. The line begins with Portuguese gentlemen and their attendants painted on screens, and finishes with sketches of Commodore Perry's officers and their accoutrements. Clothes also signal group differences within societies. The sari is worn in different ways in different parts of India. Even today, some Christian clergymen set themselves apart from other men by wearing cassocks, dark suits and clerical collars. Kilts, kimonos and the kente of West Africa, trousers, breeches and dhotis; uniforms and academic robes, top hats and spats have long made vivid the divisions of mankind. At a very deep level language itself divides men and makes them different. It is not just that grammatical structures, vowel sounds, accents vary enormously. The differences of language go deeper than these. They literally make (or fail to make) some thoughts possible. As anyone who has tried to translate poetry has probably found out, in some languages we cannot find exact representations of shades of thought we wish to express or structures which have the force of those with which we are familiar.

We have long taken this huge variety for granted. Our museums, libraries and books of reference are crammed with evidence of it. Tourist agencies exploit it: we pay to go to remote parts of the world to see how different they are from what we know. But why do we more and more avidly seek what is different? Why do we cherish and savour human variety? Perhaps because it is in danger as never before. An interesting cultural change is now beginning to appear right round the world. A new uniformity of human experience is in the making, apparently universal in scope. The world has recently — perhaps even suddenly — begun to seem much less varied, less differentiated, less picturesque, more bland, and perhaps a little more grey. 'Recently' and 'suddenly' are historical shorthand. The last century or so, in which this can be detected, is only recent or sudden by comparison with thousands of years of civilised life during which there was little to check currents moving towards diversification. It has only become too obvious a change to be ignored in the last two or three decades — when, incidentally, it became much more rapid. This may be why we have begun to value diversity more in those same few decades.

The simplest explanation is technological. If machines are to be efficient, there is little scope except in their detailed decoration for the preservation of traditional style or material. In consequence, a motor car looks much like any other motor car the world over, a ship is like a ship, an aeroplane like an aeroplane. What is more, a common technology standardises much else. Different routines and new patterns of work follow the arrival of new machines in a peasant economy, or of air-conditioning in a hot climate, or of cheap hydroelectrical power in a country poor in fossil fuels. Ballpoint pens, carbon paper and typewriters have all changed communication and the telephone does so even faster. Communications technology, indeed, makes the point most clearly. First writing and then printing helped to standardise forms, but recent innovations (particularly since the onset of satellites) have disrupted settled ways and traditions and imposed standard patterns much more suddenly and radically. They have reinforced the power of governments, have educated taste while tending to homogenise it, have disseminated new desires and ideas. More people now come to share similar impressions more rapidly than ever before. Even if new ideas make for change, moreover, it is often change in a common direction. Advertisement hoardings, transistor radios and cinemas have revolutionised men's sense of what is possible. All over the world, they have changed aspirations and expectations. Yet they have increasingly directed them towards the same goals. Television has not yet had quite the same impact outside Europe and North America, but it is likely to have it in time. Looking back, it may be that the day when the first set came to an Anatolian or Iraqi village will be seen to have heralded far more rapid change for that community than the arrival there of the first iron tool, whenever that happened, thousands of years ago.

It is easy to underrate such changes. They sometimes creep up on us unnoticed. Sometimes they are denied. To misunderstand one another is the fate of men, and there are plentiful grounds for misunderstanding in language and culture to remind us that men and their societies are still very different. So they are, of course. It is wholly reasonable to point out that uniformity does not yet go very deep; life in an African village is not much like that in Nether Stowey. Does not Islam separate the Arab world much more from the Christian than they are brought together by the motor cars so prominent in both? Are not women treated differently in Bombay, Borneo and Bournemouth? Of course, the answers to such questions must be 'yes'. But that does not mean that long-distinct cultures may not now be turning or beginning to turn on to converging courses, however vast the present gaps between them. Even if many material changes of the last few decades may well not be more than superficial, some of them already betoken transformations at much deeper levels, disturbing fundamental assumptions.

Trivial facts are often the best hints to what is going on. Let us stick to clothes. In no civilised society do people always choose all their clothes merely because they are useful, comfortable or cheap. Garments also symbolise; they are charged with messages about their wearers. Seen in this light, it is at least odd, at first sight, that the shoes, suit, shirt and tie worn by so many twentieth-century western city-dwellers in a very different climate, should have become the daily wear of thousands in modern Africa and Asia. What is the message this conveys? It is not easy to see why African women should want to wear the underwear European and North American women buy in Marks and Spencer, the Galeries Lafayette, or Macy's instead of their traditional garb. Perhaps a Japanese businessman finds his Savile Row suit[1] more convenient than the traditional robe of a gentleman in his country, but why should the Chinese of Hong Kong and Macao put on robes derived from those of medieval European clergy for the academic ceremonies of their universities? What is an official of the Nigerian parliament doing clad in the wig of an eighteenth-century Englishman? Armed forces in non-western countries prompt similar questions. The kepi survives in former French Africa. Like the Sam Browne belt elsewhere, this is probably a direct inheritance of recent colonial rule. Yet when the new post-colonial states set up their armies, they did not need sheepishly to follow the models of older nations. Their generals put on epaulettes, nevertheless, because Europeans wore them. The more dashing among post-colonial armies even adopted the beret, symbol of some crack units among the victorious armies of the Second World War, and a few, startlingly, took to kilts and glengarries.

Ceremonial occasions everywhere seem to call for unusual plumage, but that does not explain why it should be imported. It is at first sight hard to see why new nations do not turn more often to their own traditions in looking for it. African governments, for example, could, if they had wished to do so, have chosen to clothe their academic sages in the manner of witchdoctors or their soldiers in the leopard and lion skins of their own legendary heroes and warriors. But university ceremonies in Africa are usually carried out in western garb and even for dress parades African soldiers stick to uniforms of western cut (in contrast, the old imperial nations often enthusiastically maintained a version of local forms of dress when they put their subjects into uniform, as many an Indian or French colonial regiment showed). As the adoption of the bearskin by the British footguards after Waterloo (where the French Guard wore it) shows, an adoption of exotic dress is, surely, an act of homage. Few newly independent countries have failed to pay such homage to the western world in one form or another. India, perhaps, is one of the most conspicuous exceptions, but even India's soldiers tend to stick to western models, to the extent of maintaining only the Indian military dresses which had been taken up by the British. The adoption of the symbols of a cultural tradition born and fostered elsewhere is a token, however disguised and reluctant, of admiration and respect — and it is far from being a new phenomenon.[2]

Monomania can make such unconscious homage clearly apparent. Thus 'Field-Marshal' Amin promoted himself to a European rank, and solemnly conferred on himself a 'VC' — a distinction literally meaningless except against the background of a centuries-old western tradition of military honours. A more blatant example is that of the former 'Emperor' of Central Africa, Bokassa. *Imperator* was originally a Roman military title. Various European languages later derived from it their words for a very superior sort of ruler. Bokassa took both the title and its trappings by derivation, drawing deliberately upon the imperial style with which he was most familiar, the French. His coronation robes were modelled on those of the first Napoleon. He wore his crown like a medieval European king and carried in his hands a sceptre, the symbol of authority put in the hands of King David in the pictures of him which decorated medieval manuscripts, and one still given to English monarchs at their coronations. Like all rulers, Bokassa was consciously playing a role on a stage. But he chose it from an old, exotic and non-African script, the great drama of European monarchy. Written for the European theatre, it played there with great success for a thousand years, but of Africa, past or present, it had nothing to say. If we ask why Bokassa sought his symbolism in such a source, the answer can seem banal; imitation is the most sincere form of flattery. Perverse as it is, it is a claim to a share in an admired tradition, even if it is alien. It stands for something grander and more efficacious than what is locally available and so confers prestige.

Other evidence can easily be found. Since 1945, most 'prestige' buildings round the world have been imitations, more or less successful, of European or American models. Or there is the spread of some languages world-wide. Chinese is the language of a state containing more people in the world than any other, but your social contacts will be limited if you travel armed only with it. English, on the other hand, will eventually get you understood almost anywhere in the world, and Spanish, or even French, will answer almost as well. Or there are institutions. These speak explicitly of adopted aspirations and goals as well as of prestige. Why do new nations set up 'universities' which give degrees to 'bachelors', 'masters' and 'doctors', and organise themselves in 'faculties'? Institutions rooted in medieval Europe surely cannot be the only or the necessary models for organising higher studies. But such ideas as 'higher studies' or 'graduate' are themselves artefacts of a particular civilisation. Their adoption registers a successful cultural implant. Similarly, the Speaker's wig in an African parliament or that on the head of an African judge suggests respect for parliamentary democracy, or at least lip-service to it and to a tradition of jurisprudence and procedure going back to the

Middle Ages — but why? These traditions are not African and it is not obvious why more pride should be shown in them than in indigenous symbols of authority.

There is likely to be more than one explanation, of course. Inertia plays a part; many former European colonies have simply found it easier to go on in the old ways. But that can hardly be the whole story. After all, many countries have eagerly rejected a colonial past which seemed embarrassing, cumbersome or awkward. Yet some seem to have chosen deliberately to keep particular links with that past alive. They found that course more attractive. Some names, slogans, aspirations, forms and institutions appeared to them to have a superior power; they commanded the respect of civilised men in a way which alternatives did not. At times, such new nations look a little like those Germanic peoples of the fifth century who gazed in amazement at the reality of the Roman world they had invaded, and settled down to having their warlords take the title of 'Consul', and to learn to write — and so to think — in Latin.

Such parallels can seem remote and far-fetched. Yet there are also many recent and more rounded examples of change by conscious imitation. Japan today stands in the very vanguard of modernity. Yet for centuries she locked herself away from the world, above all from Europeans. They were forbidden to enter the country, the only exceptions being a few Dutch merchants who were allowed to come on an annual visit from the East Indies and to establish themselves for trade on a little island in Nagasaki harbour, Japan's only point of contact with the West. Apart from this, Japan was a closed society. The Portuguese who had been the first Europeans to go there were expelled in the seventeenth century, when Japan's rulers turned on the Christian religion some of them had at first found attractive. After that, as an island community, Japan was for about two hundred years able to protect herself against intrusion. A change came only in the middle of the nineteenth century, when Japan's modern history began. The historical can-opener was a squadron of American warships under Commodore Perry; when it sailed into Edo Bay his demands for access to the island empire could not be resisted. His guns could have devastated Edo and cut off the waterborne food the city needed. The Japanese ceded to the threat of force, though only just, and opened their country once more to trade and missionaries from the West. They had to sign 'unequal' treaties with foreign powers, effectively establishing a system of special extra-territorial rights for Europeans and restraints on the powers of the Japanese to regulate their own trade. The Japanese had their sovereignty over their own affairs restricted, though they were not invaded and colonised, and foreigners soon began to arrive in some numbers. They were not content to be victims, though. They did not propose simply to allow things to go on happening to them. Instead, they sought to choose from what the West had to offer so as to strengthen themselves against further pressure. The result was within a few decades a nation in many ways astonishingly 'western'.

To change a tradition is not an easy decision. Not all Japanese were pleased or easily convinced of the need to do so. Japanese had (and still have) a strong sense of personal identification with their culture; this sustained feelings of national pride and solidarity before the challenges of the modern era surfaced. 'Although it is not an extensive country spatially,' wrote one Japanese of his homeland early in the nineteenth century, 'it reigns over all quarters of the world, for it has never once changed its dynasty or its form of sovereignty. The various countries of the West correspond to the feet and legs of the body. That is why their ships come from afar to visit Japan.'[3]

India, almost completely under British rule by the middle of the nineteenth century, and China, at that moment being driven to grave concessions by the 'barbarians', were standing warnings that there was another side to the West. Even while the official policy was still to shut it out, some Japanese scholars had pursued knowledge of it through what was called 'Dutch learning' — the study of books in Dutch, or translated from the Dutch, since they were the only western people officially permitted to have contact with the Japanese. They learnt about medicine, science, technology, and they wondered. The traditional assumptions about the superiority of the Chinese culture so heavily drawn upon by Japan in the past began to waver. In 1811 an official 'Institute for the Investigation of Barbarian Books' had been created and some of the great feudal domains established schools of western science and languages. One can sense Japan hesitating between choices. Even before Perry, some of the clans were sending young men abroad to find out more about the source of the West's mysterious power and his own report on his mission expressed his surprise at the level of information Japanese already possessed about western countries. The West was not regarded (as in China) with contempt, even if many Japanese felt hostile to it. There were two slogans current which stood for two possible futures for Japan; *Sonno joi,* which meant roughly 'Honour the emperor, expel the barbarians', and *Wakon yosai,* or 'Eastern ethics and western science'.[4] Government policy reflected hesitation. In 1825 an imperial edict had appeared with the title 'Don't think twice' — it urged that the foreigner should be driven out. This was the seventeenth-century recipe; having saved Japan from Christianity then, it might work again. In 1842, though, after reports were received of the pressure being brought to bear by the British on China,[5] an order was promulgated that foreign ships in need might be provisioned, even though individual foreigners would not be allowed to land from them. It was hard to decide which way to go.

In the later 1850s and the 1860s the debate was thrashed out, partly in civil war. Most (though not all) of Japan's rulers agreed that *some* adoption of western models was needed; virtually everyone agreed about the superiority of the barbarians' artillery, for instance. To try to shut out the West altogether would have been very hazardous. The bombardment of Kagoshima by the British Royal Navy and the destruction of forts at Shimonoseki by a combined British, American, Dutch and French expedition brought home the hopelessness of resistance. Only too clearly, as the 'unequal' treaties showed, Japan might be driven down the road China was already travelling, bullied and exploited by superior western power. Some urged the adoption of western values — individualism and utilitarianism, or Christian idealism. The question remained: which models and what degree of adoption? For many Japanese, moreover, it was not just a matter of regaining power, but of retaining status, equality with western nations; modernisation was to be seen as a way to the recovery of self-respect.

In the end, Japan's rulers avoided China's fate not just by efforts to understand the West (they sent seven 'diplomatic-cum-study' missions to Europe and the United States between 1860 and 1867), but by falling back on Japanese history. The 'shogunate' which had governed Japan since the seventeenth century had already lost prestige because of its failure to resist the western intruders. In the winter of 1867–8, it was overthrown. The emperor, for two centuries a secluded, ceremonial, almost powerless figure at Kyoto, was now brought back to Tokyo and to the centre of the constitutional stage by the opponents of the shogunate. This was the operation now commemorated as the 'Meiji restoration', after the name of the emperor — a boy in his teens at the time, who lived to see his country transformed before he died in 1912.

The four greatest clans now surrendered their power and lands to the emperor. Japan's rulers had decided in favour of revolution, even though they called it a restoration and focused it on the central institution which expressed the particularism of Japanese history, the unbroken imperial line of descent from the Sun God. Imperial authority was needed to drive through the changes ahead and to turn to such a source was only possible in a culture already very much aware of its national identity. It was also a brave and clear-sighted decision, because it recognised the difficulty of what lay ahead. Many nations have sought the rewards of westernisation without counting (or expecting to pay) costs in giving up old ways. This was a conscious decision to modernise, even though it was one to modernise (if possible) under control. In whatever mattered for the recovery of real independence, Japan was to become more western. So, in the next three or four decades, Japan began to turn itself into an industrial nation-state.

The new order started with important assets in hand. Japan had achieved over the previous century or so a high level of capital accumulation because her population had not grown greatly. The traditional loyalties to emperor and family could easily be adapted to a conscious nationalism more like that of European states. *Sonno Kaikotu* — 'Honour the emperor over the country' — became the slogan of the samurai who were the driving force behind public policy in the early Meiji era. 'Knowledge shall be sought throughout the world so as to strengthen the foundations of imperial rule' said an official pronouncement by the emperor almost at the outset.[6] Literacy was already high at the end of the Tokugawa period; the traditional economy soon revealed considerable potential for growth; an obedient, hard-working labour force existed in huge numbers; old notions of national and personal pride could be harnessed without difficulty to the acquisition of new skills. One Japanese intellectual, Fukuzawa Yukichi, born of a samurai family, has left a moving account of the sailing across the Pacific of the first Japanese-crewed steamship. 'The voyage of Kanrin-Maru was an epoch-making venture for our nation,' he wrote, 'every member of the crew was determined to take the ship across *unassisted by a foreigner*.'[7]

Above all, there was an internal sense of the need to preserve the national identity by adaptation. Even so, the state had to do much; early Japanese industrialisation had to be stimulated in hothouse conditions, and even protection and subsidy could not easily tempt private capital away from traditional investment. Innovation on other fronts, too, had to be vigorous. Foreign experts were hired to advise the new civil service. A written constitution set up a parliament of two chambers: seeking an equivalent to the British House of Lords, the Japanese created a new peerage, too. A new civil code reflected German influence and combined protection of older Japanese custom in the management of the family, with a new emphasis on property arrangements favouring individualism and the market economy. Compulsory education, railways, universal military conscription (a startling change in a country where great pains had been taken for centuries to keep arms out of the hands of the peasants), the Gregorian calendar, newspapers (sixteen were founded in 1868) and religious toleration followed. Feudalism and the system of retainers which had kept alive the old warrior class of samurai were abandoned, and conservative rebellion was suppressed. The British helped to train a new navy (which for a long time bought its ships from British yards, too; it was only in 1905 that the Japanese laid the keel of their own first battleship). On state occasions, ladies at court began to wear the hideously unattractive garments of contemporary Europe.[8] Japanese soldiers and sailors adopted western uniforms. It reminds one of Peter the Great's efforts to modernise Russia in the early eighteenth century; his example was much in the minds of some Japanese (whose own example, in its turn, was to inspire other reformers elsewhere).

Copying the West, especially in superficial matters, nevertheless made some people unhappy. New currents of thought could not be kept out. Some, indeed, were eagerly taken up — notably those drawn from Samuel Smiles's best-selling book *Self-Help* or from notions of what Darwin was supposed to have said about the survival of the fittest. But there were out-and-out conflicts of values, too, heady debates which revealed the incompatibility of much in Japanese thinking with the universalism implicit or explicit in western ideas. The Meiji emperor himself is said to have disliked the use in his presence of the words 'East' and 'West' to signify cultural distinctions. In the year of his death an elder statesman committed suicide in order to symbolise Japanese alarm over the advance of what he saw, perhaps farsightedly, as western 'hedonism'. The gesture was peculiarly Japanese, but westernisation from above has always generated cultural shock, as the Islamic world was belatedly to show. Nor was it only Japanese who did not like what was happening: foreign admirers and connoisseurs of Japan often agreed. Kipling regretted 'this wallowing in unloveliness for the sake of recognition at the hands of men' and others deplored the loss of refinement, politeness, morals and the capacity for simple happiness which seemed to follow change.[9]

It was not long before there was a nationalist reaction. The catalyst was the failure in 1887 of attempts to negotiate away the disadvantages imposed upon Japan by the mid-century 'unequal' treaties. They were not to survive much longer, for renegotiation took place successfully in 1894, and Japan recovered full control over her own tariffs in 1911. But beyond this, antipathy to westernisation *à outrance* was widespread. Conservative misgivings tended to express themselves indirectly and cautiously rather than in rejecting change altogether; they neither stopped the Japanese reformers, nor seem to have blurred their very clear sense of just how far they needed to go. The men who presided over the first thirty or forty years of Japanese modernisation were largely drawn from the same domain lands of the old ruling class; they formed a very cohesive group. Such a continuity of élites made the management of change easier. They knew what they wanted: independence of foreigners. Foreign investment, for example, was by and large kept out of industrialisation; it was a corollary of this that the state should play a large part in it, because substantial investment resources in private hands were lacking. That meant heavy taxation; the discipline of Japan's traditional society made its imposition possible. The Japanese underwent controlled westernisation, therefore, and much was deliberately left untouched.

So, for a long time, many sides of Japanese life looked unchanged — as some things still do. A traditional role for women, established patterns of education for children, the Confucian belief in filial piety, willingness to sacrifice self to the community — all lived on. They can still give an impression that Japan is a society resting on values many of which remain alien to those of the West. Hence, in part, the lack of understanding with which many western statesmen strove to grapple with the warrior Japan of the 1930s and 1940s. Though there was much that was easily comprehensible in Japanese imperialism, there was also something else, something harder to decode which did not seem to go with the rationality of large-scale capitalism or the diplomats in top-hats and morning coats. Yet this should not have been so surprising; even in the 1930s, most urban Japanese were no more than a generation removed from the traditional patterns of rural life, and fishermen and peasants were still the most numerous occupational groups. How far change actually went and whether it had been, in the end, controlled and demarcated as the Meiji reformers hoped, is not, though, in question here. What matters for our present purpose is that what had been done was done by conscious imitation of the West. This was what had made Japan's remarkable military prowess possible.

The decision of the Meiji statesmen is an outstanding mark of the attractiveness and seductiveness of much of western civilisation to non-western societies — an attraction and seductiveness all the stronger because it included a promise to find a way to resist the West's power. That promise has been sensed by many great reformers in other traditional societies over the last two or three centuries. A history of them could begin on the fringes of Europe with Peter the Great of Russia. He was often to be evoked as an example by later non-western modernisers, though it is doubtful whether they understood much of what he actually did. Like that of Frederick the Great of Prussia (another much cited exemplar), Peter's symbolic achievement was a stimulus to those who learnt about him, often from western books and teachers. From him the line runs through nineteenth-century reformers like Mehemet Ali of Egypt, to Kemal Atatürk in twentieth-century Turkey and on to every 'Third World' leader who sets his sights on nation-building, democracy, industrialisation or anything else in the western mail-order catalogue of civilised living.

Nonetheless, conscious imitation is neither now, nor has it always been, the most important force disseminating the style, ideas and assumptions of western civilisation. The impact of western civilisation on the non-western world is much more complicated and ambiguous than that, as some facts already cited suggest. It is virtually impossible to measure objectively how far it has gone. It is not even true that the changes coming from the West have only helped to make people more alike. On the contrary, within non-western societies the onset of change has often accentuated existing contrasts or created new ones. Economic disparities which did not exist in earlier times have opened up sharply because of things which happened in the West. The life of a medieval European was probably much like that of his Asian contemporary in calorie-intake or buying power. This is certainly no longer true of their modern descendants. Attempts to offset the standardising culture of the West have sometimes led to new political fragmentation and polarisation too. Dramatic instances of outright and violent resistance to the onset of modernisation, particularly in Islamic countries, have caught the headlines increasingly in the last few years.

This underlines the unsurprising truth that the interaction of civilisations is a vast and complicated business. All we can do is to try to recognise trends. Even in the twentieth century, after all, when governments have great resources at their disposal, conscious change in social and cultural institutions is very difficult. For both good and evil, human variety is everywhere well buttressed and protected by inertia. The Indian republic's constitution enshrines the respectable western platitudes of our era — democracy, secularism, republicanism — which have won lip-service the world round. Nonetheless, though India, so far as parliamentary and political history goes, has a better track record than many new nations, it still remains very hard to believe that, for most Hindus, the existence of caste is not just as important a consideration in daily life as their formal equality before the law. The problem of the untouchable has not gone away because of a constitutional provision (though there may be grounds for believing it will be swept away by the blind forces of economic and technological change). Indian civil servants still act on what astrologers say about auspicious days (for that matter, the very timing of the moment of Independence in 1947 itself took account of it), and Mrs Gandhi was said to consult them about elections. Further, while the Indian state is, undoubtedly, formally secular, Indian society is not: cows are not treated the same way in Benares as in Brittany. The support given by inertia to old forms can also be seen in much more trivial examples, some so familiar that they are easily overlooked. Even within the same zone of civilisation, Englishmen and Frenchmen manipulate knife and fork in a different way; but they both use knives and forks, whereas most Indians, including many educated men and women, prefer their fingers. Nor has chewing-gum quite replaced betel-nut in India. As for rituals and habits connected with sexual behaviour, these remain enormously diverse right round the world.

Nonetheless, when all has been said that can be said about the survival of variety, it is more a matter of survival than of creation. Not enough new differences are appearing within our world to persuade me that human behaviour is growing more diverse and human beings less alike. The tendency of the last hundred thousand years seems to be petering out. However we exactly measure the change, we are well into a discernibly new and unique phase of history. For the first time there is a trend towards a greater cultural homogeneity than has ever before seemed possible. Traditional and local ways are giving ground, often without recognising it, before tides of global scope. For the last few centuries, civilisations have been drawn more and more into direct contact with one another and their history has gradually become world history. Communications have never before transmitted the reverberations of events so rapidly and sensitively from one side of the globe to the other. The rhythm and pace of history are not only now much faster than a century ago but are shared by many more. Isolation is now impossible. This is the main reason why the world is now growing less strange, somewhat less exciting, a little less diverse.

The explanation of this appears to me to lie in the history of the West, and at more than one level. To tie together signs of growing material uniformity round the world and the huge economic and technological influence of the West cannot be the whole story. That connexion obscures a deeper and more important change, a growing world-wide acceptance of certain ideas and institutions. But these, too, are drawn from western civilisation. In fact, it has become exactly what so many in the nineteenth century believed it ought to become: the first world civilisation. That mankind might slowly grow more alike was first recognised, though only indirectly and imprecisely, by Europeans. The very idea of civilisation, of course, is a European idea, a cultural artefact which helps to illuminate our data — though on the basis of certain European assumptions. To see something *as* a civilisation is a selective, orientating act, a way of ordering and managing history. Among the first to go beyond religion as a way to do that were men who can now be recognised as pioneering figures of the discipline of sociology. Several of them tried to fathom the general processes of history. In the eighteenth century, for instance, Turgot and Condorcet sketched stages through which they assumed every society evolved. The Scottish students of the 'natural history' of man who were their contemporaries had similar schemes in their minds. They did not minimise the obvious differences between societies, but were more interested in what they saw as common patterns of evolution. In the nineteenth century Auguste Comte (the inventor of the word 'sociology') set out at enormous length the evidence and arguments for his view that all societies went through similar phases of organisation which reflected distinct stages in the growth of the power of reason in them. Karl Marx took a different tack, but still offered a general interpretation of historical development, this time as a projection of what he believed to be European economic experience. Like Comte, he seems to have thought that changes which were necessary (in the philosophic sense) would come about in actuality by the operation of something like natural laws which operated everywhere in the world, however long circumstances might delay their unrolling in any particular place.

None of these thinkers recognised that their own visions and theories were not discoveries of universal laws but recognitions of the power of their own civilisation to impose itself on others. History seemed to point one way only because all round the world the European or western vision of the world and history, of the laws of nature and society, looked increasingly likely to displace other conceptions and values. The system by which we reckon time in years is a good example. Though some important alternatives are still in use (the Islamic, for instance) the western chronology has now spread almost world-wide. Yet it encapsulates a whole world view and a periodisation resting on Christian assumptions; why should so much of the rest of the world take up a calendar so soaked in alien categories of thought? It can hardly be because Christian dogma is taken as true. Evidently, a successful civilisation's ideas have enormous power. They impose new symbols, erase old differences, as well as making possible (and encouraging) the formal creation of new institutional arrangements which gradually ease men into new shared paths. And western civilisation has been doing all these things in the world for some centuries. It has been the major world agent of cultural change from the beginning of modern times. Most of what we now think of as traditional Ethiopian pictorial art, for instance, only goes back to the adoption of European models from Portuguese visitors in the sixteenth century. Chinoiserie or the cult of the Japanese print by Impressionists are mere episodes and fashions in the history of western art, while Indian and Japanese artists now widely adopt western styles.

Western influence can be seen at its most paradoxical in the use of western ideas and mythologies as defences against the same West which spawned them. Bodies like the United Nations Organisation or the Organisation of African Unity are sometimes seen as defences against the West but they also express its ideological and institutional dominance. The idea of such international organisations, like the idea of the state itself, originated within western civilisation. The creation of such bodies shows both the prestige of western ideas and their insinuating strength. Africans and Asians do not merely wear uniforms like those of Europeans and Americans; they have also taken up the practice of appealing to democracy, nationalism, human rights and all the rest of western political mythology.

Such dependence can go very deep. Pan-Africanism and African unity are ideas which make no sense without a pre-existing concept of Africa. But Africa is a western idea, a geographical notion originating in the thinking of Greece and Rome, and fully defined only in the modern era. Until Europeans took the idea to Africa, no African knew that he lived in a continent which could helpfully be thought of as a whole. No African knew he was an African, until his European schoolmaster told him so. Of course, this is not to say that modern Africa is just the product of Europe. Africa is the outcome of centuries of simultaneous internal development and interaction with the outside world. During those centuries, African reality powerfully and often decisively influenced the external forces which played on it. Islam was for a long time by far the most important external force shaping it; then came the new diversities added by colonial powers, but they, too, had to respond to the huge variety of the continent. Huge differences existed between, say, the British West African colonies where so much depended upon a commercial and educated native élite, and those in Central Africa or Kenya, where not only were white settlers dominant, but quite different local potentials existed. There is no need to see European influence as a *deus ex machina* explaining everything in modern Africa, a Prince Charming awakening a dusky Sleeping Beauty with a technological kiss. Nevertheless, specific decisive western influences have determined Africa's history in the last two or three centuries, and in no way more profoundly than by the introduction of new ideas — among them, a vision of Africa as a single discrete whole, materially identical with a particular geographical mass, capable of discussion in general terms and perhaps a focus for loyalty.

The cant of modern politics best shows the power of western ideas. In spite of occasional exceptions and violent reactions (especially from parts of the Islamic world) it is always interesting and revealing in an international forum when delegates stand up for the rights of women — a quintessentially western cause. The lot of most women in the countries of many of the speakers is often to act as bearers of wood and drawers of water (when not attending to the relaxation of the warrior or playing other traditional roles), and most of their fellow-countrymen are quite happy that things should stay that way.[10] If the speakers actually believe what they are saying, this only shows how complete is their surrender to alien values created by a particular civilisation at a particular time; if they do not, their hypocrisy is not only the tribute of vice to virtue, but one paid by ideological weakness to ideological strength.

Usually, of course (though not always), it is only the élites of non-western countries who talk the language of the West. Whether telling people to rally round the national flag, turn out to vote in democratic elections, or turn on home-grown exploiters in quest of a more just and equal society, they use the language of an alien world. Like the man in Molière's play who spoke prose all his life without knowing it, they are using words whose significance they do not know, or, at least, do not know through and through, as part of their own heritage. In using them, though, they have in a measure abandoned their own tradition, however unwilling to do that explicitly. A few years ago, I attended a conference to discuss the state of the humanities in the modern world. It struck me (though no one else seemed to think it remarkable) that the notion of the 'humanities' was in fact very particularly and circumstantially rooted in European culture and that it made much less sense outside that culture than within it — unless, of course, European culture was to be assumed to be, in effect, world culture. Saying this awoke some hostility. One African writer became particularly indignant. He resented the idea that much which he treasured was, in some sense, a colonial imposition, even if benevolent, that his own culture might point in very different directions from those of western letters — which had led him towards such alien conventions as the novel and to use the exotic language of Shakespeare and Milton — and that the culture of the humanities might carry moral implications often wholly at variance with the traditions of his own society. His indignation would have gladdened any Eurocentric cultural chauvinist: a victory had been won for western concepts without, somehow, my interlocutor seeing it. Yet he was, in other, more conventional and less interesting ways, very anti-western, and took care we all knew it.

It is easy to be misunderstood in such matters. People sometimes find it hard to accept that recognising a particular civilisation's historical success in spreading its ideas does not mean you admire or approve it. You would have to do so, of course, if you held the view that the course of history alone authorises moral values, but few would now agree to that. Nor has it recently been thought easy to assert that western culture is in some way better than the alternatives on offer. Fortunately, the 'success' of our civilisation does not have to be discussed in such terms. It is a matter of simple historical effectiveness. Almost all the master principles and ideas now reshaping the modern world emanate from the West; they have spread round the globe and other civilisations have crumbled before them. To acknowledge that, by itself, tells us nothing about whether the outcome is good or bad, admirable or deplorable.[11] It only registers that this is the age of the first world civilisation and it is the civilisation of the West.

'Modern' history can be defined as the approach march to the age dominated by the West. It can now be seen that for three or four centuries after 1500 or so, western civilisation was on the move towards world dominance. Some of the consequences have been indisputably good, some, equally indisputably, bad. Most of them cannot be assessed in such terms. Possibly there is an undiscovered moral calculus which should enable us to say whether it would have been in some sense morally better or worse had history taken some other course than the one which it actually did. I do not believe that there is, nor that history can be talked about in such simple terms. I doubt whether an abstraction so general as 'civilisation' can meaningfully have words like 'good' or 'bad' attached to it. It remains true that western civilisation has knowingly and unknowingly forced other civilisations to concessions such as they had never before had to make to any external force. Sometimes their own identity and coherence have almost given way in the process (as men like the Ayatollahs of Iran fear). Elsewhere things may not go so far. Yet, whatever the weight of Chinese tradition in practice, 1000 million Chinese are now formally and nominally ruled in the light of principles derived from a German philosopher of the late romantic era who was striving to understand the Europe of his day with the help of the economic science created by the first modern industrial nation, Great Britain. (It is ironic that Marx often and incidentally showed deep contempt for other, non-European, cultures.) But other countries have chosen different western teachers; their politicians try to cram the complicating and proliferating economic and social problems of their own societies into such Procrustean frameworks as are provided by Mazzinian nationalism or Natural Rights. These master categories, too, remain western, exotic to their own civilisations. Only in some Islamic countries does an intransigent and wholly alien spirit of resistance seem alive.

People have already seized on some aspects of this great change. They know, for example, that much of the last three centuries is the story of a triumph of the outright power of the West. Conquest and manipulation of the world by force, rule based on might — in short, western imperialism — is, they suggest, the only real success the West has enjoyed. This is welcome doctrine in many parts of the world and congenial to those in the West who cherish or writhe under feelings of ancestral guilt. It fits and seems to explain a lot of the facts: for a time much of the world was indeed ruled directly by Europeans, and often they could have their way with much of what they did not rule directly. Like all effective historical myths, a vision of the world-historical role of the West as an especially striking and far-flung episode in the old, old tale of sin, domination and power, has some truth at its heart.

Yet it does not go far enough. What the western impact on human history has meant is not exhausted by describing a brief era of political and military conquest, part of the complex truth though that undoubtedly is. In 1985, western Europeans rule no more of the world than they did five centuries ago, yet their mark (and that of those countries of European stocks planted overseas) is still being made afresh the world round. In 1978, for the first time, the College of Cardinals contained more non-Europeans than Europeans (fifty-six as against fifty-five) and this reflected the success of earlier transplantation of the Catholic Faith; so successful that now Europe is no longer the continent containing most baptised Roman Catholics. Yet most of the story of world Christianity is the story of a western success in spreading its ideas. The world has not conceded so much to western values and assumptions just because forced to do so by naked power, however big a part that played at times; it has for centuries been responding also to much else that came from Europe.

Some have tried to make sense of the western impact by reading it in economic terms. Essentially, they say, what has happened is that one economic system, capitalism, has triumphed over others (dispute often follows about whether this process is irresistible and necessary, or whether it could have been avoided or can be amended). But even if we can agree about a definition of 'capitalism', it is hard if not impossible to frame one which does not include much that is to be found in the economic systems of evidently 'non-western' societies. Yet their seeds of capitalism (if that is what they were) evidently did not sprout with the same vigour as in a few western countries. Why not? A close and elaborate examination of historical circumstance might give an answer, but there is no need to exclude a priori the hypothesis that a peculiar western factor was available at another level than that of economic organisation. For centuries, Europeans have looked very much alike to non-Europeans in terms of their culture and civilisation, and today some countries make little distinction between free-market American and socialist Russian exploiters and aggressors. It does not seem only to be capitalism which is the feature recognised by the rest of the world as distinctive of 'the West'.

Such over-simple views need to be recalled, if only to clear the ground a little. They leave us with the task of identifying the real nature of the western impact, and of western civilisation itself. Ahead lies a task of discovery: of what 'the West' is, of the nature of this powerful but mysterious entity which has had so vast an effect on the world. The word is packed with ambiguities and paradoxes. If it is to be used so widely, and covers so much, it is because it is felt to be needed, and needed to focus a complicated idea. Sometimes, its particular references and connotations are easy to grasp — in the Cold War, for instance. But that narrow usage is only a recent development and has already begun to look outdated. Many of the world's poorer countries see 'the West' as, simply, the rich; they would lump Cold War East and West together and throw in Japan, too, for good measure (a recent more fashionable distinction, of course, is North/South). But such distinctions cut across colour, religion and culture, leaving defenders of western values on both sides; some Latin-American countries which fall historically and culturally well within the ambit of western civilisation have been said to belong to the 'Third World'. As for the interpretation of the West in terms of imperialism it would have to include not only one country from the Cold War's 'East', Russia, but one whose racial stock is non-European, Japan. Countries seem to have been able to move into (and out of?) such categories as time passes. Yet it would be a pity to think that we were using mere Humpty-Dumpty language, meaning no more than the users wanted it to mean, when we talk about the 'West'.

Of course, it is a misleadingly simple, slippery term. There was never one simple, monolithic 'West', nor did it confront other simple monolithic abstractions like the 'East', or 'Asia', or 'Africa'. Vast dualisms of that sort get in the way of understanding historical processes in which cultures and subcultures of great specificity act and react, interplaying with one another, offering ever-new opportunities for discovery and self-discovery. Westerners, though seen as 'white men', 'hairy barbarians' (as the Chinese called them) or under any other general name, were in fact sixteenth-century Spaniards, seventeenth-century Frenchmen, nineteenth-century Scotchmen and New Englanders — and many, many other things. What they shared across the centuries was a historical role. They were all agents for the transmission of different selections from the richness of one civilisation, that of the West, to other parts of the world. For all their variety, that civilised background identifies them with the same historical process. What follows in these pages is simply a sketch of an attempt to trace the nature of that process, the emergence of the West in its history and its effects on the world, its sheer impact.

As it is in its history that western civilisation reveals itself, can be recognised and defined, enquiry has to begin with historical soundings. To expect such soundings, in an exploration on this tiny scale, to catalogue all the sources of that civilisation's supremacy would be unrealistic. All sorts of material factors would have to be taken into account, from the availability of quantities of land for easy cultivation, to the possession of certain tools at certain junctures; from patterns of climate, to obscure facts which subtly condition birth-rates. To investigate any one of them properly would be a lengthy and laborious task. Only a few of the more obvious of them can be touched on here. In men's responses to such material forces, though, in their use of them or search for protection against them, other sets of factors come into play. They are mental, spiritual, intellectual, ideological — the whole set of ideas, concepts, assumptions with which the participants in a particular civilisation are equipped by it to face the brute data of the material world. Part of that store of ideas, too, was the growing self-awareness of western civilisation, the vision that it had of itself, its own myths of what it was and where it was going. They are to be seen operating in its history, a part of its huge, complex, flawed and ambiguous triumph, for it is surely clear by now that western civilisation gave the world, among other things, an idea of what a successful society was and a notion of a burden to be shaken off — the seeds of the destruction of the West's own political dominance. That destruction by something it had itself given the world is ironical, but history is full of ironies. It's not likely our vanity will remain unscathed by looking at the past. 'I will show you fear in a handful of dust,' said the poet; there is a triumph (of a sort) in a discarded Coca-Cola can.

II
A SENSE OF DIRECTION

Like individual men and women, peoples and civilisations spin myths about what they have been and are, what they can and should do. In that way they find meaning in their experience. Some myths are very obviously about the past, about history. One of the marks of a civilisation is a wish to make sense of its past and order its knowledge of it. We cannot do without myths for that purpose; they are vital in grappling with history, for without them it would be unbearable for all but the strongest or most unimaginative souls. But such myths come in many different degrees of sophistication. At different times and in different places, people have believed that all history is explained by the movements of the planets or by racial characteristics, that it is all part of a Divine Plan, that it has been perverted from its right course by wicked men (Jesuits and Freemasons are popular choices), that everything goes in cycles of endless repetition, that it is all the reflexion of class struggle — and many, many more oddities. Sensible or not, such myths also tie us to a future. They provide signposts and links in some directions, and put obstacles in our way in others. They often generate 'philosophies of history' which attempt to rationalise what has happened. This is why the past seen through the distorting lens of our own needs and longings is just as important to us as what 'really' happened — the 'past as it really was', as the great German historian Ranke once hopefully put it.

Yet what people do and the way they see what they do are often hard to separate. One reason why history is so difficult to understand is that what happened was by no means always what was seen to happen. The storming of the Bastille was — quite rightly — seen as the symbolic end of an era; the reality was the seizure by the mob of a near-empty prison guarded by a handful of pensioners, followed by lynchings. The storming of the Winter Palace has been turned into a cinema spectacle and endlessly reproduced by painting and print to give a heroic scale, but was in fact a drawn-out, confused, hesitant process, with both defenders and attackers anxious to avoid bloodshed.[1] Yet what was seen to happen is itself an essential part of what happened in the broadest sense. This means we must seek to understand how people see their own history: the view they take of it shapes the things they feel they can and ought to do. When nineteenth-century Englishmen set about rebuilding the Houses of Parliament after the old Palace of Westminster had been burnt down, they did so in mock-medieval style; they used new ideas and iron and glass for their railway stations and the Crystal Palace, but wanted their parliament building to express the continuities of an ancient constitution. So they turned to Gothic and stone, as they did for many other public and civic buildings. Many 'new nations' formed when colonial governments withdrew have given a lot of attention to the rewriting and recovery of their real or imagined pasts; at least one, Ghana, has adopted the name of a long-extinct African polity, rather as seventeenth-century Dutchmen, also members of a 'new nation', harked back to memories of what the Romans called Batavia. Soviet Russia is the best example of all. It is formally committed to a particular account of the past without which its own history would not make sense to its rulers (though it could to other people), and its encyclopaedias and textbooks are frequently revised to maintain the plausibility of such an account.

Whole civilisations have historical myths, too, though they are much harder to pin down and identify than those of nations. How does a civilisation see its past? How, in particular, does ours? In many ways, it seems. There exist dozens, perhaps hundreds, of versions of its history. Nor are they all to be found in what is written by historians, good or bad; we could count among those versions all the summary, informal judgements made by people who consciously think about these things at all. Our view of the past as a civilisation cannot be easy to isolate; it is a question not only of formal narrative, but of untidy bundles of very deeply bedded attitudes — almost unconscious — whose total, massive inertia has kept people moving in some directions rather than others. They are a part of what a philosopher once called the 'inherited agglomerate'. We could call it an overall cast of mind, a way of seeing the world's past which colours all our particular judgements about it.

Nonetheless, to put it briefly and crudely, I believe that two central myths can be found at the heart of the western view of history. One is the idea that men are, in some sense, able to take charge of their own destinies: they are autonomous. The other is the idea that history is meaningful because it has direction; it is going somewhere. These are ideas which some people have believed they could see working themselves out almost as independent forces. Others have seen them, less mysteriously and metaphysically, simply as very strong and decisive influences on historical development: because people believed in them, they have to be taken into account as positive facts. Put thus simply, they are no doubt put too crudely. Such ideas have never been held explicitly and consistently by the majority of those who have lived within western civilisation. But in qualified forms they pop up time and time again: they are enduring in our tradition's history.

These two ideas, myths, visions, or whatever we wish to call them, appear to originate in two traditions older than our own, the Graeco-Roman and the Judaic. This is where the roots of western civilisation have long been recognised to lie. The two traditions come together most visibly in Christianity. It is literally true that we could none of us today be what we are if a handful of Jews nearly two thousand years ago had not believed that they had known a great teacher, seen him crucified, dead and buried, and then rise again to live a little while on this earth before going to dwell in glory everlastingly with their Jewish God, his father. Nor would we have become what we are today had not such obscure men had successors who, when the moment came, could become the intellectual and spiritual directors of a civilisation defined by Roman power.

The contribution made to western traditions by Greece is immense and it is rich. Views of it tend to be dominated by the achievement of a few preeminent Greek cities in their classical age of splendour in the fifth and fourth centuries BC. At the very least, we should also bear in mind a whole Greek world — Hellenistic is the conventional term — spread over all the eastern and much of the western Mediterranean, and a large part of the Near East as a result of the great conquests of Alexander the Great in the fourth century BC. In practice, though, we tend to dwell upon the giant figures of the earlier, classical age, great philosophers, mathematicians, historians, poets. In doing so, we recognise in them most easily those things which make them seem akin to ourselves, and overlook the enormous differences thus thrown into shadow. Scholarship reminds us, though, that the Greek world even of their day was more unlike our own than like it.

Selection can lead to over-idealisation of the Greek world, even at its splendid peak. One authority has suggested that its great age, the fifth century BC and a little after, can be seen as something of a *tour de force*, a triumph of intellectual effort between eras dominated by fear, guilt and unreason.[2] Even in that great age, too, much of the Greek story is one of superstition, pride and arrogance. Irrational fears could easily dominate the politics of the city-states; disbelief in the supernatural and the teaching of astronomy were made indictable offences in Athens. Greek thought was never a homogeneous bloc (only a very simple culture can be) and it was a historical continuum. Different elements were predominant in it at different times and many of the most primitive and irrational among them survived into the Christian era alongside some of its greater achievements.

This complex background has to be borne in mind, while trying to identify what it was that the Greeks left to the future civilisation of the West. The richness of their legacy has stamped itself on our language, studded as it is with words of Greek origin. Ruthless simplification and selection of themes is necessary. Yet it might be asked, why begin with the Greeks at all? After

all, more than half the history of civilisation was over by the time we reach
— say — the sixth century BC. Surely this immense stretch of time, during
which the ancient Egyptian dynasties and the empires of Mesopotamia and
Assyria flourished and fell one after another, must have also left its mark
on what was to come? We still count time with the sexagesimal scale derived
from ancient Babylonia, and the Greeks, we know, learnt about monumental
masonry from the Near East and derived the fluted column from the Egyptian motif of bundles of papyrus reed. Why start with ancient Greece? The
answer itself arises from that same long history when it is considered in a
different light. The Greeks not only took over some ideas and skills from
others, but they turned them into something entirely different, a creative,
developing culture, which can still be tapped for its vigour and creativity
today. Once the political and military structure protecting it had gone, ancient Egyptian civilisation ceased to be significant except to scholars and
cranks. Greece went on as a world influence long after the Greek cities were
themselves only ruins.

One element in that influence was the Greeks' sense of the difference
between civilisation and barbarism — or, rather, of the difference between
civilised men and barbarians. Part of the poignancy of their long struggle
with Persia is that Greeks came to feel that more was at stake in it than mere
survival; some of them — Herodotus, for example — got as far as seeing
two mental worlds in conflict and the conflict as one of freedom against
servitude. That the West stood in contrast to barbarism was an idea with a
long history ahead of it, both in secular and religious forms. It begins,
though, with the Hellenes, as the ancient Greeks called themselves. They
seem to have thought that only those who shared their language, gods and
ancestry, could live truly human lives, centered in self-direction (autonomy)
and political self-government (the city-state or *polis* invented half our political
vocabulary). They thought they were special. So, in many ways, they were.
Not until this century was political life to be a matter of active participation
for so large a proportion of the people as it could be in the *polis* but, as
always, the coin had two sides. To stress the individual's capacity for self-
rule and encourage his self-development released creativity and enriched
culture. But it also led to ferocious competition and self-aggrandisement.
Struggle encouraged excellence, of course. Professional rivalry to have trag-
edies chosen for performance in the great public festivals of Athens has left
us some of the treasures of European literature. Yet the faction and intrigue
of city-state politics was a terrible and perhaps fatal drain on the vitality of
public life.

The Greeks' sense that men — real men — were unique among animals
in their powers of self-direction led some of them almost to an idolising of
the rational intellect. The greatest Greek thinkers gave a status to rational

enquiry which it was never quite to lose in the West, in spite of ferocious attempts to overthrow it. Nor has it ever enjoyed that status in any other civilisation except our own. Socrates has remained the symbolic embodiment of this attitude, but the beginnings of Greek rationalism are to be sought back in sixth-century Ionia when men appear to have taken oriental ideas about the nature of the world, but to have stripped them of their mythological and magical settings, transforming them into rational enquiry. The Ionians virtually founded natural science, another great swing towards rationality and away from magic. If it was to prove less fruitful than the Greek contribution to philosophy (and one can agree that the bias given to that study by Plato helped to stymie scientific advance for centuries, by directing it away from observation of the material world and experiment, towards mathematics and metaphysics), it was nonetheless an immense addition to human understanding of the world. As for observation, the first great classifier and analyser of scientific data was Aristotle. Reason, even a critical, corrosive rationality, was thus part of what Greece left to the future, although it was not what many ancient Greeks would be aware of as the dominant tone of their culture.

Making lists of what our Greek heritage contains is a worthwhile activity because it reveals a lot of what we owe to them. But such lists do not tell the whole story. What the West owes to ancient Greece is not just the mass of specific artefacts and ideas which have actually survived; logic, the Parthenon, mathematical theorems, drama and so on, and the idea we have of these things. It has survived also in the idea of excellence such things expressed and it still lives in that idea today. The Greeks set up a new standard of human excellence. They gave the world a higher idea of what humanity could achieve than had been available down to their time. It was to be higher by far than many ideals to be put forward in later centuries. It inspired the Romans, the men of Byzantium and, later, those of Renaissance Italy, and still inspires some today.

This legacy has been renewed time and time again. Such renewal was sometimes desperately needed. In the Middle Ages it had to come about largely through Arab scholars — a sort of intellectual blood-transfusion by intermediaries. But since the fifteenth century or so, there is a sense in which ancient Greece has always been very familiar to western culture. We — as a society — are in a way thinking about Greece all the time. We have long had men appointed to study it and have built libraries and museums for them to do so. We are constantly rediscovering it, reinterpreting it, and reusing it. Ancient Greece has again and again been looked at by Europeans as a mirror in which to rediscover themselves. For centuries (until our own, indeed) it made up a huge central element in the educational curriculum of western civilisation. We continually reabsorb its legacy, even though the classical focus of our education (which once made this so much easier) has been abandoned.

Almost certainly, Greeks of the classical age would have seen the Jews as barbarians, yet the culture and religion of the Jewish people shaped our world just as unmistakably as that of the Greeks had done. Behind Christianity lies a rich Jewish heritage, and through Christianity it was transmitted to the future. To identify what was passed on requires (once more) ruthless selection. I wish only to select from it two great ideas which appear to me to have indelibly marked our history. The first is the idea of the bad conscience. Formulated and preached first by the Prophets, it reappears time and again throughout western history, a force always pushing out the boundaries of the morally possible. It gave Christian teaching a self-corrective bias from the start, making the achievement of higher goals feasible. In time it was to stimulate the first claimants to individual religious freedom. It has generated a nagging sense of inadequacy which has often stirred up western thought and stopped it from settling down into immobility. At its worst, it has imposed a crippling sense of guilt on individuals aware they could not meet the demands of the universal moral principles which sustained Christianity.

Yet Jewry's heart does not lie — as does that of its Christian offspring — in the salvation of the individual. God's covenant with Israel was not with individual men and women, but with a whole community. This was the root of the other great Jewish idea whose weight would shape world history, the idea of the Chosen People. It was to sustain generations of Christians in the belief that if they made their way through this vale of tears in obedience to God's law, they not only could but would reach a Promised Land of salvation. The idea inspires the story of Exodus. Thousands of years later, from the days of those who sought sanctity in suffering and poverty in the Middle Ages to those of the Pilgrim Fathers and even later, western thinkers have often looked towards a future in which, after battling through the desert, all things shall be made perfect (even, sometimes, in earthly terms). That is one reason why, unlike the histories of so many other cultures, that of the West has thrown up so many Utopias. The western view of history has always tended to be progressive — a story of a people going somewhere.

Yet there are no neat packages in the history of ideas. The ruthlessly self-assertive and confident craving of the Greeks for distinction did not obviously cohere with the disciplined community-focused striving of the Jewish tradition in its post-Hellenistic phase. Although, by the time of Christ, some Jews (the biblical King Herod was one of them) were 'hellenised' — they had, that is to say, taken to Greek ways and ideas — they were unpopular. Those Jews, often the poorer, who followed strict teachers distrusted them. Later, within Christianity, the tensions continued: 'What has Athens to do

with Jerusalem?' snarled Tertullian, choosing what seemed to him an ap-
posite antithesis. Yet both Greek and Jewish culture provided positive, active
stimuli; both gave meaning to the world of the here and now and a reason
for putting effort into it.

For most of its inhabitants that world was coterminous with the frontiers
of the great empire of Rome. During the great age of the classical Greek
city-states, not much notice was given by them to the little cities founded by
Latin tribes in central Italy. Rome was one of them. Roman institutions always
bore the stamp of Italian cultures which had preceded them, notably that
of the Etruscans, but also, as time went by, they showed the influence of
contact with the Greek cities of Italy and Sicily. Later, after a long struggle
with Catharge (the Punic Wars) which settled the fact of supremacy in the
western Mediterranean, Rome gradually revealed herself as a conquering
imperial power. *Magna Graeca*, as the Romans called the world of Greek
cities in the west, soon succumbed to the legions of the republic. The Hellenistic world of the east took longer to acquire but the process was complete
well before the birth of Christ.

Conquest and empire changed the Romans in many ways, but not least
in the way they thought of themselves, in the myths they took up to explain
themselves. Meeting the Greeks on closer and closer terms — it was something of a landmark when the Romans were admitted to the pan-Hellenic
games which brought together representatives of all the Greek cities —
encouraged the Romans to self-definition. Though they were a tough, ferocious, self-controlled, austere lot, many of them were somewhat bowled
over by the superior civilisation of the Hellenistic world. It was rich, luxu-
rious, hedonistic, complex, intelligent. Even those who had not fallen under
its spell could recognise cultural superiority when they saw it — and the
contrast must often have been galling. The Latin language was nothing like
so refined and sophisticated an instrument as the Greek. While Athens was
already a city of marble, Rome was one of brick. When the Romans sought
definition for themselves and their historic role, therefore, they were almost
bound to do so at least in part in terms of Greek culture. They eagerly took
up, for example, the legend (immortalised by their greatest poet, Virgil) that
their city had been founded by Aeneas, a fugitive from the sack of Troy.
Greek deities were equated with those of the Roman pantheon and Zeus,
chief of the gods, became Jupiter. Even under the Republic, Romans of the
ruling class took over Greek ideas and educational principles; this was when
and how, as the Roman poet Horace put it, 'captive Greece enslaved her
fierce captor'. Roman boys read Homer, and Roman art and architecture
went to Greece for their models. Thus was transferred a tradition which was
in the end to produce Caesar and Cicero. Other Romans strove to write
comedies like the Greeks. Thus the Romans' notion of what it was to be

Roman — *Romanitas* — in the end incorporated with the old Roman traditions much of the Greek heritage safeguarded by Roman imperialism.

Roman arms and government built a framework within which the Hellenistic past lived on and, eventually, turned into early Christendom. At its greatest territorial extent, the Roman Empire stretched from Scotland to the Sahara, and from Gibraltar to the Euphrates. '*Romania*' was a word which appeared in the fourth century to designate it as a whole, though by then it was no longer quite so far-flung. It incorporated the great cities of the old Hellenistic world, and that was where it found the models for the monuments which set its style — temples, forums, theatres, aqueducts. It brought prosperity not to be known again for centuries (if ever, in some) to huge areas — Sicily, Africa — and focused a complicated trading system which stretched as far as the Indian coast and central Asia. Roman coins have turned up as far away as Indo-China. Yet the empire's centre was always the Mediterranean. Its most splendid cities were all ports of the inland sea; none which were important lay far from it. Those cities formed a great cultural system, within which the Greek language could take a man anywhere in educated society, though he would also have found Latin useful in Africa and the West.

The monuments which the Romans left behind so impressed subsequent generations that they left men awestruck. It came to be believed that their great ruins must have been built by giants or magicians: anything so huge, so well thought-out, so elaborate, surely could not have been built by merely human power. Yet something more than outstanding skill in exploiting the simple technology of the day lay behind these structures. The Romans did something the Greeks had never been able to do: they brought peace, order and stability to their whole zone of civilisation. As an undivided system of government the Roman empire lasted nearly three centuries until it was split for convenience into western and eastern divisions. Of course, 'government' did not then mean what it does today. Bureaucracy was not so complete, communications were not so swift. Big concessions had to be made to local custom. In making up his mind about the extent to which he could hold out against the danger of offending Rome's subject peoples, a governor of a whole province was sometimes as much on his own as a district officer in a frontier region of India before the days of the telegraph. Pontius Pilate could not telephone to his boss in Rome for instructions: he had to make his own decision to wash his hands of a hard case in a troubled city. But the empire was a unity all the same — an area under one supreme authority and one law, and coterminous with a civilisation.

The empire and what it sheltered made the rapid spread of Christianity possible. It first took root in the large Jewish communities scattered in big cities round the Mediterranean basin (Rome itself was one place where this soon happened). That Christianity was at first only a Jewish sect is indisputable. Jesus never claimed to stand outside the Jewish tradition and the Gospels can only be understood against the background of the Old Testament. Nevertheless, once St Paul had begun to preach the Gospel to the Gentiles, it was not hard for Christianity to spread beyond the Jewish communities, because they were embedded in a larger cultural world. Ideas and men moved about easily within a culture both tolerant and religious — or, at least, credulous about the unseen. The Graeco-Roman world which received Christianity swarmed with sects and mysteries; to most people who encountered them in its first century or so, Christians must have been just the followers of one more among many spiritual and superstitious remedies peddled by oriental holy men to those seeking refuge from the uncertainties of their own world. But their faith had the inestimable advantage of offering the vanquishing of death itself, and life everlasting — a huge claim. The early Christians believed (as millions still believe) that Christ's followers were to be called to join Him in glory, to live everlastingly with Him. He had overcome death, and so would they.

There was much to offer, in a world which turned to the mystery cults and magic for its reassurance: it must be allowed, too, that at some levels Christianity seems already to have offered them, as it did later, only an alternative magic of its own, another superstition for an irrational age. That, though, was never the whole story. Christianity could take advantage of much else in the civilisation into which it was born. Once outside the Jewish communities, the early Christian proselytisers and teachers had to operate in a world whose intellectual leaders spoke, wrote and thought in Greek. When the great men we call the 'Fathers of the Church' set to work to elaborate the doctrine which would (they hoped) unquestionably distinguish their faith from mysteries and magic, they involved Christian teaching more and more with the intellectual textures Rome had inherited from Greece; so, they distinguished it more and more from its Jewish roots. A very early consequence was that Jesus, the Jewish teacher, was increasingly lost to sight behind the more awful and mysterious concept of Christ, the embodiment of the Godhead, the Son, Second Person of the Trinity. This figure was a creation of the early church, which had to argue it out of the Gospels. Like other great religions, Christianity was not founded, but made itself; in its first three or four centuries it generated its own individuality.

Sometimes the conceptual debt to Greece was very clear. Some of the Fathers deliberately sought to bring to bear on doctrine ideas which perceived Christ as the embodiment of the *Logos* — the reason which lay at the heart of God's nature. Another Greek idea, the dualism of body and soul so strongly sustained by Plato, blurred easily with the contrast of flesh and spirit so emphasised by St Paul (and perhaps, taken by him from the Old

Testament). These are deep waters, not easily sounded by laymen, or, indeed, by modern minds. But the work of the first theologians was an outstanding practical expression of the effect on new ideas of the already ancient civilisation into which Christianity was born. Through them and the church, the later West was to be tied to the Greek past. Yet there was much in that past that Christianity repudiated. It was of enormous importance, therefore, that as time went by the church found itself in the saddle, and able to use imperial authority to impose its views by political means.

The man who brought this about and, more than anyone else, made the Christian church into the legatee of Rome, was the emperor Constantine — Constantine the Great, as he came to be called (another title sometimes given to him was that of the 'thirteenth Apostle', for he claimed equal status with the Twelve). He was a Serbian. Roman politics were much confused and the empire was falling apart under rival rulers when the army hailed him as emperor at York on the death of his father in AD 306. It took Constantine another twenty years of soldiering and diplomacy to defeat his competitors and reunite the empire under one man — himself. Much earlier, though, in 312 he had ordered his soldiers to paint on their shields a Christian monogram before a battle. He seems to have been covering his bets; openmindedly, he was going to give the Christians' God a try. Certainly he knew little then about Christian doctrine. At the Milvian Bridge, just outside Rome, he won his victory; this seems to have confirmed his sympathy for the Christian faith. Christians had for some time been undergoing persecution at the hands of the imperial authorities. Constantine brought that to an end, granted them toleration once more, and gave money to their churches and clergy. After 320, the old pagan symbol of the Sun God no longer appeared on his coins and in 324 he formally declared himself a Christian. The following year he presided over the first ecumenical council of the church, held at Nicaea. Clearly, he saw himself as an emperor with a duty to preserve the faith from impurity, as well as the empire from decay. Without the continuing favour of the Christian God, already clearly shown to him at the Milvian Bridge, the empire was not likely to prosper. Constantine was a believer, certainly, though not in a very spiritual way. He was baptised shortly before his death in 337.

Constantine's conversion had momentous consequences. So had another of his decisions, the building of a new imperial capital at the entrance to the Bosphorus, the mouth of the Black Sea. The strategic importance of the site would have been obvious to so good a general, but he had more than strategy in mind. It was to be a great and spectacular city, a 'new Rome', and, Constantine hoped, a Christian city, containing no pagan statue or temple. Eventually it bore his name: Constantinople, now Istanbul. The foundation gave new clarity to an administrative division of the empire into east and west which the emperor Diocletian had initiated for convenience in 285. Then, a co-emperor had been given charge of what lay west of a line from the Danube to the coast of Dalmatia. Not all of Diocletian's successors had kept up the arrangement, but it recognised reality: east and west had become too much for one centre of government to manage. An impetus was thus given to the gradual drifting apart of a Greek-speaking east and a Latin-speaking west. When Constantine gave a splendid capital to the eastern half on the site of a Greek city, Byzantium, which had been one of the most important centres of the old Hellenistic world, this too emphasised a cultural as well as administrative distinction of east and west. From it was to emerge in the end the state known to history as the Byzantine empire.

Constantine began the process of making the empire Christian. He robed the church in the imperial purple and threw the immense weight of imperial patronage behind it. That launched a historical process which was not to be reversed. Before the end of that century, Theodosius, the last, brief ruler of a united empire stretching from Asia to the Atlantic, forbade the worship of the ancient pagan gods. The empire had officially become Christian. What did this mean?

In the first place, it meant a new kind of ideological unity. The old empire had been tolerant: if you paid proper respect to the official cult and its altar, you could believe what you liked. Christians had only been persecuted officially because they refused to do what other Romans did, and would not take part in the sacrifices to the divine emperors: the empire did not harass them because of what they believed. But from the fourth century the authorities began slowly to move towards imposing Christianity on all its subjects; like the Jewish religion, Christianity was a religion of exclusive claims, but (unlike that of the Jews) it sought to proselytise and had the power of the state behind it. Before long we hear of the harrying of priests of other cults, of pogroms of Jews. At the end of the fifth century the last pagan teachers were expelled from the academy of Athens — the Middle Ages begin, intellectually speaking, and antiquity is over. Christianity was in the saddle and was going to show itself master. The church was now tied to the glamorous and prestigious tradition of Rome, a legacy which was to be a rock to Christianity in the centuries ahead. Yet, Christians saw the church not as powerful but as weak. The faithful were, in a favourite image, the saving remnant of the Chosen, tossing in the Ark, while the floods mounted and the storms raged about them. This, of course, helps to explain why they were so harsh, intransigent, cruel, uncompromising and — if one dare say it — 'unchristian' to their fellow-men. They still lived in a world of demons and magic, where heresy or paganism threatened those who succumbed to their seductions with eternal torture in hell-fire. Theirs was an unpleasant temper, but a heroic one. At its best, it was noble. And it made possible the transmission from a dying antiquity of the cultural heritage of Jew and Greek. As there always are in great historical decisions, there were ironies in that, for, in the end and sometimes unwittingly, the church helped to destroy the framework of the classical world and consigned many of its more attractive ideals to the lumber-room of history. The greatest of English historians, Edward Gibbon, saw the story of late antiquity — the era during which the once great Roman empire crumbled into decay — as the triumph of barbarism and superstition over classical civilisation. By superstition, he meant Christianity. His was an 'enlightened', eighteenth-century view. It is too brilliant and too simple a paradox to be true, of course: Christianity in fact preserved much of the Roman past which might otherwise have gone under. Still, Gibbon's epigram reminds us that a great historical fact, the triumph of Christianity, was the triumph of the once despised religion of a tiny Jewish sect; he signals unforgettably a change of direction in the march of civilisation. Christianity nevertheless grew within the imperial civilisation, not outside it, and could not help itself becoming a great transmitter of at least some of a pagan past. Archaeologists tell us that Roman bricks were re-used in many towns to build new Christian churches, and we know of pagan temples being pillaged to provide materials. Sometimes the conversion was complete; the whole building was turned over to a new use. The earliest temple we know to have been converted in this way to Christian purposes is the Pantheon which is, in consequence, the only intact building from classical antiquity which today survives in Rome.

There is, though, another level of transmission which is more than a matter of material and style. Nearly two thousand years after Christ, and longer still after Socrates, a German said that changing the world, not understanding it, was the task of philosophers. The important thing about the Greek and Jewish ideas sheltered and cradled by the Roman empire and passed on to the later West is not simply that they helped men to understand the world but that they helped them — drove them — to change it. At first sight, that seems unlikely: no Christian (or anyone else for that matter) in late antiquity thought in terms of a better alternative to the great civilisation the empire sheltered: it was simply *the* Empire, not even described in those days as 'Roman', because none other was comparable to it and so it needed no name. Its standards were universal; other states could be assessed in the light of them. Even those who dreamed of a Judgement Day which was quickly approaching saw it as one in which all earthly powers would fade away and crumble — not as one which would replace one human order, one set of standards, by another. Educated men knew hardly anything of the worlds of Persia or India, nothing of China. Rome was all they knew. It *was* civilisation.

Many, moreover, would have thought the world was changing quite startlingly enough of its own accord in late antiquity without help being needed to further the process. At the end of the fourth century the old western Mediterranean world faced nothing less than the collapse of the framework of civilisation as it knew it. A whole world order seemed to be going under in a chaos of barbarian invasions from the north and east. What we now see is less dramatic: a collapse of political authority, rather than a cultural cataclysm. But the alarm expressed at the time is understandable. In 402 the emperor and senate had to flee to Ravenna. For eighty-odd years, while there were still western emperors (the last was deposed there in 486), that city was to be the centre of imperial rule in the West. One barbarian people, the Visigoths, sacked Rome itself in 410; another, the Vandals, repeated the performance in 455 (hence the mark left by their name on the English language). By the end of the century, the Vandals ruled what had been Roman Africa, the Visigoths dominated Spain, a new kingdom of Franks had appeared in the northern part of the old province of Gaul, with a Burgundian kingdom between it and an agglomeration of other branches of Gothic peoples, an Ostrogothic kingdom which covered Italy and much of the Balkans. A barbarian West had arisen on the ruins of the empire. True, the ruler of Italy, Theodoric, the only Ostrogoth who was a Roman citizen, had been adopted as a godson by the emperor, who had also made him consul, and (like some other barbarian generals) was called by the old Roman title of 'patrician'. He purported to govern in the emperor's name, and under his rule, while no Roman held a military command, no Ostrogoth had a post in the civil service. But that was a pretty dilute survival of the once-great Roman *imperium*. Like Theodoric's public games, held when he visited Rome, or the legend *Invicta Roma* on his coins, it says more for the empire's prestige than for its power. Admittedly, the prestige of Rome was still high. 'Our royalty is an imitation of yours, a copy of the only empire on earth', wrote Theodoric to the emperor.[3] The barbarians who had begun to press forward so much more insistently and irresistibly in the fourth century were by no means always enemies of Rome except in an objective, unconscious way, somewhat like the modern tourist who unwittingly destroys the historical treasure he seeks to share by the demands he imposes. Barbarian kings often admired Rome. They had long lived beside the empire. They wanted to share its civilisation and wealth and, as they settled down to enjoy their successes, were often willing to give up their own gods and follow that of the Christian empire. The relative paucity of the barbarian impact on the 'Romance' languages has often been pointed out; Latin made the running in settling the vernaculars of the barbarian kingdoms.

One other thing is clear. Whatever happened in the West, it was not the end of the Christian empire. Not only did barbarian rulers try to emulate it; the changes of the third and fourth centuries had already ensured that idea a firm anchorage in the East, where the wealthiest provinces and best recruiting grounds of the empire were to be found. The story of the By-zantine empire had begun. However threatened it might be, a Christian empire based on Constantinople would for a thousand years struggle to hold off the enemies of Christendom in Asia and south-east Europe. But in the West, no such state structure remained. There, the Christianity which the empire had protected had to fend for itself. From an early time, there had been distinctive Christian traditions, not only East and West, Greek and Latin, but Coptic, Nestorian, Marionite and others. Certain traditions and places had indisputable pre-eminence because of historical associations — above all, Jerusalem, where those who had known Christ had gathered after his crucifixion, and Rome, founded by St Peter, whose bones, like those of St Paul, were interred there.[4] Now, as the western empire's secular structure crumbled, the pope had increasingly to provide the leadership for the Chris-tian West which could be found nowhere else, though still provided in the East by the emperor at Constantinople.

As the barbarians pressed on the western half of the empire, and the power of the far-away emperor to protect his possessions seemed to shrink, churchmen could hardly be expected to feel very confident. The legacy from the past carried forward by Christianity and classical culture tended at that moment to show an other-worldly and passive, rather than its active, face. The transmission of ancient culture to what was later to become western Europe in an era of great barbarian invasions was a matter of survival, not of creation. The collapse of ancient certainty was a terrible experience for those raised to take the empire for granted. 'If Rome can perish, what can be safe?' St Jerome had asked. The implication was clear: nothing in this world can be taken for granted. The best for which the Christian could hope was the chance to put his soul in order in readiness for the eternity which awaited him. Some men who might have been expected to turn in earlier, less stressful times to careers which offered worldly success, can now be seen casting about for spiritual answers to their inner problems. Yet even an emphasis on surviving the uncertainties and traps of this world could foster the growth of new shoots of life which were to lead to vast changes in the actual world. Men and women stepped aside from the world to build little islands of spirituality and learning on which to keep their footing in the flood. They strove to convert barbarians, to safeguard doctrinal truth, to formulate an understanding of history which made sense of what was happening.

One such figure was St Augustine of Hippo, a gigantic influence on the later development of Christian religion and civilisation. He was an African, highly educated in the Latin literary culture which was the conventional preparation for a secular career in the late empire. Born in 354, his life coincided with the violent and terrible age when the Roman world fell apart. Christianity was not his first resort in facing it, though he had been brought up with a knowledge of Christian tradition, for his mother was a Christian. Only after he had gone to live first in Rome and then in Milan, though, did he turn to his mother's faith. At Milan he had come under the influence of the great bishop, St Ambrose, a man so powerful that he has been said to have had an authority overshadowing that of the imperial court itself.[5] Ambrose had used his spiritual authority to bring even an emperor to book; one stood before him once in his church to do public penance for wrong-doing, the first great public example of the critical power of Christianity in public affairs and the beginning of a long western tradition of confrontation between church and state. Whatever the effect of Ambrose's views on him, Augustine greatly revered him, though he seems to have been held up at the last stage of his conversion to Christianity by his own difficulty in leading a chaste life. In the end, though, Augustine became a Christian and was baptised when he was thirty-three years old. Once converted, he made rapid progress. Ordained in 391, five years later he was a bishop back in Africa, where he lived in his diocese, Hippo, until he died in 430, while his city was besieged by the Vandals.

Augustine left behind a great name as a learned man, a holy man and a bishop, and a formidable reputation as a polemicist. A large body of controversial writing testifies to this. His importance to a later age, though, is rather that in grappling with the problems which faced the church in his own age, he helped to define its course for centuries to come, by steering it away from ideas and assumptions which would have tied it to a stoic, enduring, but in the end sterile, side of the classical past.

Take Manichaeism, for example, a set of teachings said to be those of a Persian of the third century who saw history as an eternal conflict between evil and good. For a time, Augustine himself held Manichaean ideas, but turned violently against them. The Manichaean attempt to make sense of human life by seeing it in the context of a universe dominated by such a struggle was ultimately pessimistic. It undermined confidence in human autonomy. In rebutting this view of things, Augustine set out the view which has remained central to Christianity ever since: that all creation is good, and that evil is only the result of some shortcoming arising from imperfections in things created; especially, the human misuse of free will. Such distinctions may seem somewhat obscure to our age, which does not easily recognise its problems when they are cast in theological forms. Yet they had great actual relevance: they helped to settle what men felt was achievable. If you take the Manichaean view — or cast your view of history in the form of the Manichaean myth, if you prefer that language — then there is no ultimate hope that things will ever be other than they are. You may have a duty to strive for good, but not much will follow from that. The redemption of a state of things fallen or imperfect because of human action, on the other hand, is possible, even probable, according to Christian doctrine. A Christian believes that there is hope from God's grace and therefore must believe there is a case for striving: the Kingdom of God is possible.

When he attempted to make sense of what was going on round him St Augustine wrote what may be thought his greatest book: *Civitas Dei*, in English, *The City of God*. In it he integrated the story of Rome with a vision of divine purposes. For centuries, western intellectuals were to look back at the classical world from his standpoint. Bad as the events of his age might be, they were not senseless, he affirmed. They showed that even the greatest political institution known to history, the empire coterminous with civilisation itself, was dispensable. Paradoxically, the disasters falling on Rome were, he taught, another confirmation that history was meaningful, that God was working his purposes out. This was very important. For centuries, Christians were to learn from his works — enormously influential as they were — that what had happened had its place in a divine plan. History was going somewhere, even if, for Augustine, all that lay ahead was the Last Day; the Jewish idea which lies at the roots of the faith was re-asserted. The fall of Rome could be accepted because it did not involve in its disaster its legatee, the Catholic Church. Christians could transcend the history they were forced to witness, confident that its meaning was to be sought elsewhere.

Prominent among the ideas from late antiquity that lie at the roots of western civilisation and are not found elsewhere was a certain conception of a human being. The Platonic idea of a dualistic human nature, in which the soul, of divine origin, was at odds with its prison, the body, fitted easily into a vision of the individual as someone responsible for himself, not only a creature capable of autonomous direction, but the possessor of a soul precious in God's sight. From this, much else was to follow — belief that man could (and therefore ought to) regulate his own life, belief that man should be the maker of himself, and from that, in due course, would follow repeated challenges to settled pretensions, vested interest and social conformity.

The consequences of this for human history were profound. Like the overwhelming majority of human societies which have ever existed, Christian societies were to be based on the exploitation of man by man. Some people have always done better than others out of prevailing social arrangements, whether in terms of the resources they could command, including other men and women and their labour, or in prestige and influence. Yet Christianity, whatever the moral enormities (as they may seem to our complacent age) it tolerated or supported, has also thrown up correctives of them. It contained elements of criticism, of self-searching and, above all, of dogmatic moral assertion which have made it impossible for all Christians at all times to turn their backs on the possibility of reform and improvement. If you believe — as any Christian until this century was meant to believe — that the individual human soul is of infinite value, then you believe something important about human equality and human claims to equality of treatment. However remote from the actuality in which it had to be asserted, Christianity contained a transcendent principle. So, potentially, it was a source of claims to rights. That had very long-term implications. Slavery (though it is not easy to define) was an institution which, until the nineteenth century, was virtually taken for granted everywhere in the world, but then western civilisation became the only one ever to have abolished it of its own internal volition. Long before that, though, Christian ideas had affected slavery's practical working and the legal status of slaves by raising questions about their treatment — by, for example, demanding that slaves be given the chance to receive religious instruction. It is, nonetheless, the overall claim that matters: that in Christ there is neither bond nor free.[6]

Even very authoritarian regimes (some nominally Christian) have had to come to terms with such ideas and are still having to do so. They are the ultimate ground for something which still only a lucky few human beings can take for granted: a pluralist society, in which different and alternative social and moral goals may be pursued.

The Jewish legacy also gave Christianity another potential. The Chosen People were not meant just to sit down in the desert and stick it out; they were on a pilgrimage, were going somewhere, marching to a Promised Land. Inevitably that meant trying to change the world, if only to make the pilgrimage more direct and speedy. The values of Christianity demanded that Christians take part in the building of a new Jerusalem. That could mean the suppression of other possibilities which might stand in Christianity's way, of course. Here we come back to the intolerant, convinced, self-righteous Old Testament component in the equation — the urge to remake without compromise the old corrupt world into one new, purer and more just: social and practical puritanism, in fact. It fitted the Platonic dualism; grace or will could reconcile body and spirit, the beast and the intellect, and make possible the achievement of moral rectitude. Together, they spoke of the mistrust of self which later awoke so powerful a response — for instance in Rousseau. Yet in spite of Greek intimations of an austerity spurning this world and the flesh, it is the Judaic legacy which seems uppermost here. Striving puritanism has always drawn upon the Prophets (and the same puritan emphasis can be seen in the other great religion to emerge from the peoples of the Semitic tongues, Islam).

One last point. The ideas which lie at the roots of western civilisation have hardly ever received more emphatic endorsement than in something often seen as alien to them: Marxism. This may seem surprising. Part of the reason is that Marxism is now so abused and misused a term. Many people who violently disagree with one another claim to be Marxist. It is very easy to mistake one's way amid the sects. By Marxism, though, I mean the thinking which does not just pay lip-service to the ideas set out by Karl Marx and flourish his name like a talisman, but which has at its centre two convictions to which he kept coming back, however qualified and contradictory were the different statements in which he embodied them.

The first is that in the world as we know it, and as others have known it in the past, freedom is largely an illusion. The sheer weight of historical and material circumstance in which human beings are enmeshed is so great, said Marx, that most of them have very little scope to act without constraint, whatever individuals may briefly succeed in doing. This is the idea we call historical materialism. It is not reserved to Marx and his followers, and comes in many versions, hard and soft, but it is essential to their views. The other conviction which seems to be central to Marxism is that humanity's potential is such that man could assume a virtually complete control over his destiny were he to remove the hindrances actually put in the way by his social arrangements here and now. True human nature, that is to say, would then appear; men really would be free. The link between these two ideas is provided for Marx by a special view of history. This presents what is going on in the world as a working-out of the liberation of man, more or less inexorably, and independently of human will. Marxists believe that human beings who scrutinise history with the eye of faith will be able to identify themselves with it and to move with it. If they do this, they can and will increasingly escape from necessity. They will be able, one day, to run their own lives as human beings ought to do.

Perhaps not all who claim to be Marxists would agree that these are Marxism's central themes. But Marxism without them can hardly be the genuine article. Of course that does not mean that these ideas are by any means necessarily connected, nor that they are self-evident. It is indeed very hard to give considered intellectual assent to them, though many have appeared to do so. That history was the story of freedom (though in a very different way), was the belief of Marx's master, Hegel, and of many others who lived through or soon after the French Revolution. Marxism is a mythology woven round that vision, a reading of history from a particular ethical standpoint. But that does not mean that it is not easy to believe such ideas, if believing means acting in the light of the vision; if you do that, theoretical difficulties are soon forgotten. Marxism has had its successes not as philosophy but as faith; its historical role has been as an animator and inspirer of men, not as a system of scientific knowledge (though that is what Marx seems to have hoped for).

Like those of other great religions, Marxism's historical successes are based on circumstance, leadership and its essentially mythical power. And this power seems to me to be rooted in the fact that Marxism is, as it was once described, essentially a Christian heresy. It is another rewriting of the old scenario whose classical and biblical origins we looked at a little while ago, and so is a characteristic product of western civilisation. Though Marx looked at the world as an eighteenth-century materialist, he judged it in terms very like those of a Jewish prophet: he denounced a civilisation which was the greatest wealth-producer which had ever existed because it was cruel and hypocritical towards its underpaid labourers of factory and field. The world which ought to be the world in which men could rise to the full exercise of their astonishing powers of reasonable self-determination was, as he saw it, one of unreason and superstition, in which men behaved like animals to one another. From one point of view, humanity could not help this; the mills of history ground slowly and could not be hurried. Grind, though, they did — and the outcome was to be an apocalyptic transformation akin to that sought by the Jewish sectarians who so eagerly awaited the coming of the Messiah. Marx believed in a God, but called him History. The understanding of history could give men freedom even here and now, he thought, just as an understanding of God's purposes had nerved the Chosen People and braced them for what they ought to do, or as the early Christians clung to the thought of the divine plan for the Ark of the church to ride out the tempests in which the ancient world was collapsing. Freedom was something which Marx esteemed very highly in principle. He once said he had no desire to change it for equality.[7]

That the roots of Marxist ideas go far back into western culture is by no means all that there is to be said about Marxism's intellectual ancestry. Even in passing, it should be said that the immediate background against which Marx's thought is to be understood is to be found in secularised versions of many once-Christian ideas put forward by eighteenth-century philosophers. But the links and parallels with remoter ages are there and can be developed a long way. When they are, Marxism, far from being a rejection of the western tradition, as Cold War polemics sometimes suggest, seems rather to restate and summarise some of the West's most central and traditional ideas. The appalling practical outcome of the installation of Marxism in some countries as a state religion no more affects this judgement than scores of historical examples of institutionalised Christianity acting in a repressive, uncreative way in the last nineteen hundred years nullify the central messages of the Gospels. It helps to explain the irony that it is in the name of Marxism that so many contemporary revolutionaries in Asia and Africa have sought to shake off western domination. Such an adoption of a western mythology is one of the clearest and most authentic signs of surrender to western culture throughout the globe today, and, perhaps, a very old story, too. What Horace said about the defeated Greeks taking their fierce Roman captors captive might now be said of western civilisation and the world which has so eagerly borrowed its ideas — Marxism among them.

III

THE BIRTH OF THE WEST

However we define the West, its historic heartland is Europe. But Europe and the notion of Europe are both historical artefacts; once, they did not exist. For a long time after the disappearance of the western Roman empire only a few learned men, and perhaps a very few soldiers or rulers, were able to think in terms of a higher or more embracing community. Before 900 or so, there must have been very few of them indeed. Yet by the tenth century Europe and the West had been born, even if they were not remotely like what is conveyed by the words today. We can trace back many continuities still living and effective today to the centuries between, roughly, 400 and 900. Certain directions were opened up then and others were closed off. Much of the future of the world was settled by those choices. Those centuries — which, patronisingly and ambiguously, we still sometimes call the Dark Ages — produced among other things still with us the primacy of the papacy in the West, the earliest monastic structures, the English monarchy and some of its basic institutions, as well as the fundamental linguistic divisions which still form the basis of many modern European nations. At the same time there appeared feudal society, the Holy Roman Empire, the first European nobility, the French monarchy, the structure of thought which shaped European culture down to the rediscovery of Aristotle in the eleventh century, and many other things which have now disappeared but which were to have centuries of life in them, as well as enormous influence on the world. A lot of what we still live by, therefore, has roots in that age. This is why, remote as they may seem at first glance, those far-off centuries can still help us to understand our own.

Much of that extraordinarily creative period was also very troubled. Some inhabitants of the old Roman empire in the west saw the onset of the fifth century as a time of especially appalling calamity. None of them, though, had any sense of living through the birth pangs of a future Europe or dreamed that historians would look back at the age in that light. History is by no means what people are always most aware of. For all the ups and downs, and comings and goings of peoples, men and women often lived and died in remote, isolated villages, lonely valleys or clearings in the forests that then covered so much of Europe, without dreaming that historians would look back and so describe their times. Living lives shorter than their modern descendants', they can have had little sense of upheaval during the Dark Ages.

One thing which had clearly happened, though, was that the political superstructure of Roman society in the west had disappeared. This raises a most important question about the end of the old western empire: what took its place? For a long time, it cannot have seemed that anything very impressive did. The West, or large tracts of it, was deprived of the Roman state it had long taken for granted. A subsistence economy imposed strict limits on the organisation and the extent of power. Authority among the barbarian peoples must long have been a matter only of local and personal loyalties on which a warrior leader could draw in defending his own. Warbands enlarged themselves into small kingdoms on this basis, but for a long time nothing more. Nevertheless, the story of Europe begins with these little pagan units. They were the first European states. Through them the barbarians were to be civilised — which means, above all, converted to Christianity.

The church was the major instrument both in the forging of Europe and in the alchemy which produced its civilisation. It could lean on the trust of communities which recognised supernatural authority when secular power had gone. The taming of the western barbarians through their kings is one of its greatest achievements, yet the church came to owe much to kings, too. Challenged as it was by widespread adherence even in Italy to a vigorous heresy (Arianism) it mattered hugely to the Roman church that the Franks, a people who sprawled across much of western Germany, the northern Rhineland, and northern France, had a king, Clovis, who adopted Roman Christianity and enforced it in what had been Roman Gaul. In part, the clergy won such successes by exploiting barbarian admiration for Rome. What the barbarians actually knew about the amorphous mass which the western empire had become in the fifth century is very hard to see. Perhaps they never saw it as it really was. What they sensed confronting them was something fascinating with mysterious resources, power and a complicated story behind it, and huge physical monuments as its most conspicuous relics. It had glamour. They were overawed by and admired the civilisation they found and sought to learn from it. It was literate, a distinction as striking as is the possession of the techniques of telecommunication in our own day. Nor did wondering Germanic warriors distinguish two elements in it which were later to be pulled apart — Christianity and *Romanitas*, the old classical idea of what being a Roman meant. To its Christianity, since Constantine's day increasingly blended with the warp and woof of classical civilisation, they could only oppose superstition. So, slowly, the invaders were christianised, and when, in the end, Europe's future ground-plan emerges from the scatter of barbarian settlement, it is organised in a number of Christian kingdoms. Their rulers had decided to go along with the most impressive set of ideas and institutions they had ever encountered. Barbarian custom certainly survived in the Romano-Germanic kingdoms; much of it was to live on into the medieval future. Yet the representations of Woden in Germanic art were gradually transformed into images of Constantine, as those who made them slowly ceased to be simply barbarians and entered upon the heritage of Rome. The effigies of emperors appeared on the coins of Germanic kings; in 550 one of them for the first time portrayed himself in the imperial insignia.

By the end of the seventh century, Roman Christianity was the dominant form in western Europe and its great achievement in the Dark Ages would be to make a whole new world which was Christian throughout from the debris of the classical past and the cultural gifts brought by the barbarians. A new religious institution, the monastery, played a crucial part in that process. For a thousand years monasticism was to loom large in the cultural history of Europe; at times it dominated it. It is virtually impossible to imagine European culture without the monks. Yet the origins of monasticism were very far from anything like the ordered, disciplined, quiet life which we think of as typical of monks today. The first Christian monks had appeared in the Near East, in Egypt and Syria. Some of them were solitary hermits, wild and fanatical figures, their ranks no doubt reflecting the same admixture of genuine religious conviction and spiritual insight with charlatanry and downright dottiness which can be seen among India's vast population of holy men today. Some of them were men of learning and organisational ability. From the east, monasticism spread to western Europe, changing as it did so. On the continental mainland, it offered the chance of a life to which, as the old certainties of Roman life crumbled, men and women of old ruling families, the social élites of antiquity, were increasingly drawn. Its attractiveness to so many of the best and most cultivated minds of the age was of momentous significance. Gradually, monastic communities grew up which sheltered not only the life of prayer and meditation but, slowly, other things, too — writing, learning and the arts. Monasteries became cells carrying and passing on the genetic strains of a civilisation. From them men would go out to convert the pagan lands of northern Europe, while within them others maintained a living culture when its supports in the secular libraries and schools of the cities of the old classical world had collapsed.

The early history of monasticism is studded with the names of dynamic, assertive individuals, many of them easy to admire. But one stands out, perhaps the most important monk of them all and certainly a man who did much to shape the future West. This was Benedict of Nursia, better known as St Benedict. Many details of his life are still unknown — the only literary source we have for it was composed fifty years or so after the saint died — but we know that he was born about the year 480 into an aristocratic Italian family, that he opted out of the secular career which might have been open to him and, consumed by a desire for salvation, retired while still young first to a community of monks and then to a hermit's cell. We do not know whether he was ever ordained priest, but round about 520 or 530 he set up a new monastic community at Monte Cassino, between Rome and Naples — one of the great creative acts of western history, though Benedict cannot have known it.

For his monks he wrote a code of guidance and discipline: a Rule. In it was gathered together much (and presumably what St Benedict thought was the best) of earlier monastic traditions. But it was much more than a hotchpotch or mere anthology, because it had been put together by a man of spirituality and genius. Its aim was the service of God and the pursuit of individual salvation. It broke away from earlier excesses — the mortifications, self-torturings and prolonged solitudes of the desert tradition — and substituted a communal routine, directed by the abbot who ruled the monastery and was to be a father to the monks, and regulated by a timetable providing for work, prayer, worship and rest. Seven times each day his monks met to pray and sing their psalms (and so they still do). In between services they studied, carried out manual labour, ate at a common table and slept in a common dormitory. The abbey owned land which was to support the monastic community, and this could not have provided for luxury. The life was austere, highly disciplined: the monks' wills were to be bent to the community and its unvarying routine. Yet it was not a life of unattainable perfection and austerity. The background of the classical literature and philosophy of the Roman tradition and its moderation seems to have borne fruit in Benedict's Rule; it was not inhuman but was livable by ordinary men of faith and determination, for it did not ask the impossible.

As time passed, more and more communities took up Benedictine ideals and practice. The Rule was taken in the eighth century to Germany, by the greatest of English missionaries, St Boniface. The self-governing, autonomous community Benedict had designed was well fitted not only to survival in anarchic times, but to the demands of missionary and pioneering work among the heathen. It was an ark which could float in the Deluge. Thanks to St Benedict's own inspiration, moreover, it was an ark of learning as well of spirituality. Its monks studied and recopied the manuscripts which carried forward the learning of late antiquity to a post-Roman, barbarian Europe. Monks, of course, transmitted to the future only a selection from the past, partly because only a selection of it interested them and partly because they did not have access to all of it. For centuries, though, they transmitted the classical heritage to the future when almost every other tie with it in the West had snapped. This is why St Benedict (who died somewhere about 547) is so important a figure in the history of our civilisation. Benedictine monasticism is the foundation of much of western Europe.[1]

The monasteries were all the more important as fresh blows fell on Europe in the eighth and ninth centuries, completing the process which turned the descendants of former barbarians into defenders of Christendom against the new invaders. Islam calls for special attention elsewhere. But there were Hungarians, Avars and other new waves of pagan barbarians pressing from the east, too. Above all, there were the Vikings — much more dangerous than the raiding Magyars because they liked to form bases and settle, as well as being able as seafarers to strike much further afield. Charlemagne, king of the Franks from 768 to 814, is a central figure in the story of the way in which some of these threats were warded off.

Charlemagne was a great warrior, though even he could not master the Vikings. More than this, though, he was to be remembered as *Europae Pater* — father of Europe — and cannot be exclusively claimed (in spite of strenuous efforts by nationalist historians) for either French or German history. But his special standing does not rest on a bogus and anachronistic 'internationalism', either. Nor is it just a matter of his founding so much that survived to the remote future (in the United Kingdom the division of the currency into the £.s.d., which he introduced eleven hundred years ago, has only just been given up). Charlemagne had also a special place in his own day. He was the first ruler in western Europe to bear the title of 'emperor' since a Germanic warlord had deposed the last emperor in the West in 476. Other ninth-century rulers were to use the title, but they seem to have meant by it only that they were personally overlords of a number of sub-kings. Charlemagne has always been seen differently.

He was crowned by the pope himself, in Rome on Christmas Day 800. He was the first emperor to whom that had happened. Scholars have argued furiously since about what the ceremony and the title might mean. Perhaps this is not surprising. His first biographer (who knew him) makes it seem that Charlemagne himself was not quite sure what had happened. Some things are obvious: he was a Germanic king — Charlemagne had inherited his title and possessions from his father and brother, both kings of the Franks — yet claimed to be something more than just another warlord. But there was already an emperor in Byzantium: was Charlemagne saying he was a ruler of equal standing? Perhaps this is all he thought there was to it. The Byzantine emperors clearly did not like accepting him as an equal, though they called him by his title while it suited them diplomatically to do so. Their representatives at Charlemagne's court were soon taking part in ceremonies in which he was hailed as *imperator* and *basileus,* the title of the eastern emperors. His seal soon bore the words '*Renovatio Romani imperii*' — the renewal of the Roman empire.

It is tempting to reflect that when he went to Rome to help the pope, Charlemagne must have seen for himself (and was probably awed by) the mighty ruins of the imperial past, much more impressive, still with their roofs, mosaics, coloured tiles and plaster, as many of them would then have been, than they are today. The classical past of Rome was the only past, other than that of the story of God's people in the Bible, to which Europe could look back; an identification with the imperial tradition also meant identification with the classical. So imperial Rome was connected again to secular authority in the West by the coronation. Building a permanent palace at Aachen was another expression of a new sort of role (Dark Age kings and their entourages were usually ambulant, eating their way like caterpillars round their estates and those of their vassals); people at court hinted that Aachen, not Constantinople, might be Rome's true successor. Carolingian art ('Carolingian' because that was the name later given to the kings of Charlemagne's line) shows the influence of a new sense of the past in its adoption of classical models; the clothes actually worn by ninth-century Franks were not like the classical drapes on the ivories they admired.

Charlemagne was also a ruler over many peoples, another imperial reminiscence. Conquest added to the original core of Frankish territory; he came to rule Spaniards in what is now Catalonia, the descendants of other Germanic peoples in southern France and Burgundy, Italians and Lombards in central and northern Italy, Bavarians, Carinthians, Bohemians, Wends, Avars, Saxons and Danes in the east. This was a realm bigger than anything seen in the west since the Roman empire (and, incidentally, somewhat like the original EEC in its shape and extent). Within western Christendom, only the British Isles, southern Italy and the little states of the Spanish Asturias lay outside it. Though he was a good warlord, as the legends of him and his paladins were to commemorate, Charlemagne seems to have had pretensions to a new sort of rule over this mixture of peoples; he had a very ideological conception of kingship which went beyond the usual Germanic warlord's view of his role. He seems to have seen himself as a king like those depicted in the Bible, a judge and father of his subjects with, especially, responsibility for their religious faith. Christian religion was the cement of his many-peopled empire.

Charlemagne thought much about the church. His people, the Franks, had been the first of the Germanic peoples to give up the Arian version of Christianity which Rome saw as heretical, and to identify themselves with Roman Catholicism. Frankish aristocrats became bishops, and the Frankish church had prospered. Charlemagne's father and uncle had toyed with ecclesiastical reform but he eagerly threw himself into fostering the life of the church, busying himself with its doctrine and good government. The effects may not have been very visible in many village churches or private chapels, but can easily be sensed in the higher ranks of the clergy. In 789 they were admonished in a widely disseminated message to 'diligently examine their priests throughout their dioceses . . . so that they may hold the right faith, observe catholic baptism and understand well the prayers of the mass'. At least the aspiration is evident, whatever the practical effect.[2]

One especially important way in which Charlemagne benefited the church was by encouraging learning. This was not a matter of mass education, but of encouraging and protecting a handful of scholars. At Aachen he gathered learned men from many lands to transcribe sacred texts, above all the Bible, copies of which then flowed out to the great missionary monasteries of Germany. This led to a great spread of copying through other monasteries and thus to the preservation of many Latin works which would otherwise have been lost. Of all the literary work of ancient Rome now known to us, some nine-tenths survive in their earliest form in a Carolingian copy. So, the work of the Carolingian scholars and copyists determined in a broad way the intellectual and literary development of the Middle Ages. Almost incidentally, too, there also came from it a new and immeasurably clearer script than any so far available to copyists — the 'minuscule' or little hand, which revivified the making of manuscripts in the West and was the ultimate ancestor of the first Italian printing types (because, it seems, it was assumed in the fifteenth century to be much more ancient than it was).

The eighth-century scribes who solved the problem of creating an easily legible alphabet which would stand up to the test of survival in recognisable form even when copied by those of inferior skill were responding to something more than the needs of simple piety. The 'Carolingian Renaissance', as it has been called — a 'Renaissance' because its contribution to the recovery of the classics reminded nineteenth-century scholars of the humanist rediscovery of Greece and Rome in the later Middle Ages — mixed up politics, learning and religion. The church provided an enduring underpinning for conquest. In Germany, for example, Charlemagne followed up his military successes against the Saxons by setting up bishoprics and missionary centres among them. Once they had accepted Christianity, relapse was punished as seriously as rebellion. This worked. Saxony was bullied and evangelised into loyalty and piety. To convert the heathen was to bring them under the sway of the empire as well as of the church. It was also to bring them within the pale of civilisation. The missions of the Dark Ages in which English missionaries had joined with the Frankish church had been the first stirrings outwards of a civilisation which was to impose itself on the whole world. Charlemagne's conquests in Germany carried the frontier of Roman Christianity still further outwards.

The 'Carolingian Renaissance' must be seen in this setting. A missionary church needed books as manuals of practice, as training aids, as propaganda. So, moreover, did Carolingian kingship: what better teaching for subjects was there than that to be found in the stories of righteous kings set over Israel by God Himself? The authority of the Carolingians was already buttressed (no one was quite clear about how or to what extent) by the sacred quality which the church gave to their coronations. In 754, the founder of their line, Charlemagne's father, together with his two sons, Charlemagne and Carloman, had been anointed by the pope with the sacred oil as David had been in the Old Testament: this was a new ceremony. After this, the authority of the Carolingian kings must have had a quality somewhat above that of mere Germanic warlords, even though that was what Charlemagne still was in the eyes of many of his great men.

The 'special relationship' between the Frankish monarchy and the papacy, the uniquely important western bishopric of Rome, is another fixed point in the making of Europe. The imperial past of the city, even in its decay, and the vigour of its bishops in exploiting their heritage of special sanctity as the successors of St Peter and the custodians of the place of both his martyrdom and that of St Paul, counted for much. In addition, there was a story put about since the seventh century that the emperor Constantine had conferred upon the pope primacy over the eastern churches and dominion over all Italy. More realistically, the collapse of imperial government in the West had as a matter of necessity imposed new secular and administrative responsibilities on the popes. They had soon come to act with small regard for an ineffective representative of the authority of Constantinople who lingered on at Ravenna. This was the background to the military help given by Charlemagne's father to the pope against the Lombard kings who had come to dominate Italy, and his subsequent endowment of the papacy with lands stretching far north of Rome itself, the basis of the later Papal States, the Temporal Power of the papacy. The ties of Christianity and the church with the first political structure in the West which transcended barbarian kingship were thus complicated and many-layered. That may make it less surprising that Pope Hadrian I, who came to the throne in 772 (the same year in which Charlemagne, after his brother's death, came to rule over all the Frankish lands), was the first pope to date his official documents without a reference to the reigning emperor at Constantinople.

In the end, a new empire was to emerge in the West as an enduring institution — albeit one which was for much of its life to have more form than substance. Vague as the meaning of Charlemagne's title might be, from his coronation by the pope there ultimately sprang the Holy Roman Empire (a name not used until the twelfth century). It was to have a thousand years of life and its story starts with Charlemagne because of his imperial title and because the German and Italian parts of his heritage formed its territorial core. A hundred and fifty years later — in 962, to be exact — Otto the Saxon was crowned emperor, like his great predecessor, by the pope at Rome. After him, the imperial title was passed down along a succession of rulers until 1805, when it was brought to an end by another *arriviste* emperor, Napoleon of France. For a thousand years, though, there was at least in name and often in reality a western empire again, at first claiming equal status with Byzantium, and then outliving it for three hundred and fifty years. 'It was neither Holy, nor Roman, nor an Empire' goes the old quip. Well, perhaps so. But if it is recognised that it was inseparably associated with the idea of the protection of the church and Christian kingship, then 'Holy' is only an exaggerated description of the idea at its heart. As for 'Roman', it was the inheritor of Rome in the West; no rival was conceivable. It could be called an 'Empire' because of that fact, and because the emperor was quite a different sort of ruler from an ordinary king, ruling many peoples, even if by Otto's day they were only to be found in Germany and Italy. By then, the old western Frankish lands had long since broken away; they were called 'Frankia' and were not to be reunited with the rest of the Carolingian inheritance until, tentatively and contractually, by the setting-up of European economic institutions in the 1950s.

Of course, we must not be taken in by words. In the Middle Ages, just as today, they were used as political tools and have to be understood as such. The emperors did not always have much power. Nor, even, did later Frankish kings: something of a collapse of central authority followed Charlemagne's reign, partly because of the Viking onslaughts which threw responsibility on local magnates, partly because the roots of what was later called 'feudal' society were nourished by disorder which led men to bind themselves to strong lords for protection. Nor should the material achievement of the Carolingians and Ottonians be rated too highly. Charlemagne made Aachen a centre of learning and by western European standards of the time embellished it magnificently. But judged against the Constantinople or Córdoba of those days — let alone against the Roman past — it looks provincial and small.[3] Nevertheless, an idea was established there on which the self-confidence of later Europe, the Europe of the High Middle Ages, was to be built. The inheritances of classical Rome and of Christianity — the Empire and the Papacy — were the foundations of a new emerging Christendom, one distinct from the Christian communities of eastern lands. This was why the age of Charlemagne was so important. During it there emerges for the first time a new unity of civilisation in western Europe, focused on the ecclesiastical centre of Rome and on political and military power north of the Alps.

This civilisation, even in Charlemagne's day, already reached beyond the formal limits of his own empire (whose neat boundaries on many modern maps are misleadingly definite, for we have to come almost to modern times before political frontiers as we know them begin to be realities). Even then, one important centre of Christian civilisation (on which his own encouragement of learning drew, as had done the conversion of Germany), lay outside the Frankish lands, to the north, across the Channel, in the British Isles, the nucleus of a future nation and a world power. The collapse of Roman imperial rule in Britannia had been more complete than anywhere else in western Europe. After three centuries and more of its use, the Latin language disappeared there, whereas it remained in Spain and France, as well as in Italy, the basis for future vernaculars. But it is unlikely that it was experienced as a cataclysm. Certainly what happened did not happen quickly. To talk of the German peoples, who, from the early fifth century onwards slipped up the eastern and southern estuaries of England in growing numbers, as 'invaders' may be precisely true, but suggests a suddenness and violence which are not always justified. They sometimes met resistance, but in some places new Germanic arrivals and the Roman-British natives may well have been settled peacefully side-by-side even before Roman rule was formally withdrawn. So, at least, archaeological evidence suggests.

Nonetheless, the old Roman province of Britain was abandoned by the dying western empire of the fifth century, formal ties between it and the mainland disappeared, and a handful of barbarian kingdoms grew up, some of them with names commemorated to this day by those of English counties — Essex, Sussex, Kent, for instance. This took a long time, but it had happened by the beginning of the seventh century. Just before that, in 597, a Roman mission had begun the evangelising of the island from Canterbury, from that moment the animating centre of the church in England. Its rapid success was followed by a period of competition during which England's cultural and political, as well as religious, future hung in the balance; nevertheless, by the end of the next century the Romans had outdistanced the Celtic church in their rivalry for primacy in England.[4] Soon a great missionary movement back to the continent would be launched from what had only recently been a cultural backwater. So successful, too, was the recivilising of these islands that Charlemagne drew upon England for the scholarship he needed to revitalise the Frankish church. England, we may say, was part of Europe from the start.

Like their continental neighbours, the English people suffered badly from the onslaught of the Norsemen. In the ninth century, much of the island was conquered and settled by the Danes. The struggle with them came to a head under the king who has the best claim to be the first English national hero who actually existed: Alfred the Great, king of Wessex and founder of the national monarchy, though he himself never ruled all England. He is also something of an index of just how far European civilisation had come by his day. One of his main concerns was to repair the damage done to religion and learning by the destruction of so many monasteries in the Viking attacks. There was more than a practcial idea of their usefulness to government in this, and more than naive piety. Alfred was a thinker. He pondered for himself the old philosophical questions of free will, necessity and divine purpose and he wanted to bring the literature which dealt with them to his people. It was, of course, in Latin. He had himself as a boy gone twice to Rome (and, indeed the pope had given him the honorary dignity of Roman consul) and he taught himself Latin (Charlemagne had tried to learn it, too, though we are told, without much success). Latin, through which lay access to the heritage of civilisation, was not easily learnt; there were not many teachers about. So, Alfred conceived the great scheme of translating the books 'most necessary for all men to know' into English; as many free-born English youths as possible were to be schooled at least so far as to read English writing and thus to be able to share in the heritage of the classical past. It was a marvellous idea, nothing less than the first programme of national education. And as the texts chosen for translation made clear, it took it for granted that the heart of civilisation was to be found in Christianity and classical culture. Alfred himself translated the philosopher Boethius, a book by Pope Gregory the Great which told bishops what they should do to teach their flocks, a history of the ancient world by Orosius, and the book which is the fountainhead of all English historical scholarship, Bede's *Ecclesiastical History of the English People*. Alfred's intellectual ambition, like his political and military achievement, was heroic. It showed the same mingling of Roman and Christian tradition as could be found at the Carolingian court (with which Alfred had close ties). In that mingling lay the foundations of medieval Christendom, the cradle of modern Europe.

The 'Middle Ages' — a term whose own appearance in the fifteenth century registers that some people thought the centuries it denoted were already over — lasted a long time. At a minimum we can think of five centuries after 900. That would be an arbitrary date to choose, though. Many historians would see AD 1000 or 1100 as more useful points of vantage.[5] Whatever date we choose, at some point a qualitative change becomes apparent. A vast structure was to be built on the foundations laid in the Dark Ages and the outcome was a mature western Europe. Its political, material and cultural (and even geographical) definition owed much to forces from the outside, but that can wait for later consideration. Only one thing need be stressed here: Europe was practically defined long before its inhabitants had anything like a modern idea of it. Even in, say, 1500, few people would have used the word 'Europe' to denote the largest collective entity to which they felt they belonged; they would have preferred an older one: 'Christendom'.

That word, too, is a latecomer. It cannot firmly be identified until the eleventh century. For a long time, in spite of the spreading geographical grasp of the church, it did not connote territorial extent. This should not surprise us, for men in the Middle Ages did not think readily of societies occupying defined spaces. Christendom was at first a community of persons, those who shared the Christian faith, whether in its Roman, Orthodox, Coptic or any other form, and whether they lived under Christian rulers or, as in parts of nearer Asia or Spain, under pagans. Potentially, of course, the whole world was capable of inclusion in Christendom. Only gradually did this idea become narrower. It stabilised somewhat as it became possible to sense some sort of boundary between the Christian world and the rest; particularly in the face of Islam, the meaning became a little firmer. But new ideas took root slowly. No doubt, even in the eleventh century, most Europeans might, as a matter of fact, never have heard of the Byzantine empire and would have assumed Christendom to be coterminous with the sphere of the Roman church, but at that time their educated betters at least should not have accepted such a narrow view. Four centuries later, the idea of Christendom was still hazy, but a great deal had happened to sanction a working definition of it as the region within the ecclesiastical jurisdiction of the Roman Catholic church. Probably most Europeans by then thought of it in that way.

Christendom by 1500 covered the area which inherited through a Latin-based culture the traditions of the ancient classical past. Much of its boundary was well defined by the sea or by Islam. In that last fact lies the revelation that the mature idea of Christendom was a confession of failure, a relinquishing of a universal view and a recognition of the reality of pressure from outside. By 1500 only Christian princes ruled the lands within it, some linked in ties of dependence to one another, but all acknowledging formally the spiritual supremacy of the pope in Rome and (most of the time) some vague, ill-defined primacy in the ruler who inherited a wraith-like version of Charlemagne's supremacy, the Holy Roman Emperor.

Clearly, a very deep separation from the 'other' Christendom of the eastern churches and the Byzantine empire had occurred long before this definition was complete. The division rooted in the cultural difference of the Greek east and the Latin west of the old Roman empire, and institutionalised by Diocletian and Constantine, had been deepened by different historical experiences as the centuries passed. Geographical and ethnic divergences were made more important by theological schism, a very effective cultural separator. So two zones of civilisation matured in different ways. From difference stemmed distrust, incomprehension and, in the end, conflict; it was a western Christian army which, in 1204, was the first to sack Christian Constantinople. One very important, perhaps essential, contribution to this estrangement and to the shaping of western Europe as a distinct civilisation was made by the internal dynamic of the Roman church itself.

The long domination of western European civilisation by religion may have been logically inescapable, given the nature of Christianity. Both east and west, it made exclusive institutional claims. Theoretically at least, they were in the last resort incompatible with those of any other religion. Practical concession was possible, of course. Barbarian custom — a midwinter festival, cult-worship at a sacred place, popular ritual — could be tolerated in practice, if it could be absorbed into a Christian conceptual framework and dressed up in Christian theology. Until the eleventh century, this allowed much practical and local variety in western European religious practice. Local liturgies and rites survived (a 'Mozarabic' rite going back to Visigothic times is still celebrated today at Toledo, though almost as an antiquarian indulgence) and bishops, kings and magnates took their own decisions about discipline and morals. All this changed, though, with a rise in the pretensions of the medieval papacy which gave a quite new intransigence to western Christianity and gave it a new uniformity and power. The outcome was medieval civilisation as we now think of it.

The change owed much to monks, above all to the Benedictines of the abbey of Cluny, a Burgundian house near Mâcon, founded at the beginning of the tenth century. That community quickly won itself a name for strictness of discipline, for splendid liturgical embellishment of worship, for good economic management and for — above all — independence of the local lay bigwigs. Cluniac ideals spread quickly. By the eleventh century there were many Cluniac houses; they attracted recruits and endowment from noble families, and their influence was great throughout both ecclesiastical and lay society. Kings and princes often listened to Cluniac monks as advisers and counsellors.

Of all those faithful to Cluniac ideals, none was more important and effective than Pope Gregory VII. He is one of the great revolutionaries of European history. Hildebrand, as he was known before his enthronement, had been a monk and was a great admirer of Cluny. Through him, the Cluniac ideal touched the church at its very heart, for he stood for nearly a quarter of a century at the elbow of popes as a trusted counsellor before he was himself elected to the papacy in 1073. He almost at once launched a campaign to discipline and revitalise the clergy. They were to be men apart, a *militia Christi,* 'Christ's soldiers'. Gregory may be said virtually to have invented the idea that Christian society consisted of two distinct orders, lay and clerical. He denounced sexual incontinence (at that time concubinage was widely tolerated among ecclesiastics), simony (the sale for money or other personal gain of spiritual things) and, above all, lay interference with the church. More than an abstract issue of theology or law was involved. At the heart of the matter lay wealth and resources: were laymen — kings and magnates — or churchmen — bishops and abbots — to control them?

This is why the issue of lay-clerical relations blew up into a great struggle with kings and emperors. Its most dramatic episodes have gone down in history books as what is called the Investiture Contest — a row over who should invest an abbot or bishop with his ring and staff and receive his homage before his consecration. Gregory forbade churchmen to receive investiture from laymen, because it was likely to lead to the lay manipulation of the church. Twice Gregory excommunicated an emperor, once humbling him by making him wait for him barefoot in the snow outside his residence. Yet at the end of his life Gregory was driven from his own capital by imperial troops and he died in exile. The struggle over lay investiture went on for a long time after that. Formally at least, the papacy appeared in the end to have won, but the issue was blurred and it is not easy to say that anyone actually surrendered. The details, in any case, are less important than what was at stake for western Christendom. Gregory had wanted not merely to assert the independence of the church, but its separation from and superiority to the lay world. His efforts to achieve this were enormously creative acts, though the outcome was in a way quite unlike anything Gregory can have intended. Hildebrandine reform divided every Christian community into two — lay and clerical — as he wished, but the tension between them was time and again to prove the catalyst of liberties for the laity. Gregory had gone much further than merely distinguishing, though; he had made claims which, exaggerated yet more by some of his successors, led to assertions of much more than the independence and spiritual superiority of the church. Gregory said that rulers, if erring, might be deposed — a shocking idea for a society deeply respectful of oaths of fealty, social ties of the utmost importance. By the thirteenth century, Gregory's successors were claiming ultimate monarchical authority over all men.

Paradoxically, such claims were to help to give European history a unique twist in the direction of freedom. From centuries of contest and sometimes overt struggle between what were later called church and state, Europe derived a tension which in the long run told in favour of liberty and pluralism. There could be no development of monarchy in the West towards such a unification of lay and spiritual authority in the same man as was to be seen at Constantinople. Moreover, when strong men, clerical or lay, fell out, they had to bid for support and make concessions when they did so. Their quarrels left interstices where liberties could take root and survive. This meant that, at the political and legal level, self-critical adjustment within medieval European civilisation was often made easier and was protected by circumstance which allowed scope for self-interest and self-seeking.

The preservation of an idea of liberty and its transmission to the future thus owes an incalculable amount to the quarrels of church and state. They might spring immediately from disputes over wealth and power, but they were latent, too, in the clash of principles between the spiritual supremacy of Rome and the realities of secular power. The great philosophical and legal minds of the Middle Ages returned again and again to the issue. The separation of temporalities from spiritualities when a bishop was inducted to his see, the definition of clerical immunities, and many other theoretical achievements express a tension which cropped up over and over again in medieval life. There was conflict after conflict between individual kings and their bishops (from one of them, Canterbury gained the martyr who made it the greatest English centre of pilgrimage in the Middle Ages), local magnates and abbots, quite apart from the great struggle of pope and emperor. Such struggles bred opportunities which helped to keep a civilisation open to new developments, alive and dynamic.

Meanwhile, the church itself was transformed and through it Europe. A growing papal bureaucracy — the Roman *curia,* or court — gave a new cohesion and central direction to its affairs. From all over Europe, first parchment and then paper flowed in a rising flood to Rome, all in the international language which bound the continent together, Latin. Churchmen and pilgrims circulated endlessly along the appalling roads, many leading to Rome, and this, too, testified to a new unity in the continent's life, for all its local diversity. New religious orders — Cistercians, Dominicans, Franciscans — revivified spiritual life and developed new kinds of evangelical and intellectual expertise. Architecture underwent a great blossoming; a great era of cathedral building began in the twelfth century. Doctrine was changed, too — the curious theory of transubstantiation, that by a mystical process the body and blood of Christ are actually present in the bread and wine of the communion service, was imposed from the thirteenth century — and frequent individual confession gave the church a formidable new instrument of discipline. Clerical celibacy at last became the norm, the clergy were distinguished from the laity as those of the eastern Orthodox churches were never to be. The new universities, which first appeared in the thirteenth century, were clerical corporations and all education was in clerical hands. Europe west of the Elbe was by then already a zone of civilisation permeated by Christianity as never before.

Laymen and clergy alike took for granted the claims of the church to the custody of unique truths. Their quarrels were usually about practical applications. This argument underlines one of the most sinister outcomes of the strengthening of the church. From the thirteenth century onwards we hear much more about the persecution of heresy. It had begun to develop in a way unparalleled since the fifth century, but it was always a feature of medieval Christianity that it aspired to an ideologically exclusive community.

Hinduism, Confucianism, Buddhism, Shintoism seem to have no difficulty in coexisting with other beliefs in the same society and even Islam has a hierarchy of toleration; but Christianity demanded adherence and belief — and, increasingly, pure belief. Hence the pursuit of heresy. The joining of church and state in western Christendom to suppress by force dissent which might endanger either of them was for a long time pretty effective.

It was not, though, just because of ideological conformity, or through its institutions and politics, that medieval civilisation can be described as permeated by religion. It is worth repeating: men thought of themselves as Christians living in Christendom, not as Europeans living in Europe, and the huge implications of that were everywhere actually visible. There were more clergy about in the streets in those days, more religious houses of nuns and monks; in hundreds of towns and cities the tower or steeple of the church or cathedral was the tallest landmark. The greatest works of art and engineering of the age (and the largest single investments of capital) were the Romanesque and Gothic cathedrals which for many northern Europeans defined for centuries what ecclesiastical architecture should be. Even the daily timetable was set by the bells of parish belfries or monasteries announcing the hour of another office: an important focus in an age when clocks were few.

And, of course, religion went deeper than this. Medieval Christianity coloured men's views at every level. It had taken over superstition and tradition; pagan rites had been christianised, and pagan festivals absorbed into the calendar of the church. The Christian mentality seeped into the popular imagination and intellect through the stories told in stained glass, the statuary and carving of the great churches, the homilies of the preachers. As it did so, it changed men's minds. Whatever may be thought of the bilious comments of some medieval clergymen on women, for example, the image of the Blessed Virgin which looked down from thousands of cathedral windows, façades and altarpieces was never that of a fertility goddess, but a female embodiment of ideas of intercession and mediation, a focus of honour and devotion. It was not a worship of fecundity which lay at the heart of superstitious exaggeration of her role, but a promise of understanding rooted in maternal tenderness. Like the specific authorisation and institutionalising of new roles for women in the religious life — and a handful of outstanding women won recognition for their achievements as administrators or scholars — such influence slowly educated Christendom in the evolution of a respect for women (and a safeguarding of their rights) unknown in the other great historic civilisations. From respect followed a real independence, however limited it may look from the perspective of today. Chaucer's Wife of Bath is not easy to imagine in Ottoman Turkey or Confucian China.[6]

Her case may remind us, moreover, that by Chaucer's day the church had also completed a takeover of marriage, one of the most fundamental of all human institutions. Religion not only defined, prescribed and explained the tests which validated the proper arrangements for the union of man and woman, but built outwards from this to colonise huge areas of life. Ecclesiastical law — and courts staffed by clergy, in which clergy were judges — regulated not only marriage, but much of family life, inheritance, and a huge area of personal conduct and belief. It is an extraordinary fact that this practical domination of so much personal and public behaviour (to say nothing of the formal apparatus imposing uniformity of belief and religious observance) never quite stifled either dissent or disagreement. Partly, no doubt, this was because the physical and political problems of doing so effectively were very great, particularly after Gutenberg had brought together a number of existing processes to create the modern printing-press.[7] Neither, though, did it prevent evolution towards a society more varied and pluralist, even in sectarian terms. The Protestant Reformation of the sixteenth century was a great upheaval which in the end shattered the world of Christian religious unity. Martin Luther, the man we rightly think of as its dominating personality, was an intensely medieval figure. He jeered at Copernicus for wanting to prove the earth goes round the sun. He was a monk, obsessed as many medieval churchmen before him had been, with the contrast between what Christian society was and what it proclaimed itself to be. But, unlike his predecessors, he survived and succeeded because it suited certain lay rulers to support him as none of his predecessors had been supported, and because of the distracting pressure of Ottoman imperialism. So, from one point of view, begins the modern world — almost all of whose ultimate values Luther would have abhorred — and so we tend to forget he was a man of the Middle Ages.[8]

At the deepest level, it is in its Christian nature that the explanation of the success of medieval society in shaping the future must lie. At such a level, too, we can recognise again the legacy of a very distant past. It can be seen, for instance, in the fact that the Christian world view of the Middle Ages was integrated and rational. It gave an account of all creation which was intellectually defensible. It might be grounded in mystery, but its articulation and structure were comprehensible and logical. The ways of God might be ultimately unfathomable, but they were not unreasonable. Though rationalism had always been contested by some, this was what the early Christian Fathers had taught of the divine *Logos,* what Augustine had argued with the aid of Roman history, and what the great scholastic thinkers of the Middle Ages brought to a peak of refinement in the philosophic system we call Thomism, after St Thomas Aquinas. The idea that faith was reasonable was to triumph. This was to lead to something very different from the barbaric rituals and incomprehensible deities of oriental temples. And it was different, ultimately, because at its roots, it was Greek.

Furthermore, this was an active, questing, striving religious culture. Christian clergy were forever trying to make over things again, to make things new. The idea that history was a pilgrimage towards salvation was never lost to sight. Christianity was almost obsessively self-critical: hence much of the long-drawn-out story of self-sought martyrdom and unwilling heresy as reformer after reformer railed against the church as it was in the cause of the church as it might be. Its search to change the world, and its self-criticism, ensured that medieval civilisation never lost the capacity for self-renewal, though, in the end, that renewal was only achieved after the shattering of its formal and structural unity in the Reformation.

The 'Protestant ethic' came, in due course, to be held responsible for the later idolisation of the individual in western culture. That was exaggerated. It may now be more helpful to remember that Protestantism, too, was a transmitter of a medieval heritage, as the personality and outlook of Luther reveal. At the heart of Christianity, once St Paul had done his work, there lay always the concept of the supreme, infinite value of the individual soul. This was the tap-root of respect for the individual in the here-and-now, a respect buttressed by Roman concepts of law and legal rights, and by the emphasis on moral autonomy which went back to ancient Greece. It was a standing argument — even if occasionally near-silent — against conformity and a fundamental challenge to all settled social and political pretensions. Even highly authoritarian regimes had to respect it by appropriate forms.[9] Secularised in later times, it was to be a huge source of creative energy within western civilisation. Its importance can easily be sensed by considering the absence in other great cultures — Islam, Hindu India, China — of such an emphasis. In their histories there are certainly striking individuals, lauded for great deeds, but there is little respect for individuality itself. All those cultures stressed social harmony, order and cohesion, and the values which went with them. In none of them was the safeguarding of individual rights to be given much attention until the coming of western ideas.

The West first expressed its moral bias towards safeguarding the individual (which it has now communicated to so much of the rest of the world, at least in form) in a religious mode.[10] Christianity was one — if only one — of the complex sources of a certain predisposition in western European society to evolve towards variety and pluralism, towards greater and more widespread acceptance that men might make different choices of personal and social goals, and agreement that it is licit to pursue them. Even medieval Europeans could choose between the lay and religious lives; those alternatives, nonetheless, were still related to the same, single over-arching view of society and its end, the salvation of souls. What had still to be accepted was that disagreement could be tolerated about final ends, fundamental assumptions, values. A society which can sustain such an acceptance of disagreement and divergence without falling to pieces under the strains of the conflicts they engender must be able to tap energies and intellectual resources left unexploited in more homogeneous cultures.

Truly open societies tolerant of such variety only emerge at a very recent date. They are still very few. Political institutions only slowly reflect changing social facts. Largely ineffectual laws on blasphemy remained on the English statute book as atrophied relics of a theocentric age long after there was any realistic will to enforce them. Social practice is a better guide to the pace of change and the operation of the bias given to Europe's medieval civilisation by its rationalism and individualism. Part of the story of the preservation of the inherently individualist message of the Gospels is that of dissenters, cranks, ascetics, heretics who time and again confronted the church itself and charged it with illegitimate compromise with the political order. But political compromise and shrewd recognitions of reality had helped, too.

Of course, there are many dangers in trying to sum up anything so complex. The easiest trap to fall into is that of judging the past in terms other than its own, by awarding it marks either for following or for departing from the way historians now think history was going — by relating it to what 'ought' to have happened. To do so is fatal to historical understanding. We can avoid it by continuing to remember that most men and women who lived and died in those remote centuries could have sensed virtually nothing of what later historians would say was important or 'really' happening in their age. If we are going to give good marks and bad then at least it should be on the basis of the awareness, standards and aspirations of those who lived at the time. But I am not much interested in good and bad marks anyway; real connexions with later times are what matter. For present purposes what is interesting about the civilisation of the Middle Ages is its factual linkage with what followed. Much of the later dynamism of the West rests on what was done in the Middle Ages to prepare its material, institutional, cultural and psychological foundations. Whether this was for the ultimate good or ill of mankind need not concern us here. What matters is the relation of cause and effect. In making judgements about that, our knowledge of what came later is inescapable, so, in that sense at least, we have to judge levels of importance; but we should try to make them judgements about instrumental importance, not about moral or aesthetic value.

The most obvious achievement of the Middle Ages is very physical and down-to-earth: by 1500 western Europe was supporting many more people than ever before. The evidence is patchy and hard to interpret, but it seems likely that by then there were about eighty million Europeans.[11] That figure had been achieved despite a terrible setback in the fourteenth century, when a succession of disasters (which we tend, somewhat misleadingly, to recall under the name of one of them, 'the Black Death') had harshly corrected a precarious over-population. By 1500 the trend was upward again. Such an absolute growth in vitality and human capital was only possible because western Europeans had learnt how to grow more food. They had some natural advantages — richer soils, abundant rainfall and a longer growing season than lands further east. But these advantages had to be exploited. Much has been claimed for Dark Age technological innovation — the wheeled, mould-board plough which could manage heavier soils, the horse-collar and horseshoe — but it seems likely that the basic explanation for rising output was the breaking-in of more land, adding to the area which could be sown, and slowly improving the way it was cultivated (which, of course, also often depended on technology). It is possible, too, that the diet of Europeans, given the particular circumstances of their agriculture and its provision of non-cereals, may also be something to be taken into account.[12] Another, though much smaller, contribution to a larger food supply was the still infant development of long-distance trade. This, though by 1500 only on a small scale, made it possible once again to rely in some places (as some areas in the ancient world had relied) upon distant suppliers for some foods. So, the Middle Ages was a time of major economic achievement.

What was happening was that Europe was already drawing ahead of other civilisations in her energy resources, command of working capital and real income *per capita*. What is more, she was on the eve of adding hugely to her available resources by discovery, and of startling further development of international trade. By 1700 Europe was to be visibly ahead of all other centres of civilisation in the wealth of her inhabitants. She would also be ahead in such cultural indices as the diffusion of education and literacy, and, if 'ahead' is the right word, in the evolution of a more and more autonomous market, distinct from the feudal carapace which had cramped virtually all economic processes in the early Middle Ages. The roots of this all lay in late medieval Europe and it is not possible to limit the explanation to material and technical factors, whatever their importance. We have also to take account of social, institutional and cultural facts which made it possible for Europe to edge its way out of the population trap which weighed down other civilisations.

Clearly, like most economic advances, this one was inseparable from social change. The fourteenth-century population collapse made it impossible, for example, for all landowners to keep their serfs tied to their manors. Labour being scarce, men who ran away might expect to find employment for wages — even those who stayed on the spot could now ask for them. In England, in particular, the old rigidities of rural society began to crumble at an early date. Whatever the term 'feudal society' may mean — and it is, after all, an invention of lawyers and historians — by the sixteenth century it was no longer a sufficient term to describe society there. Few European countries, though, were altogether untouched by such changes. They were part of a general liberation of the economy; it was well on the way to autonomy everywhere in western Europe by 1500, if autonomy means regulation by prices providing relatively undistorted signals of demand and a substantial degree of security for property against arbitrary confiscation by king, lord or robber.

This reminds us of another indicator of economic change: the late medieval growth of towns. There is an old and deeply rooted European tradition which distrusts urban life as a nursery of subversion and innovation. 'Town air makes a man free' said an old German proverb, and not everyone thought that a good thing. It was sometimes a literal truth, nonetheless, for those who shook off formal, legal ties when they left the manorial estate for the town, and the idea of the 'citizen' or 'burgher', the town-dweller enjoying rights and privileges shared with his fellow citizens, was an important step towards the idea of individual liberty. The slow multiplication in numbers and growth in the size of the towns in the Middle Ages was in fact a concomitant, even if not a necessary one, of the slow growth of the agrarian economy. By 1500, many Europeans, though still only a minority, lived in towns, important nuclei of a new kind of life unlike either that of the Dark Age peasant or that of the urban proletariates of the great Hellenistic cities. Towns sheltered and nurtured the recovery of commercial life, to whose collapse in the west in late antiquity the medieval fairs had been for a long time the only effective response. Ports were especially important. But cities like Venice and Lübeck, or Florence and Bruges for that matter, had more than economic significance. They could offer a security and richness of experience unknown in the Dark Ages, expressing in civic festivals, holidays, religious and secular ceremonies an independence of a new kind. A few of them, mostly in Italy, had at an early date crystallised a cultural and artistic life of unprecedented intensity, which made them the cradles of what we look back upon as the Renaissance. They expressed their new vigour in better building — not just in new civic buildings such as guildhalls and exchanges, nor merely in the town palaces of the wealthy, but also in improved and more comfortable homes for many of their citizens. In the north, where easily worked stone was not readily to hand, the three centuries after 1200 saw the slow rise of brick buildings, often with tiled roofs. Both represented not only an increase in comfort, but also in safety from fire (and therefore greater security for society's capital investment in housing), as well as conditions more favourable to improved public health, slow though that was in making itself apparent.[13]

This appropriately reminds us of the Middle Ages' long-underrated technological advances. By 1400 the bigger, more seaworthy ships which were to be the carriers of a new age of seaborne commerce were already beginning to be built. A hundred years later, the best western European artificers and engineers were better than those of Islam, from whom they had once had to learn, and had also left behind the Chinese, who had been the first to achieve many important inventions and discoveries. That widening gap has two sides, though; it is another story and part of the future. What is more interesting is that technical achievements, too, register the unique accumulation of capital which was to sustain economic growth on an unprecedentedly fast and unprecedentedly effective scale in the future. This process was far from complete by 1500. Agriculture could not by itself provide profits for investment on a scale to assure sustained growth. The development of manufacturing capital and the expansion of extra-European trade had only just begun. But begun they had. Their momentum was to endure.

The Middle Ages had also witnessed a great political and organisational achievement. The semi-tribal, semi-patriarchal divisions of barbarian Europe had evolved into complex structures capable of major feats of administration and political control. Huns, Vikings, Saracens and the rest of the peoples who harassed early Europe had ultimately been held off. Kings had been able increasingly to play off their strong men against one another, or to beat them in battle (in the fifteenth century they had a new 'last argument of kings' at their disposal: cannon which could destroy the feudal stronghold). In a period of conspicuous and famous political disorder like the Wars of the Roses, it is easy to overlook a truth which stares at us from the pages of Shakespeare's plays: the disputants were fighting for the *crown* (or for control of it). Kingly power was worth having, even if some kings were weak.[14] In many countries a 'King's Peace' was a reality, somewhat restraining evildoers and making possible the enforcement of the rights of property which underpinned economic growth. Often, they were able to turn anarchic energies against foreigners. Europe, in short, was beginning to emerge as a system of separate states. There was no overreaching, ideologically standardising empire to hold them in awe and from which there could be no escape.[15] The Holy Roman Empire could never be that; what Europe had later to face was the threatening aggrandisement of individual components of its system, sometimes dynasties, sometimes states. Habsburg Spain and Bourbon France were the first two candidates for the role of makers of a new European order; happily for Europe, neither was successful. Nor were later contestants, thanks to a widespread acceptance of a European balance of power. But that lay ahead; all that is clear is that by 1500 a few rulers already presided over areas something like those of modern nation-states — Portugal, Spain,

France and England.[16] The 'Hundred Years War' between the two last was perhaps the first war of nationalities.

Within such polities, there were some institutions which, though remote from those of their modern successors, were to develop and survive into modern times. The English parliament is the most famous example. Similar bodies existed in other countries, though for the most part they have disappeared. Still, it is a great thing for an age to have invented representative government, for this in the end is what the medieval parliaments meant. The roots of some of them might lie back in the Dark Ages, but they were already a long way from those barbaric centuries and hint at a coming age when similar institutions would be carried round the world. The western state form and representative government would not be the only medieval legacies to world history, though. What was more important, the world was to inherit a certain idea of the individual as a creature of potentially limitless spiritual value, whose status could and ought to be defined and protected by a pattern of legal rights. Somehow, however improbably, the European mix had turned out to be one which could nourish a dynamic rather than a static future.

IV
THE WORLD'S DEBATE

What could medieval Europe (which took a long time even to become aware of itself as an entity) easily know of other civilisations? By what means and routes could it get knowledge of them? Look at the map. To the north there lay nothing — or worse than nothing: for centuries, barbarian peoples who, until civilised by the church, were only a menace. In the east, across the great plains, came recurrent waves of other, mounted barbarians: Huns, Avars, Mongols, and so on. True, in the eastern Mediterranean there was a civilisation preserved by the old eastern half of the Roman empire after its western counterpart had collapsed, that of Byzantium. It enriched western Europe's art and, somewhat, its thinking, but for all sorts of reasons of geography, language, politics and theology, the civilisations of Byzantine and Roman Christendom drew more and more apart as the centuries passed.[1] The importance to western Europe of the Orthodox world was largely as a go-between and buffer. Byzantium stood between western Christendom and Asia. The eastern empire's armies were protective barriers and its peoples were middlemen; along the conduits which they kept open just a little trade and culture trickled through to the West. Constantinople was a focus of routes along which, in the later Middle Ages, a few travellers made their ways to further Asia. The Polos were the most celebrated, Innocent IV sent numerous emissaries to the Tatars, and there was a remarkable Franciscan friar, William of Roebruck, who visited the Grand Khan of the Mongols — but for the most part, Asia beyond Byzantium remained unknown to western Europeans, a world of elephants and other wonders almost as remote as sub-Saharan Africa.

The one great exception to this ignorance, the one non-Christian civilisation with which the West was in direct contact, and through which it was further linked at one remove to Asia and Africa, was that of Islam. The word means 'submission' or 'obedience'. Islam is the way of submission to the will of Allah, the one God, and obedience to his law, which (it is believed by the Islamic faithful) was finally declared to mankind by the last and greatest of a long line of holy men, among whom were the Jewish patriarchs, the prophets of the Old Testament, and the Jesus who is worshipped as God (wrongly and blasphemously, think Muslims) by Christians. This great man was Muhammad, the Prophet so holy that his face still may not be depicted in any image. His life, work and teaching have had more impact on Europe and later western civilisation than those of any other non-European since Jesus Christ — and are still having it.

In about 570 (the exact year is not known) Muhammad was born in the Hejaz of poor parents. They belonged to one of the many Bedouin tribes of the huge peninsula of Arabia. The nomadic, pastoralist society of the desert was under increasing strain while the young Muhammad was growing up as an orphan. The old values and loyalties of tribal society were challenged by the commerce which brought expansion and prosperity to the caravan towns and the ports of the Red Sea. The central explanation of Muhammad's success seems to have been his skill in articulating beliefs and moral principles which enabled the peoples of Arabia to grapple with these changes. He did it in two ways, by providing them with a holy book to guide them, and by launching his people on a process of conquest which was in the end to spread Islamic empire from Delhi to Spain, and from the Yemen to the Danube.

The holy book of Islam is the text called the Koran, composed from the insights, judgements and aphorisms recited for over twenty years by Muhammad to his first followers. Like the Prophet himself, they believed them to have been literally inspired by God. They were first put together after his death, but there is no reason to doubt that they contain Muhammad's authentic message: there is but one God, Allah, and Muhammad is his prophet. Uncompromisingly monotheistic, Islam teaches that this is the same God in whom Jews and Christians also believe, though in an erroneous and improper way. Beyond this, the Koran also teaches that Allah is to be served by prayer and observance of his law, a far-reaching series of prescriptions which grew until it covered every aspect of social life, from food and drink to marriage and inheritance. Islam was therefore not only a creed, but a community governed by a law. It was a religion of action as well as of theological belief. Its adherents were enjoined to live in a certain way in a society which preserved many of the traditional patriarchal ways of the desert. Nonetheless, in the last resort Islam placed the brotherhood of the faithful above the ties of kinship which were the essence of tribal society. Yet this is not such a change as might be thought. Unlike Christianity, which relentlessly pressed its adherents towards the contemplation of themselves as individuals, Islam asserted the importance of the group as kinship obligations had done in Bedouin society.

Nonetheless, there are in Islam interesting and suggestive parallels with Christianity. Both faiths make — or made — absolute demands on the intellect; they require acknowledgement that they are true. Both are monotheistic, in this respect similarly indebted to roots deep in the cultural inheritance of the tribal societies of the Middle East which spoke Semitic languages. Both are religions of the Book — the Christian Bible and the Muslim Koran. Yet western Christianity and Islam turned out very differently as political forces. No doubt this is because of the very different cultural and historical contexts in which they matured and developed. Christianity was cradled by the cities of the Roman empire, Islam by the desert. But there was something else, too: Islam knew nothing of the potentials for conflict between the laws of God and those of Caesar which were built into Roman Christianity from the start.

Muhammad's teaching was not at once widely welcomed. Monotheism and the relegation of kinship to a secondary role soon brought conflict with traditional Arabian society, pagan and polytheistic as it was. Even in the Prophet's own lifetime, Islam moved from conversion of the infidel (which he had enjoined) to conquest. So Muhammad combined, as it were, the roles of spiritual leader and political sovereign.[2] From Medina, the town in which he had settled in 622 (the year now taken as the beginning of the Muslim calendar) he subdued first Mecca, an ancient place of pilgrimage, and then the tribes of Arabia. At his death in 632 the fate of Islam still seemed to hang in the balance, threatened as it was with disunity and division among his followers. Yet it survived. 'Caliphs', who inherited the Prophet's spiritual and religious leadership and interpreted his works authoritatively, were the community's focus. The first caliphs were drawn from Muhammad's own following, and were related to him by blood or marriage, but this came to an end when the last of them was killed in 661. Within Islam, argument has gone on ever since about the legitimacy of later caliphs. By then, though, Islam had already embarked upon a remoulding of the world more far-reaching and spectacular than any other achieved before modern times, and the divine authorisation of its state forms could be inferred from its victories and imperial success.

Muslim tradition says that during his lifetime the Prophet had sent letters to the emperors of Rome and Persia summoning them to accept Islam or suffer the consequences of unbelief. Islam's revitalisation of the Arab peoples was in fact soon followed by an astonishingly rapid series of conquests. The Arabs were driven by the spur of over-population in the barren peninsula of Arabia. It helped to recruit Arab armies, as did Muhammad's assurance that to die fighting the infidel was a sure path to paradise. Holy War was the invention of Islam.

Once beyond the confines of Arabia itself, the Arabs were fortunate in their neighbours' weakness. Already when Muhammad died, the eastern empire of Byzantium had for decades been slogging it out with the Sassanid empire of Persia; both great states had been gravely strained in the process.

When the fighting among the Arab peoples spilt over into Iraq and Syria, it broke into lands where the grip of the emperors at Constantinople and Ctesiphon was already loosened; discontented subject peoples were often ready to cast off masters who could not protect them, and to accept new ones who could.

So began the great era of Arab conquest. Jerusalem was captured by Islamic armies in 638, a great symbolic event. To the north they spread into Syria, driving back the frontiers of Christendom in the east as far as Anatolia. Soon, they seized the Byzantine inheritance of the former Roman possessions in Egypt and North Africa, so outflanking western Christendom. In 673–8 they attacked Constantinople itself, though without success. Meanwhile, further east, Sassanid Persia had already collapsed long before. Kabul was taken by the Muslims in 664. For over half a century attempts were made by them to invade India. Finally, Islamic armies crossed the Hindu Kush and then the Indus, and conquered Sind. There is even a story that one Arab army got to China. What is certain is that another reached Talas, in the high Pamirs, and defeated a Chinese army there in 751, so that Turkestan and much of Sinkiang underwent Islamicisation. Eventually something like a formal frontier for Islam appeared in the region of the Oxus.

These great conquests made Islamic civilisation much more than its Arabian origins would by themselves have allowed. Many different peoples were converted; many contributions would now be made to a new cultural mix and to a new religious community looking far beyond the originally Arab master race. By then, too, the relationship of western Christendom and Islam had been defined. They had first met on the battlefield, and it went on like that for centuries. The Muslim conquest of Africa had been followed by sea crossings to Europe, a leap across the Straits to Spain, the shattering of the old Christian Visigothic kingdoms of the peninsula, the raiding of the coasts of Italy and France. Arabs and Moors were just as frightening to Europeans as Huns or Vikings. Popular tradition soon gave them a role which absorbs deeds done by others: by the eleventh century, when the *Song of Roland,* the great epic of medieval chivalry, had settled down into more or less its final form, bardic exaggeration had made a heroic struggle against overwhelming Arab forces out of what was in fact a skirmish with Basque mountaineers in 778. Nowadays such epics are forgotten except by scholars, but the folk memory of centuries of strife lingers on, just recognisable in the Sicilian puppet plays about Charlemagne and his Paladins, the fiestas of little Spanish towns in which tourists now enjoy processions of armies and mock battles of 'Moors' and 'Christians', or the South American dances which set Christians led by 'Santiago' against 'Moors' led by Pontius Pilate.

It is not hard to understand the fright that Islam caused. It was difficult to live-and-let-live while the Arabs were still moving forward. While even the mighty Chinese empire was finding it hard to stop them in the east (as late as 758 Arabs looted and burned Canton, we are told), the overrunning of Spain was being followed by thrusts into France. In fact, when an Arab force turned back from Poitiers in 732, the threat had already reached its European high-water mark, but nobody knew that at the time. Charles Martel's victory could have been judged just another frontier encounter, and for years raids into France went on. It took great efforts, too, to confine the Arabs to southern Italy; without them, all Italy might have been Muslim. As it was, in the late ninth century Arab emirates appeared briefly at Taranto and Bari; and in Rome, St Peter's was sacked in 846. Further west, even when Islam was confined to the Iberian peninsula (and within it was making no serious attempt to settle lands north of the Duero) the little Christian statelets hanging on in northern Spain by no means had it their own way. Frontier raiding and skirmishing hardly ever stopped. Charlemagne could not do much more than organise a frontier province in Catalonia, the Spanish March, to serve (like the Dane March in the east) as a military shield to the west. Two civilisations, without thinking much of alternatives, first defined their relationship in terms of conflict.

Yet this was only the obvious, most dramatic, side of the story. It indicates just one thread in the complicated pattern of Muslim and Christian relationships which evolved across the centuries. Certainly, the Islamic onslaught of the seventh to ninth centuries was one of the most important of the processes hammering Europe into a certain shape. The word 'Europeans' (*Europeenses* in Latin) seems to appear for the first time in an eighth-century reference to Charles Martel's victory at Tours. All collectivities become more self-aware in the presence of an external challenge, and self-awareness promotes cohesiveness. European consciousness could hardly have evolved so early — or perhaps at all — without the threat posed by Islam. A territorial sense was sharpened. But something else was going on, too.

Islamic civilisation, after all, did not entail the extinction of Christians or Christian culture in the conquered areas. In the east, it was not Christianity but the Byzantine state which had been rolled back by the Arab armies. For a long time, Islam was tolerant. The Prophet had said that the Jews and Christians, Peoples of the Book, were not pagan. Christian communities lived on, taxed, but otherwise undisturbed, in lands the Arabs conquered. Sometimes they welcomed the change. Not all Christian churches had found Orthodox domination pleasant. It was only the later behaviour of invaders from western Europe which turned Muslim fury loose on their Christian neighbours in Palestine and Syria. In southern Spain, a large majority of the Christian population accepted conversion, and no doubt tax advantages had something to do with that, but those who remained Christians (the 'Mozarabs') were not persecuted until well into the ninth century. At a distance, too, good manners were maintained between Christian and Muslim rulers and the culture of the caliphates (first centred at Damascus, later at Baghdad) was cosmopolitan. Harun-al-Raschid sent presents to Charlemagne, if we are to believe Einhard, and the emperor was in fact *invited* to intervene in Spain by the son of a former emir of Córdoba.

The fact that, in time, this tolerance towards Christians was to weaken should remind us that during the long centuries we call the Middle Ages, Islamic civilisation was itself a changing entity. It was, for one thing, long at work absorbing influences — Hellenistic, Persian — from the lands to which it spread. Yet none of this was understood in the West, where men saw Islam (somewhat uncomprehendingly) as a monolithic whole, whatever their local experiences and responses to it. At the start, Islam simply seemed a threat. Many western Europeans in the eighth and ninth centuries must often have felt like the occupants of a beleaguered fortress. When an Arab or Viking raiding party came along, there were only two courses, to fight or pay ransom. Both were tried (Danegeld was the name given to the tribute paid to the Scandinavian invaders of England). The struggle against Islam endured, and in the end became Europe's first great common cause. Unlike the resistance to the Norsemen, it persistently retained a religious dimension; the Scandinavian kings were to be converted, but 'Moors' were not. What is more, the conflict disputed the future of what had once been Christian lands. It hardened as Christian Europe itself crystallised a sense of greater ideological unity in the eleventh and twelfth centuries, the era when the first great Christian counter-offensive began.

By then, Europe was long used to fighting. There were plenty of willing warriors about. The Frankish adoption of the stirrup led eventually to the emergence of mounted warriors as the backbone of their army; this created a class of professional soldiers dependent on kings and lords who could afford to maintain them. The slowly improving agriculture of north-western Europe gradually made that easier. So there appeared on the stage of history the original knights — the ancestors of the later European nobility. They were land-hungry fellows, happy to fight for estates to bequeath to their children in an age when land was the only good security. Some of them belonged to a group of semi-tamed descendants of Scandinavian barbarians who have gone down in history under the name of the Normans. Like their remote 'Varangian' (that is, Frankish) cousins who were pushing along the eastern rivers into the mysterious lands which were later to be Russia, they were resourceful and determined. In the tenth century, they had settled in northern France. Soon they cast off their Scandinavian ties, taking up the Frankish tongue of the day along with the Christian religion. In 1066 some Normans followed their duke to England, seeking to satisfy their economic needs there. But there were limits to what England could provide. It was a

Christian state already and William the Conqueror had some legal claim to the English crown, so his new realm could not just be treated as conqueror's booty by his countrymen. To the south lay more promising prospects. When other Normans found what they wanted there, they almost unconsciously opened another chapter in the long story of interplay and conflict between western Christendom and Islam.

Its focus was Sicily, the largest of Mediterranean islands and from ancient times — the sixth and fifth centuries BC, when Greeks came there to found new cities — a place of civilisation and wealth. The eastern Byzantine empire had managed to hang on to Sicily when the western empire collapsed. For roughly three centuries thereafter it was ruled as a dependency of Constantinople, with Greek as its language of government and its bishops looking to the Patriarch at Constantinople, not the bishop of Rome, for leadership and authority. Arabs sometimes raided its coast, but full-scale Islamic conquest of Sicily did not begin until 827. It took over a century to eliminate Christian resistance, but the Byzantine grip on the island was almost gone by 900. In the process, Syracuse, for fifteen hundred years a great metropolis, had been so destroyed that (it was said) no living thing remained there. Yet for all the ferocity of conquest, once conquered, the islanders seemed to settle down pretty quietly under Islamic rule, perhaps reconciled to it by taxation lighter than that of Byzantium and by integration into the great commercial world of Islam with its splendid markets and suppliers of beautiful goods, a world so much richer in what it could offer than western Europe. By then, Sicily was already a very mixed-up society. Native-born Sicilians of ancient Sicel descent mingled as fellow-islanders with Arabs, Berbers, Greeks black Africans, Jews, Persians, Slavs and Lombards. Palermo, the Arab capital, had hundreds of mosques and was probably bigger than any Christian city of the age except Constantinople.

In Sicily as elsewhere, the Arabs were not only appropriators but carriers of civilisation. As in Spain and North Africa, they patched up the wreckage of Roman irrigation with techniques of their own; they brought oranges, lemons, melons to the island, probably introduced the cultivation of rice, and certainly that of cotton and silk. By and large, Muslim Sicily was a rich and improving economy, so far as we can now judge. Its mines, mineral deposits and skills flourished. Fortune turned against its inhabitants only when Islamic rulers on the African mainland began, in the tenth century, to fall out with one another and with dissident subjects who had religious grievances against orthodox Islam. By the middle of the eleventh, Muslim Sicily was no longer, as it had been, firmly integrated into a political sphere of influence whose centre was Tunisia. That area and much of North Africa had more or less collapsed into semi-anarchy. Two major centres of Islamic power, each with a caliphate, existed, one at each end of the Mediterranean, in Cairo and in Córdoba, but neither could control what lay between them. Berbers and Bedouins together ravaged the once prosperous Muslim towns of Tunisia. Muslim Sicily was, for the first time, separated from the Islamic power of Africa. It was this, fundamentally, which made it possible for a Christian reconquest of the island to begin.

Byzantium had first go, sending an expedition in the 1030s to take advantage of quarrels between Muslim notables on the island in alliance with the emir, who wanted help against his rebels. But Byzantium's day in the western Mediterranean was over; this attempt could not be followed up. Naval desperadoes from Pisa and Genoa were now making the running in expeditions against the Muslims and a long quarrel between the Latin church of Rome and Greek Orthodoxy led the pope to back other reconquerors of the former Byzantine lands than the Byzantine emperors themselves. Foremost among these were the Normans, already well established in southern Italy.

The Christian reconquest of Muslim Sicily began when a Norman, Roger d'Hauteville, landed near Messina with a small force in 1060. It was merely a reconnaissance party and stayed only a few hours. Early the following year, a larger party of Normans arrived. They came to an island which still sheltered a hybrid culture, though one in which Islam had become the dominant strain. There had been heavy immigration by Muslim settlers who spread out into the countryside as peasant farmers. Arabic had become the language of government. Not surprisingly, then, Norman Sicily long bore the marks of its Islamic inheritance. Roger, who became ruler of the island and 'Count of Sicily' in 1072, employed Muslim officials, accountants and soldiers. Coins struck by Norman rulers had Arabic inscriptions; some even carried the words 'Muhammad is the Apostle of God'. The first Norman governor of Palermo called himself emir, a title later borne by first ministers of the Sicilian crown. Muslims, though penalised by taxes (like Jews) were allowed to worship and follow their own law in courts presided over by their own judges. There were not many Normans, after all, and it took thirty years or so for the main Muslim strongholds to be eliminated. Prudence dictated conciliation, not only of Muslim but of Greek Orthodox believers.

The result was Norman Sicily, a society which for a century mingled Greek and Arab with Roman and north European traditions in a unique blend. Roger might appoint a Latin archbishop to the see of Palermo, but he endowed Greek monasteries with land. His successors (he died in 1101) ruled the island from the former Arab capital of Palermo. His son, Roger II, knew both Greek and Arabic, was said to keep a harem in the Islamic style, and modelled his own royal role on that of the Byzantine emperors. After 1130, when he was crowned in a magnificent ceremony in the former mosque which had been made into the cathedral of Palermo, he was king of what was simply and distinctively called the *Regnum* — 'the Kingdom'. He extended his authority to North Africa and even Corfu. But, unlike almost all other contemporary rulers, he played no direct part in the Crusades, and indeed showed little interest in them except in so far as they afforded him chances of gain while other people were busy elsewhere.

Crusading was something new, an idea emerging in the late eleventh century, though only in a vaguely defined way: Latin had no distinct word for what we call a 'crusade' until after 1200. The essence of a crusade was a military expedition with a symbolic and religious purpose, usually the freeing of Christian lands from the infidel, and it is the clearest evidence of the hardening of Europe's response to Islam into one of simple, ignorant hostility. Charlemagne's attempts to push back the Muslims in Spain had been an early precursor of the idea and it had been fed by later 'holy wars' with Islam in Spain. In Frankish times the church had already begun to bless the weapons of the Christian warrior who defended Christian people from the heathen. It was one way, undoubtedly, for the church to try to come to grips with the problem of disorder in a society with a plentiful supply of armed thugs who respected neither laymen nor churchmen when in a predatory mood; it was a step towards taming them. Not surprisingly, then, the descent of the Normans on Sicily was encouraged and in part justified by the knowledge that the island had once been Christian (though no one much respected the erstwhile claims of the emperor at Constantinople).

Nonetheless, the idea of crusade only appears with final clarity when the focus is the Holy Land itself. In the eleventh century a new force within Islam had replaced the old caliphate of Baghdad and posed a new threat to Christendom. This was the appearance of the Seljuk Turks as dominant within Islam. Originally from central Asia, they established themselves in Asia Minor, Jerusalem and Egypt. It was in response to an appeal by the eastern emperor for help against them that Pope Urban launched the First Crusade in 1095 by his preaching at the Synod of Clermont. Invoking the memory of Charlemagne, a great spreader of the faith by conquest and Christian rule, he associated a military foray to the east with the old idea of pilgrimage to Jerusalem, the Holy City. Quite soon, the idea that the liberation of the Holy Sepulchre was the goal of crusaders overshadowed any other. It was enormously effective. Pilgrimages had always been works of merit and the military pilgrimage to recover the sepulchre of Christ from the heathen assured spiritual reward as did no other. In 1096, there began the first of a series of great popular movements which were to testify time after time to the strength of the crusading ideal in the next couple of centuries.

Crusading, though, was never merely a matter of devotion and popular fervour tapped by magnetic preaching. Behind it lay other forces. Historians have spent much time unravelling and identifying them. Some have stressed a growing pressure on food supply, increasingly felt in western Europe from the eleventh century onwards, as population at last began to rise again and land became even more precious. Clearing forest and waste seemed to have gone as far as it could, given existing methods and tools. Some men looked for land in the east, along the Baltic coast, others to the south; that was why the Normans had turned to southern Italy and Sicily, and why Frenchmen went to the wars in Spain. Not surprisingly, others easily had their gaze diverted elsewhere across the sea, to the Levant. Among the crowds who in 1096 began to move towards Syria and Palestine were thousands of soldiers drawn above all from the Norman-French gentry and nobility. Remembering earlier times, when population pressure drove the Vikings out on to the seas, some historians have seen the crusades as the last of the northern barbarians' irruptions into richer lands.

Covetousness as well as land hunger helps to explain the later widening of the purposes of crusades so that they came to be preached against others than Muslims — against heretics, for example. Crusades seemed to offer so much to those who took part in them. Some were moved by the prospect of plunder (perhaps of the cities of the Byzantine empire) and slaves. The Genoese, anxious to transport the crusaders in their ships, thought of future territorial and commercial privileges in the Levant. All the time, though, religious faith sustained and underlay the movement, and it was a faith all the stronger, no doubt, because of the huge ignorance among the crusaders of the religion against which they were to struggle.[3] Blind faith gave men clear consciences in doing what they might have hesitated to do without it; above all, it offered the hope of eternal salvation for those who died in the service of the Cross. It was, of course, a complicating factor that a Christian empire already existed in the east; Byzantium. If historic claims meant anything, the lands in Syria and Palestine disputed by the crusaders belonged to the old empire. But even before the First Crusade, the Normans had followed their seizure of the old Sicilian territories of the eastern empire by moves further east, nibbling away at other Byzantine possessions. Latin and Greek Christianity had drifted too far apart for the Franks to understand what the empire stood for, or view its peoples as anything but alien.

What else, besides Byzantium, faced the crusaders? By the early twelfth century, the caliphate of Baghdad was long past its peak. The Arab world at least was in disarray, even if the Seljuk Turks had given a new military impetus to Islam. So the early crusaders had successes, in spite of mishaps on the way. Jerusalem, the Holy City itself, was retaken by them, a feat accompanied by appalling massacres of Jewish and Muslim women, children and non-combatants. The crusaders often behaved very badly. Like later settlers of non-European lands they could be ruthless (because their position was precarious), cruel (because their consciences were easy and, anyway, they were far from Europe and its restraints), and disregarding of the interests of pagans whom they felt to be inferior. 'Christians are right, pagans are wrong,' says the *Song of Roland* and that sums up the Christian warriors' attitude very well.[4] We must not judge them too hardly. They clung to what justified them in their own eyes: the ways in which they were different from the natives. They did not, though, hesitate to ally with those 'natives' when it suited their political ends, and they deeply respected them as soldiers.

How did the Muslims see them? Their reaction, too, was a fairly simple one. For all the variety of Englishmen and Germans, Frenchmen and Italians, the crusaders were to Muslims (as to the Byzantines) simply 'Franks', a word which was to go round the world. They were, in our terms, just 'westerners'; for all the differences between them, they were defined by a common creed, an alien setting and a historic role. They felt all these with great intensity. What is more, their identity in the eyes of Muslims solidified as, time and time again, the hatred awoken by the appalling behaviour of crusaders wore away any understanding among their enemies that great differences might exist in their ranks.[5]

In the end, the crusades failed. There was never enough sustained support from Europe to keep the Frankish grip on the recovered lands once the Muslims had rallied — and rally they did, notably under the leadership and generalship of the almost legendary Saladin, the Kurdish leader who recovered Jerusalem for Islam. He so fascinated his Frankish opponents that some of them came to believe he must be a secret Christian; by the fourteenth century his birth was legendarily attributed to the shipwreck of his mother — supposedly a French noblewoman — on the coast of Egypt. It was a subtle form of cultural self-congratulation. Another, more important part of the story of Islamic recovery, though, was the mastery by Islam in 1260 of the Mongol threat which had overshadowed both it and Christendom.

By then, the inherent weakness of the Christians of 'Outremer' ('Beyond the sea') had been amply demonstrated. A handful of new principalities on western European lines had been set up in Palestine and Syria. They were intensely artificial, something of a *tour de force*, sustained by tiny numbers of Franks. While they lasted, they depended on fresh supplies of manpower from Europe. Appropriately, the great remaining symbols of what they once were are the ruins of huge fortresses. Within the Christian statelets grave divisions tended to appear and reappear between those settled (and sometimes raised) in Outremer and new arrivals from Europe who, with each crusade, showed they had learnt nothing or only very little from their predecessors' failures. There was, furthermore, a long, distracting, bitter and internecine struggle between Franks and the emperors at Constantinople. It need not cause surprise, then, that the crusades ended in failure.

Yet they left their mark on the shape of a future West, and on world history, too. Gibbon was right when he called the crusades 'the World's Debate', for great issues were at stake. The most obvious immediate outcome was a deeper rift than ever between Christendom and Islam; the intransigent crusader spirit hardened the Islamic response and revivified Islamic zeal. Muslims in the Near East began to persecute their Christian subjects. This spelt disaster for many of the old Christian communities which had survived in Egypt, Syria, Palestine, and Iraq. The same hardening of attitudes helped (in the end) the Ottoman Turks towards the final overthrow of Byzantium. But that was still a long way ahead in 1244, when the Christians gave up Jerusalem once more and for the last time. The first, perhaps premature, wave of European expansion had burst long since. Now it was on the ebb. In spite of further spasms of crusading effort, the Holy City was to remain under Muslim rule until 1917. Ultimately, all the crusaders' efforts had proved abortive.

What must seem in retrospect a much more important immediate political outcome of the crusades was the mortal wound they inflicted on the eastern Christian empire. Byzantium had been the greatest of all Christian powers, and once the shield of the West. Yet the West had neither understood nor trusted her. The Sicilian Normans happily waged war to win further Byzantine islands, while Genoese, Pisans and Venetians wormed their way into the empire's commercial life. The worst blow by far ever struck against Byzantium was delivered by the Franks when, in 1204, a crusading army sacked Christian Constantinople. For more than half a century after this appalling event, the city was ruled by Franks as a part of a new 'Latin empire' (*Romania*). The Greek emperor came back in 1261, but by then the old imperial power was broken; Byzantium's end at the hands of Muslim enemies was only a matter of time. With that power, too, had disappeared the shield of eastern and Danubian Europe; thus the crusades led in the end to two hundred years of Turkish domination of the Balkans and all it entailed.

As for the crusaders' positive role in channelling Islamic influences into the culture of western Europe, it was small. Like all settlers, they had to adapt to the demands of a frontier environment: the climate, the available diet, the local customs, and so on. But Outremer was an extraordinary sort of frontier, both psychologically and physically. For one thing, it was inhabited by peoples some of whom were the heirs of far higher levels of civilisation than those familiar to many crusaders in their homelands. The Franks found more advanced administrative techniques in the Levant than any they knew at home. Outremer had more cities than western Europe, and they were richer, bigger and more ancient; the crusaders, for all their castle-building, lived on an urbanised frontier. The Levant seaports were great cosmopolitan cities that nothing in western Europe, even the rising Venice, could rival, and Jerusalem, Antioch and other cities had histories some of which went back further than that of Rome itself. The crusaders never had much of a grip on the hinterland and as time went by they more and more fell back on the cities, trying to make them feel like home by giving them 'burgesses' and holding ceremonies of state like western coronations and crown-wearings. It does not sound very convincing. The Franks were always superimposed on the Levant; they never rooted themselves in it.

Yet Outremer was a frontier and frontiers change men in subtle ways. Settlers who go to live on them take along assumptions about ways of doing things which they think are best, and then find they have to change, adapt and sometimes discard them because of local circumstances. The crusaders had to work very hard to keep their own ways but often succeeded in doing so. Some of them took to locally-born wives and concubines, Arab clothes and cooking, and adopted Near Eastern pleasures such as those of bathing; perhaps, too, this is where the four-poster bed enters European furnishing. Yet all this did not go very deep. They showed hardly a trace of interest in native and Muslim culture and science, and (except in military architecture) their technical and artistic achievement now looks feeble. Outremer remained provincial, its intellectual life that of a Frankish colony .[6]

Given that so much which they found in Outremer was better than what the crusaders knew at home, and that Islamic civilisation was in many ways so unquestionably superior to that of the Christian West, this may seem curious. Elsewhere, certainly, Islam was changing western culture at very deep levels throughout the crusading era. This was almost always a one-way affair. Islam was itself the direct source and origin of some of these changes, but the Islamic world was also a great transmission system for influences coming both from further east, and from the Hellenistic past of the Near Eastern world. Besides being a determining influence on Islam's own evolution, the re-copying of the works of Greek scientists and philosophers made them again accessible to the Latin West.

Some places were especially important as places where contact was easy and such things were most easily passed on — the court of Palermo was one (and much distrusted because of it). In Sicily, of course, not only Muslim, but Byzantine civilisation played upon the culture of the Normans and we can trace the effect in such works of art as the coronation cope of Roger II which passed to the Habsburgs, or clerical vestments of Byzantine origin embroidered in Arabic. Churches were decorated with Arabic inscriptions and in the Palace Chapel at Palermo are paintings and carvings of turbaned chess-players, dromedaries, veiled houris. Arab craftsmen made a water clock for Roger II's palace and Greek classical authors were translated into Latin at his court. Unfortunately, the cultural matrix of Norman Sicily did not hold together long enough for it to produce the effect upon western

Christian culture which its vigorous variety suggests. In the twelfth century, baronial ambitions and a new popular antagonism to Muslims (which may have owed something to a growing influx of north European immigrants often deliberately settled by the Norman kings on former Muslim lands) broke the equilibrium of tolerance. Slowly, bureaucracy and culture were latinised and the island was christianised. True, the kings of Sicily would still wear oriental clothes, keep Muslim concubines and bodyguards, and abbots would be found who would let their serfs swear on the Koran. In 1189, an Arab doctor and astrologer appear to have been present at the deathbed of William II, to judge by a manuscript from the following century. But William had no children and after him his kingdom drifted into the orbit of new rulers, the German Hohenstaufen emperors.

It was by one of them, Frederick II, *stupor mundi* ('wonder of the world') as he was called, that the last Muslim communities were fully absorbed into the kingdom. Frederick's laws were fierce towards heretics, but he harried his Muslim subjects because they rebelled, not because they were Muslims. That tolerance was one reason why some Christians distrusted him. To them, his own views were suspect and his behaviour scandalous; he liked discussing religious and philosophical questions with Jewish and Muslim philosophers, kept a crack corps of Muslim soldiers, maintained a harem and took too many baths to be thought reliable. At his court could be found Michael Scot, a physician and astrologer who was also a noted translator from Arabic and Greek and an authority on Aristotle and the Persian scholar Averroës; Dante consigned him with the wizards to hell. That Frederick should have attracted so much attention for his feared infidelities and irregularities only shows how far things had moved in a century. A hundred years earlier and the blending of cultures of Norman Sicily had been taken for granted. By the thirteenth century it could no longer be so. Norman Sicily did not survive long enough to be the major channel by which Islamic civilisation irrigated the western mind. That was to be in Spain.

It is still easy to sense the power, wealth and elegance of Islamic Spain. The Alhambra of Granada or the Mezquita of Córdoba are only the most spectacular of many physical monuments it has left behind. Splendid as they are, though, even they do not reveal the whole story. The 'Moors' (as successive Arab and Berber rulers in Spain came to be somewhat misleadingly lumped together) were part of a wider Islamic world. Not only did *Al-Andalus* — the Arabic word for Spain — embrace more in the peninsula than is covered by the modern word 'Andalusia', but it was part of an Islamic 'West' which at its height embraced much of North Africa and Sicily, too. It was also a part of an even larger economic sphere. After the Abbasid revolution of 750, the Islamic world was a single commercial entity, a free trade area with all that implied for goods and travellers, stretching as far as Persia in the east. Within it ran Islamic law, which was not territorial, but personal. Travel within it was, if slow, administratively unhindered. Many of its inhabitants were Arabised and spoke Arabic, but ethnic groups within it were effectively equal: only faith divided men legally. Al-Andalus was, thus, part of a bigger world, a world of ideas — a civilisation, in fact.

It was also the most splendid exemplar of that civilisation in the West. Roughly speaking, the history of Al-Andalus can be divided into three phases. From Tarik's arrival until about 850 the conquered territories were formally organised as part of the Ummayad caliphate, whose centre was Damascus. Then follows another distinguishable century and a half in which Muslim government was consolidated in the peninsula by a branch of the Ummayad family and its own caliphate, based on Córdoba, made its appearance in 929, legitimising the local dynasty's authority. In that age it is possible that Al-Andalus was the most powerful state in Europe. It was an era which lasted until decline set in sometime after 1000, and the unity of the Córdoba caliphate gave way to the ethnic and tribal divisions it could no longer contain. After that, we are into the long last phase of Muslim Spain, ending only in 1492, during which Islam was in retreat before a Christian reconquest, in spite of occasional vigorous spurts of recovery.

The most splendid metropolitan centres of Al-Andalus were Córdoba and Seville. Indeed, they were among the greatest of all Islamic cities, Seville being said to be more like Damascus than Damascus itself. To them — and to Toledo and Granada too — scholars and intellectuals were drawn from all over Europe, for they had great libraries and schools. They were meeting-places of civilisation, drawing, through Islamic culture, upon the Hellenistic past as well as the skills and science of Asia. Madrid sheltered a school of astronomers, while Seville first drew together a significant group of students and expositors of Aristotle. From the mid-tenth to the mid-thirteenth centuries, Muslim, Christian and Jewish scholars were used to working together in Spain, to their great mutual benefit. The Jews were especially important; for some time they were virtually the only Europeans among whom could be found readers of Arabic. One of the great stimuli to co-operation was the desire of Christian Europeans to gain access to the knowledge of science contained in the Arabic versions of Greek books which the Muslims were quickly known to possess. Toledo became one of the great centres of co-operative translation when it had passed back into Christian hands.

In this way, Greek, Persian and Indian science, retranslated out of Arabic into Latin, reached western Christendom. So did some of the technology of China, notably, the ability to make paper, and perhaps the knowledge of gunpowder.[8] Our modern numerals were another of the benefits to be drawn by Europe from this exchange, and one of the earliest. Known in the eastern Islamic countries at an earlier date, the originally Indian numbers turn up in Christian Spain in the ninth century (including the zero, a word derived from the Arabic *sifr*, meaning 'void'). A book on calculation in them by the great Arab scholar Al-Kwarizmi was translated into Latin in Toledo and the numbers became known throughout Europe as 'Toledo numbers'. Their exact shapes took a long time to settle, but it seems likely that the majority of them had already taken their present form in medieval Spain. Their adoption in the West opened new paths: our mental habits would be very different were we forced to make do with Roman numeration for multiplication, fractions and so on; perhaps we should never have arrived at logarithms.

Gradually, an intellectual community grew up which stretched across frontiers and was not troubled by differences of religious faith. Virtually all over Spain, learned men and scientists held broadly similar Aristotelian views about the general structure of the natural world. Such views seemed to conflict with neither Christian nor Islamic theology. Dante, in the greatest Christian poem of the Middle Ages, even placed the Muslim sages Avicenna and Averroës (as well as the hero Saladin) in limbo with the sages and heroes of the classical world of Greece and Rome.[9] Learned men, often respectful of Islam as no soldier could be, were of course a minority, but they had great importance for the subsequent development of European thought. The emphasis on alchemy and astrology in the Middle Ages, and the blurring of the boundary between astrology and astronomy owe much to them. It has been claimed that it was Islamic influence which set in train the events which led to the emergence of modern science. The development of the scholastic method so crucial in the evolution of the European university has itself been traced to origins in Islamic legal studies.[10] However difficult to measure the Islamic cultural impact may be, it was certainly more than a simple aggregated effect of independent elements.

Convivencia (living together), as the experience of Spain when its three major faiths had to live side-by-side has been called by a nineteenth-century historian, had other cultural expressions, too. There was, for instance, a great interpenetration of artistic styles in Al-Andalus, as the 'Mozarabic' work of the Christians living under Arab rule, or the Islamic influence on ceramics, show. Muslim influence on agriculture and agricultural technology had vast effects, and even today the Spanish landscape still shows traces of its medieval orientalisation. Olives, apricots, rice, sugar, oranges and lemons were all brought to the peninsula by the Muslims, and so was the *noria,* the water-wheel which may well be the original model for all later geared machinery in Europe. As for language, only Latin has given more words to Castilian than Arabic, and from Castilian many of those words were to pass into other European tongues.[11]

Besides such fertilisations, there were also Arab legacies of pleasure to

Christian Europe. Arab musical instruments (among them lute, rebec and guitar) are one sign, but there was also the taste for those oranges and lemons, sugar and olives; cooking in olive oil came to Spain by the same route. The two societies could often relax together and share the good things of life, once away from the frontier zone. An old drawing on a manuscript shows a Christian knight quietly playing chess with his Muslim equal. In the great poem of medieval Spain, the hero, the *Cid campeador,* moves easily in a world of Christians and Muslims alike (as did his real-life original, albeit somewhat less nobly and disinterestedly). Men on both sides of the frontier knew that they had to put up with their neighbours and to respect workable arrangements when they had been made if life was to be tolerable. Alfonso VI of Castile, the king who received the surrender of Toledo in 1085 and so gave back to that great Muslim city the role as a Christian capital which it had enjoyed in Visigothic times, nevertheless prided himself on being a king over three religions — much to the irritation of his more enthusiastically pious wife and her advisers. For all the military struggles and the almost continuous disorder, peaceful relations were usually possible between individual Christians and Muslims in settled areas — as our chess-playing knight and his Moorish host suggest.

Even in Spain, though, the story could never settle down to perfect peacefulness. Kings might stay at peace, but frontiersmen and town militias were usually carrying on a sporadic warfare of raids and sieges. This was the soil in which princely ambitions grew. In the end Spain turned out to be the theatre of the most unambiguous and unqualified struggle of all between Islam and Christianity. Finally, there was no compromise. In human terms, Islamic Spain was in the end obliterated, whatever its enduring traces in monuments and mentality. The only Arabic-speakers or Muslims likely to be found in modern Spain are tourists. This was the outcome of what came to be seen as the great national epic of Spanish history, the Reconquest.

Like those of the crusades, the roots of the Reconquest were very deep and very mixed. Spain had already received Christianity in Roman times. The first Spanish pope was installed at Rome in 366. By the seventh century the legend was current that the Apostle St James had visited the country; in the ninth century his tomb (it was said) was found at Compostela. A Spanish prince seized the opportunity to build a shrine, declaring St James — Santiago, as he came to be called by the Spanish — patron of Spain and, significantly, slayer of the Moors. The idea of a conscious effort to recover the once Christian lands had by then been formed by Spanish Christians, though it was, of course, founded on a misapprehension — that the Christians of the Reconquest and the old Gothic élites of pre-Islamic Spain were the same sort of people. Religious fervour was soon at work to fuel campaigns against the Moors but was never the whole story of the Reconquest. The essence of that story is the transfer of political control in Spain from Muslim to Christian rulers. To that process there contributed greedy princes, fanatical bigots, roughneck French knights looking for fighting, Castilian squires seeking land and booty, as well as selfless heroes, saints and martyrs. At the end of the eleventh century Spain also began to undergo the influences which disciplined and centralised the religious life of Christendom in the wake of the Gregorian reforms. The story, then, is culturally as well as politically complex. Logged by signs like the decline of Visigothic script and the building of Romanesque churches, the goals, methods, means and ends of the reconquerors subtly changed and shifted as time went by. Nor did they always seem to be winning; there were swings of fortune, Muslim recoveries. Nevertheless, by the eleventh century (when a majority of the people of Al-Andalus was Muslim), Islam's peak in Spain was passed.

Thereafter, with the collapse of the caliphate, disunity kept Islamic Spain strategically on the defensive (as was the eastern Islamic world then, too, grappling with crusaders, Mongols and Turks, so that help was not easy to find). After the Christian capture of Toledo there was one last great Islamic resurgence at the end of the twelfth century under the Almohads, a Berber dynasty from North Africa. At one time the once great caliphate was little more than a satellite of North African Islamic power, so weakened was it. But Berber and Moorish help only enabled the Muslim cause to recover briefly before, in 1212, in the great battle of Las Navas de Tolosa, the Christians overthrew the Berber army. Traditionally, this has been seen as the decisive victory of the Reconquest. From that time, the Christians were faced only by rival Arab rulers with occasional and limited support from Africa. Córdoba and Seville fell to Castile by the middle of the thirteenth century and that left only two or three minor states, already vassal-kingdoms of Castile, to stand up for Islam in Spain. The most important of them was the emirate of Granada. Outside these states, all Spain was by 1252 ruled by Christian princes. A last great Islamic invasion of the peninsula from Africa took place in 1340 — a crusade in reverse — and failed. But the end was still a long time coming, for Christian Spain was long divided and preoccupied with other matters.

In this drawn-out story there was much that is exciting and tragic and much that is interesting and fascinating. From one point of view the Reconquest was only the extreme expression of a widely shared European attitude to Islam; it embodied the crusading spirit and was self-justified by the consciousness of doing God's work. But though more than merely a Spanish phenomenon, it was also to come to be seen as the supreme, the unique achievement of Spanish history. Time and again in her history, Spain seems for a moment to have achieved real definition as a nation just because of the presence of an enemy; the Reconquest provides the first example of that. It has marked Spain's destiny right down to our own day. Because of the Reconquest, a unique intertwining of religion with Spanish national character took place. The nation's history became involved with that of intransigent, militant Catholicism as did that of no other country. Spain became the land of saints and soldiers, where religion has been a matter of politics (and of rather bloody politics) right down to this century, so that the Civil War of 1936–9 was idealised by the nationalist victors as a *cruzada* — a crusade.

One result was intolerance. Popular and official persecution of Muslims, Jews and Moriscos (converted Moors) began well before the Reconquest was complete. Attitudes had changed since the days of successful *convivencia*. Later, in the sixteenth century, even after the Islamic severity awoken by the crusades, Christians in the east were still practising their own religion and living in communities under their own religious leaders; at the same moment ruthless intolerance was successfully being imposed in Spain.

The end came at last (if a date has to be put on it) when on 2 January 1492 Granada surrendered to the army of Isabella of Castile and Ferdinand of Aragon, the 'Catholic Monarchs', as they were called. After military conquest came a radical ideological clean-up. A Final Solution could now be imposed. Jews who refused to be baptised were expelled that same year. Promises to respect the rights of the Muslim subjects of the Catholic Monarchs were ignored. Ten years later the Muslims of Castile were compelled to go into exile if they did not accept baptism. Other purges would follow. Even the Moriscos would have to go in the end. But the central story of the Reconquest was by then over and with it the Spanish crusade against Islam; a different sort of crusade, against heterodoxy and dissent, replaced it almost imperceptibly and, tragically, it was to continue through much of Spain's later history.

Of course, it was a long time before people could see that the struggle against Islam was over. For a few decades it looked as if it might be carried further south still. The pope blessed an African crusade in 1494. A few Spaniards crossed to the North African shore, seized little towns there, and dug themselves in, feebly imitating the earlier Christian states in the Levant. Charles V led expeditions against Tunis and Algiers. Like those earlier kingdoms and princedoms in the Levant, the Spanish North African conquests were lost again before long, and soon Spanish soldiers and sailors were fighting to hold back the fiercest Islamic threat yet, that of the Ottoman Turks whose naval power hung over the West like a cloud until their defeat at Lepanto in 1571.

Even Lepanto, though, was not the final spasm, the last kick of the crusading impulse. Melilla, Mers-el-Kebir, Oran and the rest of them (like Ceuta, which the Portuguese had won nearly a century earlier, in 1415) are part, also, of another story just beginning at the end of the Reconquest, the establishment of European overseas empire. For the moment, it only need be noted that because the African settlements did not prosper, and Spanish rulers were soon to be lured away from Africa by the dream of dynastic aggrandisement in Italy, Europe was in due course left defined in the west by that most natural of all boundaries, its coast. For the first time, as a French scholar has pointed out,[12] the straits of Gibraltar became a political frontier. He might have added that they became a frontier of civilisation, as well, as they had not been before. The Reconquest thus brought about a greater tidying-up of the map than anyone might have expected. It had been a search for a clear boundary; now, one had been achieved. An untidy, blurred zone across which for centuries filaments connecting two civilisations had run back and forth was replaced by the sharp line of the sea coast. Europe's limits in the west were set by salt water; within them by 1500 lay half the Christian world. Its other half, though, faced a far less-defined region, the Slav east.

V

DEFINING A WORLD

Europeans have long been unsure about where Europe 'ends' in the east. In the west and to the south, the sea provides a splendid marker — as *Finisterrae,* the 'end of the earth', or Cape Finisterre, reminds us — but to the east the plains roll on and on and the horizon is awfully remote. Metternich, a Rhineland nobleman who was Chancellor of the Habsburg empire in the early nineteenth century, thought that Asia began just beyond his office windows in Vienna. There was something to be said for the idea; after all, Islam had twice been carried to the very gates of the city by Turkish armies. Before it was rolled back — a long business, starting in the late seventeenth century and ending in our own — Ottoman rule long gave the Balkans and south-eastern Europe histories very different from those of western Europe. But you can take other views of Europe's limits to the southeast. Not only political and military history, but language, geography and religion have all left other sorts of boundaries in that region. Further north, things are vaguer and more difficult still. Roughly speaking, Europe's great northern plain broadens out steadily as it goes east from northern France and the Low Countries until it ends, sprawling across Russia, up against the mountains of the Urals and the Caucasus. Much of it imposes a harsh life on those who live there, especially in winter. But it offers great opportunities, too, above all in cultivatable land. So it has always tempted intruders and settlers from the west, and nomads and raiders from the east. Charlemagne's men carried forward the frontier of Frankish Christianity on the Danish 'Mark'; from the eleventh century onwards, later German settlers pushed on across Mark Brandenburg and into Pomerania and, from the thirteenth century, into Prussia. Further south, in Moravia, they had long before that already bumped into members of another group of peoples, the Slavs, who had settled on the plains centuries before.

Much more obviously than that of some other peoples, the history of the Slavs seems to have been shaped at crucial moments by outstanding individuals. Climate, geography, resources, culture mattered in the east as much as and sometimes more than elsewhere. Nonetheless, those great spaces also seem to have favoured strong rulers. In the history of the most important

Slav nation, Russia, it is easy to recall Ivan the Terrible, Peter the Great, Lenin, Stalin. Perhaps no one is more important in Russian history, though, than a man who, unlike them, was not a Russian, and indeed never went to Russia at all. Yet he exercised huge if indirect influence upon her through other men. By helping to shape their ideas and ideology, his influence has left its mark on Russian government today. He was intellectually gifted and given to pontificating on philosophical issues, courageous, a dreamer of dreams who was willing to fight to give them reality, but he was also ungrateful and ungenerous; he could turn on those who served him, and bullied and blackmailed those whose independence of mind he feared. Those who seemed to threaten his plans he ruthlessly sought to destroy. Yet his work laid foundations at the deepest level for a Russia we can still recognise. This was Justinian, emperor at Byzantium from 527 to 565.

At the time it must have seemed Justinian's most notable achievement that he did so much to reunite and rebuild the Roman empire. In spite of some successes, though, he did not complete this, nor did he destroy the power of Persia which hung over the empire like a menacing cloud in the east. What now seems more important is that it was under him that the shape and character of the Byzantine empire were settled, the matrix of eastern Christian civilisation. From the first formal recognition of administrative convenience under Diocletian, politics and circumstance had again and again helped to separate the eastern from the western half of the empire. First, co-emperors became normal; then the western empire dissolved into a set of fragments while the eastern survived broadly intact as a large entity, with big provinces in the Balkans, Greece, Asia Minor and Africa, but only claims to former imperial territories further west. Justinian's most lasting achievements were not to lie in recovering these, in spite of some successful campaigns. What mattered more was his contribution to a distinctively Byzantine imperial style.

Justinian inaugurated what has been called, somewhat clumsily, 'caesaropontifical autocracy' — an attempt to get into a single term the theory that secular and spiritual power are one. It was an idea which failed to take root in western Europe (though, naturally, there were always rulers there who favoured it) but it triumphed completely in the eastern Roman empire. To say that the emperor was head of both church and state, though true, hardly does justice either to the idea or to the Byzantium which expressed it — indeed, the difference between church and state which most of us make without thinking does not really fit the life of the eastern empire, which was in theory a monolithic Christian community, church and state in one. This idea has been transmitted to our own day through the Orthodox churches. Their view of the duty they owe to the ruler has always been far less independent than that taken by the Roman Catholic church and its later offshoots in the West. The leaders of the Orthodox churches have usually found it possible to accept the moral authority of their rulers even when they were infidels — or, as today in Russia — self-proclaimed atheists.

Justinian's empire was, as it was to remain for nearly a thousand years, both a Christian empire and the inheritor of Rome. It kept up the old Roman titles to show it. But Byzantium was the child of the late Roman empire; it was not the myths of republican Rome and its virtue which sustained it, but the supreme authority which the imperial office had drawn to itself as the centuries had passed, the side of the 'Roman' tradition which had always been most easily influenced by the ideas of the east. This was the Rome of despotic monarchs to whom semi-divine status was attributed and to whom ritual honours were paid. The nimbus which had surrounded the representations of Persian monarchs had been taken up by them and passed into Byzantine iconography, whose emperors stand in the mosaics and paintings beside figures of saints, and even Christ himself, similarly haloed.

Eastern Orthodoxy was not at first obviously or irrevocably divided in theology from western Christendom, and at first little was at stake between them except ecclesiastical independence and the claims of papal authority. Yet attitudes deeply rooted in the very origins of the Christian churches opened the way to an eventual descent into (at some moments) schism. Strategic and political factors, too, pulled west and east apart. Justinian's campaigns recovered Italy from the Ostrogoths and restored imperial power there for a time. For centuries after this, Byzantium was still to rule some Italians, as it was to rule Sicilians, Africans and Asians as well as Greeks. Yet it lost control of its western territories bit by bit, and physical contact with them became much harder in the sixth and seventh centuries as a wedge of pagan peoples virtually ended imperial control of the Balkans and Peloponnese, except for a few coastal towns. These were the peoples who later became lumped together as 'Slavs'. After that, it was easier still for Frankish and Greek Christendom to drift apart, even in the face of the threat from Islam. Charlemagne dabbled in diplomacy with the great Harun-al-Raschid, caliph of Baghdad (who does not seem to have been much impressed) because Harun threatened the eastern empire, not the Frankish.

The Christian eastern empire of Byzantium, more and more distinct, was to survive until the middle of the fifteenth century. As the crusades showed, it was small thanks to the Christian West that it did so. Yet it long served western Europe well, by blunting the shock of Islamic onslaught. The story of the relations of the two halves of what ought to have been a united Christendom soon becomes a sad one, as first the Normans, then the crusaders, and then the sea-dog merchants of Venice and Genoa nibbled and munched away at Byzantium's possessions and trade. Yet, for a long time, if there were eclipses of the imperial power, there were also waves of recovery. In the ninth century, Byzantium began to shake off the effects of the Arab conquests — which had cost it virtually all its North African and Levantine provinces — and to reassert its influence in the Balkans. It was, after all, in Charlemagne's day the greatest state west of China. The imperial palace at Constantinople may well have been as big as some whole cities in western Europe. In the eleventh century, though, things worsened again. The papacy and the Orthodox churches were by then in actual schism. In 1071 the Byzantine army suffered the shattering defeat of Manzikert at the hands of the Turks, which meant that Asia Minor was from that time virtually lost to it. A Byzantine emperor's plea for help led to the First Crusade. And then — one more crucial date — in 1204 came the most appalling event of all, when Constantinople itself was sacked — by Christians. Refusal of tribute to it led a crusading army to turn on its fellow-believers, robbing, burning, pillaging and raping through the 'second Rome'. It was a mortal wound, although the empire lingered on for another two and a half centuries.

This long story of disaster and decline, though, obscures a brilliant and complex civilisation, its style and character shaped by the empire's diverse provinces and peoples and by its contacts with Asia. They had given it a cosmopolitanism always lacking in western Europe. Byzantium borrowed from the Persians, Arabs and Turks with whom she struggled, and she enriched her own civilisation in the process. The most important legatee of that civilisation was Slav Europe, for from Byzantium sprang the christianising of the Slav peoples (the peoples who speak languages of the group we call Slavonic) and therefore much of what has made Slav Europe different from western Europe. This is the basic reason why it is hard to make up our minds to this day whether Russia does, or does not, form part of the West.

Slav origins are very obscure, but there have been Slavs in eastern Europe for a long time. Harried by nomadic invaders from the east who time and time again swept across the lands where they settled, they somehow hung on to them. By the year 500, Slav migrants occupied the northern bank of the Danube from Belgrade to the sea. Like other peoples with whom their history was much mixed up they gave a lot of trouble to the eastern empire. Although they were farmers and pastoralists, living in tribes without much political organisation, they joined the ranks of the nomadic Avars who besieged Constantinople itself in 626, and they took over most of those Greek cities which could not be reinforced from the sea by Byzantine naval power. By then there were Slavs settled not only over much of the great plains of Poland, the Ukraine and northern Russia, but also scattered along the Adriatic coast and over parts of central Europe. The story is tantalisingly vague. Given such success in establishing themselves, though, it is ironical that so vigorous a group of peoples should have given the term 'slave' to western European languages.[1]

The Slav migrations were mostly over and done when, in 865, a Bulgarian prince was converted to Christianity. This was a seminal event of Slav history. The Bulgars (as the Greeks called them), ethnically related to the Huns, had come in the seventh century to dominate the Slavs of the lower Danube valley, only to be slavicised by them as time went by. The outcome was the first true Slav state, a Bulgarian monarchy, and the conversion of its khan, Boris, was a major stroke of Byzantine diplomacy; even if Christian Bulgaria was often to trouble future emperors, it was not to fall within the western, Roman sphere of influence. More important still, it began the process by which the Slav peoples entered the orbit of Christian civilisation. A Slav monarchy had now adopted it in its Greek version. The developing Slav cultures were thus linked to the eastern churches which were more and more distinct from the traditions of the Latin West. That gave the Slavs access not just to a special theological or liturgical mode, but to legal and philosophical ideas, cultural models drawn from Byzantium.

Many legends have grown up about two brothers who did more than anyone else to make Slav Europe Christian, the Greek monks St Cyril and St Methodius. Cyril seems to have served as an emissary to the Arabs and a missionary to the Khazars, an important power on the lower Volga, before he and Methodius were sent by the emperor to Moravia. There, he invented Glagolitic, a script in which Slav speech could be written down; it made Slav literature possible. Glagolitic was later set aside, though, in favour of a scrips based on Greek characters; it is the origin of modern written Russian and Bulgarian and is called Cyrillic, in honour of the saint. Together with Christianity, it spread rapidly among the Slavs, producing a Slavonic liturgy and Bible.

Writing and literacy crystallise culture, fixing it as it has not previously been fixed. From the moment writing appears there will be records; people will then have a new definition in their ideas of what can and ought to be done. Moreover, literacy means selectivity; the stabilising of language cuts off some possibilities of influence from the outside and opens others. For the Slavs, literacy meant that the models on which, for centuries, their learned men, their lawyers, their statesmen would draw would be those of the eastern Rome — the Greek heritage of Byzantium, not the Latin heritage of the Catholic church of the west. So, in the end, the Orthodox sphere of Christian civilisation which was slowly extending itself to the north of Byzantium, into the Slav lands, was to move more and more to its own rhythms, out of phase with what was happening in western Europe. The Orthodox Slav world was to have no Renaissance, no Reformation, no Counter-Reformation — the list of experiences it did not share with the West is very long; only the Slav lands which were converted to Roman Catholicism — Poland and Bohemia above all — were to share directly, for good or ill, in the history of western Europe.

But this is getting ahead of the story. Cyril and Methodius were also great missionaries. They carried forward the work of christianising the Slavs by converting their princes. Right down to the sixteenth century, Christian conversion usually worked like that: Constantine's decision had made the Roman empire Christian, and the views of princes tended to settle these matters until Christianity spread across the oceans in the modern era and mass evangelisation became more common. Until recent times, in religion as in much else, you converted kings, princes, men of war, and the rest followed. This was the way the Franks in the west had become Catholics — through the conversion of their leader Clovis — and the same process was at work in the east. But there it had an extra dimension, because the Byzantine tradition focused both secular and spiritual power in the same ruler. Whether western European barbarian kings found it easy to admit it or not, they were in the eyes of the church only trustees for the spiritual health of their peoples, answerable not only to God for it, but, sometimes, to God's representative on earth, the Vicar of Christ who sat in Rome. Eastern Orthodox emperors had no such earthly superior.

The most important Slav conversions of all took place towards the end of the tenth century — in about 986 — in a principality centred on a trading city on the Dnieper, Kiev Rus. With that name, the idea of Russia enters history. Western Europeans have never really been able to make up their minds about where to put Russia on their mental maps. Is she — indeed, is Slav Europe — a part of Europe at all? Is she, as she now looks to many Asians, a part of the West? Or does she belong (as many North Americans and western Europeans have thought and still think) to a non-western, semi-Asiatic 'East'? Is she something different from either, *sui generis*? The agonisings of Russians themselves about this question, particularly in the nineteenth century, show that the difficulty emphatically does not simply lie in the difference made by the Revolution of 1917, when a power committed to ideological opposition to capitalism was installed in Russia. Far less is it just a matter of the 'Iron Curtain' and the consequences of victory in 1945. It is a question with much deeper roots. Only in the eighteenth century was Russia's ruling house at last recognised in western Europe as a member of that gilded circle of dynasties which governed Europe. No one quite understood even then what went on in Muscovy; hence the delay in acknowledging the Romanovs who had held the throne since 1613. The Russian empire was — well, oriental or Asiatic. The ambiguity had long persisted.

Kiev was the first focus of anything we can call Russia. In the eighth century, the Slav peoples of north Russia and the Ukraine had faced an onslaught of Scandinavian peoples from the north somewhat like that faced by western Europe. Vikings, Norsemen, Danes, Normans in the west, they were called 'Varangians' in the east, where they penetrated much further inland. Their boats were ideal for exploiting the great rivers of Russia. Hundreds of miles up the Dvina they could easily cross to the headwaters of the Dnieper to drift down that great highway to the south. Or they could move inland up the Volkhar to reach the headwaters of the Volga system. By the middle of the ninth century, some of them had even turned up in Baghdad. In 860 an expedition of two hundred of their ships raided and terrorised the imperial city of Byzantium itself. The Byzantines called these fierce barbarians 'Rhos'.

By about that time, legend says, a Varangian prince called Rurik had set up his court at Norgaard: all those noblemen of later Russian history who bore the title 'prince' were to claim descent from his house. Soon, this Viking capital was transferred to Kiev, the Varangians were increasingly mingled with their Slav subjects, and the lineal ancestor of the Russian state had come into existence — Kiev Rus. For a long time, it can have been little more than a market, or semi-permanent fair, tapped by the local bigwigs to satisfy their needs. It remained for a long time pagan — officially, until 986 or so, and unofficially, no doubt, much longer. It must have been pretty barbaric until old ties with Scandinavia dwindled. Historians have judged that there was little notable cultural change in Scandinavia and the nature of its civilisation during the whole of the first millennium of the Christian era, but Byzantium had much more to offer. Links with it multiplied, in spite of the recurrent fighting. Byzantine diplomacy sought to use the Varangians against other enemies. Whether there were Byzantine missionaries we do not know, but Christianity reached Kiev before 900, probably from Bulgaria. A Kievan princess, Olga, regent for her infant son (he was incidentally, the first Kievan prince to have a Slav name — Sviatoslav) became a Christian. But still, in the middle of the tenth century, the fate of a future Russia was unsettled.

It is fascinating to pause and think how things might have been otherwise. Protected from Islam by the Khazar peoples to the south-east, Russia was a great prize awaiting the shaping power of civilisation. If Islam were ruled out, China was too far away to compete, so there were only two possible candidates, the Catholic Latin West and the Orthodox Greek East. Both were Christian, but they were very different. A decision could not be put off for very long, for the Catholics had already coverted the Slavs of Poland and Bohemia, and German settlements (and new bishoprics) were appearing in Bohemia and the Baltic lands. Already, the two Christian traditions were bitterly antagonistic. To whom was the great Russian future to go? No one saw it like that then, of course, but that is how we can see it now.

The man who decided was St Vladimir, a prince who by 980 emerged after ferocious dynastic infighting as top dog in Kiev Rus. Though a pagan, he was a grandson of St Olga. He was also formally an ally of the Byzantine emperor, and he began to think about other religions. He was a pretty rough, tough character, and Russians treasure the story that Islam was rejected by him because it forbade alcohol. It may have been so. What is more certain is that he sent some sort of commission to visit the Christian churches of other countries. The Germans, they said, had nothing to offer and the Bulgarians smelt. But in Constantinople, their hearts were won. It was there — probably in the church of Hagia Sophia — that, they said, 'we knew not whether we were in heaven or earth, for on earth there is no such vision or beauty, and we do not know how to describe it; we know only that there God dwells among men.' Vladimir seems to have dallied some time before accepting Orthodox Christianity for himself and his people. There were political and diplomatic considerations to weigh. Nevertheless, in the end he did so, marrying a Byzantine princess, the emperor's sister, to show it.

Vladimir's decision settled that the future Russia was to be Christian and Orthodox. It was a choice of civilisations and the climax of the most splendid and long-drawn-out public relations campaign in history. For centuries, the incense and chanting had risen in Hagia Sophia, the gorgeously clad processions of priests and acolytes had wound about the streets, and the physical rituals surrounding the appearance of the emperor in public had stamped a culture with God's own authority. It had been a huge and sustained effort, and it paid off in the impact it made on the minds of those barbarians sent by Vladimir to tell him how to choose. It must also have been the outcome of political calculations on both sides: Kiev Rus was worth a nuptial mass to Byzantium — even a princess. But beyond all this, Vladimir's decision mattered because of what was to come. He had made the single decision which, more than any other, shaped Russia's future.

There followed the conversion of his people and, therefore, their civilisation. Unpleasant as Vladimir was (and he was very harsh in imposing his new faith on his subjects), his countrymen were right to canonise him two hundred years later; saints need not always be good men; it is sufficient if their lives express the workings of God. He had settled that Russia should be Christian, and by not making her Catholic, he contributed another layer to the Russian enigma: is she part of the West?

Geography has to be part of the answer. Russia was born into exposure and virtual isolation. No great physical markers cradled her first statelets. Around Kiev Rus stretched the vast, anonymous plains of the east. But she had formed on a trade route and that made Kiev very open to outside influences, even somewhat cosmopolitan. An eleventh-century Kievan prince married a daughter of a Norwegian king, and his son a Byzantine princess. An Anglo-Saxon royal family took refuge at that court. Elsewhere in Russia,

German merchants appeared and settled, particularly in the northern town of Novgorod. Yet when the strength of Kiev ebbed and Muscovy and Novgorod became more important, the future Russian monarchy was still unprotected by geography and undefined by clear boundaries. You had to go as far as the Urals in the east, or the marshes of the Pripet and the line of the Don in the west to find any. Russian state power was slowly secreted, crystallised, solidified into little islands in an ocean of land.

Across the plains came enemies, as well as traders and friends. From the east, for centuries, came first Turkic peoples from the steppes, then the Mongols or the Tatars. From the west came the Germans: settlers, Catholic missionaries and, above all, the Teutonic Knights. These formidable warriors were the cutting-edge of European expansion to the east, another part of the first wave of European expansion expressed also in the crusades to the Holy Land. Like the 'military orders' of other lands — those of Santiago de Compostela in the Reconquest, of St John of Jerusalem, or the Templars — they were crusaders. They were military monks, taking certain religious vows, bound to obey their priors or commanders for the advancement of the faith. Their advance guards in the east protected the settlers of the *Drang nach Osten*, the drive to the east by the Germans who founded the Baltic cities and imposed their overlordship on Polish, Lithuanian and Latvian peasants, christianising the Baltic hinterland as they did so.

Such crusaders were seen by the Russians as enemies and invaders. It did not matter that they were Christians and claimed to be spreading the faith: the Orthodox Slavs were Christians, too, but were pretty sure that their Catholic attackers did not see them as such. What was worse, not only did the Germans press forward into Slav lands, enslaving the population and seizing the soil, but they did so while the Tatars were harrying Orthodox Russia from the east. Catholic western European and pagan Asiatic savaged and tore at Slavs at the same time, and nature offered no defence — except sheer space — to the plainsmen. All they could turn to was military power: the strength of princes whose resources and authority could enable them to survive. So, if Russia survived at all, it would be as a nation made by the state — a state which could offer the military power needed for survival, and whose rulers would buttress that power with the autocratic claims of Orthodoxy. From the start the pressure of her enemies drove Russia towards centralisation and the ruthless assertion of state power.[2]

A hardening of autocratic authority was not all that was born of centuries of invasion and harrying from east and west. A deep new psychological distrust of western Europe took over which has revived again and again to hinder the passage of ideas from west to east. It explains in part a long debate which raged among Russian intellectuals in the nineteenth century; should Russia go forward as a nation by consciously adopting western European ideas and methods (this was the 'westerniser' view)? Or should she turn inwards, searching her history for her own institutions and traditions as guides (the 'slavophil' view)?

We cannot too often recall how insecurity and distrust of western Europe shaped the answers to such questions. Russia and the Russian state was in large part defined by conflict with western Europeans (Poles might be Slavs, but they were also Catholics, tied to the Latin West). What is more, Christian though they called themselves, in Russian eyes, those western Europeans cynically and perversely exploited the dangers Russia faced from the pagan barbarians of Asia. This was a recurrent nightmare. Russia had always had at least two frontiers: an Asian and a European. Her way of dealing with that problem has been for centuries the same — to push them as far away from the home base as possible. Space and military power alone could give plain-dwellers protection. But there was always the nightmare that the two threats, east and west, might again coincide.

In 1938, Russian cinemas began to show one of the greatest films of a great director, Eisenstein's *Alexander Nevsky*. The thirteenth-century prince who gave his name to it was a grand duke of Novgorod. He came to the throne at a terrible time. In 1240 the Mongols had captured Kiev, got within sixty miles of Novgorod, and set themselves up as rulers of southern Russia and overlords of the Russian princes. But there were other dangers, and Nevsky deliberately chose to collaborate with the Tatars in order to fight off first the Swedes and then the Germans. Thanks to him, Novgorod survived. With Nevsky's son, who was prince of Muscovy, the curve turned upward again and the slow consolidation of Muscovy began. In the film's twentieth-century treatment of this story, the pagan Tatars appear cruel, aggressive, rapacious. But they are not the main villains. The truly wicked are the Christian Germans who, clad in outlandish and sinister armour, cruelly menace the Slav townsfolk, brutally confident in the superiority of their arms in battle, cynically exploiting the specious cloak of religion. That film was made while the prospects of collective restraint on Hitler and collective security in Europe were crumbling day by day. The point was obvious: a new threat from the west was on the way and Russians must brace themselves. The German infantry of Eisenstein's movie were dressed in helmets like those of the German armies which had shattered Russian strength in 1917 and imposed the savage peace of Brest-Litovsk the following year. The successors of those armies in fact came within an ace of a repeat performance in 1941. What was more, there were new Tatars in the background when Eisenstein made his film. In 1936 fighting broke out between Russians and Japanese in Mongolia. Not much was known about it at the time, and the Russians seem to have kept their end up pretty well, but their rulers knew and recognised an old danger: an alliance of western Europe and Asia against Russia.

It was another sign of the Russian worries about the east that a couple of years later the Russian invasion of Poland in 1939 was, it seems, delayed a few days because of the need to settle with a Japanese threat to Mongolia.[3] This is the background to be borne in mind when we are puzzled by what seems to us the wholly disproportionate Soviet fear shown in recent years of a German-led western Europe on the one hand and a resurgent China on the other. History is stronger than Marxist ideology.

Fashionable history is not so keen on dates which 'begin' or 'end' epochs as it was when I was a schoolboy, but they are still useful in pegging out our historical maps. 1453 is a very good one for in that year it was settled that Russia was to be the big brother of the Orthodox family. Nine hundred years after Justinian, Constantinople, the second Rome, fell to an infidel army. After the grave damage done to her in the crusading era and the subsequent failure of the crusaders to hold off the Muslims, the Byzantine empire had recovered its capital and lingered on, from time to time given a little breathing-space, but more and more closely hemmed into a smaller and smaller area. In the fifteenth century efforts to reunite the Catholic and Orthodox churches failed. So Byzantium faced the last Islamic onslaught, this time by the 'Ottoman', or 'Osmanli' Turks, alone. Crusades in the east and Reconquest in the west had provoked a spirit of counter-crusade within Islam and these formidable warriors were its westward striking force.

The end of the old empire, when it came, was not dishonourable. On the evening of 28 May, Constantine XI — the eightieth emperor since his name-sake Constantine the Great made the empire Christian — took communion in Hagia Sophia, and then went out to lead his soldiers. Early the following morning (no one knows exactly how or when) he died fighting the Turkish final assault. A few hours later, the conquerors entered the city. As the looting and massacre died down, their leader went straight to Hagia Sophia, said his prayers and set up his triumphal throne. The great cathedral became a mosque. A thousand years of Christian empire came to an end, and with it there died, so it appeared, the legacy of Rome in the east.

The conqueror was the Ottoman sultan Mehmet II. His people had a wonderful record of military success behind them and further successes were to come. They were the last non-Europeans before this century to force European states onto the defensive. Like many other nomadic peoples of Central Asian origin, they were by origin migrant warriors who seized op-portunities as empires crumbled, marching in to live among their debris. In the fifteenth century they were solidly established in, and dominated, An-atolia, the major and Asiatic part of modern Turkey. They showed an es-pecially strong commitment to Islam. By 1400 that faith was more than seven hundred years old. Like Roman and Orthodox Christendom, it had known ups and downs. From the fifteenth century a new wave of Islamic expansion can be seen to be rolling in, first in the old Middle Eastern lands, and among the islands of the Aegean, where western European had already replaced Byzantine rule. In the sixteenth century a great new Persian Islamic empire was to rise under the leadership of the Safavid dynasty (also Turkish in origin). Further east still, conquest in the twelfth century had already installed Muslim sultans at Delhi, but soon after 1500, Babur, roughly the contemporary of our own Tudor king, Henry VIII (and one of the most attractive of great rulers), created the Mogul empire of India, another major focus of Muslim power. Of this new Islamic surge of conquest the Ottoman Turks were a part. In near Asia, eastern Europe and the eastern Mediterranean, they offset the retreat of Islam in the west before the Reconquest.

The Islamic resurgence not only threw up new barriers of communication with east Asia (so that the Europeans were driven to look for ways round them), and disrupted sea communication in the Mediterranean, as the Arab invasions had not done, but eventually carried Turkish power far into Europe. It had never been as threatened since Charles Martel turned back the Moorish armies at Tours. By 1500 the Turks had swallowed mainland Greece, Bosnia, Herzegovina, Albania and the Ionian islands. Many of the inhabitants of the Balkans were converted to Islam. The Turks even captured the Italian port of Otranto and held it for a year. On they went, wiping out the army of Hungary at Mohacs Field in 1526, conquering that nation and going on to besiege Vienna. True, they did not take it. Nor did they take Malta in 1565, and they had suffered setbacks even in lands long islamicised (the Emperor Charles V had managed to seize Tunis for a time in 1535). The early sixteenth century in fact saw the Ottoman empire at its zenith (all the Muslim lands of North Africa except Morocco had by then fallen under its sway), and even beginning its decline. Though it seemed to be pressing harder than ever on a divided Christendom, soon after 1600 Islam was no longer by then the military threat which it had been for so much of the Middle Ages. True, the Turks had added Cyprus and Crete to their bag and were still fanning out in the Balkans. But a very acute or knowledgeable observer could have seen the significance of the language of a treaty made in 1606, the first negotiated with, not dictated to, a ruler no longer contemptuously referred to as 'King of Vienna' but as an equal, the 'Roman Emperor'. In 1683, finally, the Turks were back again at the gates of Vienna and once more failed to take it. The Ottoman star had at last begun visibly to wane. That campaign had been the last great Ottoman effort.

Their record of success had by then had gigantic repercussions. The Turkish conquests explain why Metternich thought Asia began just east of Vienna, for into the lands they conquered the Turks not only brought Islam (there are flourishing Muslim communities in Yugoslavia to this day) but methods of government which emphasised the difference between this part of Europe and what was to be found further west. This was known long ago. A seventeenth-century English traveller in Hungary rather quaintly (and with some exaggeration) put it like this: 'a man ... before he comes to Buda seems to enter upon a new stage of the world, quite different from that of western countries: for he then bids adieu to hair on the head, bands, cuffs, hats, gloves, beds, beer: and enters upon habits, manners and a course of life which, with no great variety, but under some conformity extend into China and the utmost parts of Asia.'[4] That was to underrate the diversity of the East, but he had a point. In the nineteenth century, you could still buy a Serbian girl for a concubine in the slave markets of Belgrade (Sir Samuel Baker, the great explorer, not only did, but married his purchase). You would find in the Balkans none of the civic privileges, representative institutions, and individual liberties of medieval western Europe. But neither would you have found the serfdom and seigneurial jurisdiction of the West; peasants enjoyed a form of hereditary tenure and greater freedom than under Byzantine rule. Nor were they harshly taxed, and many of them rose high in the service of the empire. Nor, incidentally, would you find under Ottoman rule religious intolerance such as that spawned by the western church. Christians and Jews suffered certain disabilities as communities in Turkish law, paid special tribute, and were second-class subjects, but the practice of their religions was allowed. Indeed, Turkish government liked to deal with its subjects as religious communities through their religious leaders. When, eventually, the Turks went away, the Christian communities they had ruled for centuries were still there, their culture and language intact. It was very different from what Christian rule did to Islam in Sicily and Spain.

Most of the Turks' European subjects were Orthodox Christians who already, even before the Ottoman conquests, belonged to a civilisation distinct from that of western Europe. Furthermore, almost all of them spoke languages very unlike the Latin and Teutonic tongues of the west. Geography, too, makes their part of Europe look away from the west. Its main natural outlet is the Danube valley, surrounded for the most part by mountains. The highlands which dominate the whole Balkan peninsula restrict communication and make it difficult to penetrate. So probably there would always have been a different sort of Europe in the east, even without centuries of Ottoman domination. But the Turks were still ruling much of it only a century ago and it is difficult to believe that their conquests did not deepen the still older differences. As frontiersmen in a zone of endemic warfare, as oppressed Christians, who were not top dogs but underlings, as objects of interest to European diplomats, south-eastern Europeans led lives quite different from those of western Europeans for three hundred years or so — and all that was on top of differences there long before.

The Turkish conquests in Europe had great implications for Russia. With the eastern empire gone and western Europe in disarray, Moscow remained the only possible protector of Orthodox Christians. The enormous consequences of Vladimir's conversion now begin to be apparent. Already, in 1448, Muscovy had cast off the ecclesiastical authority of the Patriarch of Constantinople. 'Two Romes have fallen,' wrote a monk to the Muscovite ruler early in the sixteenth century, 'and the third stands, and a fourth there shall not be . . . You are the only Christian tsar in the world.'[5] To western ears such words sound extraordinary. But they made sense in the context of Orthodox assumptions: the Roman church had betrayed the Faith (though some Orthodox churchmen thought Byzantium had earned her punishment at the hands of the infidel because of deathbed hopes of compromising with Catholicism), and the ruler of an Orthodox state had theological duties — and authority — quite as important as those which were secular.

By coincidence, the collapse came at a moment when, under the leadership of the princes of Muscovy, the Russians were at last fighting their way clear of their enemies. In 1462 there came to the throne of Muscovy a statebuilder somewhat like the English Tudors or the French Bourbon kings. He is remembered as Ivan the Great. He consolidated the territory of his state not only at the expense of foreigners like the Catholic duchy of Lithuania and the Tatars, but at that of Russian trading republics like Pskov and Novgorod. From its central position, it has been well said, Muscovite power spread like a forest fire. When Ivan came to the throne his principality extended over something like 415,000 square miles; at his death, he ruled lands which — in theory — stretched as far east as the Urals. His successors carried on the good work. The Urals were crossed in 1480. Another decisive step was the conquest of the Tatar capital of Kazan in 1552. From there the advance went down the Volga to Astrakhan and the Caspian. By 1600, Russia had about 2 million square miles of territory. Ahead lay Asia, where she was to press forward in a colonial movement, populating new territories and upholding her flank of the great western counter-attack against the Muslim world, but by advance across land rather than across the seas. In Europe itself, successes were achieved by wresting territory from others, notably the Ottoman empire and Poland in the eighteenth century. But Russia's largest territorial acquisitions were in Asia — and they had even greater implication for the future. Already in 1600, territories which stretched across the Urals into Siberia and across the Volga to the shores of the Caspian were ruled from Moscow. By 1638 Russian settlers had reached the Sea of Okhotsk; this was much further from Moscow than Oregon is from Massachusetts. On they went, reaching the Bering Straits in 1649. Russian claims to a Pacific coastline and to territories belonging to China began in the seventeenth century. There were Russian subjects on the Pacific coast before there were any on the Black Sea. Russia's eighteenth-century aggression westward for a time obscured this oriental thrust, even when it resulted in settlements as far away as Alaska, but in the nineteenth century came another, more visible, surge eastwards, in Central Asia, the Far East and North America. The Central Asian peoples were subdued in a series of campaigns; the Kazaks in the 1850s, the Uzbeks in the 1870s. It was a little like British advances had been in India in the first half of the century, when the need for security had led to fresh annexations, but it was part, too, of the centuries-old movement outwards of Europeans at the expense of weaker peoples. Early in the twentieth century there were to be short-lived Russian attempts to control northern Iran and Manchuria, performances to be repeated in the Second World War and after. More recently still, a Russian army of occupation has arrived in Afghanistan, from which British policy had striven to exclude Russian power all through the nineteenth century. Only the California settlements turned out to be a flash in the pan, and Alaska was sold to the United States in 1867.

Such an extension created a Russian empire with world-scale responsibilities and entanglements. The greatest state sharing frontiers with Russia was (and still is) China. They were soon in conflict, but in the seventeenth century, and for a long time afterwards, the Manchu emperors of China were well able to look after themselves. A Russian emissary who turned up at Peking in 1654 and refused to perform formal obeisance (the kowtow) was sent away without being received at court. In 1676 another Russian who refused to kneel when receiving presents for the tsar from the emperor was similarly sent away. Soon the Russians were driven away from posts they had set up on the lower Amur river. In 1689 they abandoned by treaty their post at Albazin, though they won trading rights at Peking, where a Russian hostel sheltered envoys (who by now agreed to perform the kowtow). In 1727 a further treaty defined the border of the two empires, excluding the Russians from Mongolia.

Partly in response to the Russian stirrings and partly in response to British advances in India, the Ching emperors began to enlarge their empire again in the eighteenth century, adding huge areas on the frontier of Sinkiang to their domains and exercising more power in Tibet, East Turkestan, Mongolia and Manchuria than any Chinese rulers had done ever before. But the tide turned against China in the nineteenth century. When that happened she lost far more territory to Russia than to any other European power. The ending in 1856 of the Crimean War, which had tied Russia up in conflict with England, France and Turkey, released her energies for further expansion eastwards. She won major cessions from China in Central Asia in 1861. By then, the eyes of the Russians were turned to the Far East again, too. Manchuria and Korea (a Chinese tributary) fascinated them. 'We shall make

Manchuria a second Bukhara,' one Russian general dreamed.[6] As China reeled in the 1890s under defeat at the hands of the Japanese and humiliation by other western states the Russians installed themselves in the important strategic harbour of Port Arthur. They began to build a railway across Manchuria to their own Far Eastern province and Vladivostok. Railways had made campaigning in Asia easier; in 1891, the building of the most famous of them all, the Trans-Siberian, was started. When completed in 1915 you could at last go from Russia to the Pacific in the same train and the line was almost at once put to a strategical use not envisaged when it was projected, the movement of the products of American and Japanese industry from the port of Vladivostok to the Russian armies fighting Germany in Europe.

A year before that, when the Great War had begun, the Russian empire took up one-sixth of the world's land surface. This was not quite so large as the British (which covered a fifth of it), but Russian territory lay in one consolidated mass under one government. True, there had recently been setbacks. One, very bad indeed, came when defeat by the Japanese in 1905 forced the abandonment of Russian designs on Manchuria and Korea. But Russia was still in 1914 a great Asian power, and so she has remained. Her imperialism there is part of the world impact of the West. Though utterly unlike the American vice-royalties of Spain, the Portuguese oceanic empire, the Asian trading network of the Dutch, or the British Raj in India, Russian empire, too, was a carrier of western civilisation. Whatever the disputes of Russian 'westernisers' and 'slavophils' over their cultural destiny at home, and however alien Russia's ways might seem to western European and American liberals, she looked western to those who met her in Asia. 'In Europe', wrote Dostoevsky, 'we were Asiatics, whereas in Asia we, too, are Europeans.'[7]

Russia's ambiguity can be traced back a long way. It shows in its central institutions, in the nature of Russian government itself. Muscovite ideologists who were keen on promoting their grand prince's authority began to use the title of 'Tsar' more and more in the fifteenth century and soon began to seek recognition of it from western rulers. It went along with and helped to justify the transformation of a princely state into an empire of many peoples, heir to the Golden Horde and its successor states. Ivan the Great was the first Russian ruler to call himself 'Tsar', and the first western acknowledgement that this was the title of the ruler of Muscovy came in a diplomatic document of 1514. Then, in 1547, shortly before the conquest of the Kazan khanate, a Russian ruler for the first time took the title of 'Tsar' formally at his coronation. So what was once the name of the Roman family of the Caesars survived the empire in which it had become the title of a ruler to pass into yet another empire's terminology. Ivan married a niece of the last eastern emperor, too; it may have been because of her that he adopted for the royal seal the Byzantine symbol of sovereignty, the double-headed eagle which gradually became part of the heraldic insignia of the Russian monarchy, and as such survived until 1917.[8]

Time and time again, twists and turns in the road of Russian history have emphasised its difference from western Europe. The Tatars had devastated the Russian towns just as those of western Europe were showing their greatest vigour and independence. The continued consolidation of the state territory by centuries of acquisition from neighbours confirmed the military and autocratic bias of the regime. For good or ill, Russia carried forward into its era of expansion none of the western and 'feudal' stress on individual status and privilege, none of the tension of religious and secular, none of the 'liberties' of the western cities, none of the emphasis on group and corporate rights which led to the representation of 'estates' of the realm in parliamentary or quasi-parliamentary bodies in the West. Because she was Orthodox and had no Reformation, so Russia had no slowly emerging tradition of religious pluralism. Her Scientific Revolution and her Enlightenment had to be imported. When she first industrialised it was to be on the basis of a serf economy such as had virtually disappeared in other centres of industrialisation, and serfdom was actually to increase its extent and its grip on Russian society at a time when it was in retreat in western European countries. Long to be preoccupied with Asia, which she penetrated by land, Russia played only a tiny part in the exploration and exploitation of the oceans. Drawn, inevitably, into the European diplomatic system, she was to remain ideologically aloof from it, even while using its language and forms, distanced mentally as well as geographically from the West and still debating right down to the present whether she is of it or not.

In the eighteenth century, Peter the Great moved the Russian capital to St Petersburg. There then began two centuries during which Russia's rulers often seemed to be trying to identify her firmly with the West. But in 1918, when the struggle with Germany had taken yet another twist, the capital was moved back to Moscow. And there it stayed, in the sometime village which had seen itself as the Third Rome and was now once more the self-proclaimed metropolitan see of an international religion. The first and second socialist internationals had passed away, but it was in Moscow that the third was formally created in 1918, the practical and official embodiment of the claim of Russia to lead international communism. It, too, has now gone, but the claim is still made, even if more and more strongly challenged in recent years.

And we still do not know the answer to our queries. When Russia looks westward, she appears uneasy, threatened by lands from which a mortal danger has all too often come. Yet Russian expansion in Asia has long been justified as progressive, advanced, 'western', as it were. Seen from Asia, though — or sometimes from Africa, or from South America — she looks western in another way, often enough as just another exploiter. It is still hard to say where Europe 'ends' in the east.

VI
AN EXPLORING
CIVILISATION

Disinterested intellectual curiosity surely plays a smaller part in the pursuit of knowledge than we like to think. Even the great gesture of President Kennedy's suggestion to his fellow Americans that they try to put men on the moon within the decade was not just the result of an urge to see how far the technology could be pushed. It was also a grab at international prestige and national self-esteem, while in the background was the need to mobilise resources for rocket development which might not have been made available just for an armaments programme. Just as practical and political in their origin were the oceanic voyages which began in the fifteenth century to open up the world and then with startling suddenness and rapidity to unify it. For the first time, and very quickly, the globe became an entity. Much of it was still unmapped a century after Columbus, but by then it was potentially mappable because the world had been circumnavigated. Thousands of years of civilisation had gone by without this happening. Yet, within a single century or so, mankind began to live in one world, not several as hitherto. Why did this happen so suddenly?

One fact about this change is so obvious that it is easily overlooked: the exploring was done exclusively by Europeans. What is more, the voyages of discovery were the beginning of a new era, one of world-wide expansion by Europeans, leading in due course to an outright, if temporary, European economic and political domination of the globe. That domination lies at the heart of the historical role of the West in world history, though it is not its essence. Why were fifteenth-century Europeans the only human beings to launch such a movement? We know enough about the seafaring history of other civilisations for this to be a sensible question. Long, mysterious voyages in open canoes were made by the peoples of the south Pacific. For centuries Chinese seamen had used much the same navigational aids as Europeans, some of them at an earlier date. The Ming emperors had skilful admirals, ocean-going junks which were probably the largest ships in the world of their time, and experienced crews. They sent expeditions round South-East Asia to India, the Persian Gulf and Arabia. One commander, Ching Ho, took a huge fleet as far as the East African coast, a major feat of long-distance navigation.[1] Yet in 1480, the Ming court decided not to continue such maritime enterprise. A century later the Nanking yards could no longer build ocean-going ships and it was not to be the Chinese who discovered America or Australia. Soon, the great voyages of Ching Ho were virtually forgotten by his countrymen. The Arabs of the Gulf and southern Arabian ports, too, were accomplished sailors. They went to Java and Canton to sell slaves and spices and further down the African coast than the Chinese (though they do not seem to have rounded the Cape of Good Hope). Arab cartography was better than that of Europe for most of the Middle Ages, and Arab sailors had known about the magnet long before it travelled further west. Yet, though some of them knew the earth was a sphere, Islamic scientists declared the exploration of the oceans to be impossible. The Ottoman fleets swept the surface of the eastern Mediterranean but did not venture into the Atlantic. As a result, centuries later, when the ports of China and India were full of European and North American shipping, no junk or dhow had ever been seen in Seville, Bristol or Boston.

This difference, for all its strangeness, seems to have been accepted for centuries as unremarkable. The massive indifference of some civilisations and their lack of curiosity about other worlds is a vast subject. Why, until very recently, did Islamic scholars show no wish to translate Latin or western European texts into Arabic? Why when the English poet Dryden could confidently write a play focused on the succession in Delhi after the death of the Mogul emperor Aurungzebe, is it a safe guess that no Indian writer ever thought of a play about the equally dramatic politics of the English seventeenth-century court? It is at least clear that an explanation of European inquisitiveness and adventurousness must lie deeper than economics, important though they may have been. It was not just greed which made Europeans feel they could go out and take the world. The love of gain is confined to no particular people or culture. It was shared in the fifteenth century by many an Arab, Gujarati or Chinese merchant. Some Europeans wanted more. They wanted to explore. The idea of dominating nature was already about in their culture, waiting to be put into use; what could be a more immediate expression of it than getting a grip on the map, on the very surface of the globe itself?

Already by 1400 or so some European peoples had proven records of maritime enterprise. Besides the Venetians and Genoese, who had long dominated the trade of the Black Sea, Levant and eastern Mediterranean, there were the spectacularly enterprising Catalans from the medieval kingdom of Aragon. In northern waters, too, well-established trades had long existed. The Hansa merchants had linked the Baltic to the Rhineland and the English were used to bringing their wine from Gascony. So were laid the foundations of confidence on which an age of expansion was to be built.[2]

Soon, enterprise was reinforced by technical progress. Though the Chinese had invented or discovered the lodestone and knew about the grid system of mapping, Europeans perfected the compass and became much better surveyors and cartographers in the later Middle Ages. By 1450 or so Europeans had an undoubted technical lead over any possible rivals in the business of exploration. Their instrumentation was to grow better still as maritime success fed on success. Firearms are another part of the story. The Jesuit missionaries who went to China in the seventeenth century were able to teach their hosts how to cast guns much better than those they already possessed. Metal-casting in China had been for centuries ahead of Europe's, and gunpowder had long been known there, but, for some reason, Chinese firearms had not been brought to the European level of perfection. So the Chinese had to borrow European skills. Meanwhile the superiority of European guns and gunnery turned European ships into floating artillery platforms, more formidable than anything which could be brought against them. The great ship of the Tudor navy, the *Henri Grâce à Dieu,* had 156 guns altogether, tiny though some of them were.

It is still not easy, nevertheless, to believe Europeans would have crossed the oceans so eagerly had not a resurgent Islam seemed to bar the best land and sea routes to Asia and to the grain and timber of south Russia. This was a key circumstance. Already, at the end of the thirteenth century, the first expedition had left Genoa to find an ocean route round Africa to the Indies; the then current presumption that India could not be reached by sea direct from Europe thus came under scrutiny. It seems to have been the Majorcan mystic, Raymond Lull, who is the first person recorded to have made the suggestion of sailing to India round Africa.[3] In the fifteenth century a second wave of European civilisation, gathering since the ebb of the crusading era, began at last to roll steadily outwards, but it could not roll as easily in some directions as in others. Christian Europe was faced in the Balkans by Islam and was forced onto the defensive in the Mediterranean even before the fall of Constantinople in 1453 to the Turk. Europe's land limits were filled up by the end of the century; the Iberian peninsula was by then Christian and a frontier of sorts between Catholic Poland and Orthodox Russia halted growth in the east.

There was an economic change, too. While Byzantium survived, it had been possible to maintain some land contact with the Asian suppliers of the luxuries (particularly spices) which Europeans prized and of the bulk goods most easily bought round the Black Sea coast. After the Turkish conquest, those goods had either to be bought at high prices, found elsewhere, or obtained by a new route direct from Asia. Above all, this encouraged hopes of finding a direct route to the Spice Islands. What is more, it was known that the Mediterranean had been dependent on African gold, and fourteenth-century geographers speculated about the fabulous wealth of the Mandingo empire of Mali. There were hints of other excitements, too — of the kingdom of Prester John, the legendary Christian prince who some crusaders had hoped might come to their aid, thought by some to be the mysterious Christian kingdom of Ethiopia. Finally, for the men who still dreamed of crusades there was even the prospect of turning the Turks' flank.

Expansion and exploration were thus responses to many challenges. What was decisive was that those challenges were offered to a much more confident, capable and responsive society than could be found in other parts of the world at that time. And it was to grow more capable and more confident as new knowledge was assimilated. A cumulative process was at work. Knowledge built on knowledge and even incomplete (and sometimes erroneous) information stimulated further investigation. In a very real sense, too, the work of the great explorers and geographers was part of the more general transformation in European culture which we loosely call the Renaissance. It expresses the same intellectual and spiritual vigour which is embodied in the work of, say, Leonardo and, like the artistic manifestations of the age, its sources lie far in the past.

Interest in the outside world was by 1400 stirring in several of the royal courts of medieval Europe. The story of conscious efforts of discovery can nevertheless be begun with the Portuguese, a people few in numbers but fecund in achievement. 'God gave them a small country as a cradle but all the world as a grave,' as one of them wrote in the seventeenth century. The Reconquest was over in Portugal long before it closed in Spain and as the Spanish reserved the final conquest of Granada to themselves, there was no outlet on the mainland for the crusading fervour of the Portuguese. This practical frustration helped to inspire a series of successful expeditions to North Africa and Morocco in the fifteenth century. It was further south, though, that a great series of Portuguese voyages of discovery was to change the history of the world. They are traditionally associated with the name of a remarkable prince, Henry the Navigator, as he came to be somewhat oddly called by the English — Dom Enrique to the Portuguese.[4]

As the third son of the king of Portugal, Henry was always unlikely to succeed to the throne. This removed one pressure to marry and he remained a lifelong bachelor, living a life of austerity, personal abstinence, chastity and strict religion. He was born into the late medieval world of chivalric and crusading enthusiasm, and took part in three overseas expeditions against the Moors, the first with his father and brothers to North Africa in 1415. Each prince carried on that adventure a fragment of the True Cross given them by their English mother. The climax of the voyage was the capture of the city of Ceuta. It was a great event in Henry's personal life, for here, as he had asked, he was dubbed knight with a full chivalric ceremony. He then retired, as it were, from the normal occupations of a medieval prince. He went to the south coast of Portugal and, somewhere in the neighbourhood of Sagres, the southernmost cape of the Algarve, presided over a court, of a somewhat eccentric flavour, that was to be the focus of Henry's attention as well as his residence for most of the rest of his life. From it he organised the ships, supplies and information needed to send out expeditions year after year, down the west coast of Africa and westward into the Atlantic. This was easier for him than for other princes, because he controlled the revenues of one of the richest of medieval orders of chivalry, the Order of Christ. Later, too, by royal decree, control of the whole African and oceanic trade was conferred upon Henry in 1448; that brought him payments for licences and permits, and forfeits from illegal traders, if caught. Yet Henry never had enough money for all he wanted to do.

With hindsight, knowing what the 'Guinea trade' later became, some historians have seen the fundamental explanation of Henry's efforts in a wish to fill his coffers. Certainly, he sought wealth. A prince who kept up a large household of noblemen and retainers needed money even if he did not want to send out expeditions to explore the African coast and Atlantic islands. There was the gold which came from somewhere south of the Sahara, and the possibility of trade with the East, above all in spices, the indispensable, most highly prized of all international commodities in the Middle Ages. Moreover, Henry was interested in colonisation; he planted sugar beet and vines from Crete in Madeira to launch what became a model development and lasting contribution to the happiness of mankind; within a few years, moreover, Madeira was also exporting wheat. Yet economics were not what set Henry off. Even the search for gold can only be fully understood in the light of something else, the idea of crusade. After all, to cut off Islam's supplies of gold at source was to inflict on it a grievous strategical wound. When Portugal began again to mint (from African gold) a gold coinage, the standard piece was called the *Cruzada* — the 'Crusade'.

The starting-point for understanding Henry's dogged passion for exploration lies in forces whose operation is not easy to comprehend nowadays: chivalry and religion. Henry was a medieval man and therefore a Christian. He once said that the proper purpose in life was to serve God and achieve honour and he took care to have his actions authorised by the publication of papal bulls drafted very specifically. One, *Romanus Pontifex*, 'rightly termed the charter of Portuguese imperialism',[5] awarded to the Portuguese a monopoly of navigation, trade, fishing and conquest between Cape Bojador and the 'Indies'. These documents stressed the service to Christianity of such arrangements; Henry could continue to believe in wars of conquest and the conversion of the heathen, even when trade and slaving had become the order of the day. He at least had much else in mind: reaching the domains of Prester John, winning lands from Islam, opening a road to the East where, it was vaguely known, could be found other Christians, the descendants of those converted by St Thomas on the Malabar coast. With their aid perhaps, Islam could be caught in a strategy of envelopment.

The recent technical advances in ships and sailing were available to underpin Henry's efforts. Navigation had begun to be made easier by the adoption of the magnet by European sailors in the late twelfth century; its ultimate source may well have been China. A device called Jacob's Staff (it was invented by a Jew) was available to captains soon after 1300; with it they could check the altitude of sun or star much more simply than the complicated astrolabe permitted. Ship-handling had become easier with the adoption of the stern-post rudder, instead of an oar over the side. New kinds of sails and rigging were more important still. Medieval sailing was usually a coast-hugging business; that was how most maritime trade was carried on in the Mediterranean and how the Portuguese pushed down the coast of Africa. The technique presented real difficulties on the homeward run from Africa, though, because ships then ran into head winds and contrary currents, tough going for the small, square-rigged medieval cog. Then someone invented the caravel, essentially a leaner, sleeker, three-masted ship with new 'lateen' sails like those of the galleys of the eastern Mediterranean. With them, captains could sail closer to the wind. They could also venture further out into the Atlantic and pick up favourable winds to get them home more easily by way of the Azores, which were under Portuguese control from 1451 or so. As other changes followed the lines of the medieval cog were gradually lost in the evolution of a ship whose basic form was to be little changed for the next three centuries.

Almost every year, from 1418 onwards, Portuguese expeditions added to European knowledge of the world. In that year the exploration of the Madeiras began; their colonisation and that of the Azores was not long in following.[6] Soon, expeditions began to push down the African coast. At first they were unsuccessful, but in 1434, after more than ten years' effort, one doubled Cape Bojador, or, as it was ominously called, 'Cape Nun' — 'Cape Nothing'. Unknown coasts and waters lay ahead, but it may have been the most important achievement of all the Henrician voyages, for it passed a great psychological barrier. The Cape had been a legendary limit to European voyages southwards. Beyond it, some believed, the sea boiled and men turned black in the sun. But now things changed. Expeditions began to go down the Guinea coast. The pope sanctioned Henry's view of them, as part of the struggle against the 'Moors', by allowing that those who died on Henry's voyages might be regarded as having died on crusade. When, in 1441, a ship brought back black men, they were described as prisoners of war and taken to be Muslims. Three years later, the first sale of slaves in Portugal took place. The West African slave trade had begun, and it was quickly found that there were plenty of Africans willing to sell the victims to the traders. The business was soon justified, as was the use of force against blacks, by the argument that it made conversion to Christianity possible. Soon it became big business.[7]

A little gold dust was the next indication of the wealth which might be tapped by successful explorers. After that, maritime enterprise could draw on much more support. By the mid-1440s others besides Henry's captains were taking ships to the Guinea coast and it seems that a net return was already being achieved on a successful voyage. Expeditions grew in size and frequency as people began to grasp that Henry's vision was revealing a new source of wealth. By 1450 the Portuguese had reached the Senegal river, then the Gambia. The mainland had at last ceased to be the depressing desert. Increasingly it ran eastward, and soon again to the south. A fort was built in 1448 on the island of Arguin; it became the first permanent European settlement in West Africa. By the time Henry died in 1460, his ships had reached Sierra Leone.

Thus, like Luther in the next century, Henry helped to launch modern history without any intention of doing so. There was only a brief slackening of effort at his death and then the advance went on. The Equator was crossed, and the Gold Coast reached in the 1470s; the Congo was discovered in 1485. In 1487 two expeditions were launched with the old aims of making contact with Prester John and opening the route to India, and this time they were linked deliberately with the intention of cutting in on the Asian spice trade. One went by land; Pedro de Covilha, a Portuguese, made his way from Cairo to Aden and took ship there for India. (He got there, but was diverted on the way home by royal order to the court of the emperor of Ethiopia who treated him well, giving him an estate and a wife, but never allowed him to come home. So he died there some thirty years later.) The other, in two little ships of fifty tons or so apiece, was that of Bartolomeu Diaz, who was to be the first European to sail round the Cape of Tempests — or, as it was to be called after his return, the Cape of Good Hope, the hope being that of reaching India by sea. True, he did so only as a result of storms and he sailed only a few hundred miles past it to the east before his angry crew forced him to turn back. Nevertheless, it was now clear that a ship might sail direct from Africa to the Indies. In July 1497 four ships put out of Lisbon under the command of Vasco da Gama. He rounded the Cape and picked up a Muslim pilot on the eastern coast for the last leg of the journey. In May 1498 he dropped anchor in Indian waters. On his return, da Gama's hold was crammed with jewels and, above all, spices — pepper, cloves, cinnamon.

Lisbon was to become the major European entrepôt of Asian trade. Pepper there would cost a fifth of its price in Venice. The Portuguese were careful quickly to block the Red Sea route by which it had got to Egypt, the Venetian source, and though after a few decades they were neither able to keep it blocked, nor to establish a watertight monopoly on the Asiatic spice trade, they did very well. It was only a comparatively small boast that the Portuguese king soon called himself 'Lord of Guinea and of the Conquest, of the Navigation and Commerce of Ethiopia, Arabia, Persia and India', though at that time there was probably not a Portuguese ship in the Indian ocean.[8] But sheer violence and naval power soon transformed the Portuguese age of discovery into the age of Portuguese empire: within a few years Portugal was trading regularly with the Malabar coast, had built ports there and dominated Indian waters with the fire-power of her ships. Soon, a Portuguese squadron appeared in Canton.

In the eastern seas which the Portuguese were to dominate for the next century, empire was not territorial, but naval and commercial. It rested on the control of the surface of the sea from a few key centres of commerce.

The first strategic base the Portuguese seized was Goa (1510); it was followed by Ormuz (1515), at the mouth of the Persian Gulf, channelling almost all the trade between India and Persia and Malacca (1519), the focus of the Indonesian spice trade. There were already Portuguese ports on the East African coast. Licences were imposed on Asian ships and traders. Later, after an abortive attempt to establish themselves at Canton, the Portuguese settled at Macao where, after 1557, their presence was tolerated by the Chinese empire. From Macao, they traded with Japan, establishing themselves at Nagasaki in 1571.[9] In the end they were over-extended for Portugal's tiny manpower (over forty ports and forts existed by 1600), but it was a great achievement, all the more striking in that its roots lie so deep in the Christian civilisation of the Middle Ages.

The historical consequences — the outward surge of commercial capitalism, the spread of Christianity round the globe, the building of overseas empires and the transformation of the balance of world political power — were enormous. So was the impact on men's minds. In large measure, the world exists in the minds of men, for it is what we see or sense. Directly, this cannot provide much help in organising geographical knowledge. It has to be abstracted into statements which can then be set out in forms which are easily visualised — maps. In the Middle Ages, few people unconcerned directly with navigation or scholarship could ever have seen a map. Printing de-professionalised and democratised geographical knowledge. Now, we all have mental maps. In the age of exploration fewer men had them but those who did found they changed startlingly.

What happened is not easily or simply dated. In about 1400 a Florentine coming home to Italy from Constantinople had brought with him a copy of one of the great Greek scientific texts, Ptolemy's *Geographia*. Memories of it had lingered in European and Arab geographical thought for more than a thousand years. Within a few years, it was translated into Latin, which made it much more accessible, and in 1472 it was printed; there were six more editions before the end of the century, most of them supplemented with maps. It is true that Ptolemy's world map, made in the second century AD, had one huge error: he believed that the Indian ocean was a vast lake, completely surrounded by land, and therefore inaccessible by sea. If he had been right, you could have got to China from Africa by land around the southern shore of the ocean. Yet in other ways his summary was by no means a bad one, given what could then be known by someone in the Mediterranean world. The Canary islands, Iceland, even Ceylon, all appear on Ptolemaic maps.

The next great step forward followed when the Portuguese, having dis-covered the eastward bend of the Guinea coast, set aside Ptolemy's views of what happened if you followed the African shoreline. They in fact revived an earlier Greek view, that of Strabo, that Africa could be sailed round; they were right, even though Strabo was quite wrong about distances and pro-portions. Yet it was basically on the Ptolemaic conception of the world that the Genoese sailor whom we call Columbus relied when he set off in 1492 to try to reach Asia by sailing westwards. The ancient Greeks had known that the world was a sphere; Columbus seems to have differed only in think-ing it somewhat pear-shaped.

By then, eighty years of Portuguese enterprise had provided a mass of information. Though much slower, the process was like the first explorations by men in space, in that each achievement seemed a little less surprising than the last. The most famous landfall of the age of discovery was finally made in the west, though, in a hitherto unknown hemisphere, and it was a fluke. Under the flag of the crown of Castile, Columbus landed on 12 October 1492 on an island in the Bahamas which he called San Salvador, and from there went on to Cuba and Hispaniola (the island now divided between Haiti and the Dominican Republic). So, he discovered the Americas, though he did not think that was what he had done. Like Henry the Navigator, Co-lumbus achieved something other than he had intended; he was trying to go somewhere else. There was an old idea, drawing on Aristotle and Seneca for its support, that you could get to Asia by sailing west across the Atlantic. Columbus's son says (significantly) that he picked it up in Portugal, 'where the Admiral began to think that, if men could sail so far south, one might also sail west and find lands in that quarter'.[10] His voyage, too, thus owed something to the long efforts of Henry the Navigator.

Even after three further voyages, Columbus still would not concede that he had not reached Asia's off-shore islands. Nor did he ever do so. The 'West Indies' is a name which commemorates his delusion to this day. So the first 'discovery' of the New World was in one important sense nothing of the sort; the man who made it believed he had reached a part of the Old World, not a new one.[11] But others soon realised that he had not reached Asia or even its islands. Another Italian and an acquaintance of Columbus, Amerigo Vespucci, seems to have been sure that he had himself done so a few years later (though he may have been lying). There is much argument about his voyages across the Atlantic; he was never in command and even the number of them is disputed. From one voyage, though, which probably discovered the mouth of the Amazon before turning north, he returned convinced that he had touched the extreme east of Asia. In 1501–2 another expedition, in the Portuguese service which he took part in, sailed further south. In 1505 a little book appeared in Florence with a letter by him in it about his voyages. It bore the title *Mundus Novus* — 'New World'. Only two years after Columbus's first landfall one of the councillors of the crown of Castile had already used a similar expression in a manuscript. What did it mean?

Those words are, in fact, a clue to the real discovery of the age, one which took place in men's minds. Europe began to take in the great new idea that there was a world elsewhere. The idea got about that a whole continent, not just a few islands, lay across the western route to Asia. It was soon suggested that this should be named after Vespucci. So it appeared on a map in 1507: America.[12] Later the name was extended to cover the northern continent, already reached by the Cabots, father and son, in 1497, though they then thought, like Columbus, that they had touched on the territories of the great Khan of the Mongols. The fate of a second expedition under the elder Cabot is unclear, but there is no evidence that he changed his view.[13] The Dutchman Gerhard Kremer, known to us as Mercator, was the first man to print a map which named a North and a South America.

Direct eastward contact with Asia and two new continents discovered in the six years between 1492 and 1498: this was to change the world. And it was to do so very rapidly. Most obviously and immediately, it encouraged explorers to go further still. The circumnavigation of the globe was the next obvious goal; thirty years after Columbus's first voyage it was done, by a Spanish ship which had set out under another of those great Portuguese captains, Magellan. He was killed in the Philippines, but his name is commemorated in that of the straits he discovered and sailed through. After that great achievement the pace of conscious exploration quickened more and more. At the beginning of the eighteenth century it was finally shown that Asia was not connected to North America. Soon after, Australia was circumnavigated. The nineteenth century brought the deep penetration of the African and Central Asian unknown. Twentieth-century western man seemed to be left with very little to find out about the surface of the earth, or at least about the shape of its land masses, once the two poles had been reached by explorers. And so he turned to space and other planets, not just because he had the technology, but also because he had the urge to continue the centuries-old drive to explore.

Long before this, the great discoveries had immense political consequences. It seems amazing that fifteenth-century Europeans should have been so far-sighted and prudent that in 1481 the pope prohibited the sale of firearms to Africans (not that the ban was effective for long). The first treaty between European nations about trade outside European waters had been made three years earlier by Portugal and Spain: it had dawned that there were new dangers of conflict in a world becoming wider every year. Admittedly, the Spanish and Portuguese, two powerful peoples, did not take any other Europeans into account when, in 1494, they made the Treaty of Tordesillas,[14] which effectively divided the unknown world between them along a line of longitude, running about 1500 miles west of the Cape Verde islands and the Azores; all lands discovered to the east of it were to belong to Portugal, to the west to Spain. In spite of the pope's approval, interloping nations soon made nonsense of this agreement. Nevertheless, it is a landmark of great psychological and political importance: Europeans, who by then had not even gone round the globe, had decided to divide between themselves all its undiscovered and unappropriated lands and peoples. The potential implications were vast. Yet that decision, for all its implicit arrogance, rested on solid grounds for confidence. The conquest of the high seas was the first and greatest of all the triumphs over natural forces which were to lead to the domination by western civilisation of the whole globe. Knowledge is power, and the knowledge won by the first systematic explorers — not only of the geographical location of hitherto unknown lands, but of winds, navigational techniques, and trade routes safe from interference — had opened the way to the age of western world hegemony.

Europeans were now to take a new view of themselves and their relation to the other peoples of the globe. Maps are the best clue to this change, too. They are always more than mere factual statements. They are translations of reality into forms we can master; they are fictions and acts of imagination communicating more than scientific data. So they reflect changes in our pictures of reality. The world is not only what exists 'out there'; it is also the picture we have of it in our minds which enables us to take a grip on material actuality. In taking that grip, our apprehension of that actuality changes — and so does a wide range of our assumptions and beliefs.

One crucial mental change was the final emergence of the notion of Europe from the idea of Christendom. Maps show the difference between the two.

After the age of discovery, Jerusalem, where the founder of Christianity had taught and died, could no longer be treated as the centre of the world — where it appeared on many medieval maps. Soon it was Europe which stood at the centre of Europeans' maps. The final key to a new mental picture was provided by the discovery of the Americas. Somewhere about 1500 European map-makers had established the broad layout of the world map with which we are familiar. In the fifteenth century, Europe had usually been placed in the top left-hand corner of attempts to lay out the known world, with the large masses of Asia and Africa sprawled across the rest of the surface. The natural centre of such maps might be in any of several places. Then the American discoveries slowly began to effect a shift in the conventional arrangement; more and more space had to be given to the land masses of North and South America as their true extent became better known. Juan de la Cosa, who had sailed with Columbus on his second voyage, was the first man to incorporate knowledge of his discoveries (as well as those of John Cabot's voyage of 1497) in a world map he made in 1500 which already shows the shift of Europe towards a world-central position. Maps on similar lines soon followed from other map-makers, incorporating fresh facts as they became available.

By the middle of the century the new geographical view of the world had come to be taken for granted. It was given its canonical expression in the work of Mercator — a great admirer of Ptolemy, it may be remarked. He polished up the new visualisation of the world map into the one we know best in the course of attempting to solve a very practical problem: how to find a way of representing without distortion the globe as a flat surface on which courses could be logged and plotted. To take to sea a globe which was big enough to be of navigational use was impracticable. Mercator's new 'projection', first used in a map in 1568, was to serve for four hundred years with great success. Basically, he turned the globe into a cylinder. Cut down one side and unrolled, this gave you a grid of lines of longitude and latitude which would always tell you where you were with reference to the poles. What it could not do was provide accurate comparisons of surface area because, of course, the ends of the cylinder are lines; the poles, though, should be points. Mercator's picture of the world therefore becomes very distorted as you get a long way away from the Equator. But it still provided a good scientific basis for the calculation of position and direction on the high seas.

Of course, it also did something else: it impressed itself upon the minds of men who were in no way concerned with navigation, and drove home the idea that the land surface of the globe was naturally grouped about a European centre. So Europe came to stand in some men's minds at the centre of the world. No doubt this led Europeans for centuries to absorb unconsciously from their atlases the idea that this was somehow the natural order of things. It did not often occur to them that you could have centred Mercator's projection in, say, China, or even Hawaii, and that Europeans might then have felt very different. The idea still hangs about, even today.[15] Most people like to think of themselves at the centre of things. The Chinese long believed they lived in what they called the 'Middle' — or 'Centre' — 'Kingdom'. Mercator helped his own civilisation to take what is now called a 'Eurocentric' view of the world. Much later, it was reinforced by the adoption world-wide of the Greenwich Meridian, which came about in 1884 after difficulties had arisen in timetabling the Canadian Pacific Railway which led one of its engineers to launch a campaign for the international regulation of time-zones. This was, if you like, a mental or moral distortion. But perhaps it was inevitable to a projection invented in Europe, and technically and scientifically it served well and long. It is hardly Mercator's fault that we now need projections which provide information other than that which he sought to provide, about population distribution, for example, or accurate proportional representation of areas, or gross national product. All maps are conventional and selective.

The ultimate origins of a change in men's minds, though, lie deeper than maps. They can be traced at least to the thirteenth and fourteenth centuries.[16] Even then, to a few people, the European continent was beginning to be clearly identifiable as an area to all intents and purposes identical with Christendom, and so (though no one had the concept to hand) the seat of a distinctive civilisation. Such hints of this sort as have been detected suggest the presence of seeds likely to be fostered by much which was going on in the later Middle Ages.[17] Meanwhile Christianity had been extended to every corner of Europe.[18] The Christian churches of Asia, though, had been the victims first of Muslim response to the crusaders' brutality, and then of the rise of the Ottoman Turks and the destruction of the Byzantine empire. Non-European Christianity had therefore never looked less impressive than at the beginning of the sixteenth century, and that gave even more importance to its Catholic and west European form. Finally, Europe's economic life, growing richer in these centuries, was giving the continent a new sort of homogeneity.

All these facts meant that fifteenth-century Europe was a unity in quite a new way. Some churchmen, statesmen and polemicists began to work out and make suggestions about the implications of this.[19] They were not always fully aware of what they were doing. But 'Europe' slowly became interchangeable with the concept 'Christendom', and 'European' with 'Christian'. In common parlance, Christendom no longer extended to the Christians under Ottoman rule, who were not regarded as Europeans. Maps, which had begun in the fourteenth century to distinguish symbolically between political authorities in different places, began in the next to mark off a Christendom confined to Europe, from the area dominated by Islam.

With a growing self-consciousness went a growing sense of superiority. New knowledge of other continents seemed to bear this out, and ancient conceptions began to stir and to be given new applications. The old antithesis of civilised and barbarian rooted in Greek origin had never quite disappeared. The legend of Noah's sons implied superiority in the descendants of Japheth, at least over those of Ham. An Englishman, Purchas, writing in 1625, gave a remarkable expression to a new European confidence:

> Europe is taught the way to scale heaven, not by mathematical principles, but by divine verity. Jesus Christ is their way, their truth, their life; who hath long been given a bill of divorce to ungrateful Asia, where He was born, and Africa, the place of his flight and refuge, and is become almost wholly and only European. For little do we find of this name in Asia, less in Africa, and nothing at all in America, but later European gleanings.[20]

The sense of identity, of a special nature, derived from religion, was by then no longer new. It was reflected in the transition from the idea of Christendom to that of Europe. What is new in such a statement is the confidence it shows at a moral and mythical level, and its attachment to place and people, to Europe and Europeans. It shows Europeans who are beginning to feel they have little to learn from the rest of the world. What is more, they are making a spiritual takeover bid for it; even Christ 'is become almost wholly and only European'. When another half-century or so had gone by, the replacement of 'Christendom' by 'Europe' as a political term, too, was well under way, in England and Holland, at least.[21].

The cultivated European's view of universal history at about the same time might be found in the work of a French clergyman, Jacques Bénigne Bossuet, bishop of Meaux. He was a learned and thoughtful man, but it was probably less his learning than his eloquent and fashionably successful preaching before the Court which led to his appointment as tutor to the king's son, the dauphin, in 1670. He was to hold the post for eleven years. During that time, one of the books he wrote for his pupil's instruction was a *Discourse on Universal History*. He singled out religion and the story of great empires as the key themes for his royal pupil's attention — 'les deux points sur lesquels roulent les choses humaines'[22] — and, in the light of this judgement, not the least interesting feature of his book is the fact that the history of most of the world finds no place in it.

It is focused on the tradition which Europe inherits — the tradition which leads to Bossuet and his master, Louis XIV — the Judaeo-Roman tradition. We learn from Bossuet much of the kings of Israel and the great days of

Rome, something, even, of Assyria, Persia and Egypt, whose histories impinge on those of the Jews and Greeks, but nothing, for instance, of China, whose empire was already nearly two thousand years old when he wrote. Yet Bossuet was the dauphin's tutor when Louis XIV solemnly received the first ambassadors to Europe from Siam, a tributary state of the Chinese empire. He must have known of the avidly studied Jesuit missionaries' reports from the Chinese imperial court and may, perhaps, have heard of the concessions in behaviour and dress which some of those Jesuits were making to a civilisation they had learned to admire. Why does he show so little concern for its role in the story of mankind, then? The reasons must be a reflexion of the emotional and logical self-sufficiency already achieved by European culture. The essential meaning of history, for Bossuet and his contemporaries, was to be found in the Christian story, which culminated in the Europe of his day and perhaps even in a Catholic monarch who saw himself as the 'Sun King' — *le roi soleil*. Only a little while before this had men learned that they lived in a heliocentric universe, that the planets revolved about the sun, which now stood at the centre of the celestial map in as unquestioned a way as Europe stood at the centre of Mercator's. Now a king, the most powerful in Europe, could accept the theory as an image of his own position.

Nowadays, people have come to use a specially minted word to summarise this state of mind — 'Eurocentrism'. It means 'putting Europe at the centre of things' and its usual implication is that to do so is wrong. But, of course, if we are merely talking about facts, about what happened, and not about the value we place on them, then it is quite correct to put Europe at the centre of the story in modern times. From the age of discovery onwards, Europe, and those countries which are descended from the European stocks, have been the mainspring of history, and to that extent (and no further) Purchas, Bossuet and others were sensing the truth. It was from Europe that the discoverers, *conquistadores*, settlers and traders had gone *out*: they created a world of which Europe was the centre, the Americas and Asia the periphery. Eurocentrism, nevertheless, at an early date went revealingly beyond the mere facts of power and influence (which, in any case, were only just beginning to show themselves). What Purchas and the rest felt was a qualitative superiority.

It must at once be said that that sense of superiority had its challengers at a very early date. In the sixteenth century, Montaigne reminded his readers that it might only be that a sense of perspective was missing. 'We ... wonder at the miraculous invention of our artilerie', he wrote, 'and are amazed at the rare device of Printing: when as unknown to us, other men, and an other end of the world named China, knew and had perfect use of both, a thousand years before.'[23] Yet this judgement, too, was over-simple.

Printing might have long been known there, but it had not produced in China the liberating effects it had in Europe. Nor could reminders of the past achievements of other cultures account, as time went by, for a widening gap of achievement, which in many ways still remains to be explained. It is clear, though, that Europeans rapidly became more and more conscious of that gap, almost from the moment at which reports began to come home about what the discoverers had found. That is the main reason why the voyages of discovery, as much as the rediscovery of antiquity by the humanists, are a turning-point in Europe's cultural and intellectual history. Four-fifths of the globe is covered by sea and already by 1600 the Europeans had no rivals upon it except in the land-locked Mediterranean.

VII

NEW WORLDS

Ask anyone in the world to name an American city: if he has heard of only one it will probably be New York. Once it was called New Amsterdam, and all over the United States you can find similar names: New Orleans, New Jersey, New Hampshire — and, of course, New England. Canada's old name was New France. South of the Rio Grande lay the great Spanish viceroyalty of New Spain, and further south again, New Granada. The Spanish had founded New Vizcaya, New Galicia, New Castile and a New Toledo, too. There must be more to this quirk of place-name history than a simple inability to think of something different. Those names stamp 'Europe' — and a European intention to maintain a European civilisation — on the New World. The same was later to be true on the other side of the globe — in New Zealand, New South Wales, New Caledonia. In the Americas as elsewhere, Europeans did not succumb to what they found, but strove to master it, whatever concessions they made on the way. They were determined to keep their end up.

The first great effort since the crusades to transplant European civilisation overseas changed world history more than any since. The Americas came to shelter two distinct, but clearly related, varieties of European civilisation — north and south of, roughly, the Rio Grande. The south came first; to all intents and purposes the story there begins a century before that in the north. In due course, the Portuguese and Spaniards built empires on the central and southern mainland of the American continents which led to something which the nineteenth-century French emperor Napoleon III could call 'Latin America'.

Seen from Europe and North America, Latin America was defined by the use of Portuguese (in Brazil) and Spanish (elsewhere) as the dominating languages, by the superiority everywhere in the continent of Roman Catholic Christianity, and by governmental arrangements derived from those of European absolutist monarchy. Later, those countries took up some of the language and concepts of more recent European politics. Radical, liberal republican, anti-clerical, democratic — these were words familiar to the politicians of an independent Latin America. North of the Rio Grande, things look somewhat different. Though there were once Spanish settlements over much of what is now the southern United States, and the French once held Louisiana, two predominantly English-speaking countries of mixed but over-whelmingly European stock now divide most of the northern continent between them. In them, too, Christianity is the predominating religion, but within a society more blatantly secularised. Christianity's particular forms in North America, moreover, are much shaped by Protestantism, by a tradition of religious pluralism, and by a very different social structure. As for law, government, politics, they reflect the Europe of constitutional, individualistic political culture; that of England, in short, rather than that of continental Europe.

North and south, though, both Americas are part of the western world, whatever the differences between them. In one, the descendants of the aboriginal inhabitants have been in large measure officially ignored, in the other they were all but wiped out; both attitudes now seem arrogant but they speak of great self-confidence. The modern Americas are great creative achievements of a civilisation or, rather, of two selected, edited versions of that civilisation, operating in different environments. That they succeeded was not just a matter of accident. It can tell us some important things about our civilisation and why it is dominant in our age.

Exploration in the Caribbean and Central America was followed by empire much more rapidly than exploration further north. The origins of impe-rialism are even more complicated than those of the urge to explore. True, both stories began with the Portuguese, who had provided indispensable example and experience of settlement in the planting of the Atlantic islands with settlers, a task they shared with the Spanish. For a long time the Iberians had had no competitors and, among them, the Portuguese remained for most of the fifteenth century pre-eminent in the infant colonial enterprises in Madeira, the Canaries and the Azores. Among other European peoples with a potential for assertiveness and expansion those of central and eastern Europe were by 1500 pretty well boxed in. The Ottoman conquests and the rise of Muscovy had put new barriers in the way to movement southeast and east. The old maritime powers were in decline: Venice and Genoa, long deeply committed to the eastern Mediterranean, were now more or less bottled up there. Past their commercial prime, they faced the Ottoman threat to their remaining possessions. Further west, too, they had formidable rivals, first in Catalonia, then in the crown of Aragon, and eventually in the united power of Aragon and Castile which we can call 'Spain'. In northern waters, the Scandinavians, notwithstanding Viking and Norse traditions of enter-prise and piracy, seem to have been preoccupied with commercial possibilities nearer home — supplying raw materials to northern Europe where an important Baltic trade had developed, institutionalised in the mercantile empire of the Hansa towns.

England and France were better, and even admirably, sited for oceanic adventure, with excellent harbours. At the end of the fifteenth century, some Englishmen and Frenchmen were just beginning to look beyond the traditional horizons of their trade and fishery. In 1497 John Cabot was backed to sail from Bristol to make his landfall in Labrador, and only a few years later his son helped to open up sea communication with Muscovy around the North Cape. Yet the mixture of forces in England and France had not been and was still not yet quite right for them to challenge the Iberian lead. In Portugal, it was right by 1450, in Spain, as the Reconquest came to an end. Both countries were admirably placed for physical access to the oceans: the winds alone settled that.

Spain, though, had a special stimulus. The long conflict with Islam had uniquely tempered her people for the adventure of empire. They looked forward eagerly to further campaigns against the infidel. It was clear that a more formidable enemy than it had faced in the west during the last centuries of Muslim Spain now faced Christendom in the eastern Mediterranean, threatening at one moment the holy city of Rome itself. But that is still not the whole explanation. The Reconquest had not only awakened crusading impulses, it had transformed Spanish society. Medieval Castile had, over the centuries of Reconquest, turned itself into a specialised fighting and conquering machine. It could function superbly so long as fighters were needed and more land was available to reward them. But as Reconquest neared its close, the chances it offered of winning glory and estates at the same time began to wane. If adventure outwards came to a stop, then its landless squires and yeomen would be pitted against one another by magnates out for their own ends. The conquest of Granada had been the last opportunity inside Spain to give the war machine something to do. When it was over, no further outlet was available in Spain and the land-hungry *hidalgo* of Castile had to look elsewhere. The brief African adventures were not enough. Yet the state of mind which sustained the Reconquest was still alive as the sixteenth century opened; if only it could be utilised, it would generate the psychic energy great enterprises require.

Significantly, it was in the Christian camp outside Granada, within sight of the towers of that last Muslim stronghold, that the decision was taken to give Columbus the ships and money he asked for. He was commissioned to act as viceroy or governor in any islands or mainlands he might discover, and was given a letter to present to the great Khan. His expedition was equipped as a thanks-offering. In the August following the fall of the last Moorish capital in Spain — seven months and a day later — he set sail.

Eighty years later, a Spanish empire stretched across half the world. Philip II of Spain, great-grandson of the Catholic Monarchs, ruled lands on which (as his English contemporary Walter Raleigh remarked) the sun never set. With, as it must have seemed to some, almost providential appropriateness, Columbus had opened the way to a vast new territory available for missionary work, adventure and personal advancement to a European society which had, for centuries, been 'conquering, administering, christianising and Europeanising' the Muslim inhabitants of Spain.[1]

One other fact has to be taken into account as a part of the background to the character Spanish imperialism was to assume. No one knew it, but just as the first age of European empire was about to begin, so was a great age of religious struggle within Christendom. The Protestant Reformation enormously magnified and envenomed religious conflict and conflict in the name of religion; it raised religious emotions to new intensities and gave European rulers new issues to quarrel about. The Counter-Reformation and a vast remaking of the Roman Catholic vision of the church were a result. Wars of religion (some religious only in name, but some in savage reality) were to soak European battlefields with blood for a century and more. This, too, was to shape the way Iberian imperialism soon developed.

The Portuguese had made the first treaty about trade outside European waters with the Spanish in 1479 — a landmark in international affairs, if one thinks about it for a moment — and then in 1494, two years after Columbus had landed in Cuba, came the Treaty of Tordesillas which divided the world east and west between them. The Portuguese, even before the voyage of Vasco da Gama, were pretty sure that the way to wealth lay eastward and do not seem to have minded giving Spanish enterprise this final shove, in the wake of Columbus, westward towards America. The treaty was not, in fact, to reserve the 'New World' for Spain, because it was only a few years later that a Portuguese expedition came across land east of the treaty line but in the Americas, the future Brazil. As a result Brazilians, uniquely among South Americans, still speak Portuguese today. But it was the Spanish who for over a century dominated the fate of the New World. The Portuguese had planted settlers in the Atlantic islands, and were later to do so in Brazil, but the more important Portuguese oceanic empire was Asian and African; it was a matter of forts, fleets and trading-posts, not of communities of colonists seizing land and building a new society on it. The Spanish, on the other hand, were not after trade: they wanted outright possession.

They began with the islands of the Caribbean. Some were drawn to them by the hope of gold, some because they wanted land to farm and for stock-raising. On Hispaniola in 1496 they founded Santo Domingo, the first European city in America and, one might say, the last city created in the Middle Ages. In 1523, the corner-stone of its cathedral was laid; in 1538 the first

university in the New World was founded there, a century before Harvard.
Cities were a sign (to the Indians, especially) that the Spanish were not going
to go away.[2] Architecture was the most successful art practised in the colonised New World south of the Rio Grande for three centuries after the Conquest; the Spaniards seem to have felt a need to show they could build as
splendidly as their predecessors. Meanwhile, in 1511 Cuba was settled, and
promised to be a richer, more rewarding colony than Hispaniola. Soon,
expeditions went further. The ruthless Balboa founded Darien on the mainland in 1513. Six years later, he crossed the isthmus of Panama and became
the first European captain to see the Pacific shores of the Americas. The
hope of finding a strait through the isthmus quickly led other explorers to
the mainland of Central America. Soon, the Spanish had come to stay on
the mainland, too. The brief, heroic age of the *conquistadores* was beginning.

They were by any standards remarkable men. It is tempting to think of
them as very modern, for they built the first European territorial empires
overseas. Yet they can only be wholly understood against a background of
medieval aggressiveness. The *conquistadores* are one evolutionary stage in a
continuum which runs from the crusaders down to people like Clive in India
in the eighteenth century, and Rhodes in Africa in the nineteenth. To some
of their personal motives we can at once respond; others are alien to us.
Many of them responded to a medieval urge to repeat the legendary deeds
of paladins and heroes; significantly, the reading, printing and writing of
new romances on traditional lines seems to have been very frequent in the
first half-century or so of Spanish America. Many of them also saw what
they did as a way to make a raid on accumulated wealth, many as a way of
getting land. Always, though, there was the Cross in the background, sometimes as an inspiration, sometimes as an excuse. They were continuators of
the Reconquest.

The most famous of all the *conquistadores* set out from Cuba in 1519 with
a few hundred men, flouting the authority under which he operated and
later burning his boats so that his men could not go back when (on Good
Friday) they landed on the Mexican coast at what is now Vera Cruz. This
was Hernán Cortés, whose conquest of Mexico and destruction of the Aztec
empire is the best-known and most dramatic of all episodes in the history
of Spanish America. He was not merely out for personal wealth and security;
Cortés was also confident that his cause was the cause of Castile and the
Faith. He carried always on his person an image of the Blessed Virgin and
his standard bore the injunction to follow the Cross, and the historic slogan
'in this sign shall we conquer'. He was also sure that glory should be sought
for its own sake and is reported to have said, with satisfaction, that he was
outdoing the deeds of the Romans.

The sixteen horses Cortés had with him were a great advantage; they astonished the Indians who had never seen before a beast that could divide itself into another beast and a man — which was what they thought was happening when a Spaniard dismounted. They were probably influenced, too, by the coincidence (lucky for the Spanish) of Cortés' arrival with a prophecy that the Aztec god Quetzalcoatl would return in 1519 and would be fair-skinned. It was also a help that Aztec rule had antagonised other Mexican peoples who welcomed Spanish assistance against it. As for the morale of his own men, it must have improved dramatically as the march proceeded. As one of his companions put it, 'We saw so many cities and towns settled on the water, and on land other great habitations, and that causeway, so straight and so level, leading to Mexico, [that] we were struck with admiration and we said that it was all like those things of enchantment which are told in the books of Amadis . . . there were some soldiers who even asked whether all that they saw might not be a dream.'[3] But what mattered most was the enterprise, courage and drive of their leader.

It is not now easy to offer Cortés unqualified admiration, but he was true to his religion as well as to his ambition, and strove, even at great risk, to serve God as well as Mammon. Driven, at the crucial moment, by a sense of desperate isolation and danger, he cut out his path to fame by cunningly imprisoning the Aztec ruler Montezuma (whom he had at first tried to convert) in his own capital, and ended by destroying a civilisation and — as Cortés himself put it — 'the most beautiful city in the world'. Few men have done as much. On its site Cortés began to build a new Spanish city. His reward was to be made Governor and Captain-General of New Spain.

Cortés was the greatest of the *conquistadores*, but there were many others. Alvarado in Guatemala, Francisco Pizarro in Peru, his enemy Almagro and his brother Gonzalo Pizarro in the upper Amazon basin are the most famous. The deeds of such men have thrown many others into shadow. Comparatively few of them, though, actually reaped the huge rewards which were available. The beneficiaries were more likely to be the merchants and bureaucrats who followed them. But their work was irreversible, once the discovery of the silver of Mexico and Peru removed the danger that the new empire would always be a drain on the resources of Spain. The *conquistadores* built on a scale such as no one had ever seen before. By 1600 the Spanish ruled, in name at least, much of what is now the south-western United States, almost all of Mexico, Central America, the islands of the Caribbean and what is now Venezuela, Colombia, Ecuador, Peru, Chile and the coasts of Argentina and Uruguay. To create this huge structure, the *conquistadores* overthrew the Aztec and Inca empires, two complex social and governmental systems with great resources behind them. And they and their successors were often almost uncontrollable by the governments at home.[4]

From the first, the new order displayed an ambivalence — or, perhaps, incoherence — towards the native cultures it disturbed, and this may have had wide historical implications. Though Pope Alexander VI had been pleased to hear that there were already living in the Caribbean settlements native peoples who believed in one God and seemed 'sufficiently disposed to embrace the Catholic faith and to be trained in good morals',[5] the settlers were quickly disappointed by their apparent unwillingness to adopt Spanish ways — for that was the way they saw it. Some of them soon began to say the Indians were not capable of such a change. They were stigmatised as creatures lower in the scale of creation than true humans, lacking something which true human beings had in them which made civilisation possible. Ferdinand of Aragon ordered the Casa de Contratación to send white slave women to the Indies because some Spaniards there were marrying Indians who were 'far from being rational creatures'.

Such attitudes were in due course carried over from the islands to the American mainland. Though, at first, the Spanish in Mexico were somewhat awed by the glamour of some native institutions and by the plenteousness of gold, once they came into intimate touch with native custom, tradition and religion they treated them with contempt and sometimes (as they did the Aztec sacrificial rites) with horror. Other Europeans in other lands, at other times, were to show similar divergences. For centuries, Europeans had admired from afar the pomp, wealth and power of non-European empires. They continued to do so for some time after they encountered them at first hand. Rarely, though, did they feel spiritually intimidated and they tended to respect other cultures less and less as time passed. Wherever they went — to Isfahan, Delhi, Canton — Europeans were sure their own achievements, values and religion were best. One reason why the Spaniards built cities was that they could be sure that in them they were still European.

That, though, is not the whole story. The ambiguities went deeper. The rightness of offering an alien religion to the aboriginal Americans was indeed unquestioned, but how to do so was much debated. Religion was part of the justification of empire; everyone knew that the crown of Castile had a duty to propagate the Faith in its new possessions. The papal bulls which demarcated Spanish authority overseas in 1493 specifically entrusted to it the conversion of its new subjects to Christianity. A new crusade — for that was how many Spaniards saw it, being medieval men — opened a new hemisphere to a force hitherto largely confined to Europe; the universal claims of Catholic Christianity were now to be given global play. Cortés himself asked his king to send out priests to Mexico and wanted to found monasteries there, supported by tithes. The cross was for *all* men and so the Americans were to be converted, like it or not. Many natives obviously did not mind; of those who objected, we hear and know much less.

Yet converting the Indians was no simple matter. They did not seem to like life on the estates granted to Spanish settlers where, roughly speaking, they were serfs obliged to labour for their masters. Doubts were soon raised by reports that the Indians rejected the civilised benefits offered to them: they would neither work nor give up their vices — perhaps they were, after all, irredeemable? Special laws were passed to regulate their lives. One of the first enquiries by questionnaire ever mounted by a government was launched in 1516 by three Jeronimite friars sent out to find out what the colonists thought. Only one man — a Dominican — whom they questioned thought the Indians ready for liberty. It is hardly surprising that it should have been a friar who said so, for it was among the clergy — and particularly the mendicant orders — that the Indians found their only protectors.

Among the Franciscans and Dominicans who carried the cross into the new Spanish empire in the first phase of evangelisation were conscientious and devoted missionaries. Some of them set to work to learn and write down the Indians' languages, to record Indian history and custom, to encourage Indian crafts and traditions. They had a practical aim. They wanted to use analogies with Christianity in native religion (the Aztecs, for instance, associated the sign of the cross with gods of wind and rain, and had another god, they believed, who had been born of a virgin). Missionaries laboriously worked out a way of using Aztec pictographs to convey Christian ideas such as 'soul' which had no local equivalent. All that could be done to bring to the Indians what was in the friars' eyes the most precious of all the gifts that Christendom could offer, the Gospel, was done. And as they grew closer to the Indians and understood them better, some of the clergy came to sympathise more and more with them. They even tried to keep other Spaniards from contact with them. The hardbitten soldier settlers who ran the new empire often treated the Indians appallingly — and not just in Mexico, but elsewhere as the conquest was extended. But the clergy were moved to rebuke and oppose them by more than mere human feeling.

The roots of their concern were theological. They lay in medieval Christianity and tangled scholastic argument about how non-Christian peoples should be treated by Christian rulers who subjugated them. Debate on this theme began again in 1511. In that year, the first sermon against the way the Spanish treated their new subjects was preached in Santo Domingo. 'By what right or justice,' asked the Dominican Montesinos, 'do you keep these Indians in such a cruel and horrible servitude? . . . Are not these men? Have they not rational souls? Are you not bound to love them as you love yourselves? . . . Be certain that in such a state as this, you can no more be saved than Moors or Turks'.[6] It was the most terrible threat the age could utter, and it was employed to defend the Indians.

There followed the first attempt to restrain the settlers, the 'Laws of Burgos' of 1512. Evidently, the crown did not think that the threat of damnation would alone suffice. In the following year came a strange phenomenon, the adoption of 'the Requirement' — a long legal document which was meant to be read aloud to Indians in the Americas before hostilities were begun against them. What Indians made of it — it began with a brief history of the world and the papacy, all in Spanish — is difficult to conceive. But it expressed a deep concern with moral justification for the use of force and with legality; significantly, the Indians were to be asked to allow the Christian faith to be promoted among them and to acknowledge the over-lordship of the crown of Castile. Only if they refused could armed force justifiably be employed against them, said the Spanish lawyers.

Later, there were to be more laws to protect Indians. But enforcement was hard. When the first Viceroy of Peru tried to apply them, his fellow-countrymen killed him. Yet doubts continued and flowered into bad consciences, not only among the clergy, but also among royal officials and ministers in Spain. Not only individuals, but the crown itself enquired into what a colonising nation should try to do in its colonies. In the end, the emperor Charles V suspended all further expeditions to the Americas until a jury of theologians, lawyers and officials had heard a great debate at Valladolid in 1550 on what is to modern ears an extraordinarily scholastic and medieval question: whether the American natives were, like the men whom Aristotle had described as 'slaves by nature', creatures lacking the natural reason which would enable them to govern their own lives, and therefore rightly be governed by others for their good.[7] The declaration of the papal bull *Sublimus Deus* in 1537 that 'the Indians are *truly men* and . . . are not only capable of understanding the Catholic faith, but, according to our information, . . . desire exceedingly to receive it' seems not to have been enough. It left open the question: what sort of men? Souls they might have, and so they might be capable of salvation. But, besides this essential attribute of humanity, what else did they share with other men — with Spaniards, for instance?

One side of this debate was taken by a great Dominican who became famous as the friend of the Indians, Bartolomé de Las Casas. For centuries, his strictures on the behaviour of the colonists provided ammunition to critics of Spain: they forgot that Las Casas, too, was a Spaniard. He was so appalled by what some of his countrymen had done in the Indies, he said, that he began a great history in order to explain God's actions should it prove that He had decided to destroy Spain because of her sons' behaviour in America.

Las Casas had gone out to Hispaniola as a settler in 1502 and was the first man to be ordained in the New World. In 1519, at Barcelona, he first disputed the 'Aristotelian' hypothesis that the Indians were slaves by nature. Later, as bishop of Chiapa in Mexico, he fought to uphold the rights of the Indians against settlers who exploited them, refusing absolution to Spaniards who could not satisfy him at confession about their treatment of the Indians.

For half a century, he took the Indians' part in America and Spain, preaching, arguing, lobbying. 'God created them simple people and without guile,' he wrote. 'They are now obedient and faithful to their natural lords and to the Christians whom they serve. They are now submissive, patient, peaceful and virtuous. Nor are they quarrelsome, rancorous, querulous or vengeful. Moreover, they are more delicate than princes and die easily from work or illness. They neither possess nor desire to possess worldly wealth. Surely these people would be the most blessed in the world if only they worshipped the true God.'[8]

The passion of Las Casas and men like him was nonetheless balanced by the unshakeable confidence of others in the rightness of what they, the conquerors, were doing. It was in some ways a prefiguring of a conflict between the moral imperatives of European civilisation and the self-assuredness of settlers which was to break out time and time again in the next three centuries, and all round the world. Here is one of the confident views, that of a historian of the age, Lopez de Gómara: 'The Spaniards gave beasts of burden to relieve the natives of drudgery, wool to wear for modesty's sake if they liked rather than as a necessity, and meat to eat which they were without. The Spaniards showed them the use of iron and oil lamps to improve their way of living; they gave them a system of money so that they would know how to buy and sell and what they had owed.[9] They taught them Latin and other subjects, which are worth a lot more than all the silver taken from them, because with literacy they became men whereas the silver was of little or no advantage to them. And so they were benefited by being conquered and, even more, by becoming Christians.' Such arguments led to something just as new as the first scrutiny by a colonising government of the ethical imperatives which should govern its actions and something much more sinister, the first attempt by intellectual argument to stigmatise a whole race as inferior. This was what was implied in the great debate at Vallodolid. A great ruler had ordered that conquests in his name should come to a halt until his learned men satisfied him about the justice of the way they had been carried out. Though formally inconclusive, the debate is a remarkable landmark in the thinking of a civilisation. In it, Las Casas did not reject the Aristotelian hypothesis upheld by his opponent that there existed beings who were by nature slaves, incapable of a full, autonomous, human life. But he would not admit it applied to his Indians; if they seemed deficient in reason, he argued, it was only because they had hitherto lacked occasion to develop it. He had been arguing for more than thirty years that Aristotle's argument did not apply to the Indians, ever since the meeting of the first council on Indian affairs, and himself used Aristotelian arguments to support his case.[10] The debate had no clear outcome before the tribunal of learned men. Yet the crown seems to have accepted Las Casas' arguments, to judge by further laws of 1573 forbidding conversion by force in the new discoveries, and recommending protection of Indians' rights. Unfortunately, the conscious attempts of the crown to control its subjects had been (and went on being) too feeble to restrain the men on the spot in the violent early days of settlement.

Other things besides conversion came with Spanish conquest: probably the most immediately damaging was the unwitting introduction of European disease. Almost incidentally and by accident, Cortés' expedition wiped out much of the Mexican population — perhaps a half in some places — because among his followers there was one who had smallpox. A collapse of population in the Caribbean had followed within half a century of Columbus. This may well have owed much also to the appalling way in which many Spanish ruthlessly exploited native labour by a system hard to distinguish in practice from slavery itself. To this day a common word for 'peasant' in South American countries is *péon* — the 'pawn', the lowest valued piece in the game of chess.

The clergy, by and large, were the only effective local champions of the Indian cause. Though there were divisions within the church about how and what Indians should be taught, they never lacked friends among the clergy, whose efforts to meet Indian needs left an astonishing mark on American life. Quite physically and literally, much of what can be seen today of the Spanish impact is owed to them, especially to the regular clergy — Franciscans, Dominicans and Augustinians — who were the spearhead of the church in Spanish America. With special privileges which made them somewhat independent of the bishops (though many friars became bishops, among them Las Casas himself), they built churches with huge compounds where services could be held and sermons preached to huge number of souls. There was no chance of getting such congregations indoors. They built schools, hospitals, whole towns, too, even aqueducts. Finding that Indian villages, like Spanish towns, were often grouped about a central square or *plaza mayor*, other clergy built so that many Mexican towns look like old Spanish towns to this day. One Franciscan, Father Tembleque, spent seventeen years on his own directing Indians in the building of more than thirty miles of aqueduct to bring water to his flock — and he had no architectural or engineering training.[11]

The missionaries changed Indian life as they worked. They did not consider future amateurs of native art and archaeology as they destroyed what they thought of as 'idols' and 'temples'. Because they confronted so many languages, and rarely imposed their own except on the Indian élite, they sometimes chose one among the native languages for promotion, and so subtly affected native society at a deep level. They made Indians wear clothes and imposed on them a European sexual morality. In other ways, though, they opposed their hispanisation. The first schools in the New World were founded in the 1520s by Franciscans but teaching came to be in native languages or Latin, not in Spanish. Europeans were kept out of the Indian villages founded by the friars because they might set a bad example.

Occasionally, churchmen, too, were unrestrained and ruthless as they strove to root out idolatry.[12] This, though, seems linked in time to a gradual decline in the fervour for popular evangelism which appeared in Europe itself as the Counter-Reformation took the church further and further towards a rigid authoritarianism and formalism. Such forces, like the earlier missionary zeal, tended to spread through all the Spanish New World, although with local variations. The American hierarchy became more interested in its place in creole society than in winning Indian souls. Even the religious orders quarrelled more and more as time went by. The Inquisition had little to do in America, as heretics were few and far between, but it obsessively concerned itself with trivia. Significantly, too, the church began to worry more about miscegenation. The voices in favour of the Indians and interest in their culture did not die out, but they grew weaker as time went by.

So, for all the noble efforts and purity of principle among the missionaries, the church in the end helped to build a two-tier society. In much of Latin America, an Iberian ruling class presided over a non-Spanish-speaking Indian population excluded socially and economically from wealth and power. Not till the late seventeenth century did a native priest become a bishop in Mexico: native Roman Catholic bishops in Africa, India and China had been appointed before that. For all the early efforts of the missionary clergy, what were founded in the Americas were not native, but colonial churches, characteristic products of the mother countries. They celebrated divine office as splendidly as possible in order to impress the Indian imagination, introduced processions and confraternities, and even successfully inoculated native custom with such extraordinary manifestations of Christendom's past as *Las Marismas* — the dances of 'Moors and Christians' which were essentially mock combats in which the 'Christians' were led by St James, patron of Spain, and the 'Moors' by, at times, and of all people, Pontius Pilate. The end-result was much of what can still be seen in modern Latin America. In its making we must never forget that its origins were shaped by medieval men — by men who took for granted the unity of Christendom, huge disparities of rank and status, dreams of universal empire, and the unquestionable superiority of their religion.

They implanted a culture which, at one remove, was to evolve in a way which reflected with surprising fidelity the evolution of the Catholic Europe from which it had sprung. Counter-Reformation authoritarianism, the decadence of Spain, Enlightenment ideas, the nationalism of the French Revolution, positivism, socialism and many other phenomena were in due course to colour 'Latin American' civilisation. It was, of course, the creole, Spanish- and Portuguese-speaking stratum of that civilisation which showed such influences most clearly. At its other pole, the Indian culture, too, underwent change, but by and large regressively: the springs which had welled up in the brilliant indigenous civilisations of pre-Columban America seemed to dry up or go underground. Although miscegenation did a lot to blur the division for individuals (and for all the importance attached to creole blood, Spanish and Portuguese Americans never resisted inter-marriage and inter-breeding with other stocks so vigorously as did Anglo-Saxons) the Indians became, for the most part, bearers of wood and drawers of water for a society shaped predominantly by élites of European origin who saw their civilisation in terms of its European institutions — state, church and cities. Only in the plastic arts, as many Mexican churches show, in a Counter-Reformation baroque suffused with the colour and vigour of Indian work, was some sort of positive fusion achieved within the structures of formal culture.

All this, for good or evil, was the work of the colonial Spanish and Portuguese. They were shaping the future Latin America for about twice as long as the independent states of post-colonial South American history have lasted. For three hundred years the Spanish and Portuguese American possessions were evolving into new nations. When they emerged into independence, their élites shared assumptions which are 'western', for all the suppressed peasant cultures and such debts to Africa as are very visible in Brazil and the Caribbean. It is a curious mixture — but an implantation of western civilisation such as most of Asia and Africa were never to know. It was an exemplary achievement, even if criticised: the Spanish and Portuguese empires long set a standard of what empire might be. They were the first real European maritime empires (that of Venice was so different in scale and nature as to be incomparable) and the first of a global age.

As everyone knows, the evolution of new Americans looks very different north of the Rio Grande. So does the story of empire. There were, of course, some similarities. One was that both American continents were seized by Europeans who were, in the main, looking for land, by would-be settlers. The first wave of European expansion had receded as population pressure declined in the wake of the Black Death, but that pressure was building up again by the sixteenth century and was much talked about in England towards the end of it, when colonisation overseas was seen as one remedy. That was one reason, perhaps the simplest, why Europeans only really began to settle in North America more than a century after Columbus. The different phasing of settlement, south and north, was one of the first great historical differences between the two continents. From it flowed much else.

By the time settlement in the north began, the Reformation had taken place and the ideal of a united Christendom had been shattered. What is more, the Europeans who eventually did most to shape the northern continent's future came from Protestant churches and from societies where the social certainties of the Middle Ages — what we might crudely call 'feudal' ideas — were much less evident than in Spain.

It was not that the Spanish were not interested in North America. Spain did not surrender Florida until 1819 and at that time still formally ruled over parts of no fewer than nine future states of the American Republic. Spanish missionaries left their mark all over the south-west United States and California. And there were other would-be colonialists. Part of California was also for a time to be claimed by the Russians; they had settlements there as late as the 1840s, and did not sell Alaska to the United States until 1867. The French founded Canada, and many Canadians still prefer to speak French. Yet all these possibilities were in due course extinguished by the vigorous demographic and historical currents rolling outwards from the original English settlements on the Atlantic seaboard.

The original roots from which the modern United States stem are over-whelmingly Anglo-Saxon, however later refreshed and supplemented. Probably by the middle of the nineteenth century most United States citizens already had other than British blood in their veins. Nonetheless, down to that time there had only been one president who did not have a British surname (Van Buren: 1837–41) — and the next one (Roosevelt: 1901–9) to follow him did not take office for another sixty years. The fact that the continent was dominated for a long time by a people of English tradition inclined them to continue many English practices. The village green of England was reproduced in New England townships just as the *plaza mayor* of Spain had found a new home in Mexico. Less tangible things, too, sur-vived: English political and commercial practice, English ideas of law, Prot-estant notions of religion. All of them, of course, were profoundly altered by being applied in a new environment and increasingly at the hands of those who were not of British stock. But what they kept out of North Amer-ican history is almost as important as what they built into it. The absolute state and the Counter-Reformation were hardly to touch America north of the Rio Grande. Slavery in the Carolinas or Georgia was not the same thing as the Spanish *encomienda*. The whole basis of British America, too, was, from the start, marked by the institution of important checks on the power of the crown and its officers. The usual way in which the English crown set up colonial government was to devolve responsibility by means of a charter. These important documents not only conferred legal authority on the gov-ernment and the only titles to the soil, but immunities from particular English laws and special privileges. They were buttresses of independence and self-government.

Another important face differentiating the results of European impact in North and South America was what the Europeans found there. Nothing like the glittering civilisations of Aztec or Inca existed north of Mexico. There were no monumental buildings and, indeed, not much permanent building at all. The native peoples were illiterate. Most of their cultures were those of neolithic savages. Whatever Europeans may have hoped for, they found little to loot, not much to admire. Indeed, the continent was astonishingly empty. There were not many natives there at all; perhaps a million, spread over the whole of it. There was no large labour force to exploit as there was at first in the Caribbean; men had to till their own fields — or import black slaves to do it. Throw in geographical, zoological, botanical and climatic differences, and it is easy to see why North and South America were certain to diverge in their development when exposed to transformation by Europeans — and Europeans so different in their own traditions.

The story of enduring settlement in what is now the territory of the United States begins in 1607 with an expedition which planted a settlement at Jamestown in modern Virginia.[13] Half of those there died in its first year. A hundred and fifty years later, thirteen English American colonies were solidly established along the whole Atlantic coastline from Florida (still Spanish) as far north as what is now the state of Maine. They ran inland for the most part as far as the Blue Ridge and Appalachian mountains. About two million free men and women lived in them, predominantly British in origin, but many also of Dutch, German and French Huguenot descent. There were also black slaves.

This varied population and the contrasts within the territory it occupied already suggest North America's enormous variety. The thirteen colonies were different from one another on many other counts, though. Their economies grew out of different opportunities, stimuli, challenges, potentials. Their constitutions and political arrangements, though all subordinate to the English crown, had many individual features. Cultural and ideological temper varied greatly from one colony to another, a fact that often reflected the religious variety from which they sprang. One colony, Maryland, had been specifically founded for Roman Catholics while others (notably the New England colonies) were deeply marked by a stern — and sometimes exclusive — Protestantism. Yet Rhode Island and Pennsylvania were tolerant and prided themselves on being so.

This implied a great cultural diversity. Many believed it would assert itself when royal government was withdrawn, as it was after the defeat of British arms in the War of American Independence, and that, for political and economic reasons, too, the new confederation would fly apart. Yet the former colonies were to remain united. It helped them, of course, that no European power could get near enough to them to exploit their divisions. But it was also true that they had somehow devised constitutional arrangements which could take account of diversity and which embodied an important degree of ideological agreement between the former colonies.

American nationalism was going to take a long time to make a new nation out of such diversity, but it would never have done so had not there been a real contribution to it from what the colonies shared beyond the experience of struggle in common. That shared heritage was nerved and animated by certain attitudes and myths; they not only served a pioneering society in its earliest years but in much later times, too. The men and women who first came to the wilderness which was all that, often, North America seemed to offer, came with minds braced to grapple with it by the religious and social order they knew at home. The first was the firmer stay. The Bible, much read by Protestant preachers, and by many Protestant laymen too, provided them with the imagery of the Chosen People, making their way through tribulation to glory, to a new Jerusalem, a city builded on a hill, in a much-quoted Puritan image. The Pilgrim Fathers, who founded Plymouth Plantation in 1620, were not to loom large in the historiography of the American nation until after independence. Nonetheless, like other New Englanders, they had a consciousness of serving a higher power's designs, the self-righteousness of the justified, and a passionate conviction that what they did was part of a Divine Plan which has coloured the American vision of American history down to the present day. The chronicle of Plymouth Plantation was written by its first leader and governor, William Bradford, and its pages are suffused with the conviction that (in his words), 'out of small beginnings greater things have been produced by His hand that made all things of nothing, and gives being to all things that are; and as one small candle may light a thousand; so the light kindled here hath shone unto many, yes, in some sort, to our whole nation'.[14]

This suggests, correctly, that though Iberians and Anglo-Saxons both felt superior to the natives of America, the differences in the way they expressed it were considerable, both in their deeds and their words. Although eye-witnesses in the early Virginian settlements drew attention to the skill of the North American Indians in the management of a harsh environment, the natives found among the Anglo-Saxon clergy no such protectors as the missionary friars or Las Casas; the wild idea that the 'Indians' might all be descendants of a Welsh migration or of the lost Ten Tribes of Israel might seem flattering, but did not help them in practice. Such delusions were much less influential than the reports of Indian barbarism, savagery and cruelty which soon got back to England. Massacres of settlers there were, but it tended to be overlooked that early clashes often arose because of the intrusive greed of the settlers (sometimes themselves desperate to secure food supplies for over-populated communities, it must be allowed). As one historian, impatient of what he calls the 'cant', put it, these were wars of Puritan conquest.[15] A tendency soon made itself apparent, reminiscent of some episodes in the history of the Spanish New World and brutally foreshadowing what was later to be seen many times elsewhere in the course of European overseas settlement; it came to be believed by many white Americans that the natives of North America were irredeemable savages, a lower species, as a more biologically conscious later age might put it.

The Puritanism which provided the ideological drive in so many of the northern settlements was intellectually well-prepared to give short shrift to any case which might be put on the Indians' behalf. God's 'wonder-working Providence' which watched over the early colonies was a great ease to tender consciences — if, indeed, many were tender in this matter. Some of the Puritan clergy, for instance, went so far as to advocate that the Indians (whom they saw as children of the devil) should be wiped out and their lands appropriated. The argument was a simple one, with a wide appeal, to judge by what is said to have been agreed at one New England meeting:

1 The earth is the Lord's and the fullness thereof. Voted.
2 The Lord may give the earth or any part of it to his chosen people. Voted.
3 We are his chosen people. Voted.[16]

Such attitudes did not always or necessarily lead to aggression against the Indians (though reprisals for Indian attacks were savage). A certain smugness was just as characteristic. The 'hand of God was eminently seen in thinning the Indians, to make room for the English' wrote one commentator. 'It . . . pleased Almighty God to send unusual sicknesses amongst them, as the Smallpox, to lessen their Numbers; so that the English, in comparison to the Spaniards, have had little Indian blood to answer for.'[17]

Perhaps Protestantism, with its strong Old Testament emphasis and the predominance it gave to the individualistic myth of the saving remnant, was bound to care less for the Indians as an object of missionary activity than the Roman Catholic church of Spanish America, less absorbed with the importance of individual conversion, and more concerned to provide the means of salvation to the many. It is certainly true that the much smaller French North American settlement (no doubt in part because it was so much smaller) enjoyed better relations with the Indians, and that in these relations a significant part was played by missionaries. The Spanish crown, too, was from the start determined to apply Christian principles to its new colonial problems and, at least on paper, it could do so. It had unusual powers, conceded by the pope, to appoint clergy in its new domains. The English crown could do little with its much more independent, chartered colonists and proprietors and America was still without resident bishops of the Church of England when the American colonies broke away from the mother-country at the end of the eighteenth century, two and three-quarter centuries after the establishment of the Spanish Roman Catholic hierarchy in Mexico. For a long time, too, the private missionary efforts of Englishmen in North America were of little importance, though the scrupulous care with which William Penn conducted business with the Pennsylvania Indians is, of course, legendary. This celebrated example, nonetheless, only throws into sharper relief the behaviour of settlers in other of the English colonies.

Thus was embedded an interesting contrast between the two major theatres of the first phase of European settlement overseas: at a time when Europe was tearing itself apart in religious and civil wars, the antitheses which helped to produce them were being planted in the two Americas. Each, as it were, was based on a selection of Europe's civilisation, a selection both in time and in social reality. Yet both led to the Europeanisation and christianisation of whole continents. This had enormous implications.

So did another result of European action in North and South America, the introduction and settlement of other racial stocks. Although some of these, in British Caribbean territories, were to include Asians, the most important addition, other than themselves, which Europeans made to the American ethnic mix was African. The story began with the introduction of African slaves to the Caribbean and Brazil early in the sixteenth century. By 1600 African slaves were the mainstay of the plantation economy of Brazil's coastal provinces and it is said that there were then between 13,000 and 15,000 of them. They came from West Africa, the Congo, Angola and even the western Sudan. In the main, though, West Africa provided the slaves who were shipped further north to the Caribbean sugar islands and British North America in the seventeenth and eighteenth centuries. The consequences were to be immense. Brazil today provides what is practically the only example of a large state based on an ethnic 'mix' which is virtually complete — and successful. In contrast, it need only be recalled that as a result of the decisions of Elizabethan Englishmen the United States were forced in the nineteenth century to fight what was, in proportion to their population, the bloodiest war of their whole history — and a civil war, at that.

By that time much more was at stake than the narrow coastal strip of the thirteen colonies of pre-revolutionary North America and its tiny population. The United States which fought the War between the States, the Civil War, or the War for the Union (as it is variously named) already by 1861 stretched from the Atlantic to the Pacific ocean and had a population of more than thirty million. The republic was already a young giant, though too remote to have any direct influence on Europe's affairs. But the world influence which she was to have was immense, and the establishment of a continental state in North America — something not achieved in Latin America — is one of the key facts of modern history. Hypothetical speculation may help to put this in perspective. If the North had not won the war and preserved the Union, then France and England would have been unlikely to have won the First World War; if they *had*, nevertheless, done so, it is highly unlikely that American support would have been available against Germany in the Second. If a northern and a southern state had both emerged from the war, then it is doubtful that North America would have enjoyed an era of internal peace from 1865 to the present day, or that the unified domestic market which sustains the greatest industrial economy in the world would have come into existence — and so on, and so on.

In 1861, the new continental state had still to mature. Its communications network was incomplete, great tracts of its territories had still to be brought under regular government, and its population still had its greatest growth ahead. Nevertheless, those processes were visibly under way. Diplomacy had removed some obstacles: the Louisiana Purchase was the greatest real estate transaction in history, and negotiations with the British, Russians, Mexicans and Spanish followed it. So did war and outright aggression against Mexico (from which — if Texas is included — the United States took nearly a million square miles of territory) and against the aboriginal Indians of the plains. But Americans felt few stirrings of conscience. It appeared to them self-evident that they were meant to fill up a continent from sea to sea, that they had a manifest destiny to occupy land which was God-given, to exploit its resources, to people it with free men living under free institutions. It never seemed to occur to anyone to ask on what grounds it was asserted that there was a natural right of Americans to move westwards, any more than it occurred to anyone to ask why Dutch farmers had the right to take up land in South Africa, Spaniards in Mexico, Englishmen in Australia, or Russians in Siberia.

It was not only Americans who were unquestioning, then. Others, too, saw something very like a hidden hand at work in the great processes of history of which the filling-up of America was one. In 1835 one of the most profound observers of his age, the French historian and sociologist Alexis de Tocqueville, published a book about *Democracy in America* in which he made a startling judgement:

There are at the present time two great nations in the world, which started from different points, but seem to tend towards the same end. I allude to the Russians and the Americans. Both of them have grown up unnoticed; and while the attention of mankind was directed elsewhere, they have suddenly placed themselves in the front rank among the nations, and the world learned their existence and their greatness at the same time.

All other nations seem to have nearly reached their natural limits, and they have only to maintain their power; but these are still in the act of growth. All the others have stopped, or continue to advance with extreme difficulty; these alone are proceeding with ease and celerity along a path to which no limit can be perceived. The American struggles against the obstacles that nature opposes to him; the adversaries of the Russian are men. The former combats the wilderness with all its arms. The conquests of the American are therefore gained by the plough-share; those of the Russian by the sword. The Anglo-American relies upon personal interest to accomplish his ends and gives free scope to the unguided strength and common sense of the people; the Russian centres all the authority of society in a single arm. The principal instrument of the former is freedom; of the latter servitude. Their starting-point is different and their courses are not the same; yet each of them seems marked out by the will of Heaven to sway the destinies of half the globe.

One last point remains to be made about the European settlement of the New Worlds, north and south, of the Americas. However defined and qualified, it was part of a one-way transformation of the globe. European culture — even on its colonial frontiers — for a long time made few conscious concessions. When influences begin to flow back from overseas to Europe itself, the first and strongest came from new consumer products — potatoes, tobacco, coffee, tea, rubber — or from familiar ones in a new abundance (precious metals above all). These were not the fruits of the interplay of civilisations, but of the simple exploitation of the resources of other lands. Next in importance may be ranked the political repercussions of colonial involvements. Europeans had new interests to fight over, to put it at its simplest. Stylistic and intellectual influences — eighteenth-century chinoiserie, the Japanese print or African mask a hundred and fifty years later, a craze like Zen Buddhism in the twentieth century — are only marginal. Once the Ottoman era was over, the non-western world was to have no direct influence on the West of any magnitude comparable to that of the West upon it until, thanks to oil, it acquired in the twentieth century that of sheer economic power. What mattered long before that, was the indirect influence of the New Worlds on Europe — the enormous difference they made by giving Europeans new issues to quarrel over and dispute.

The lack of direct influence might be inferred, curiously, from the processes of discovery itself. It had always been (and went on being) one-way. Europeans went out to the world; it did not come to them. Few non-

Europeans other than Turks even entered Europe, except as exotic imports and visitors (like the Siamese ambassadors to Louis XIV or the American Indian 'Kings' who came to Queen Anne's court), body servants or slaves. And we still do not really know why.

VIII
A NEW AGE

Outside the National Gallery in Trafalgar Square stands a fine statue of a bad king: James II. Like many princes of the later seventeenth century, he is got up in what his age thought of as typical Roman garb. His contemporaries sought to dignify and honour their notables by putting them on a level with the giants of classical antiquity. It was a conventional form of flattery, repeated all over Europe. Louis XIV in dozens of statues, pictures and other representations, the Great Elector of Brandenburg outside the palace of Charlottenburg in Berlin — and many others, buskined and periwigged in anachronistic splendour — show the grip upon the mind of an age of a certain idea of greatness and a certain estimation of what human achievement might be. The greatest monument to that idea is the splendid palace of Versailles, for a century the seat of government of the greatest power in Europe, and something more, too. Versailles was the focus of an idea of monarchy, the stage for the pageant of a great court whose style told Europe what its rulers ought to aim at: glory and power.

Each age of European history has been similarly stamped by ideas Europeans took for granted, and this has meant that Europe has affected the world differently at different times. The first Spaniards in America were medieval men, with medieval minds. Yet the final organisation of the last unmapped and unabsorbed tracts of North and South America took place in the age of steam. Europe's ascent to world dominion took more than four centuries. That gave time for many things to change. The Iberians of 1500 were not like the nineteenth-century British who ran the Raj in India, nor like the Americans who built missions and hospitals in China, nor like the French who taught Racine to West Africans. Though those who came later clearly belonged to the same civilisation and often looked back to the first European conquests as first steps on the road they had themselves to travel, they had different minds and outlooks, different conceptions of the possible from those of their predecessors.

The first signs of the West's seemingly unique powers of continuous self-transformation can be discerned a long way back — well before Columbus' voyages, in fact. But changes in ideas — especially in shared, collective ideas

— are not only very hard to measure, pin down and define but sometimes hard to spot when they take place. They are often slow and uneven. It is difficult to agree over what the historians should be talking about. Clearly, educated twentieth-century Europeans do not share the views of medieval Europeans about witches and wizards. For that matter, few of us even share the views of eighteenth-century people about such matters. The eighteenth century still had plenty that was barbaric and superstitious about it. Well after 1700, in many European countries, men and women were burned, drowned or lynched for their supposed acquaintance with the black arts. Dr Johnson was taken to be touched by Queen Anne for the scrofula, because, as an anointed monarch, she was supposed to have a healing power; Louis XVI of France touched over 2000 people for the 'King's Evil', the day after his coronation in 1744, and as late as 1825 people talked of resuming the practice at the coronation of the last French king of his line, Charles X. Though people poked fun at them, we must not underestimate the slowness with which such practices ceased to be credible.[1] It is one of those things which makes it hazardous to say exactly how the thinking of different ages differs or to generalise about it. Nevertheless, long-term cultural changes *can* be observed and historians have to try to measure them. Within the last five hundred years or so the West somehow acquired a mentality unlike any that had been seen hitherto. It not only vastly expanded the capacities of European civilisation, liberating it to think new thoughts and envisage new possibilities, but also transformed that civilisation's view of itself.

In 1500, in spite of some innovations, Europe was still living on a stock of concepts and ideas which had been remarkably stable for centuries. This stock had three main sources: the classical heritage of Greece and Rome, the barbarian cultures of the Dark Ages from which it derived many social relationships and much of the law and custom ruling daily life, and Christianity. The last was the most obvious. It pervaded everything else. Most men and women, of course, did not think in such terms because they did not conceptualise at all. The few who did probably usually shared a general picture of a world created by God, inhabited by men made in His image who had the duty to obey His laws until they died, when they would go before Him for judgement. Men's eyes tended to return to what faced them in the next world. Here on earth they thought they should keep things going much as they were (a few Utopians notwithstanding), avoiding any disturbance of the established order which could not be justified by custom or religion. One or two sceptics had already made their appearance, and there was even just a little — very cautious — questioning of whether there was, in fact, life after death. Nonetheless, the mental world inhabited by the great discoverers, the *conquistadores* and the founders of the first overseas European empires can be not unfairly summarised in such terms as these.

Even by 1800, though, such a description of prevailing attitudes in Europe and North America would have been already obsolete. The Protestant Reformation and the political re-arrangements which followed from it; together with the practical concerns of diplomats who sought co-operation with the Turks, shattered the old ideal of Europe as an undivided Christendom. Protestantism has been seen as an unleashing of a process of liberation, too. It favoured new speculations about history, even justifying in some people's eyes the idea that change for the better might be sought in this world. Other, vaguer landmarks of change can be seen in those fruitful and well-known stirrings of new intellectual and artistic forces and rediscoveries of older ones familiarly summed up in the word Renaissance. Then there are the voyages of discovery themselves. It was in the 1500s that an Italian historian noted that 'not only has this navigation confounded many affirmations of former writers about terrestrial things, but it has also given some anxiety to the interpretation of Holy Scriptures'.[2]

Traditionally, another major phase in our cultural history has been called 'Enlightenment' — an image taken up in many languages: *lumières, Aufklärung, illuminismo* all express the sense of a new light flooding into hitherto darkened places. They came into familiar use in the eighteenth century. Enlightenment suggested the removal of ignorance by knowledge and of superstition and fear by reasonableness and commonsense. It was summed up by Kant as 'the removal of self-imposed tutelage', though it cannot be contained in any single formula. One modern scholar has helpfully described it as 'an attitude of mind'.[3] It was much indebted to new knowledge and speculation, though most educated people probably knew little that was precise about that. Nevertheless, cheaper printing and spreading literacy were giving new ideas wider circulation than anything other than the Bible had ever hitherto enjoyed, and thousands of Europeans in Europe and outside it came in the eighteenth century to feel that they were part of a self-conscious, self-regarding movement in which educated men could thoughtfully and openly reject much of what they had inherited from earlier times. They felt, too, that they need no longer distrust the spread of knowledge; indeed, the idea that new knowledge was, in its social tendency, fundamentally progressive was another characteristic of 'Enlightenment'. *Aude sapere* — 'dare to know' — was one of its slogans.

Four changes which we owe to the Enlightenment seem to me to have been particularly important in changing minds and attitudes. One was a new emphasis and encouragement given to science and the manipulation of the natural world — in itself a very complicated subject, because many 'enlightened' attitudes themselves grow from an increasing awareness of what science had uncovered; the relation of the two is reciprocal. The second must be a new scepticism, a reinforcement of the old self-critical faculty in western civilisation, but this time in a way which began to sap formal religious belief. The third great change was that Enlightenment helped people to want to be more humane. Finally, and most important of all, was something to which all these three changes themselves contributed, the growth of the idea that Progress was normal. But nothing is simple in the history of ideas; to separate any of these four changes from the other (or from much else) is only tolerable because a story has to be organised if it is to be understood.

The word 'scientist' did not exist until the nineteenth century. Now, there are said to be more scientists alive and working than have lived and died in the whole of human history before the present and science has no difficulty in impressing us. Its attitude towards nature was once confined to a few Europeans, but is now shared by millions round the world. It has given the West an enormous advantage in tapping the world's resources and so is a part of the story of western dominance. Much of the world now seeks to remove that dominance by mobilising science against it. And science has also given mankind a new faith. That may well prove to have been its most decisive impact on the non-western worlds as well as on the West.

Modern science emerged from an intellectual revolution first clearly evident in the seventeenth century. The changes of that age made possible a new approach to the physical world, one to be popularised in the Enlightenment. Of course, the new outlook had roots in the past. A faith in science, though, or true science itself, probably did not exist in medieval Europe. Islamic and Chinese science, Indian mathematics, were, it is true, then well developed in many of their branches. Something of what they had to offer came to Europeans through their contacts with Islam, above all in Spain. The Greeks, too, had left fruitful ideas behind them and had recorded useful information; much of this, hoarded or rediscovered by Byzantine and Islamic scholars, found its way to Europe. Nevertheless, there was a lot of rubbish mixed up with it, and the Greeks had not arrived at the experimental method. Science as we know it is an artefact of post-Renaissance western culture. It came into being first in Europe, long after Islamic and Byzantine scholarship had yielded up all they could which was likely to be of use from the legacy of the ancient world.

Whether we should speak of the 'discovery' of modern science, or of its 'invention', the first signs of it are to be found in new observations (some of them, it may be noted, only available because of the voyages of discovery which revealed new stars in the southern hemisphere and the variation of magnetic from true north). From observation and recording there can follow questioning, interpretation and then (one must hope) understanding. That basic set of ideas is a very old one: in our own tradition it goes back beyond Aristotle, a great assembler of facts, to the Ionian Greeks. In other cultures, observation as a prelude to understanding is even more ancient: the astronomy of the Babylonians provides some of the earliest accurate observations of the stars as well as the basis of our own measurement of time. The aspiration to rational understanding latent in careful observations, though, remained for a long time pre-scientific. The learned men of the Middle Ages worked away (by no means so uncreatively as was once believed) but did not have an adequate technology to support their work. Another limitation was more theoretical. For all that had been learnt from the Arabs, and despite a healthy emphasis in some of its branches on definition and diagnosis, medieval science rested on untested assumptions, not only because the means of testing them did not exist but also because the wish to test them did not emerge. True experiment — the testing of hypotheses by replicable means — took a long time to appear. The most important contribution of the Middle Ages to the later scientific development of western civilisation lay in advances on other fronts: the training of generations of Europe's best minds in the rational disciplines of scholastic thinking, and the steady accumulation of technological and instrumental skill which slowly built up a numerous population of artificers and craftsmen. That, more or less, was the story until the sixteenth and seventeenth centuries. For all the interest of the Renaissance masters in descriptive studies or in the solution of practical problems in the arts, and for all the new geographical knowledge of the age, the majority of even educated Europeans in 1600 still drew their world picture from the great medieval synthesis of Aristotle and the Bible. That picture centred the whole universe on the earth, as well as the life of the earth, upon man, its only rational inhabitant. The first intellectual achievement of a new age was to make it unreasonable to hold such a view.

As every schoolchild knows, an intellectual barrier was crossed and the nature of civilisation altered for ever by the work of the great astronomers and cosmographers — Copernicus, Kepler, Galileo and many others. There is neither time nor space here to do justice to what they did. The essential drive of their work, though, was towards providing simpler, more generalised, explanations of the way the physical universe worked than those previously available. They led the European mind towards the acceptance of general explicatory principles, whose validity could be tested by observation of facts. Mature science rests on the principle that the most general interpretation which can be provided for a variety of observed facts is probably the most correct. Widespread acceptance of such a view may well have been more important than the much-discussed symbolic struggle between religion and science over the heliocentricity of the universe, which looms so large in traditional accounts of western intellectual history.

The immediate practical and material repercussions of the great astronomical advances in European life were in fact less than those of the voyages of discovery. Nevertheless, the men who made them also made a difference to the practical management of the world. Galileo (to take one of the most remarkable of them) advised the Venetians on naval engineering, laid the foundations of modern mechanics, improved the practice of gunnery, and invented the thermometer. All investigations of nature increasingly depended upon material and technological advances, too — above all, on the development of new instruments. Who the artisans and craftsmen were whose work with the lenses they cut and polished led to the invention of the telescope, we rarely know, but they provided the indispensable tool for astronomical observation and made possible Galileo's confirmation of the Copernican heliocentric system. At the same time, the application of optical technology to the magnifying of very small objects (and, eventually, the invention of the microscope) was enormously to advance anatomy and biology. Better clocks, meanwhile, provided better ways of measuring time, another addition to instrumentation which gradually gave man a stronger grip on his environment.

Better instrumentation above all favoured the investigation of nature by systematic experiment. When later men came to look back for the secular saints and Fathers of Science, they often picked on Francis Bacon, sometime Lord Chancellor of England.[4] Fondly supposed by later admirers to be the author of the plays of Shakespeare, his undeniable intellectual energy was coupled with many unlikeable personal traits. Yet he seems to have been a visionary, glimpsing not so much what science would discover as what it would become: a faith. 'The true and lawful end of the sciences', he wrote, 'is that human life be enriched by new discoveries and powers.' Through them could be achieved 'a restitution and reinvigorating (in great part) of man to the sovereignty and power . . . which he had in his first creation.' This was ambitious indeed — nothing less than the redemption of mankind from the consequence of Adam's Fall — but Bacon was sure it could be done through organised research; he was here, too, a prophetic figure, precursor of later scientific societies and institutes.

Bacon's attitude expressed a new confidence in the truths conveyed by science ('natural philosophy' — knowledge of the natural world — was for a long time the usual name for it). In very broad terms, Christian and medieval Europe had observed the natural world with bemused awe as evidence of God's mysterious ways. What lay at the heart of the new science was a transition from this to a conscious and continuous search for ways to manipulate nature in the interest of mankind. Both Bacon's role in bringing this about (in his days his writings were largely ignored, it seems) and his modernity have been exaggerated. His message stood foursquare in a most ancient tradition: the first chapter of Genesis said that man was to subdue the earth. Yet in the eighteenth century Bacon came to be treated as an almost mythological figure, a secular prophet, because he embodied the sense of scientific revolution. He did so not only in his vision of what science might do but in his advocacy of observation and experiment instead of deduction from *a priori* principles. Appropriately, he is said to have died a scientific martyr, having caught cold while stuffing a fowl with snow one bitter March day, in order to observe the effects of refrigeration upon the flesh. Forty years later his central ideas were commonplaces of scientific discourse. 'The management of this great machine of the world' said an English scientist in the 1660s, 'can be explained only by the experimental and mechanical philosophers.'[5] Ever since the seventeenth century the scientist has been a man who asks questions by means of experiment. That idea lies at the heart of the intellectual world we still inhabit.

It is easier to say this than it is to summarise the precise ways in which science began to move forward. The main fields of endeavour are clear enough. The studies of the early investigators had medical, mechanical, mathematical, astronomical and cosmological bias. With better instruments, they went further and faster in them as time went by. But it was some time before a precise line of demarcation between the scientist and the philosopher was achieved. Great names dominate this re-direction of the activities of the European mind; important as what they did was, though, they are even more interesting as markers in a slower, greater, almost geological shift in the intellectual foundations of a whole civilisation. A momentous change had come about when what scientists did came to be taken for granted, even by those who understood little or nothing of it. The crucial change in the making of the modern mind was the widespread acceptance of the idea that the world is essentially rational and explicable, though very wonderful and complicated.

A unique contribution to this outcome was made by one man, Isaac Newton. His fame was immense, for his genius expressed itself across a wide range of physical and mathematical sciences. A great experimentalist, laymen remember him for the theory of universal gravitation which revealed and explained action at a distance, though the forces involved might be too weak for direct observation. And it is right that he should be so remembered; gravitation was a model instance, a conception of integrating power. It explained the universe in terms of a single physical principle. He exemplified a fundamental characteristic of the classical conception of science, its power to reveal general laws which govern our universe.

Of course, to say that is to fall into a one-sided emphasis. It is too small a part of what Newton did. If the impact of the work of so complex and rich a thinker can be summed up in a simple statement, though, it can only be at some such level of generality. He gave men grounds for hoping that the mysteries of nature could, given time, all be explained, because they must be manifestations not of incomprehensible, arbitrary will, but of ordered, regular principles. In the end, those principles might reveal even the nature of the Creator himself. 'The spacious firmament on high' as Addison put it, visibly set out in its order the majesty of God. It could reveal its message (he went on in another verse of that incomparable hymn) to 'Reason's Ear'.

By the middle of the eighteenth century the idea that nature was essentially knowable, because regular and rational, had come to be accepted by many of the educated. 'Laws of nature' were taken for granted. Slowly and increasingly they displaced in men's minds the old primacy of the laws of God and the action of his Providence. Sometimes the image of a great machine was used to convey the sense that nature made up a complete, integrated, rational system which could, therefore, be subjected to predictive observation. The acceptance of the scientific vision of nature also led ineluctably to the key modern idea that nature can be totally manipulated. If her operations were regular, and her regularities could be observed, measured and understood, then they could be put to use. Of course, human history had long pointed in this direction. Bacon may have been the prophet of the idea, but the first men who discovered that boiling water would soften foodstuffs, or that gravity operating through a counter-balance could help to raise water from one level to another, had unwittingly prepared the way for it. Only in the modern era, though, is this notion systematically grasped.

In due course, it even came to be advocated that nature should be managed as a moral duty; not only the book of Genesis but the parable of the talents could be said to teach that. Gradually, men became conscious exploiters of the environment, conscious managers of resources. Time itself became easier to use when made more precisely measurable. It could be spent more or less profitably, more or less efficiently, and as people grasped this they prized time more as a commodity. But to use time better was only one more way to tap the wealth and power which lay in nature. Men sought eagerly for others. Organised science was more and more evidently seen as the supreme way to do this and some curious paradoxes followed. Astonishingly, when men were at last sent to the moon and then brought safely back to earth again, some felt that the adventure lacked unpredictability and, therefore, excitement. Science was by 1969 so trusted that it was almost inconceivable that the operation should fail (except through human or mechanical breakdown), so carefully had the relevant information been assembled and scrutinised, and so thoroughly had all the technical problems been faced.[6]

Obviously, the interplay of early science with society was never one-way. Some circumstances in the early modern age must have been especially propitious for the rise of science. To go beyond this and to be more precise, though, is less easy. Suggestions that the apple fell on Newton's head (to cite a long-lived piece of folklore) because the class-relationships of the time demanded it have never seemed very plausible. Even conscious experiments which aim at important practical effects do not always clearly stem from social demands. Yet that there was a significant relationship between the ability of European craftsmen to provide good instrumentation and the direction of scientific investigation cannot be doubted. At a more general level, we can point to growing evidence of a widely-diffused if vague awareness that science *might* render important economic and technical benefits. This is why public authorities frequently encouraged scientific work by the foundation or patronage of learned bodies. The Royal Society received its Charter from Charles II in 1662 and the French *Académie des Sciences* was regulated and endowed by Louis XIV four years later. Scientists were also often consulted by governments about such practical matters as navigation and shipbuilding. In 1675 Charles II founded the Royal Observatory at Greenwich, with the interests of his sailors in mind. By the early nineteenth century, official and public support had become unsurprising and was a pre-requisite for the foundation of many scientific and technological establishments.

Given the steady realisation of its promise, it is hardly surprising that by the mid-nineteenth century some intellectuals felt an almost boundless enthusiasm for the science which seemed to offer so much. Some people have used the word 'scientism' to express it. It boils down to the belief that there is ultimately nothing men cannot achieve within the physical universe if only they approach their task seriously and methodically and are able and willing to put sufficient material and technical resources to work. This premise inspired the industrial society whose achievements Marx so admired, albeit reluctantly. It has gone on since his day to do things even more amazing than he dreamed of — putting men on the moon is only the most spectacular. It has generated a dream which animates the only major literary art-form to be invented in the West since the novel: utopian science-fiction. Even when qualified and cautiously expressed, so colossal a confidence is now a key component of the western outlook, and an idea which has now gone round the world. Even as doubts have arisen about science in the western countries which were its birthplace, they hardly touch the popular faith in it, while official rhetoric takes it for granted that science is not only one of the most powerful but one of the most benevolent forces at work in the world.

In the early eighteenth century, science tended also to promote a more fundamental scepticism about traditional religion. Many scientists found it easy to integrate their work with Christian beliefs; they took it that in some, not very clear but sure, way the nature of the universe was ultimately benevolent. God the Creator could not be presumed to have intended evil or suffering; the workings of his marvellous machine, moreover, increasingly

exemplified what could easily be seen as a wonderful prescience and ingenuity in the promotion of the well-being of his creatures. The problem of
evil was still there, but for a long time discoveries of the richness and intricate
majesty of the natural order seemed to increase men's confidence that evil's
existence could not be a result of God's Will. The idea of natural laws, God-
given rules, was rooted deep in the Christian past. Science gave this a new
plausibility. This was why it appealed to men of the Enlightenment. But did
the observation that there were laws entail a belief in the existence of a lawgiver? And even if it did, much that was actually taught by the religious
establishments of all Christian countries could, clearly, only with difficulty
be reconciled with the observations of scientists.

Here were problems which would grow more urgent as time went by. For
most educated people in the eighteenth century, it mattered more that a
fundamentally optimistic view of the natural world was rapidly extended to
include society; or, rather, society was brought by some thinkers within the
scope of a benevolent natural system. Men began to envisage the possibility
of 'sciences of man'; by 1800, the foundations of the modern disciplines of
sociology, anthropology and economics were in place. The 'natural historians' of humanity, as they were sometimes called, took it for granted that the
'natural' progress of societies was from lower to higher forms. Adam Smith
argued that general laws governed the economy, if left without interference
by men, and that their operation demonstrated that the search for the grat-
ification of individual appetites and the competition of individuals for goods
could have a harmonious outcome. Egoism was harmless in its general bearing; social harmony could result from the resolution of conflicts. Self-interest
and the social were, by the operation of natural laws, surely the same? Doubts
about this convenient harmony were to take a long time to spread so widely
as the optimism it generated. What was happening was that the growing
awareness of what science could do was enormously reinforcing an existing
self-confidence. Western civilisation had an innate dynamic drive whose
deepest source was its sense of direction and purpose, a confidence in its
destiny as a chosen vessel. This came from Christianity. And now it was fed
by the growing experience of success and the new sense of mastery over
nature. Both stimulated the notion that the story of mankind, at least in its
most recent decades, was the story of progress — an idea treasured by many
of the thinkers of the Enlightenment.

This encouraged a revaluation of the European past which was to become
almost a touchstone of Enlightenment. It had begun with the Renaissance
idolisation of classical antiquity. That led to the invention of various terms
which we now translate as 'the Middle Ages' — but the middle of what? The
answer was: a tract of time between two civilisations worthy of admiration,
that of classical Greece and Rome and that of the humanist Europe which

was striving to recover or surpass ancient glories. In between those two eras, some came to think, there lay either a void, when nothing worthy of note to civilised man was going on, or, worse still, barbarism, cruelty, ignorance, superstition. This devaluation of a thousand years of European history came to be widely accepted. But even in the seventeenth century signs of another, related change could be seen in a notable literary dispute in France between two camps identified as 'Ancients' and 'Moderns'. The question at issue was whether the literary achievements of the day could surpass those of the great writers of antiquity or fell short of them. At first sight, the theme does not seem momentous, but the row was in part one sign of a new self-confidence about modern times and a modern culture's view of itself. By the middle of the next century, when Voltaire wrote his book about the *Age of Louis XIV,* he was confident not only that it could be compared with other 'happy ages when the arts were brought to perfection and . . . are an example to posterity', but that it was the one which most nearly approached perfection, because (he said) 'rational philosophy only came to light in this period; and . . . a general revolution took place in our arts, minds and customs, as in our government, which will serve as an internal token of the true glory of our country.'[7]

Voltaire himself came to embody for many people the essence of the Enlightenment. He was sceptical and irreverent, a man felt to be deeply committed to a quarrel with the Roman Catholic church, even if he claimed to believe in God. He was also in a measure a social critic, though far from a revolutionary, who discerned much in his own day that was, in his eyes, indefensible. Much of what he championed, as well as much of the growing social content which began to appear in Enlightenment ideas in the eighteenth century, can best be seen in an enterprise which may be thought the most characteristic product of the Enlightenment and was certainly one of the great achievements of European culture. This was the *Encyclopédie,* the great Encyclopedia devised and directed by Diderot and d'Alembert, which eventually took up thirty-five volumes (including plates and indexes) published between 1751 and 1780. It was stuffed with useful and practical information on a vast range of subjects in articles by more than a hundred and fifty contributors, and was central to the life of cultivated France, even though officially frowned upon and soon banned by the French censor. It may also have been the most important single conduit through which French thought — the most advanced of the age — flowed out to other countries. Simply to turn the pages of its volumes or to look at their splendid plates does not easily reveal what it was that made its critics see it as subversive or why its contributors (or some of them) saw it as a *machine de guerre* against obscurantism, intolerance, superstition, credulity, injustice. Yet that was what article after article revealed. Time and again, a seemingly innocent factual exposition suddenly revealed by an ironic comparison, a brilliant paradox, or simply a logical deduction, the unreasonableness and brutality of much the eighteenth century took for granted. The *Encyclopédie* called out for reform. In it, the innate drive of the rationalism and humanitarianism towards social action became explicit, however unfair and superficial some of its expressions in that work might in fact be.

To realise in practice the aspirations of Enlightenment culture would have taken a long time; it has, indeed, never been completed. Nevertheless, from the eighteenth century onwards, Enlightenment ideas were never to be banished from the European mind; their victory was to this extent irreversible. Yet it is important also to recognise that there was a sense in which Enlightenment ideas did *not* win outright, or at least did not win a simple victory. It is an important sense, too, because it showed the power of European culture to throw up its own critics and secrete its own antibodies.

In 1749 the Academy of Dijon offered a prize for an essay on the question whether the restoration of sciences and the arts had benefited morals. That they had done so could hardly be questioned by anyone who called himself 'enlightened'. But the competition was won by an essayist who said emphatically that they had not. He argued that the growth of the arts and of man's power to master, manipulate and exploit nature — all that was usually meant by 'civilisation' was not, in fact, a good thing. And so he knocked the bottom out of some of the most fundamental assumptions of the Enlightenment outlook. This anonymous — but quickly identified — writer was a Swiss, Geneva-born, but living in France, Jean Jacques Rousseau. When he published his essay in 1750, he was thirty-eight years of age, half-way through his life. Until then, he had lived mainly on other people's goodwill or by writing (often about music, though on other topics, too; he had contributed to the great Encyclopedia itself). He was to go on to write a best-selling novel, another book which is almost the foundation of modern child-centred educational theory (*Emile*), a great, somewhat unreliable and fascinating autobiography, many discussions of theological and moral questions, and a body of political writings which includes one clear masterpiece, his most notorious work, *Du Contrat Social*.[8] Through these books and writings he became one of the most influential men who have ever lived.

Rousseau was, of course, himself a product of the Enlightenment culture, though sawing away at the branch on which he was sitting. He quarrelled violently with almost all 'philosophers' with whom he came in contact (especially if they awoke his resentment and suspicion of patronage by trying to help him in his pretty continual difficulties). In part, this was a matter of temperament and personality; for one given to self-scrutiny, he was not very good at managing his life. He abandoned to the foundling hospital the five children he had by his mistress (a girl who seduced Boswell, to his alarm, it seems when he was escorting her to England at Rousseau's request). Only women with strong maternal feelings (towards him) seem to have been able to put up with Rousseau for long. Almost certainly he was somewhat mad for much of the last decade or so of his life. He must have been intolerable. Yet he was a genius.

More than any other man, Rousseau foreshadows that profound welling-up of human energies and creativity which we call Romanticism. Explicitly or implicitly, what he wrote almost always controverted received wisdom. This won him condemnation by clericals and monarchists — like many of the *philosophes*. But what is striking is that many of the *philosophes*, too, came to condemn him. He rejected too many of their own central assumptions — that (to take a few instances at random) governments ought to seek rationally to satisfy the tastes and needs of educated, cultivated men; that the wishes and desires of the uneducated and poor should only be attended to as a matter of prudence or charity; and that in moral questions the head was a better guide than the heart. The key to Rousseau's thinking and standpoint is that he was the philosopher of moral sentiment. For him, personal, social, educational, political decisions could not be justified unless rooted in the impulses of a good motive and good feeling. Not what you did, but your motive for doing it was what mattered. This was an intensely individualist and personal way of approaching the world. As some of his critics saw, Jean Jacques was, in a way, applying outside religion and theology the principles of individual conscience and justification by faith which lay at the heart of Protestantism. But that was far from all. He was also the apostle of a new kind of collective, socialising morality, a man who struggled to find institutions able to resist the cancer of egotism, that pursuit of self-interest which he saw around him in every society he looked at.

The first chapter of *Du Contrat Social* begins with some of the most famous words ever written on the subject of politics: 'Man is born free, and every-where he is in chains.'[9] Everywhere, those words were taken out of context (and are usually still so taken): few people went (or go) on to note that Rousseau next says that he thinks he can show how this state of things may be justified — 'render it legitimate' is the way he put it. That famous sentence has usually been seen, instead, as a summons to revolution. Given the mood and tone of what follows, this is understandable. Before Rousseau there had been defenders and justifiers of revolutions, but he for the first time set out a literally limitless justification of resistance to authority. Like his 1750 essay, *Du Contrat Social* explored a large theme (was it ever possible to give authority a just and moral foundation?), but what people remembered about it was that it seemed to show that no existing state could be justified. If you felt intolerable moral oppression or outrage to your principles, Rousseau ap-peared to say, then you were justified in rebellion, for only your moral adhesion could make authority over you legitimate. Feeling ought to be all, moreover, not only in politics, but in morals, aesthetics, education, work: in a good heart lay the only proper authentication of values. So, Jack might well be not just as good as, but better than, his master, for his heart was probably less corrupted than his master's by wealth, luxury and education.

The dynamic which drove Jean Jacques to preach as he did can be argued about. One interpretation must be that he distilled his message from the envy, spite and rancour of an embittered, socially insecure personality. Another is that he is one of those prophetic, moralising figures who from time to time turn up in western history to recall some insight or emphasis in the western heritage which can be turned against its actual and existential expression in their own day. What is clear is that his revolutionary input into our culture has remained effective down to the present day. One can trace it everywhere, through subsequent western history, from the French Revolution to high-minded justifications of free love, from artless verse to the cult of the primitive, from totalitarian educational policy to arguments for breast-feeding (a practice Rousseau strenuously advocated), from respect for the unique, individual insight to indulgence of simple uncouthness. Would-be Rousseaus, alas, have been with us ever since his day; it is debatable whether his influence has been, on the whole, beneficial or pernicious. What is incontestable is that it has been vast.

Of course, few men can change the current of their time single-handed. There are signs that eighteenth-century Europe was ready to respond to such a message as Rousseau's — changes in art, religion, poetry which suggest that an age of sentiment was on the way already when he began to be famous. Yet unquestionably his influence told heavily, not least on a new emphasis of the second half of the century, a new humanitarianism. It is hardly a change to be regretted. That eighteenth-century society was casually brutal and deliberately cruel needs no demonstration. Whatever the elegance of the *salon,* and the restraint of polite manners, it was a century in which Englishmen baited bulls and rabbled wizards, Poles and Spaniards burnt witches, and ladies of the French court paid high prices for good seats from which to see a man who had attempted to kill the king branded in the hand, his limbs broken on the wheel and molten wax and lead poured into his wounds before he was drawn — disembowelled — and torn apart by four horses at the end of the proceedings. It was an age when very few countries had given up torture as a part of the process of investigation, as well as of punishment. Even in England — one of those few countries — a sailor could literally be flogged to death for a breach of discipline, though that might not be the formal intention of his sentence.

Many of the Enlightenment's thinkers threw themselves into struggles against such evils. Voltaire was already famous as a poet, playwright, wit, historian and philosopher before, in the 1760s, he secured himself a place as a secular saint by his denunciation of a judicial murder and the reversal of the verdict which was almost entirely due to his press campaign. More than anyone else, he associated humanitarianism in a general way with the progress of human understanding. Cesare Beccaria, a Milanese nobleman, won himself a permanent place in the history of reform by writing the first book on crimes and punishments which condemned torture and is the foundation both of utilitarian and of humane penology. Many other names could be cited. But perhaps the clearest sign of a new humanitarian concern was the emergence in the eighteenth century of a campaign to abolish salvery. It was a familiar institution in all continents, even in Europe, though it had been tempered there by increasing application of the principle that fellow-Christians should not be enslaved by Christians. Nonetheless, one Tudor statue actually provided for men to be enslaved as a punishment[10] and at the beginning of the eighteenth century only a few Europeans could have been found to argue against slavery in principle.

In the previous century, though, a great increase in the Atlantic slave trade had begun. It has been estimated that something like eleven million Africans altogether were, over three hundred years or so, taken by force and fraud from West Africa by the slavers. Against this background, more attention began to be given to the theoretical basis upon which slavery had to rest, above all to the idea of innate differences between black men and white. One of the earliest attempts to delimit the argument was by asserting that to buy slaves to whom the vendor had a valid title of property was not wrong, but to buy those who were not slaves already certainly was. This was not likely to prove satisfactory for long, once attention was more closely directed to the institution, nor did it. Churchmen, in particular, began to turn their attention more and more to the actual situation of black slaves in the French Caribbean islands as the new century unfolded. There was uneasiness, too, when the trade appeared to be in danger of extending itself to metropolitan France. But all the time, the growing black population of the colonies excited greater fears of rebellion among the settlers — and so drove them to more brutal treatment of their blacks — while the actual economic importance of the trade as a vested interest was more and more evident.

By mid-century, the elements of an attack on slavery were beginning to be evident. The first anti-slavery publications came from England. In 1748, though, came the first notable criticism of black slavery by a *philosophe*, an ironic chapter (misunderstood by many readers) by Montesquieu, in his great book *L'esprit des lois*.[11] The *Encylopédie* followed, repeating Montesquieu's arguments more forcefully, and Voltaire maintained a running fire. The most celebrated case against slavery, as well as against the general effects of European colonialism, was nevertheless made in a book which bore the name of a *philosophe* hack writer, the abbé Raynal who in 1770 published a *Histoire philosophique et politique des établissemens et du commerce des Européens dans les deux Indes* which in the next twenty years went through thirty editions, was translated widely into other languages and was placed on the Index (for anti-clericalism).[12] A few years later, in 1776, a gathering of American politicians, the Second Continental Congress, resolved to stop the further importation of slaves into the Thirteen Colonies, then on the eve of independence from Great Britain (though this was later set aside by the makers of the United States Constitution). Thomas Jefferson, drafter of the Declaration of Independence, denounced slavery to his countrymen and wanted to include in that document an attack on George III for allowing the slave trade but his colleagues struck it out. The tide, though, was flowing against slavery as the century came to an end, even if circumstances had by then only permitted the abolition of the trade in one country — Denmark.

Men of the Enlightenment were, of course, not simple, two-dimensional creatures, moved wholly by simple rationalism and humanitarianism. Thomas Jefferson expressed much of the age: a faith in reason; a belief in science and gadgetry; a humanitarianism which made him denounce slavery. Yet he freed only some of his slaves (at his death he still owned over two hundred) and was never able to believe that it was safe for his countrymen to embark upon emancipation if it meant that the blacks would be released into a society dominated by white men. It appears impossible to sum up the culture of an age under simple labels and harder still to assess its significance. Is the slow decline of a general acceptance that the universe is God-centred just as, more, or less, important than the later acceptance for the first time by millions of people of the idea that there will always be enough to eat and they need never fear a starving tomorrow? Is it more important that millions of people come to believe that literacy is a necessary skill, or that a relatively few influential people begin to hold the revolutionary idea that the natural and obvious role of governments is to provide steadily improving material well-being for their subjects? I don't find it easy to say. Such changes, nonetheless, constitute a revolution in the history of mankind that first became apparent in the European Enlightenment.

In the Enlightenment, one of the master-concepts of European culture in the modern era, the enormously influential idea of Progress, emerged clearly for the first time. Though obviously owing much to the Judaeo-Christian myths which stressed the direction and purposefulness of history, it remains a very complicated idea with intellectual origins difficult to disentangle. The growth of the idea that the world was becoming increasingly controllable by men's wills and by reason, for example, did not find reinforcement only in scientific advances, but had a social dimension. It could actually be seen: for example, in Europe's growing capacity to contain epidemic disease through administrative, rather than medical, measures. Control by quarantine of migration from plague-stricken areas began in the fourteenth century in Italy. By 1700 it had become much more widely accepted; even soldiers were used to maintain quarantine on the Hapsburg Military Border, where look-outs within musket shot of one another ran for more than a thousand miles, interspersed with stations where inspections and fumigations could be carried out. Undoubtedly, such arrangements were far from perfect. Yet western Europe had no serious outbreak of plague after 1720. It was a striking, visible example of the deliberate choice of practical solutions to a problem once thought to be unavoidable, a visitation of God's Wrath, and it pointed to improvement in the life of human beings.[13]

Yet the idea of progress, apparently so simply and easily confirmed by daily experience, is, like the idolisation of science, as much a matter of faith as of empirical demonstration.[14] It often involves at least three propositions not necessarily connected but jumbled together. They were so jumbled from the start, in fact, by the eighteenth-century thinkers who first explicitly set out the idea. One is that progress in the sense of both material and moral improvement has occurred and is occurring. The second is that it does so inevitably and will go on doing so. As one French writer, Condorcet, put it in a passage written when he was hiding as a political outlaw during the Revolution, men could be sure that 'nature has set no term to the perfection of human faculties, that the perfectibility of man is truly indefinite; and that the progress of this perfectibility . . . will doubtless vary in speed, but . . . will never be reversed.'[15] The third proposition is that because progress means an increase in human happiness, therefore, it ought to be sought by men and governments.

Such ideas have no single origin, even if it is easy to see that some of their sources are more important than others. The genealogy of ideas is as complicated as the genetics of real life. Ideas crop up again and again across the centuries in new guises, often barely recognisable. Deep in the western vision of a world waiting to be improved and rebuilt in the name of progress and by means of science, the weight and influence of Europe's classical and Christian past can still be felt. Those in other parts of the world who called all western-Europeans 'Franks' or 'Feringhi' without distinction of nationality were being more profound than they knew. They were saying that what united westerners, a certain attitude, mattered more than what divided them. Remote from one another as they may seem, and though they would hardly have recognised it, the twelfth-century crusader and the nineteenth-century Massachusetts merchant trading to China shared something they did not share with Saracen or Chinese. Both, in what they did, expressed — sometimes corruptly, sometimes coarsely or crudely — a sense of direction and goals, the ever-renewed, nagging, energetic, western sense that something has to be *done*. Life is real, life is earnest; life is struggle, even with oneself. The Chosen People have not simply to sit down and wait for salvation: they are going somewhere, and on their own feet. And their progress along the road demonstrates more and more clearly that they are on the right one.

By the middle of the nineteenth century, a civilisation had emerged from the Judaeo-Christian and medieval mould which no longer merely accepted change; it has actually come to seek eagerly to bring it about. Western men and women institutionalised change. They directed their research to its achievement. They consciously innovated because they believed that change was progressive and marked the way history was going. They were optimistic about it. In that lies the key to the immense adaptability of modern western civilisation. Sometimes it makes the western achievement look almost like a summing-up of the whole human story. Human beings are change-making animals. Once free of their non-human past, they were always re-making environments to suit them or adapting their ways to new environments. So they spread the world round and may now spread to other planets. Western technology is only the culminating point of a continuous development going back to the utilisation of fire. Together with much else, it is now the property of the entire human race, because it was carried round the world by a civilisation which proved more enterprising, adaptable and confident than any other. It was a civilisation which believed in the gospel of Progress. Paradoxically, that belief is now nowhere more strongly held than by societies which are in other, more obvious and more superficial ways profoundly 'anti-western'.

IX

HISTORY SPEEDS UP

The finest and most popular poet of Victorian England, Tennyson, confidently assured his readers that fifty years of Europe were better than a cycle of Cathay. They would have found nothing strange in that. The Victorians liked to contrast their civilisation with those in other parts of the world. They spoke of movement and immobility, dynamism and stagnation, the living and the dead. The difference they sensed and thus expressed between the energies of different cultures is hardly surprising, given the way they saw the recent past. From about 1450 or so, the story of Europe and the new world it had made overseas had been not only one of change, but of change which had accelerated and had spread to change other cultures, too, at a faster and faster pace. Europe was the dynamo which powered this acceleration. By the middle of the nineteenth century that was obvious. Few Victorians felt many misgivings over possible costs; most thinking people in the western world took it for granted that the world was getting better, and the quicker the better. Progress was the idol of the day; 'the march of mind' was another of Tennyson's phrases.[1] Unprogressive societies were to be pitied and, possibly, condemned. Another way of describing what was going on is to say that in the nineteenth century we have for the first time a world history to explain which is a single process, the global consequences of the change to 'modern' Europe — that is, to a Europe which is a world force, and itself undergoing change at a faster rate than ever.

Progress had become a matter of faith long before really spectacular improvements in human well-being could be discerned. Twentieth-century man can take the idea of abundance for granted as only a tiny minority of his predecessors could do. This may seem ludicrous: after all, we live in a world where millions are hungry. Other millions, nonetheless, live in sight of or have heard about the many countries which have far more material goods than they need to live tolerable lives. The idea of abundance has got about; it is much more widespread than the reality. It has spread worldwide only pretty recently: say, in the last two or three decades. Cheap consumer goods, increasingly advertised, lavishly displayed and sold the world over, are one explanation. Even communist societies try to make them available and promise to their subjects that one day they will be. Millions have learnt that an improving standard of living is possible; when that happens, almost inevitably some among those millions go on to question why it is not in fact available. This can be revolutionary; over much of the world the idea that a man should see his standard of living improve during his lifetime, almost without effort on his part, simply because of the irresistible movement of the social process, is startlingly new.

Developed, free-market countries have longer been familiar, sometimes for generations, with material improvement. Yet it is relatively new, even for them, as a matter of mass experience and they, too, find the social and political effects of the assumption of material progress disturbing. After taking for granted as individuals a steadily rising level of personal consumption, people have begun to expect more social goods as well in the form of schools, hospitals, and services of all kinds, whether provided by the market or by some system of public services. The assumption of abundance encourages utopian visions of societies where material wealth is perfectly deployed to produce the ideal environment. Such mythologies are outstandingly powerful forces of political and social change. They are one of the deep ways in which the West is changing the world, infections, transmitted to non-western countries almost incidentally, like the smallpox and 'flu which devastated South Sea islands two hundred years ago, destabilising them and overthrowing traditional ways.

The material roots of such changes in attitudes go back a long way. One of the earliest indicators is sheer population growth. In five hundred years — let us say from 1400 to 1900 — Europe underwent a demographic revolution: in round terms, its population went up from 60 to nearly 400 millions, which meant it had a larger share of the world's population than ever before,[2] without taking into account people of European stocks overseas. Such change was not only unprecedentedly fast but registered a radical transformation in the nature of population growth; it had become apparently uninterruptible and irreversible. In earlier times — and still today in some parts of the world — it is a stop-go affair: occasional surges alternate with bad setbacks or stagnation. Now, though, we have become used to continuous curves of rising numbers, broken only by local recessions and varying only in rate.

Population rises because more babies are born or because people live longer (which can also sometimes mean more births). Increased likelihood of survival has mattered more in the population history of the West in the last century and a half. By 1900 most European countries had been liberated from the danger of recurrent famine. In pre-industrial Europe every winter starved people to death, so narrow was the margin of survival for the poor; for centuries it had been so and seemed likely so always to remain. Every few years, too, there would be widespread death; thousands could then be expected to die of hunger or the disease which followed it. Malthus, at the beginning of the nineteenth century, explained the sad cycle in which population would grow until all the land which could produce food was used to do so; disaster in the shape of a bad harvest would then, he said, cut supplies back sharply and so people would die — in particular, babies and young children, whose lives were specially precarious — and so there would be fewer parents for the next generation and population would fall again.

By 1900, while periodic famines still took place in Africa and Asia, and even in Russia, dearth had ceased to interrupt European population growth as a whole. Among other new forces at work were the growth of scientific and medical knowledge and improvements in sanitation which meant that larger towns and cities could control or escape epidemic illness. But famine's disappearance is the key. There was at last more food to go round. We all nowadays have much more to eat than our ancestors five hundred years ago. By modern yardsticks, all European countries then were poor. Of course, there were always rich people who had enough while others went without. What matters is that whole societies then had too little.

The huge change in European history which the rise in population implies therefore rests on having more food. First, Europeans learnt to grow more food than before on a given area of land; next, they found ways of getting food from other parts of the world. An agricultural revolution explains the first. Historians now sometimes reject that term: they think it suggests too sudden and violent a change for something which began in the Middle Ages and took centuries.[3] That is a reasonable point; it is a story of cumulative change, a slow accretion of benefits without sudden or dramatic swings. Yet the effects were truly revolutionary.

Their essence was that ways were found of making land yield more. For most of human history (and until very recent times in some places) the only way of growing more food was to cultivate more land. This was how the slowly growing European population of the early Middle Ages was fed, by clearing forests and wastes or by migration to new cultivatable tracts in the east. But there comes a point at which taking in new land is too difficult and expensive to be worthwhile. The heart of the agricultural developments which began in Europe at least as early as the fifteenth century, and have since spread round the world, was that ways were found of growing more on the same area of land. Some of the first signs were improvements through better land management, better tillage, better animal husbandry. From Flanders, new techniques spread across the Channel to England, into Germany and eastern Europe. Meanwhile, new crops were being introduced elsewhere (for example, rice in Italy). Next came new rotations of crops, the beginnings of agricultural chemistry, the selection of the best strains of vegetables and animal life for particular conditions and a hundred-and-one applications of ingenuity to traditional practice which steadily improved yield over the centuries. The rise is still going on, now outside the western world, as dramatic improvements in this century which rest on chemistry and genetics can demonstrate. The effect on rural life was, almost everywhere, revolutionary. Even the physical appearance of animals altered. But that was not all. Such changes made a new scale of city life possible, changed population structures, modified political relations, opened the way to industrialisation and helped to give the western world — where this great change began — a margin of economic superiority which it has still not lost.

The other element in the resources equation was that Europeans not only grew more food, but also brought more from abroad. In part this was because bulk transport became easier as the centuries went by. Even in the Middle Ages, there were small transfers from producers with surpluses to customers far away. Venice and Genoa were the great carriers of that age, though the trade they handled may not seem very impressive in retrospect. Two or three modern containers hold as much as a whole ship of those days: one modern ship could carry all the tonnage landed in a year on the quays of medieval Venice. A man could then build a life on one successful voyage. Large-scale overseas and inter-continental trade, though, only became possible with the age of discoveries. They enormously increased Europe's potential resource base, giving her new fishing and whaling grounds, the northern forest frontiers which supplied so much more than timber (furs, beeswax, tar, hemp among other things), the tropical lands where plantation products could be grown, and, mainly in the nineteenth century, the great grain-growing reserves and pastures of the Americas, Australasia and South Africa.[4] One estimate is that the average area of land available *per capita* to western Europeans was 24 acres in 1500: the discoveries raised that figure to 148.

At this point the story of growing plenty becomes tangled with the story of industrialisation. We now live, in the West, in industrial societies, and we take it for granted. So do many millions of other human beings in the rest of the world. Not long ago, it could not be taken for granted anywhere. Industrial society existed nowhere on earth. No one even conceived it as possible. The story of its appearance begins to surface first in the interstices of a largely rural economy, in medieval Italian and late-medieval Flemish towns where cloth workers first came together in large numbers. That led to bigger enterprises. A few people put several looms under one roof; dyers and bleachers found that bigger vats and larger quantities of cloth for processing were more economical. Such business found more complicated commercial organisation useful. More working capital was needed to hold together the spreading networks of trade which distributed a growing quantity of manufactured goods, still tiny by modern standards though it was.

Meanwhile, something else was happening. Slowly, very slowly, artificers, smiths, engineers were accumulating technological know-how. One of the unique — and puzzling — features of Europe's history is its long and apparently uninterrupted technological advance.[5] Knowledge was acquired slowly about the working of materials with greater precision, about the engineering of large buildings, about the recovery and use of minerals. For centuries, metallurgy in the West had trailed behind or only occasionally challenged that of China, but in the late Middle Ages, Europe began to draw ahead. With more metal came new machines: mechanical clocks made their appearance in the thirteenth century. It was a very slow process. Only gradually does it become clear that the curve is rising more sharply.

As the centuries pass the machines begin to dominate the picture. The systematic tapping of non-human energy began in prehistory, when primitive men killed animals with bows or pitfalls, and used levers to handle the carcasses. Fire was used technologically, too, to harden sticks, and later to bake bricks. It also made accessible new sources of food by cooking; thus it recruited human energy as well as enabling it to be saved by providing warmth and protection. Then came agriculture and the harnessing of animal power. Boats and sails and the use of currents and winds, made navigation possible. Nevertheless, remarkable as all these achievements were, for thousands of years they still left human or animal muscle as the main source of power for machines, with only such improvements as might be made in utilising it through better tackle, harness and tools. Even the watermill and the windmill, important as they were, gave only a limited extension to man's powers of exploiting natural facts. Only in the last two or three centuries have things completely changed.

The herald of the energy revolution of early modern times was the discovery of gunpowder, which tapped the expansive power of burning gases. For a long time, though, that could hardly be significant except as a very specialised tool — a weapon. What changed technological history was the coming of steam power. Its principles had been understood by some Greeks two or three centuries before Christ, but they lacked the technology to put it to significant use. In the seventeenth and eighteenth centuries the essential engineering to make efficient engines became at last available. Falling water, used to drive water-wheels, was still the general source of power in many industries well into the nineteenth century, but when it came, steampower came with a rush. From about 1830 it swelled suddenly in importance as a source of energy until it dominated manufacturing and transport. By then, the world had undergone unprecedented change. The first industrial societies had been born.

In 1830 or so, a Frenchman invented the useful phrase 'Industrial Revolution'; it implied that what was going on rivalled or perhaps surpassed in importance the recent great French Revolution which still haunted every-one's minds. Only a couple of years later, in 1833, a bishop of Calcutta looking round him at a sub-continent barely touched by western technology could rhapsodise over the likely effects of steam navigation upon it in terms strikingly prophetic of the world-wide impact to come: 'the entrance and forerunner of all missions, education, commerce, agriculture, science, lit-erature, policy, legislation, everything.'[6] Yet steam was only the beginning of the most dynamic phase of the energy revolution; it was soon to be followed by the coming of electricity (often generated by steam), by internal-combustion engines which burnt fossil fuel products directly, and by nuclear power. All these innovations, like the harnessing of steam, were achieved in the West. This effect was a cumulative effect. Industrialisation followed an exponential curve; it is one of the markers of an acceleration of history.

Other things had to be added to more abundant energy to make an in-dustrial society. One is the bringing together of large numbers of producers in bigger units — what was soon called the factory system. Another is a stream of new inventions which applied machinery, technology, and power from new sources to old handicrafts. There had also to be liquid capital for investment; sometimes private persons found it, sometimes the state. All this points to something else: Europe was somehow already equipped to respond to the challenge presented by the windfalls of history in a creative and flexible way. It did not consume its new wealth, but used it as development capital. Again, the roots lie deep and go beyond material factors. A certain social and political order seems to have been required for take-off into sustained growth. Property and profit had to be protected if investors were to be venturesome; possibilities of diffusing and exploiting innovations had to exist, certain overheads had to be undertaken by the public authorities. Such factors are difficult to weigh. Somewhere in the special cultural and social evolution of Europe and the Americas, though, lie explanations why tech-nology and plentiful seams of coal were exploited there to produce a steam-powered society and not in China — though the Chinese had advanced metallurgical skills in ancient times and Marco Polo had seen them burning coal in the thirteenth century.

The whole change left a physical trail along which we still live. The first modern industrial areas, where new towns housed large new populations of factory-workers, were in the English North and Midlands. Pottery, textile, coal, iron districts appeared there with a dramatic suddenness which shook contemporaries. Yet their scale can easily be exaggerated. The first industrial enterprises were tiny, almost lost in still overwhelmingly rural societies. For a long time, they made little difference to the way most of the world looked and the way most men got their living. Yet within two centuries there was a complete break with what had been taken for granted by Europeans for ages. It would be startling to those born in the old pre-industrial world. Only a century or so ago people living in Devon villages could still remember the arrival of the first carts there, and with them the end of the pack-horse commercial network.[7] Though, when the twentieth century began, the age of steam and iron had still not yet been overtaken by a second industrial revolution based on electricity, oil and chemicals, the contrast with 1800 was already vast. Then, no industrial nation had existed anywhere in the world; in 1900 there were three major industrial powers, the United Kingdom, Germany and the United States. France was only narrowly in a different category, while among smaller countries Belgium can be counted as an industrial nation, given its economic 'mix'. Scandinavia, Switzerland, Spain, Italy and Russia all had substantial industrial regions. Outside Europe, too, Japan had begun to industrialise.

The world's first modern societies had also created the first true world markets. Since 1700 trade had grown at an unprecedented and accelerating rate, first as new resources were exploited and then as technical change began to revolutionise transport and communications. In the nineteenth century, bigger and faster ships made bulk-carrying easier, first between European ports and then across the oceans; food and timber could be brought in unprecedented quantities from other continents. Then there were the railways. With the steamships, they turned Argentina, the United States, Canada, New Zealand into Europe's butchers, grocers and granaries within a century. The United States was spanned from sea to sea in 1869 and six years later the first load of refrigerated meat went from Kansas to New York. The Canadian Pacific Railway was completed in 1885 and the Trans-Siberian in 1915. The first trains ran from Adelaide to Brisbane, though Australia was not spanned from west to east until 1917. It is hardly surprising that great schemes were nurtured for a 'Cape to Cairo' railway to run the length of Africa, or a Berlin-Baghdad line. Meanwhile, the internal networks of the major countries left fewer and fewer areas untouched and isolated. Other communications, too, were becoming available. In 1870 a direct cable began to operate between London and Bombay; two years later there was a telegraph service between London and Adelaide. The Suez Canal was opened in 1869 and shortened the England-India passage by over 5000 miles.

Transport and communications cannot alone explain the building of the first world economic system. Why, after all, should food and raw materials from far-off places have been available to Europeans? The basic answer must be that Europeans willed it so, and they had the physical, economic and psychological power to give their will effect. By many particular decisions, informally and formally, consciously and unconsciously, they created over two or three centuries world-wide economic interdependence — the phenomenon Marx labelled the bourgeois period of history. By 1900 the system was as complete as it ever was to be; it is the only global economic system there has ever been. It rested on the international market which was shattered in the First World War and which we have been making sporadic efforts to restore ever since. In that market Europe bought food and raw materials from other parts of the world and paid for them with manufactures and capital investment. Her manufactures and the services which she offered in shipping, banking, insurance and so on were, by 1900, generating capital, much of which Europe exported.

Many people in western countries were therefore dependent or semi-dependent on industrialisation for their livelihood. Many of them still worked in small units, but more and more in large factories. Even service units, like shops or offices, were beginning to grow larger — office blocks and department stores were appearing. A new scale of town life had appeared, too, and with it new styles of living. In the nineteenth century cities had grown faster than ever before, not just because there were more factory workers, but also because industrial society needed large workforces to service its needs as well as to make goods in its factories, and because it could afford to feed, clothe and house more people.

The western world had suddenly and unprecedentedly become much richer. This was the most obvious result of industrialisation, changing everything. Wealth brought with it power, and it was not always more power for established élites. Much of nineteenth-century history is the story of struggle between land-based wealth and commercial or industrial money. You could measure the change in many ways. It was in the 1820s that the word 'millionaire' first began to be used in England. But perhaps one of the most meaningful changes is one of the least observed: by 1900 many people, and not just a few cranks, were beginning to envisage the practical possibility of abolishing absolute poverty and the horror of penniless old age for those without families to support them.

For a long time the new wealth was no more equally shared than the old. The gap between the richest and poorest may even have widened dramatically during the nineteenth century, given the new goods which wealth could buy. In 1800, it could not have bought you much effective medicine that was not also available to someone with very modest means, simply because there was little effective medicine to buy. A steady wage could give you a warm room, dry clothes and sufficient food; beyond this money could do little to give you health or healing. By 1900 things had changed. Both the well-off and the modestly-off could buy aspirins (an unqualified addition to human welfare) but the rich could also buy much better surgery and nursing, more specialised medication, more knowledgeable medical advice, better diagnosis. On the other hand, virtually everybody, but the poor most of all, had benefited from the decline in infectious diseases which had come with better drains and diet. Similarly, everyone benefited from the new availability of cheap transport; rich men had an advantage in local travel, thanks to the horses and motorcars they could afford, but trains gave even the low-paid the fastest land transport available.

The whole complicated question of how life in western countries was changed by industrialisation does not suggest that there are many simple and unquestionable truths. Nonetheless, industrial societies had by 1900 already shown that they could offer more physical well-being to their members than the non-industrialised; death-rates were lower and people lived longer in the industrial cities of Germany than on the farms of Hungary. They had also shown that the horrifying conditions of much early industrialisation were not inevitable; industrial society could be progressive. Manchester in 1900 may not have been a very jolly place, but it was a lot cleaner and healthier than the city Engels depicted in the 1840s. Industrialisation, in fact, had been astonishingly successful, for all its costs. True, suffering and injustice had not disappeared. New relationships spawned by new industrial processes changed old and familiar loyalties; wage dependency became the commonest form of relations between master and man. The family began to undergo radical change. Such things caused painful adjustments which must be given their full weight. But when they have been allowed for, it remains true that industrial society offered mankind a greater mastery of the natural world, a greater share of its potential riches, an enrichment of human intercommunication and an increase of human possibilities greater and more varied than any society had ever done before. That it should strengthen a belief in the inevitability of Progress is wholly comprehensible.

Not surprisingly, many Europeans and Americans gloried in the change. Even in 1776 Adam Smith had proudly noted by how much the real wealth of an English tradesman outstripped that of an African prince. His chosen title speaks for an age: *The Wealth of Nations*. But perhaps the most telling admiration is that which is reluctant. Karl Marx hated much about the process of industrialisation as he saw it, but he was second to none in recognising its achievement and potential, even as early as 1848. In *The Communist Manifesto* of that year, he reluctantly but admiringly acknowledged that the bourgeoisie which made industrial society was the first class to show the real extent of what humans might do.

It has executed works more marvellous than the building of Egyptian pyramids, Roman aqueducts and Gothic cathedrals; it has carried out expeditions surpassing by far the tribal migrations and the Crusades. The subjugation of the forces of nature, the invention of machinery, the application of chemistry to industry and agriculture, steamships, railways, electric telegraphs, the clearing of whole continents for cultivation, the making of navigable waterways, huge populations sprung up as if by magic out of the earth — what earlier generations had the remotest inkling that such productive powers slumbered within the womb of associated labour?

What was more, Marx thought, this would continue, for the bourgeois epoch was a continual revolution. All nations, even the most barbarian, were dragged by it into the orbit of civilisation by which, of course, Marx meant the civilisation of the West. Here, at least, he has not been proved wrong.

Material changes did not leave ideas about government and society undisturbed. This, too, had a world-wide significance; the West first invented modern politics and then exported them to the rest of the world. Politics are a western artefact, not to be taken for granted. Not all cultures have had such a thing. Of course — as the word suggests — in some of the Greek city-states, and for a long time under the Roman republic, politics had existed. It was a way of managing collective affairs so that different interests could be given a hand in them without falling into violent conflict. We may now think that a pretty narrow view was taken of the interests which ought to be consulted and that ancient politicians were often not very successful in achieving their end. Nevertheless, one can recognise in those societies something that is absent from, say, ancient Persia, and it is the essence of what many of us still believe politics to be. Such politics require some kind of forum or marketplace for arguing and bargaining, even if those taking part are relatively few. Politics also implied agreement that there is an area of collective activities, however restricted it may be, about which disagreement can be legitimate. It assumes, therefore, that there exists a public good which is more than a mere summary of individuals' appetites.

There is another way of using the word 'politics' which sometimes blurs our sense of its uniqueness. This use simply denotes the intrigues and jostlings for power within closed circles — courts of kings, the board of directors of a company, or the executive of a trades union, for example. Such struggles lack the element of legitimate public debate which must surely be part of true politics. To confuse the 'politics' of courts and cabals, committees and smoke-filled rooms with real and public politics obscures the fact that, for most of human history, and in most societies, politics as we know them today in the West did not exist. They never existed within the great oriental monarchies, for instance, and only occasionally and to a limited extent can you see them in medieval Europe. There does not seem to be much chance of them in Soviet Russia. True politics require a recognised right to debate the public good and to struggle, within limits set by the law, to influence affairs. Nevertheless, although this has been very unusual until very recent times, a wish to run things on these lines seems now to have spread somewhat over more of the world than ever before, and it spread from the West.

Of the changes which have led to the appearance of our modern political culture the Reformation was one of the most important: for the first time it forced Europeans consciously to accept that laws would have to be made to take account of the fact that men disagreed about where ultimate authority lay in matters of religious belief. Another important change was the crystallisation of new demands for influence and recognition as a result of manifold economic growth. Together with many other secondary forces, such as the provocative effect of higher taxation, the growing ambition and competence of governments and, therefore, growing fear of them, and new loyalties to new entities (nations as well as churches), they provided an encouraging environment for the re-emergence of true politics. There were issues for people to get their teeth into. Together, they explain the acceptance by western peoples in the nineteenth century of the myth that history was the story not only of Progress but of political liberty.

Traditionally, three great revolutions falling almost within a hundred years of one another have been seen as the landmarks of the beginning of the modern political era. The English Revolution of 1688–9, the American Revolution of 1776–83 and the French Revolution which is conventionally thought to begin in 1789 and ends according to your choice in any of several years between 1794 and 1871, were all events which changed the history of the world. All three were true revolutions; they transferred power from some people to others by force or the threat of force, when argument and negotiation had failed to do it. Nevertheless, they also launched the era of modern politics, and the assumption of the legitimacy of disagreement. To see this, it is important to be clear about one difference between the British and American revolutions on the one hand and the French on the other. All revolutions try to find new principles for legitimising authority, but that does not take us far: their differences usually matter more than this similarity. The 'Glorious Revolution' of 1688 was about which Englishmen should have the last word in English and Irish affairs. The American Revolution turned out in the end to be about nationhood — whether Englishmen or Americans should have the last word in American affairs (though it took a long time for most of those involved to see it like that). To answer these questions, Englishmen and Americans had to identify anew those who were entitled to debate political questions and to redefine the forums within which they could do so. The heart of their politics, though, lay in keeping most other things much as they were. Once the question of sovereignty was settled, political debate was largely about making arrangements so that governments in both England and the United States should interfere with individuals as little as possible.

In this sense people have correctly called those two revolutions 'conservative'. It is a reasonable label, provided we do not overlook the fact that

183

the protection of existing individual rights in those two countries was in the end to release waves of revolutionary change on other parts of the world with effects that were far from conservative. Englishmen in 1688 and Americans in 1776 wanted to safeguard existing freedoms — whether legal, customary or simply practical — which had for a time seemed threatened by government. This has been obscured by the fact that the Americans tried to strengthen their case by appealing to principles which they said were universal. It is true, also, that these revolutions' principles were in later times to inspire other peoples. The exemplary effect of the American Revolution is well-known and was all the more forceful because the deposition of a monarch was not, as in 1688, followed by his replacement by another, but by the setting up of a republic. As for the American claim of a right to pursue 'happiness', of course it was an appeal to a widely-accepted Enlightenment shibboleth. But it was the happiness of particular, existing white Americans which the Founding Fathers had in mind — not the abstract rights of negroes or Red Indians. Their appeal to such general principles has always to be understood in the particular context. At much the same time, Frenchmen, Hungarians, Belgians (usually of noble birth) were protesting on traditional and prescriptive grounds against their rulers' attempts to tax *them* — the essential issue at stake in the American Revolution and one alive in most European countries in the later eighteenth century, when governments were trying to find new ways to tap their subjects' wealth. But the Americans could not take their stand on medieval 'liberties' and 'privileges', though some of them tried to make some play with their charters.

The French Revolution was quite different. For one thing, it took place in a country where (unlike Great Britain or the Thirteen Colonies) much of the Middle Ages was still in full swing. The year after it broke out, a man was burned alive (for robbery with violence) in Paris.[8] Not twenty years earlier, in 1774, the French king, at his coronation, still took an oath to extirpate heresy. Many of his subjects were still serfs at law. That law provided no equality before its processes to those whose lives it regulated. No united legal entity called France existed, either; in some of its provinces the king of France was only a duke. Moreover, the French monarchy was a great international power and French culture permeated the age. But its setting was not the only reason why the French Revolution was so different from others. It differed in scope, too (a fact which owed much to its setting).

In recent years historians have paid more attention than was traditional to showing that France was changed less by the Revolution than revolutionaries hoped or counter-revolutionaries feared. 'A brief explosion on the surface of our history' is one recent French description.[9] Perhaps that puts it a little strongly; nevertheless, the paradox can be reasonably argued. What cannot be questioned, though, is the psychological impression the French

Revolution produced at home and abroad. It was a huge shock to accepted thinking, seemingly a cataclysm of almost unprecedented changes. By modern standards, its violence was materially and comparatively less than legend suggests. Fewer Frenchmen died in the worst months of the Terror than in the week's fighting which suppressed the Paris Commune of 1871. Fewer people fled abroad from France to escape revolutionary government than emigrated from the American colonies during the American Revolution to escape the bullying and harassment of their more patriotic neighbours. What produced the impression of upheaval was the formal, ritual challenge which the French Revolution presented to the existing world. Hitherto, only the English — well-known as a cantankerous, ungovernable people — had brought monarchs to trial and killed them: now a king anointed from the vessel which, it is said, was used at the coronation of Clovis, king of the Franks, was tried by those speaking in the name of the Nation, and then killed on the scaffold. The new French state rejected the Christian religion in a way unparalleled since the days of Julian the Apostate. Even the Christian calendar was thrown overboard; a new world was declared to have begun with the 'Year One' (actually only defined after it was over, in the 'Year Two'), and 'Windy', 'Flowering', 'Rainy' and nine other new names were given to the months.

Such acts proclaimed the supremacy of will — allegedly a national will — over tradition, religion, natural law, the settled order of things. This was the spectre which stalked behind all the varied and frightening manifestations of the Revolution. It released on the world a new conception of the possibilities of social change. It also identified politics as the proper instrument for achieving such change, for challenging and infringing vested rights and interests. Political demands henceforth soon ceased to be about what you were entitled to by law or tradition, and were increasingly about what you wanted and believed you were entitled to on some other ground (probably moral). Some had put forward claims of this sort in earlier times but between 1789 and 1799 they became the basis of a new ideology of Revolution.

Political language still shows this. 'Left' and 'Right' were terms invented in France in 1789 to provide a shorthand summary of what was going on then in the National Assembly, where the opponents of further change sat on the right of the president, and those who thought they were for it on his left. This classification is one of France's great cultural exports. In due course it crept into the affairs of all other European countries, even when (as in Great Britain) it did not fit the political facts very well. It spread because the great issues of principle of the French Revolution — the equality of individuals before the law and national sovereignty — were (though already largely settled in England and North America) divisive issues in virtually every other continental European country for the next century or more. But of course the division also embodies more than this. It embodies also the idea that politics has a single central issue. In the broadest sense of the terms, that issue is one between overall change and stability, liberalism and conservatism, advance and immobility, such opposing pairs being understood to be all-embracing. Men on the Left were committed to the Future, men on the Right to the Past. Like all great and useful myths, it was an oversimplification: one can be revolutionary in politics and austerely conventional in one's view of morals, and politically conservative while collecting avant-garde art. Yet, it was a great aid to political activity, which in most civilised countries gradually became a way of achieving peaceful change by competition between those who sought change and those who feared it.

This was a great step in the history and political culture of mankind. In the long run even the most successful political systems, those of Great Britain and the United States, for example, could not remain wholly immune from it. It was reflected in the slow diffusion of new ideals of government. Authority, after all, has not had unchanging tasks throughout history; it responds to social necessity. At times government has been simply a matter of keeping order, at others of maintaining administrative regularity; both are little more than practical expressions of a general concern with the defences of society. At times, though, administration is transcended, and we arrive at policy directed to general goals. That is the way in which government is thought of in most modern western societies. It assumes that the public good rather than that of the governors should be the aim of policy, a revolutionary idea in Europe at first, and then round the world. It rests, of course, not only on the assumption that a public good exists and can be identified, but that things can be changed.

The French Revolution has been seen both as the culmination of a historical era — a huge welling-up of aspirations, designs, hopes, ideals characteristic of the Enlightenment — and as the inauguration of a new phase of history. The French have always been pretty sure of themselves as guides and models for nations and peoples less fortunately endowed with a gift for civilisation and many of the revolutionaries believed that what they were about was of universal significance. Robespierre, in his dampening way, directed his auditors to seriousness in their deliberations, as befitted men who were defining the interests of the world.[10] Nevertheless, few even among the most revolutionary of Frenchmen actually saw just how innovative they were being. Time and again they tried to draw up declarations of rights which every citizen should enjoy and which should be safe from those in power. Yet this was inconsistent with others among their aims. Such declarations were always soon set aside, not just by strong men who found them a hindrance, but because it was illogical to say that there were fundamental rights which could not be touched by popular sovereignty when their definition itself rested on the popular will. What popular sovereignty could do, it could undo — as the Founding Fathers of the United States and the writers of *The Federalist Papers* had recognised and striven to grapple with. If the popular will could justify any change, then it could justify silencing the press, imprisonment without trial, a ban on the exercise of religion — and often did. Nonetheless, in spite of such awkwardnesses, the dynamic view of politics — the assertion that it was essentially a way forward, a device to aid the seekers after light as they struggled down the road of history towards a better society — was very rich in consequences. It was in Europe in the nineteenth century that its classical standards of measurement were worked out: the extent of participation in the constitutional process, the extent of equal treatment before the law, the reality of national sovereignty, the extinction of all other claims to independent authority within the state.

Since then, the notion of politics as debate about liberating change has gone round the world, justifying and promoting the means for the overthrow of the past (often at grave cost) in every continent. One consequence is that we are all democratic now. Almost everywhere, elections are *de rigueur:* parliaments, or something dressed up to look like them, can be found in the most unlikely places. That they are often shams, marking the absence of a true political life, does not affect the main point: even sham politics embody the western myth that politics is the best instrument for achieving a better society. We owe this, too, mainly to the French, whose nineteenth-century thinkers and politicians pressed further and more continuously than any others to institutionalise this view, to the British, who implanted it in their empire, and to the Americans who have poured money into sustaining the myth all over the world. Whatever the trend in the long run (and democracy often seems to tend to stability rather than change), this has released a profoundly disruptive force on the non-western world in the last century or so.

I have already suggested that certain central, very important elements in western civilisation are religious, above all the non-rational faith that life should be directed by overriding, transcendental values which legitimise goals in the here-and-now. Nowadays these present themselves in forms, often political, which are far different from the 'other worldliness' of traditional religion. Yet they can have the same function. The moral equivalents of heaven and hell — destinations, both of them — have been for the last century or so defined in the West by new, secular creeds. Some, narrowly Utopian, have briefly flourished, and then withered. Others have prospered. Two, nationalism and socialism, seem to have had a specially notable impact.

These are loose terms. To take nationalism first, the simplest way of pinning it down is to point out that it is now taken for granted that (in the absence of overwhelmingly powerful practical constraints) if a people feels itself to be a people, it ought not to be governed by outsiders. A fact, the existence of what is felt to be a people, entails the application of a universal moral principle — that one people ought not to govern another without its consent. We argue about the test to be applied or about whether a group is a people or not, rather than about the principle which should apply if it is one. Clearly, it is a very sweeping principle: hence many of the problems nationalism causes. It opens the door to endless argument about what constitutes a people, and what can be recognised as a valid expression of its will — as Palestine or Ulster show only too clearly.

Such argument seems less surprising than the unthinking acceptance of the principle which makes it possible. For no one now (or almost no one) argues about the basic idea. Morally and conceptually, nationalism has won. Little more than a century ago — less in some countries, even in Europe — this idea was still not generally accepted. Even when they recognised the Poles to be a nation, many people did not then think it followed that they had a right to self-government. As for those who were felt obviously *not* to constitute a nation — the Irish, for example —they clearly had no such right. The rights conferred by European public law upon rulers and dynasties were in those days still thought to establish decisive claims. True, this certainty had already begun to crumble. If you want a single milestone or marker, let it again be the French Revolution, for it launched the idea of national sovereignty as a revolutionary principle, not only in Europe, but also in South America and the Middle East.

Politically speaking, nationalism is the master-idea of the last century and a half. Its first great triumphs came in Europe. Between 1815, when the Congress of Vienna resettled the European system, and 1919, when the Peace Conference of Paris tried to do so again, the map of Europe was so redrawn that, from end to end, the continent was formally organised as a collection of nation-states. Not all of them were viable; some were to prove inadequate solutions to the problems nationality posed. 1939 was to bring a new war — the last, one must fervently hope — over the German question. But at least by 1919 the national principle had triumphed in Europe. Greece had been the first 'new nation' to emerge (from Ottoman Europe) after 1815. Belgium separated itself from the Netherlands in 1830. Italy completed its national unification in 1870, and Germany the following year. By then, Romania had emerged as an autonomous entity within the Ottoman empire: by 1914, Montenegro, Albania, Bulgaria had all come into being. By then, too, Norway had separated herself from Sweden. The first Great War was meant to be the final settlement. Poland rose from the tomb of the eighteenth-century partitions; Yugoslavia, Czechoslovakia, Austria and Hungary purported to provide a national structure amid the chaos left by the disappearance of the Habsburg and Ottoman empires. From the Tsarist empire there broke away Finland, Estonia, Latvia, Lithuania (and, for a time, it seemed likely that there would be others). The patchwork Europe which resulted was studded with irredentist enclaves, areas of mixed population, potential trouble for the future. Nevertheless, formal nationalism had triumphed. It had replaced dynasticism as the organising principle of the European system.

The rapidity with which nationalism was accepted as a principle was shown by its early adoption by conservatives. Cavour used it to launch Italy on the road to unification under the house of Savoy, and Bismarck to make a German Empire dominated by Prussia. It could also be seen in the ideological debate which accompanied the American Civil War: in essence what was at stake was a decision on where nationhood (and therefore sovereignty) lay: North, South, or in both. It could also be seen, perhaps most remarkably, in the craze over the most charismatic of all revolutionaries, Garibaldi, who was identified wholly and completely with the cause not merely of Italian nationality, but of nationality everywhere it was oppressed. His international celebrity, far more potent than that of Che Guevara a century later, is all the more ironical given his own disappointment with the outcome of Italy's Risorgimento.[11]

From Europe and North America the contagion spread abroad. The Wars of Liberation in South America were its first triumph, but its victories were in the end world-wide. Everywhere, it is now assumed that the burden of proof does not lie with the advocates of nationalism, but with their opponents. All that nationalists need do is to draw attention to the fact of vociferous desire. If this needs some propping up, they turn to history, which 'new' nations nowadays invent as vigorously as did the seventeenth-century Dutch burghers who, having just shaken off Spanish rule, commissioned paintings of imaginary incidents from the rebellion of the Batavii against the Romans in 69 BC, and built legends about the heroes Friso and Baeto.

Nationalism has thus turned the world upside down; it has been the most powerful revolutionary force in the world for a century or more. It has far out-stripped Communism as a change-maker — Communists have often only been riders clinging to the back of a nationalist tiger. Nationalism shattered the state-forms of the dynastic era. It led to European civil wars between states whose real interest lay in avoiding conflict, and these spread worldwide. It has continued to undermine the structures left behind by these struggles, and even deeply-rooted historical nation states — such as England, France and Spain — have been disrupted by them. Outside Europe, from the launching of the Latin-American independence movements early in the nineteenth century onwards, European empires have been blighted by it so that their solid-seeming pomp of yesterday is, indeed, one with Nineveh and Tyre. In the United States, a war costing proportionately more lives than any other in the country's history had to be fought to establish that the country was one nation and not two. Nationalism is the triumphant creed of the age.

This is surely an outstanding example of the cultural hegemony of the West. It is easy to see why the western idolisation of nationalism proved irresistible in the non-western world. Though it shows the prestige and attractive power of western civilisation, nationalism can be a weapon against the West; it helps to undermine actual western political and economic hegemony. Conscious export efforts by the West helped to bring this about. Sometimes a missionary impulse was at work; many Europeans and North Americans at different times fanned the flames of Asiatic or African patriotism and nationalism because they believed national self-assertiveness to be the wave of the future or, even more speculatively, part of the overall progressive march of mankind. Sometimes it merely registered diplomatic or strategic opportunism.

In fact, literate Asiatics and Africans did not usually require much encouragement to take up nationalist causes. They felt (though this could not be proved) that their peoples could not step forward onto the stage of modern history and enjoy the advantages of economic and social progress until the imperialist grip had been prised away. Only national self-determination could open the way to a progressive epoch of history. All blessings would follow once alien power were removed. It did not matter much that at the same time others among their fellow-countrymen rallied to the nationalist cause and opposed the foreigner (Confucian Chinese or Islamic fundamentalists, for example) for conservative reasons, wanting to keep things as they were. Nor did it matter that (as in India) no such nation as now claimed self-determination had ever been heard or dreamed of (let alone identified) until the idea was introduced by foreigners. The nationalist fervour of a man such as Nehru or Sun-Yet-sen came from the association of nationalism with a general progressive cause. It was because of what it promised for national self-assertion and revitalisation that many Chinese turned in the end to communism. Everywhere, too, the daily contact with European institutions of those in the governing élite fed nationalist aspirations.[12] Even the symbols of Asian and African nationalism today — flags, statues, ceremonies — show their essentially western origins.[13]

Sometimes the nationalists seemed quickly to be shown to be right (though more often about the future than the past). Once embarked on the nationalist road, some new states discovered, to their leaders' pleasure, that nationalism was one of the most effective devices for the tapping of collective energies to appear since the great world religions. War has been a frequent outcome and proof of it. But there are also examples of nationalism focusing great economic and material efforts, making acceptable privation and discipline on a scale which recalls the building of the pyramids. It was nationalism which first put men on the moon. At least as often, though, nationalism has resulted in new tensions, even injustices, as efforts have been made to give substance to a myth at the cost of minorities. But the failures — if that is the word — of nationalism to deliver what it once appeared to promise to the new nations of the post-1945 world in no way diminish the historical importance of the idea.

For the past, too, can be transformed by nationalism as can the present. For centuries, the Jewish people — self-conscious if ever a people was — had preserved its identity successfully by means of its cult practices and traditions. At the end of the nineteenth century some Jews took up the idea of national self-determination and Zionism was born. In part, no doubt, because of the decline of orthodox religious belief, the new faith was warmly welcomed in some Jewish circles. But there was more to it than that. It seemed to provide practical safeguards some Jews felt they lacked, and was an idea which was respectable and fashionable; self-determination was the shibboleth of the age. It is striking that for all the opposition aroused by proposals to give the Jews any particular homeland (several were suggested, Argentine and Uganda among them, before Palestine was settled upon), there was frequent acceptance (even among Nazis) of the proposition that they had a right to a homeland somewhere, that is, that a nation should express itself in a territorial state. Zionism has now triumphed. The state of Israel came into existence in 1947 — to be challenged immediately by another nationalism, that of the Palestinians. They, too, claim that the existence of a state is the necessary expression of their nationhood. Israel is now seen by many Arabs as the latest form of western imperialism, a latter-day version of Outremer, and perhaps as temporary.

The Jews' view of their past has meanwhile been adapted to fit modern nationalism. Masada is a place of pilgrimage, whose associations are now deliberately cultivated and arranged to shape the minds and acts of modern men and women. The vows which the Israeli army used to impose on its recruits there marked the subordination of an old tradition to a new myth: that of the nation. Whatever Masada was 1900 years ago, it is now a shrine to a different cause from that envisaged by those who lived and died in the dramatic siege. It is almost as if the British were to start pilgrimages to Stonehenge in order to link Boadicea's rebellion against the Romans with their exasperations with the Common Market. Nationalist shrines are not so prominent in the lives of older and more complacent nations; but they are important to young ones and Masada, like other places of pilgrimage, has grown up because it was needed.

Socialism is the other secular religion of the West which has been a world-changing force. In this context I mean by 'socialism' no one of the systems or ideologies which have appropriated the name but, rather, a bundle of presumptions about society rooted in an old idea: equality. They start from protests about privileges derived from legal status and go on to include, for instance, the views that material inequalities between men are not self-justifying, that they should be paid for or corrected (at least in a measure) by political action and that the provision of material welfare is a major duty of the state. For a long time confined to merely theological assertion, the spread of the moral imperative of equality and its undermining of legal privilege, ethnic standing, wealth and its practical advantages, lies at the heart of much of western history. None of these assumptions would have been widely accepted two hundred years ago; they are now the commonplaces of 'progressive' politics all round the world.

Though attempts are often made to show that such ideas are in harmony with ethical precepts of other civilisations, they arose solely in the secular, progressive culture of modern Europe. Often, they seemed to harmonise with the imperatives of nationalism. Yet socialism (so defined) is not the same, has not been as revolutionary as nationalism, and can conflict with it as it does with other western values, those of liberal individualism, for instance. Yet it is only recently that choices have appeared to be unavoidable. Often socialism seemed only to be the next logical step in a continuing historical process of liberation from old constraints. Not so very long ago, though, the western model most favoured by foreign buyers would have been *laissez-faire* capitalism (as it still is in many parts of the world). Samuel Smiles' books sold with enormous success in Japanese translation. But socialism has recently had a greater appeal. Part of the explanation rests on a misleading analogy; the modernisation of Russia came to its climax under a regime which called itself socialist and from an agrarian empire, Russia became a great industrial state, from mass illiteracy she moved to literacy, in two or three decades. Many other changes registered an example which seemed relevant to many other peoples who overlooked much that was special to Russian history.

It is easy, therefore, to see why such ideas should attract men outside the western world which created them. But the primary reason why they should have been taken up so eagerly appears to me to lie, quite simply, in their origin and context. At the time when western culture was most influential they were the latest thing in its prestigious, progressive stream of ideas. It is a revealing detail, surely, that 'progressive' is a cant term of the Left (another exported European term, we remember) all round the world. Socialism was the latest addition to the general progressive impulse provided for the last two centuries by western civilisation and by no other, and it is something which, like nationalism, really got its decisive push in 1789, even though there were not many people we should now recognise as 'socialists' about in the French Revolution. Without the impulse to bring about progress and the impetus that revolution gave to nationalism, egalitarianism would have mattered less and the world would have been a different place.

X
THE CONFIDENT
AGGRESSORS

Ask half-a-dozen people what imperialism means, and you will get half-a-dozen different answers. It connotes both a huge mass of positive facts and an equally large and much more complicated body of myth and assumption. Europe's imperial expansion was a huge and untidy business. It went on unrolling, faster and faster, for about three centuries. The final climax of the western assault on the world which had begun with the *conquistadores* came barely a hundred years ago. It was never a simple single process; it was always enormously complex, affecting different regions in different ways. All this is easily forgotten once we snuggle up in the blanket term 'imperialism'.

One rough but useful preliminary distinction can be made between territorial and commercial empire. At first there were almost two worlds of European empire, east and west. Because the Spanish who first went to the Americas were, broadly speaking, after land on which to settle while their contemporaries from Portugal in Asia and Africa, broadly speaking, were not, there were as a result for a long time two vaguely defined but different imperial spheres centred on the Atlantic and the Indian oceans. Later, things changed. Other Europeans seized large tracts of North America, Asia and Indonesia, and the Portuguese took huge areas in Brazil and Africa and settled them. Nevertheless, Europeans who went east for a long time sought markets and commodities, rather than land. India was acquired by the British almost by the way, as an offshoot of a trading company's activities, though vast, non-commercial consequences were to follow. In the nineteenth century, notably in Africa, land was increasingly to be sought for reasons of prestige, strategy and resource, as well as (where suitable) for European settlement. By then, though, the territorial-commercial distinction which dominates the sixteenth and seventeenth centuries and much of the eighteenth has really lost its usefulness.

The passing of time changed the way institutions worked, too. In the early sixteenth century, when French merchants trading at ports in the Ottoman empire sought to ensure themselves some degree of freedom from local control, it suited both the sultan's officials and the French monarchy to negotiate 'Capitulations' to define their sphere of rights and give them more independence of local law. The name derives from the *capitula,* or chapter-headings, of such treaties, and the first of them was agreed in 1536. As other nations followed suit a juridical and commercial convenience was slowly turned into a formidable apparatus of encroachment upon Ottoman sovereignty and that of other countries where the device was applied. Foreign merchants sold to Ottoman subjects the use of their privileges. They acquired property which itself became privileged. All this transformed a once acceptable commercial convention into — by the twentieth century — an affront. Yet this had not been intended or envisaged.

This instance suggests the growth in the sheer weight and power behind European imperial expansion as time passed. Mature western imperialism is really only a matter of the second half of the nineteenth century, the climax of a long effort which had checked and reversed the tendency of centuries, altering long-established patterns. And it was soon to fade away. The last, high phase of European empire extended only for sixty or seventy years before 1914. The historical forces which made it possible and which favoured or disfavoured countries taking part in it form no simple system. Deep-running, long-term economic currents were at work, set, fundamentally, by the way in which Europe's social, commercial and technical achievements slowly changed her needs and desires. But such currents work through men, and often the actual course of imperialism was only the fall-out from accidents and almost parochially trivial quarrels. The fates of whole continents could be settled by tiny bands of Europeans thousands of miles away from their homes. In the eighteenth century, a power vacuum caused by Mogul decline coincided with a series of Anglo-French wars to draw the British forward in India. A handful of men settled the sub-continent's fate in a few decades. Clive won the battle of Plassey with an army of less than three thousand which had only a few hundred Europeans in its ranks, and so shaped a big piece of world history: India's future was to be made by England, not France. The incalculable consequences of that run right down to our own day, though in 1757 all that seemed likely to follow was that the East India Company could exploit the commercial possibilities in Bengal. Clive also shows the importance of individuals to the story: personality was always an unpredictable force shaping imperialism. The history of British Africa would have been very different without Livingstone — or Rhodes.

Native peoples all round the world could be (and were) scooped up almost willy-nilly in Europeans' quarrels. As Macaulay put it in a famous phrase, red men scalped one another on the shores of the Great Lakes so that a Prussian king could keep a province stolen from his neighbour. It was an almost casual outcome of the Anglo-French struggle (itself a ramification of wars between Prussia and the House of Habsburg for hegemony in Central Europe), that English became the language of government and the predominant speech in both the great nation-states of North America. Even the emergence of the United States itself came when it did as a side-effect of Anglo-French struggle. So, men like Choiseul and Vergennes, Chatham and North, rooted in the metropolitan cultures of eighteenth-century Europe, fixed the future history of the world in certain grooves, even while their eyes were on far other immediate preoccupations.

The outcome of such diverse, complex and casual processes tended, by 1914, to look very simple on the map. Just as in the great days of Spanish conquest, or of the settlement of North America, the best evidence of western imperialism's success was sovereignty over non-European territory overseas (or, in the case of Russia, overland). By 1850, when only the shadow of Mogul authority remained, India was already almost entirely under British overlordship. Yet spectacular territorial prizes were still to be won by Europeans in Asia and Africa. The French had begun the conquest of Algeria in the 1820s and there were even earlier a few British footholds in West Africa and Dutch settlements at the Cape of Good Hope, to say nothing of old Portuguese possessions. In 1870 Africa was still the 'Dark Continent', unknown for the most part once its coasts were left behind; forty-four years later, at the outbreak of the Great War, all of it except Liberia and Ethiopia was under direct European rule, occupation or protection. In the same years, South-East Asia and Indonesia, with the exception of Siam (as Thailand was then called), had also been finally absorbed into the imperial system.[1] Persia, nominally independent, was by 1914 divided between Russia and Great Britain into 'spheres of influence'. There was talk of partitioning China; Russia had detached huge territories from her in the later nineteenth century, other states had seized Chinese ports, while British and French power had erupted into her Tibetan and Indochinese dependencies.

Although the European share of world population became larger than ever before, its peoples were always a minority of mankind; they were often very few in proportion to the great populations they encountered abroad. But industrialisation and technological change gave them a huge superiority. The fire-power of Cortés' men was multiplied a thousandfold by breech-loading, repeating small-arms, machine-guns and rifled artillery in the next three and a half centuries. In the eastern seas the Portuguese adventurers faced opponents with weapons much less inferior to their own than were those of the Aztecs to those of the Spanish. The Persians, Moguls and Arabs had guns; the Aztecs did not even have iron. Nonetheless, gun-carrying ships of the seventeenth century were already decisive against the not much less inferior weaponry of the Persians, Moguls and Arabs. Two centuries further on, paddle-steamers would make even greater havoc among Chinese junks. Railways and electric telegraphs later made the Europeans' communications swifter and safer. Armies and fleets could be assembled as needed with hitherto unimaginable rapidity. By 1900 it cost only one-sixth or one-seventh of what it had a century before to move men and supplies by sea. As for manpower, better medicine — very gradually — made the management of expeditions to the tropics much easier.[2]

Psychology may have been just as decisive as material factors. Power is both tempting and deluding. To possess it makes it easy to believe that you ought to possess it, and therefore that you need not be worried about using it to achieve good ends. Conscious power fed the self-confidence of the last age of imperialism and also dramatically increased the respect in which western nations were held by others; here was another temptation. Another element in the mentality of imperialism was the increasingly widely-shared assumption, by no means borne out by events, that only territorial sovereignty could assure access to markets and raw materials. The creation or discovery of new economic resources in the non-western world consequently led to political struggles; much of Africa's nineteenth-century history was the result of that. Most of its modern states only exist because certain boundaries were settled a century ago by Europeans wishing to divide up potential booty in an orderly way. A further internal dynamic was given to imperialism by the competitiveness and national feeling which became much more virulent in an increasingly democratic age. Rivalry between states easily became entangled with domestic politics, and European and North American politicians took up colonialism as an electioneering cry. Of course, national rivalries had been part of the story of western imperialism almost from the start, influencing its path and character. It is a good working hypothesis that the pace of any nation's expansion was likely to quicken if there was a suspected rival about, as the Dutch showed in the seventeenth century in the Indian ocean and the East Indies, the French and British in India in the next, Great Britain and the United States in North America soon after 1800, Germans, French, British, Belgians and Italians during the 'Scramble for Africa', everyone in the savaging of China. But popular politics seem to have made things worse.

Whatever western nations decided to do or not to do in other parts of the globe, the non-western world was changed willy-nilly. Western nations nevertheless had special opportunities and needs, particular geographies and histories and perceptions of them, which stamped themselves individually on the history of their empires. The geographical direction of Russian and American territorial expansion was virtually pre-determined. Unlike almost any other western peoples after 1500, they could advance to empire almost completely over dry land. Russian settlers flowed across the Urals for centuries without questioning the ethical foundations of a claim rooted in a folk-movement. Like the United States, imperial Russia absorbed a continent. Both countries did it by negotiation, by war, and by settlement. Americans always found it difficult to see what was going on as imperialism; to them it looked like a divinely authorised expression of a 'manifest destiny' to move westward. As for the subjects of the Tsar, few of them were in a position to question what was going on, even if they understood it.

For all the complications and variety hidden behind the word 'imperialism', the outcome was at one level very simple: a wider diffusion than ever of direct western government. The nineteenth-century wave of western civilisation simply obliterated or absorbed many of the crumbling polities of the non-western world. The acquisition of Hawaii, and, a little later, the Philippines, by the United States showed that the daughter nations of Europe were in business for themselves as overseas empire-builders. There were Australian and South African expansionists, too, as well as French, German and Italian. If one nation dominates the story of the high final phase of imperialism, though, it is Great Britain. After 1815 she reaped the rewards of Trafalgar, having her pick of the former Dutch and French colonial empires. The world-wide network of colonies and naval bases which resulted, and was further added to in the next two or three decades, provided the strategic framework of an enormously impressive empire, the supreme example of western imperialism. Uniquely, it came to include not only the whole of the Indian sub-continent — a tail which could tend to wag the dog, for the security of India could determine British policy elsewhere — and much of Africa, but territorially huge, self-governing colonies inhabited predominantly by settlers of European stock thanks to an unusually large emigration from the British Isles in the nineteenth century. Canada, self-governing since 1867, issued a Christmas postage stamp in 1898 showing a world map with the British empire on it in red and the words 'We hold a vaster empire than has been.'

British statesmen closely watched the needs of trade and sea-power. This was a special feature of British imperial policy. Another was the coincidence of imperial growth with the development of new constitutional checks on government at home (in contrast, the Spanish empire had grown along with monarchical absolutism). The British empire was in such respects like others only in being far from a 'typical' empire (there never was such a thing). Nor was it the outcome of coherent planning or even of simple ambitions. Nor was support for it ever solid and unquestioning. In the eighteenth century, opponents of conquest abroad (particularly in Asia) would draw on their classical education to illustrate from Roman history the theme that empire led to corruption. Later, in the 1840s and 1850s, many thinking Englishmen would actually hold that territorial empire was on the way out, and a good job too. The proprietors of the empire, Queen Victoria's British middle-class subjects, by no means gave it continuous and uncritical admiration, at least in so far as it consisted of directly ruled colonies.

On the other hand, most British believed strongly in a different sort of empire. The early nineteenth century was the heyday of what historians sometimes call the 'imperialism of Free Trade', a world force quite as important as painting the map red (or any other colour). Political and military means were used to open closed economies to western commerce. Sheer fire-power, not always employed but always implicit, at last in the nineteenth century forced open the ports of China, Japan and Siam and loosed the pressures of the western market economy and capitalism on traditional societies until then pretty much insulated from them. Further, with 'unofficial' imperialism went the impact produced by contact with the missionaries, cut-throats, philanthropists and simple adventurers who followed and accompanied the traders. Thousands of agents of change contributed in their peculiar ways to the channels by which the West reached the rest of the world. Often they sought conflicting, even incompatible, ends — another complication. Like the crusaders before them, their rivalries with one another sometimes prompted them to do deals with local potentates, and like them, they often quarrelled busily among themselves.

Look alike though they might to 'natives', the 'Franks' were thus a somewhat scratch crew. Even administrators and soldiers came from diverse backgrounds and traditions. Their ideas, so important in defining goals for their new subjects, had been formed in many different ways. Outstanding examples — a Lyautey in Morocco, or a Cromer in Egypt — are by no means the whole story. The giant viceregal and pro-consular figures — how easily the era slipped into the terminology of imperial Rome! — overshadow the men on the ground. Thousands of anonymous district officers, resident magistrates, customs officers, policemen and teachers who kept the empires running were the only direct and immediate western influences on millions of non-Europeans. Their recruitment and training and the special institutions — the public schools of England, the French *grandes écoles* — and the ideologies which shaped them are an important part of the impact of the West, and have to find a place in the explanation of the way imperialism actually worked. Yet they were also individuals, often with very different views of what their power should and could be used to do.

Take, for example, the single case of the British rulers of India, first under the East India Company and then under the crown. Which rulers do we wish to consider? Those in Calcutta, those in the country districts, or those in London? Those used to the easy, side-by-side life of eighteenth-century Anglo-India, or those who took for granted the repugnance felt by many nineteenth-century Indians and Englishmen alike at the idea of eating in one another's homes? The Victorian evangelicals, or the Company officers against whom they railed for financing Hindu temples and festivals and permitting Hindu worship in the regiments of the army? A man like Metcalfe, who gave freedom to the Indian press, or those among his successors who later in the century took it away?[3] Brigadier-General Dyer, notorious for his brutal folly at Amritsar, or the patient civil servants of the 1930s, many of them anxious to accelerate progress towards self-rule? Lord Curzon, the most viceregal of viceroys — or the British who complained so bitterly when he disciplined a regiment whose soldiers had raped some Indian women? Lord Ripon, the liberally-intentioned Viceroy, or the 'd — d nigger party' (as another Viceroy described them to him)[4] who thwarted his modest wish to give some Indian judges the same powers to try white men as those possessed by their British colleagues? And what about the other Europeans in India? Bombay had been Portuguese before it was British and a visit to Goa or Pondicherry still shows the traces of other Europeans who moulded India's future.[5]

All differences allowed for, though, it is hard to believe that most Europeans did not share in some degree a sense of superiority to their colonial subjects and those who inhabited other parts of the world. As western civilisation spread world-wide, it increasingly found the great civilisations and historic cultures it encountered to be wanting; uncivilised peoples were even more disprized. The progressive outlook itself was disrespectful of the past, even when it was a past of European origin. At the end of the nineteenth century, members of the English Fabian Society could applaud the British government's war with the Boer republics of South Africa. They saw the Boer farmers as backward, unprogressive, with unacceptable ideas about the treatment of other races. So, no doubt, they were, though not everyone was quite so sure that the imposition of Westminster liberalism by force was the answer. Such assurance has often led to fresh problems. Nonetheless, those in the radical van have usually been uncompromising in their view that other cultures should adopt western ways in many self-evidently important matters, from hygiene and monogamy to law and order, voting systems and a free press.

This was to account for much of the strength of the impact of western civilisation through empire. Liberals often sought to move mountains. They were often universalists, contemptuous of the past and little interested in the specific character of the societies they sought to improve. Just as medieval men believed that 'Christians are right, Pagans are wrong', so the nineteenth century came to think that 'progressives are right, traditionalists are wrong'. And traditionalists in non-western countries were usually much easier to override than traditionalists at home. The idea of progress sustained a secularised missionary spirit. The faith it was morally proper to spread was not just that of the Cross (though that was for a long time to continue to be part of the package), but a faith in western values — understood, of course, as universal values — and in the material bounty of western civilisation. As fresh material successes flowed from the manipulation of nature, the Europeans' belief that they ought to spread the Good News of which their culture was the carrier broadened out to sustain the myth that Christianity and material improvement were meant to go together, that men ought to be brought to share prosperity as well as truth and that western man has a duty to bring both to those unfortunate enough not to have arrived at them for themselves. This was a new kind of missionary zeal, unknown to medieval Christendom, though quite compatible with it. The Gospel, hospitals, schools, uncorrupt administration, women's rights, protection of animals — the whole benevolent but culturally arrogant bag of goods is still with us today, sustained by a conscious sense of superiority and duty.

The idea of Progress thus reinforced the tendency to assess the diversity of human achievement increasingly in terms of western goals and western standards. There had been occasional and temporary exceptions; as the Ottoman threat declined, Islam was for a while regarded with a little more tolerance and even with occasional admiration (notably for its forbearance towards the religious practices of non-Muslims, which appealed to the men of the Enlightenment). Yet while some publicists might use Islamic practice — or what they believed to be Islamic practice — as a device for criticism of their own countries, and while Muhammad enjoyed a brief vogue as a wise lawgiver, these stereotypes in the end gave way to others far less favourable. Ottoman rule was identified with despotism, cruelty, corruption. It may be significant that during the eighteenth century the European merchants of the Levant Company living at Aleppo increasingly gave up their former habit of wearing Turkish dress.

Towards those further east, Europeans usually felt similarly superior; the fact that there were so few Christians in Asia before the coming of the Jesuits and Dominicans was in itself a ground for confidence.[6] In spite of an eighteenth-century craze for China, when the supposed toleration of government by mandarins became something of a debating point in the polemics of the Enlightenment publicists, that empire was always tainted in European eyes with despotism and the evil consequences supposed to flow from it. As for India, it appears that the British there, by the 1780s, were already beginning to show a certain aloofness from Indian life, close though relations had been for many of them in earlier times, and closer though they tended to be in Portuguese and French settlements. Robert Clive used to refer to Indians with contempt and never learnt to speak any native language with ease. Gradually, even respect for the cultural achievements of the great non-European civilisations faded away.[7] China had invented printing, it was admitted, but no such intellectual and cultural explosion had followed as in

Europe. Islam had bred great scientific scholars, but science had enjoyed no such development in the Arab world as in the western and had dwindled away under Ottoman rule. Gibbon praised Muslim achievements in science and the arts, but was sure that eighteenth-century Europe represented the peak of civilisation. The Encyclopedia was contemptuous of the learning of the Brahmins.[8] Hume, the greatest of sceptics, flirted with ideas which would now be termed 'racialist' in pondering differences of cultural level.[9]

The non-western world had by then been weighed in the balance of western values and was found wanting. It was barely grasped that to employ such a standard of measurement itself distorted the judgement. When Asia, for example, was seen as a continent of strange, even beastly, religions, it was because the model of religion which was employed was that of Christianity. Asiatic religions ought to be like Christianity, with a doctrine which could be set out in a corpus of sacred writings in the custody of a priesthood which expounded them and carried out appropriate rites. Such a model, though, turned away from most of the reality and social practice of Asian religion, and opened the way to contempt for what was judged.[10]

Contempt was also increasingly felt for the seeming immobility of Asiatic societies. The stereotype of the 'unchanging East' made its appearance in the eighteenth century. In a culture more and more aware of its own capacity to change, and to change for the better, it led easily to the dismissal of Asiatic civilisations as 'stagnant' — whether by consequence of bad government, the natural depravity of their inhabitants, climate or many other causes, was much debated, but is hardly to the point here. The West made its assessments against the background of its own growing conviction that progress was possible and could — ought to — be striven for, an idea which was to prove a diabolically effective agent of disruption and corrosion.

The maturing of the western view of history as a meaningful drama into the celebration of the idea of Progress made thinking men in the West more self-confident and practical men more aggressive. Such ideas filtered down through society to be coarsened and put in cruder terms. Even if they were not always clear why, those of European stock often behaved as if they were not merely right, but were actually superior beings.[11] The West knew it was superior. This is what lay behind the nineteenth-century's idealisation of the way white men were expected to behave. They were expected to show confidence, courage, dignity because they represented a higher civilisation. Like many mythologies, this one had a capacity for self-fulfilment. It was not the same as racialism, which asserted that white people *would* behave in a certain way because of their biological nature; it was a declaration that they *ought* to do something because their civilisation demanded it of them. The evidence that this was correct was to be found in visible progress that men could see about them.

Already in 1802, the *Edinburgh Review* could confidently assert that 'Europe is the light of the world, and the ark of knowledge.' It went on to say that 'upon the welfare of Europe hangs the destiny of the most remote and savage people' (a less contestable statement, to be sure).[12] This was a cruder version of the same collective self-regard which manifested itself in Hegel's cultural ethnocentrism, and was passed on by him to Marx.[13] It is hardly surprising that at the end of the nineteenth century, a Frenchman was able to describe the relationship between the West and the rest of the world in terms which are as good a general statement as you can find of western assumptions about the human world after three centuries of expansion. 'The present-day world', he wrote, 'is composed of four different parts, in terms of civilisation. That of western civilisation — our own part. A second part is inhabited by people of a different civilisation but organised in coherent and stable societies and destined by their history and present character to govern themselves — the Chinese and Japanese people, for example. In the third part live people advanced enough in some respects, but ones which have either stagnated or have not been able to constitute themselves as unified, peaceful, progressive nations, following a regular development ... India ... before the British conquest, Java and the Indochinese peninsula present particularly this third type. Finally, a great part of the world is inhabited by barbarian tribes or savages, some given over to wars without end and to brutal customs, and others knowing so little of the arts and being so little accustomed to work and invention that they do not know how to exploit their land and its natural riches. They live in little groups, impoverished and scattered, in enormous territories which could nourish vast numbers of people with ease.' He went on to say: 'This state of the world implies for the civilised people a right of intervention ... in the affairs of the last two categories.' A few years later, a simpler categorisation — but one resting on evidently similar assumptions — was made by the British prime minister, Lord Salisbury. 'You may', he said 'roughly divide the nations of the world as the living and the dying.'[14]

Such a judgement is a long way removed from the awe felt by the first English visitors at the court of the great Mogul. It justified, if it did not generate, an urge to disturb. By 1900 many Europeans and Americans felt that they should act in a dynamic and innovative way towards other cultures. The attitude can still be seen, though it must be said that few people nowadays like to think or admit that they share such views. Nonetheless, the fundamental judgements on which they rest now provide a backbone for what we might call a philanthropic cultural imperialism. The West's most progressive thinkers still seek to export to non-western societies such homegrown products as the promotion of human rights, nationalism, Marxism, or scientific materialism. Many today preach the values of humanism, the unquestionable merits and universal applicability of democratic government and parliamentary institutions, the general authority of science, in the tones of Mr Podsnap. They believe that what they admire is universally valid and true; they do not believe that Estonians, Arabs and Indonesians may reasonably hold differing views about the nature of men, society and institutions and that those views may be worthy of respect. They provide the best evidence that the sense of Western cultural superiority is still alive and kicking, though its crude nudity is now often decorously draped in the benevolent trappings of development aid.

What is wrong with this attitude matters less here than its striking vigour and attractiveness. It has persisted through great historical transformations, taking in its stride changes from religious to secular goals within western culture, surviving the colonial world. Its roots, we have already seen, lie further back than we usually think, some of them in Christianity itself, yet they have flourished more extravagantly than ever in the context of material success, secularism and the belief in Progress which has gripped the West since the eighteenth century. Religion, though, was always until recently one of its clearest expressions.

Missionary Christianity has ebbed and flowed since the age of St Paul. The second great missionary age converted Germany and eastern Europe in the Dark Ages. A third began with the great discoveries and the irruption of Roman Catholicism into the Americas and East Asia. That was only a beginning, though. The missionary wave was to roll outwards with growing strength after the advent of religious pluralism in Europe, and the new zest given to Catholic enterprise by the Counter-Reformation. The first African bishop of the Latin rite was appointed in 1518, the first Indian in 1637, the first Chinese in 1674.[15] The Jesuits had spectacular success in Japan in the last quarter of the sixteenth century. In 1600 China already had four ordained native clergy and a century later 200,000 Christians. A seminary for training priests was established in 1664 at the old capital of Siam, Ayuthia. Further stimulants were provided by the appearance of European settlements beyond the oceans. True, the Japanese church was all but obliterated by persecution in the seventeenth century. The Jesuits at Peking, too, were ultimately disappointed in their ambitions and the propagation of Christianity was forbidden in China in 1724. The Siamese initiative withered. Yet none of this was because of hostility at home. The onset of infidelity in upperclass Europe in the eighteenth century hardly troubled such missionary work abroad.[16]

Protestant missionary work began to be significant only in the eighteenth century, first reinforcing and then overtaking the great Roman effort. The Society for the Propagation of the Gospel in Foreign Parts was founded in England in 1701. For all the flooding-in of secularism within western civilisation in the eighteenth and nineteenth centuries, they were the greatest age of Christian conversion outside it. From about 1800 or so, Africa, Asia and the Pacific islands were seen as fields ripe for harvests such as Christianity had not enjoyed since the conquest of the Americas. Technology helped to bring them in; already operating through the printing-press, in the nineteenth century it gave missionaries the use of medical science, steamships, railways. With the twentieth century the aeroplane, radio and television were to come to play their parts in the evangelising of the non-western world. In spite of setbacks, the 1960s revealed that the big battalions of Rome (almost the only Christian church still asserting with confidence the universal claims of the faith) were to be found in the former colonies of western states. Papal tours to Asia, Africa and South America awoke astonishing popular responses.

Neither the cultural and intellectual aggression implicit in this, nor its link with imperial rule, can be denied. But neither are they the whole story. The nineteenth-century upsurge of public support for missionary work may be complicated to explain, but is easy to see in action. Changes in public attitudes at home were often more important than imperial support for evangelism such as had been given in earlier times by the Catholic Monarchs or Charles V. In India, the East India Company for a long time successfully resisted the arrival of missionaries from home (though it soon introduced its own chaplains) in spite of such pleas as that of the Bishop of Oxford who in 1762 drew attention to the providences of victory in the Seven Years' War: 'A new field is now open to our labour,' he declared. 'By the blessing of God and his Majesty's arms, it stretches itself to the utmost parts of the globe. Our armies have gone before us; they have made the most distant countries accessible to our missionaries.'[17] But Protestant zeal had to be (and was) satisfied for a time by a subsidy from the English Society for Promoting Christian Knowledge to German Lutheran missionaries who worked in the Danish settlements of South India. This donation was running at £1000 a year in the 1770s, which suggests no very lively sense of urgency about the evangelisation of the sub-continent.[18] Nevertheless, the tide was beginning to flow. While one British missionary joined the Lutherans in 1788 (though he did not stay long with them), the Evangelical impulse gathered strength at home and among servants of the Company in Bengal. In 1793 clauses enjoining the Company to see to the 'religious and moral improvement' of India were struck from a bill before parliament, but in the same year a Baptist arrived to become the first English missionary in the Company's settlements. He found small welcome from his fellow countrymen and soon went off to live in a Danish settlement near Calcutta. Soon, though, the story was wholly, and quickly, changed as Evangelicalism brought public opinion formidably to bear upon the British government.

Christianity had been the original and defining matrix of western civilisation and much of its message had passed into the inherited conglomerate of the assumptions of western civilisation. The urge to bring Christian light to darkness and help to the benighted could be understood as a generous impulse even by the non-religious.

O'er heathen lands afar
Thick darkness broodeth yet

sang the missionaries (if they were English Protestants); they were sure they could penetrate that darkness by the light of Christianity, and often strove to do so at grave cost in personal suffering and self-sacrifice. Most missionaries found it easy to see their work as a spiritual crusade. Many of them also fiercely criticised what Europeans did in their colonies, judging them in the name of the western and Christian standards they expected imperial rule to uphold. Yet missionary enthusiasm was an enormous reinforcement to imperialism; European rule could be justified (as it had been in the Papal Bulls given to Henry the Navigator) if it sheltered and consolidated the victories of the Cross.

There was not, of course, anything very new in seeking to save souls, to bring light to darkness, to cast down idols. Counter-Reformation enthusiasm among the sixteenth-century Portuguese clergy had destroyed the Hindu temples at Goa, prohibited the practice of Hinduism, Buddhism or Islam there, and provoked attempts to seize all sacred books of these religions, a ban on Hindu ritual bathing, the use of force to seize orphans for conversion and the condemnation of polygamy.[19] Depressingly, it has to be acknowledged that such steps were effective. Goa was effectively Christianised within a few generations, the disappearance of *suttee* (the burning alive of a Hindu widow on her husband's funeral pyre) being balanced by the introduction of *autos-da-fé* and the burning of Jews there. The Portuguese, like less thick-skinned European missionaries in the nineteenth century, were utterly confident in destroying indigenous cultures where they conflicted with their own views of universal morality.

Such victories were not solely spiritual; they were often practically expressed in healing and education. All those who believed that the western civilisation in which they had been reared was indisputably superior to anything else the world could offer, and that it should be offered to non-Europeans, could approve. Only a few Europeans ever thought that western civilisation might learn from what could be found in the rest of the world. One of them was Sir William Jones, the 'father of Indology'.[20] He had come out to India in 1783, already an orientalist of repute (he had begun by teaching himself Hebrew and the Arabic script while at Harrow) and author of several books, including a Persian grammar. Welcomed by other Englishmen in Bengal already engaged in the scholarly study of India's history, languages and institutions under the encouragement of Warren Hastings, Jones seems to have had a galvanic and revitalising effect. In 1784, the 'Asiatick Society' was founded, a landmark in the history of Orientalism as a discipline. The first volume of the Society's publication, *Asiatic Researches*, appeared in 1789, attracting not only attention but admiration in London. Jones forcefully asserted the value of the literary and religious heritage of the Indians for its own sake. True, he continued to believe that Indians should be governed authoritatively by Englishmen enlightened by whig ideas and a grasp of just principles. Yet he made possible a revaluation of the Indian past which was to be of the greatest importance to the later development of Indian national self-esteem — a self-esteem urgently needed when Indians faced the apparently all-successful impact of western civilisation.

Yet there were hundreds of other white men in India who, if they ever looked beyond profit, could see in the country they served and exploited little but barbarism and superstition. Utilitarian and evangelical Christian alike were appalled by such things as *suttee*, female infanticide, or child marriage. So, whatever the long-term challenge it presented to imperial rule, missionary work for a long time powerfully reinforced and supplemented it. As an evangelical director of the East India Company put it, 'the ultimate objective is moral improvement. The pre-eminent excellence of the morality which the Gospel teaches, and the superior efficacy of this divine system, taken in all its parts, in ameliorating the condition of human society, cannot be denied by those who are unwilling to admit its higher claims; and on this ground only, its dissemination must be beneficial to mankind.'[21] So the general 'western-ness' of the missionary impulse fitted into a monolithic cultural imposition on many colonialised peoples. Denominational differences between missionaries did not much dilute this. Those to whom the missionaries preached were not likely to be much aware of what divided Catholics and Protestants doctrinally, however sharp an eye they might have for their respective attractiveness as sources of benefits and patronage.

Moral universalism was mightily reinforced by the growing consciousness of material superiority, undermining faster and faster any residual awe and respect among western men and women for the non-western world as the nineteenth century advanced. Growing scholarly study of other civilisations and of anthropology hardly offsets this. Admiration for the ancient wisdom of the East became a matter for cranks. Earlier enthusiasms (always unrealistic and one-eyed) for the supposed tolerance and enlightenment of China, for the uncorrupted innocence of Noble Savages in Tahiti, or for the mysterious wisdom of the Indian Brahman, dwindled away. It came to be part of the conventional wisdom that the crumbling civilisations of the East were, at best, cases for treatment, only interesting in terms of their potential for western reform or improvement. Embodying as they did in grotesque forms obstacles to progress which had long since crumbled in the West under the onslaught of revolution and improvement, they were increasingly believed to be incapable of self-change. When Shelley wanted to praise the Greeks of his day who were rebelling against the Turks he did so, significantly, by saying that they had prevented Europe from displaying the same 'stagnant' and miserable state of social institutions as China and Japan.[22]

Such judgements strengthened the conviction that should their self-improvement prove impossible, then at least those ancient lands should be exploited by those who knew how. Like the long-enduring economic mirage of great mass markets waiting for western manufactured goods, this conclusion implied a certain blindness to facts. It might be true that Asia looked cruel, superstitious and poverty-stricken, that it lacked elementary forms of civilised justice, and seemed unapt to enterprise and change. But those who so argued seemed to find it easy to forget or overlook the very recent evidence of similar 'backwardness' nearer home. After all, only a few years before the French Revolution Europeans were still being burnt for witchcraft. Russia and the United States waited until the 1860s to abolish bond-labour. In 'darkest England' millions lived in squalor. Huge popular manifestations of superstitious piety could still be seen in western countries. But the consciousness of progress could easily make men overlook such things: they were, after all, in retreat.

In practice, the story twists and turns and there are shadings and gradations to be noticed over the whole picture. One British official spoke for many when he pointed out that the presumed inferiority of Great Britain's Indian subjects laid a special duty upon the rulers, though one which could only be discharged in the longest term. 'The most desirable death for us to die of', he wrote, 'should be the improvement of the natives to such a pitch as would render it impossible for a foreign nation to retain the government.'[23] Civil servants often strove to push colonial governments in unwelcome directions. French colonial practice, for instance, came almost everywhere to reflect the official doctrine of 'assimilation' generated in Algeria — the indoctrination of native élites with the values and ways of France and the pretence that they shared fully in the metropolitan civilisation of the ruling power. The effects can still be seen in a Francophone Africa quite different from British Africa. Such policies may have been arrogant, but were not always cynical. Frenchmen understandably showed pride in a man like President Senghor of Senegal, a senator of France, a poet in its language and a Goethe scholar long before he was president of an African state.

Cultural assurance came to underpin a rich and sometimes systematic ideology of empire, of which it is easier to cite particular and incomplete statements than to find it set out comprehensively. One Victorian administrator of India, Fitzjames Stephen, concisely summed up the way it looked through one pair of British eyes in a telling passage:

The essential parts of European civilization are peace, order, the supremacy of law, the prevention of crime, the redress of wrong, the enforcement of contracts, the development and concentration of the military force of the state, the construction of public works, the collection and expenditure of the revenue required for these objects in such a way as to promote to the utmost the public interest, interfering as little as possible with the comfort or wealth of the inhabitants, and improvement of the people.[24]

One of the most striking things about this is that only the last, almost casually and half-heartedly attached, phrase about improvement goes beyond a programme which would have won the agreement of an enlightened Roman provincial governor. Yet it would have been widely accepted among those who governed India after the Mutiny. They wanted to go as little as possible beyond the simple assurance by government and other agencies of the basic preconditions of healthy social life as they saw them.[25] But that all the ends were good, and in their imposition self-evidently justified, they had no doubt.

By 1900 Europe's right to rule its

New caught, sullen peoples
Half-devil and half-child

seemed to many unquestionable. The exact context of that alarming and revealing phrase is a poem addressed by Rudyard Kipling not to his own countrymen, but to the citizens of the United States. He urged them to 'have done with childish days' (they were then still thought of as a 'young' nation) and to bear their share of 'the White Man's burden'. That burden was to 'serve your captives' need' and the civilising mission cost blood and effort. At the end of it, moreover, they need expect no thanks:

Take up the White Man's burden —
And reap his old reward:
The blame of those ye better,
The hate of those ye guard —
The cry of hosts you humour
(Ah, slowly!) towards the light: —

Why brought ye us from bondage.
Our loved Egyptian night?

Such a very purposeful, very moral vision of empire shows the complexity of cultural arrogance. Kipling tapped old western myths of pilgrimage, suf-

fering for righteousness' sake, the need for self-perfection and self-disci-
pline, the image of Exodus itself. He did not invite Americans to take up
the White Man's booty; the entitlement was to a task, not a reward. The
White Man, runs the message, is not justified by being white, by his possessions or power, or even by his intellectual and moral superiority, but by what
he does with these, by his works. There was a need for some such creed. As
one of Conrad's characters put it, 'the conquest of the earth, which mostly
means the taking it away from those who have a different complexion or
slightly flatter noses than ourselves, is not a pretty thing when you look into
it too much. What redeems it is the idea only. An idea at the back of it; not
a sentimental pretence but an idea; and an unselfish belief in the idea —
something you can set up, and bow down before, and offer a sacrifice to.'[26]

Teaching was one way of serving. The monuments of the belief that
education was the way to the minds of those held back by ignorance, or
cluttered with superstition are to be seen in schools, universities, medical
schools, technical institutes all round the non-western world. The Indian or
Gold Coast boarding school was as deliberate a recreation of the English
original, as was a *lycée* in Saigon or Morocco an attempt to duplicate the
French model. Such institutions provided access both to jobs in colonial and
commercial bureaucracies and to the power and magic of western ideas. Sons
of the native élites, and sometimes those who wished to join élites in the
making, eagerly pushed forward to enter them. Reactionaries might violently
reject them as conduits of an alien culture; others sought in them the key
to a future in a society turning westwards.

Education helped to produce a new linguistic map of the world. Spanish
and Portuguese had earlier conquered indigenous languages in Central and
Southern America; a modest foothold in the Caribbean was won by English
and French. Linguistically, Africa has been largely divided between those
two tongues: 'francophone' and 'anglophone' are terms of art used by students of African affairs to denote the areas where the language of government and higher education is one or the other. Those words are not much
used in Asia; the literate civilisations of that continent proved far more
resistant to linguistic impositions from the outside. Nevertheless, in one great
instance, India, English was diffused so effectively as still to be the primary
language of contemporary culture.[27] Sometimes only the arrival of European
languages made it possible to articulate certain thoughts. When Africans
groped for a new basis for cultural self-respect in the aftermath of the
colonial age they had to turn to a French word: *négritude*. 'Blackness', of
course, is a European notion: it is the opposite of 'whiteness', and 'blacks'
who now, quite properly, call attention to their own cultural heritage and
uniqueness, do so in terms given them by western languages.[28]

Such cultural triumphs are often overlooked, both as forces for change and as contributions to human well-being. Few western intellectuals now seem even to think it worth asking whether western influence was ever beneficial in the non-western world. There has been so much condemnation of the idealistic but arrogant case once made by zealous imperialists that it cannot now get a hearing. It is even alleged that all that the West brought to the rest of the world was disruption of settled ways, upheaval in peaceful cultures, the corruption of wholesome indigenous values, the imposition of new, incongruous ones. Undoubtedly, there was disruption in plenty. The story is more complicated than that, though.

Slavery in the Americas (mainly of black men), and the Atlantic trade from Africa which sustained it, is often held up for special censure. Setting aside its terrible cost to individuals (a cost unconcernedly imposed by every other historic civilisation there has ever been) there can be no doubt that its effects were almost always appalling. Its practitioners were ruthless and frankly exploitative — never more so than when themselves African — even if centuries of European intercourse with West Africa (by far the most important source of black slaves for the Americas) led also to some positive gains for some African coastal societies where a partial christianisation and growth in literacy were to shape later African élites. Such a point, though, is a minor one. It is more important to recall that the earliest condemnations of the slave trade came from Europeans, not from Hindus, Buddhists, Muslims (Muhammad had only laid it down that his followers should not enslave one another, and that virtue could be acquired by emancipating one's own slaves), nor from the African chiefs who sold one another's subjects — as well as their own — into slavery. Islam has indeed proved very resistant to abolitionism. In East Africa and the Sudan, the slave trade flourished more than ever in the second half of the nineteenth century; Gordon himself felt obliged to legalise it when he was at Khartoum, and after his death, under the Mahdists, the trade actually expanded there, most of the slaves sold being Ethiopian girls. At its peak, the import of slaves to Egypt from the south was running at about 10,000 a year and the three-month march northwards cannot have been much less cruel than the horrors of the 'Middle Passage'. By 1786 it was estimated, too, that 30,000 African slaves were exported annually by sea to Arabia.[29] It is not surprising that there was considerable resistance to interference with the Arab traders, or that slave-holding has died hard in the Islamic world — as a scandal a few years ago showed, when a Saudi prince announced his liberation of slaves he was not supposed to possess.

In the end, it was western power which curbed (it could never wholly eradicate) Arab slave-dealing. It was only the threat of force, after decades of diplomatic pressure, which persuaded the Sultan of Zanzibar to close his slave markets in 1873 and declare the overland traffic in slaves illegal three years later. In Egypt it was the British-dominated Khedival regime which brought it to an end just before the end of the century. The effective operation of the Turkish Constitution of 1876 — which guaranteed the personal liberty of all subjects of the empire — was non-operative until the 'Young Turks', a westernising group, seized power in 1908. It is interesting, too, that when the Italians gave up Fezzan (which they had taken from the Turks) to the Senussi during the Great War, a slave market at once reappeared there. In the 1920s, the tide in Islamic lands began to move faster as Afghanistan (1923 and 1931), Iraq (1924), Iran and Transjordan (1929) all suppressed the legal status of slavery. Ironically, in Ethiopia, one of the two black Christian states of Africa (the other being Liberia) slavery was only formally abolished at last by the Italians, when Mussolini's forces occupied the country in 1936. The last formal abolition was Mauritania's in 1980.

The possibility that it might bring an end to slavery was a reason why some Africans welcomed western civilisation to their continent, whatever their nationalist successors think of them today. Edward Blyden, a West Indian of Ibo ancestry, first went to the new country of Liberia — founded for emancipated slaves — in 1851 (he was later to be Liberian minister in London). He drew attention to the help white civilisation could offer Liberians in overcoming the slave trade and intertribal wars. On this ground at least, even while warning them against western materialism and irreligion and urging upon them the importance of their African heritage, he was sure that white influence would be a force for good. It was more than a pious hope: western capitalist society alone created a world-wide climate of opinion which makes it impossible today for those countries where slaves are still kept to admit the fact.[30]

Of course, the story is not (if the expression is momentarily permissible) one of simple black-and-white. The men of the Enlightenment whose attacks on slavery inspired its abolition by the French revolutionary assemblies nevertheless saw it restored after slave revolts in the West Indies had frightened their fellow-countrymen. (Robespierre suggested the anti-slavery lobby was promoted by the British.) The two great dates in the process of abolition are both dates in British history: 1807, when the slave trade became illegal in the British Empire, and 1833 when slavery itself followed it.[31] This was decisive not just because there were so many British and British colonial slave-owners, but also because the slave trade largely depended on sea carriage, and Great Britain, thanks to her naval power, could police the seas. The moral pressure of the Abolition Society founded in 1787 was crucial in bringing about these victories and it was fed not only by Christian concern, but by the humanitarianism of the Enlightenment; Englishmen as well as continental Europeans had read their Raynal. Sceptical historians have gone to considerable lengths to demonstrate that the British reformers had an easier time than they might have expected because the development of capitalist society was on their side.[32] This, though, hardly says enough to dispose of their unique contribution; it may even be thought to increase their entitlement to admiration on grounds of their tactical acumen in choosing a good moment and the right arguments. Nor does it dispose of the fact that western civilisation abolished slavery of its own accord and no other civilisation ever did so.

What is more, it sometimes did so at great cost. A huge and bloody war was fought by Americans about what should happen to slavery, before it was abolished in the United States as a result. Moreover, it was western countries which in the end imposed abolition of the slave trade on everybody else (though without complete success in some Islamic lands which long remained fairly impervious to this change and are not now accessible to pressures effective a century ago). Western discussion of slavery even at the height of the trade showed the self-critical power of western culture and its ability to generate correctives for its own excesses. The evangelical conscience, of which Wilberforce is the most familiar example, was only one of them, and they have not ceased to operate. The British and Foreign Anti-Slavery Society founded in 1839 has as its modern descendant the Anti-Slavery Society for the Protection of Human Rights.

As time went by, people have turned their attention to other unhappy — and sometimes unintentional — consequences of western dominance, some now past the point of reversibility. Only recently has there been much concern over environmental exploitation though it is neither new nor confined to the western era (across the centuries 670 *million* acres of woodland were cleared in southern China as Chinese migrated south, with disastrous results[33]). But more recent events have been more noticed. The whales of the south Atlantic were devastated within decades of Cook's reports of their numbers. Even by the beginning of the nineteenth century the seals and otters of the north-western Pacific coasts of America were virtually exterminated. The much-esteemed sandalwood of Hawaii and Fiji was exhausted by 1830. Now (some say) the great Brazilian rain forests are threatened and, through them, the atmosphere itself — the list can be made to go on and on. Social changes, too, have rapidly and uncontrollably followed almost casual economic innovation. In British India, the extension of a more effective system of public law and order in the nineteenth century made money-lending much safer — and one result was by 1900 a disproportionate growth in the numbers of the caste of money-lenders and peasant indebtedness. Then there was the impact of diseases carried by Europeans to other parts of the world. A catastrophic drop in population followed the Spanish occupation of the Caribbean islands; the North American Indian peoples were devastated by smallpox, measles, alcoholism; death-rates in small Melanesian and Polynesian communities shot up after the arrival of European ships carrying influenza and venereal disease. About this process, though, there is nothing that is intrinsically one-way. Malaria seems to have come to Europe from West Africa early in the Christian era, and China has always been a great reservoir of plague, transmitted time and time again to Europe, by way of the Middle East, in huge epidemics of which the Black Death is only the most notorious. And, by way of a balancing item, the medicine and biology of western science have driven back diseases formerly endemic — though this can produce new problems too.

Ambiguities also hang over the introduction of new crops and beasts and their effects in the non-western world. There was nothing new in principle about such changes; Europeans were only the latest of many middlemen. Asia's bananas, yams and taro were first brought to Africa via Madagascar, where Indonesians had planted them. Java learnt from the Yemen how to cultivate coffee; Muslims brought oranges and lemons to Europe. What the modern era changed was the scale and rapidity of such transfers, and the increase in both was a result of western manipulation of the natural order. Maize, sweet potatoes, ground nuts were taken to China, vines to Madeira, the Americas, Africa and Australia by Europeans; cassava went to West Africa, chili, potatoes and tobacco to India. Such changes sometimes created new societies. The crucial biological event in Australia's history was not the coming of the Europeans, but that of the sheep they brought there in the 1790s, because they made New South Wales a viable region of settlement, by giving it a staple product.

Sometimes, effects took a long time to be evident, but the integration of previously local markets with a world economic system almost always had enormous effects in the short or long run. Malaysia's rubber industry would not be there had not Europeans transplanted the tree from South America. Nor would they have taken the trouble to make that experiment stick if the coming of the pneumatic tyre, and a hundred and one other outlets for the use of rubber by the industrial nations, had not vastly increased demand for the raw material. So grew the rubber estates of Malaya, with great, sometimes disruptive consequences for the people who lived there. Rubber brought them new and different jobs, new relationships in their villages as a result of changes in relative wealth, the creation of new supervisory and managerial roles and greater rewards for some than for others. Rubber also brought a new dependence on the ups and downs of international demand for the crop whose tending and harvesting earn the wages of the native labour. Eventually, it even helped to give a new strategic significance to the Malayan peninsula, which became another bone to be worried over in international relations.

Sometimes the imperial impact was, in particular ways, clearly negative.

Free markets were actually restricted by the imposition of colonial rule in some parts of Africa. European goods displaced the traditional wares of local craftsmen.[34] Some artisan and small-scale Indian textile producers suffered grievously from Lancashire's competition — a fact we might remember more often, perhaps, given the rumpus now sometimes heard over cheap foreign imports to this country, though it has long been made much of (and even exaggerated) by some Indian nationalists.[35] Western imports had to be paid for, moreover. Ineluctably, many parts of the world were drawn into the conversion of their economies to the growing of major cash crops. In Africa, certain colonies came to specialise in the large-scale production of cocoa, ground-nuts, palm oil, timber. Thus they were sucked into the cycles of world commodity markets and the ups and downs of an economy whose rhythms were generated far away. Human relations became more and more monetised and this brought benefits and costs which were unequally shared. Such effects and ramifications are numberless. They appear as a result of virtually every new economic activity encouraged in other societies by the industrial nations — and, indeed, as a result of the need in colonies to meet new fiscal demands. In tropical Africa, some would migrate from French to British areas in order to earn money to pay taxes at home.

Even in an earlier age of plunder, the western impact on the rest of the world had never been simple, nor had western imperialism ever been without its troubled consciences. From Las Casas' misgivings over the treatment of the American aborigines, through the abbé Raynal's denunciations of colonial rule, through the charges levelled at Warren Hastings and the distrust of the 'nabobs' who made fortunes in India and the outcry over the cruelties of the Congo rubber plantations under Leopold — through century after century, criticism continued. By our own day, it was very loud indeed. If it seems nonetheless overdue, it should be recalled how recent was the acceptance in Europe itself of the general idea that government should seek the good of the governed — which is the idea of trusteeship, when applied to colonies. It only became conventional throughout most of Europe itself in the nineteenth century. No other imperial civilisation has ever taken it for granted. Imperial rule might often express itself in outright brutality, but that was never the whole story. Self-criticism could be built into policy, too; a difference between Afrikaaner and British notions of what was due to the black African lay at the root of the bitter story of the Anglo-Boer wars, as well as the brutal facts of strategy and commerce. The climax of self-scrutiny may have come in our own day, but many Europeans denounced imperialism long before it became part of radical chic to do so.

Western aggrandisement was no simple, straightforward process of alien imposition, but a complex, ambiguous set of forces, some counteracting and qualifying the effects of others. Everything turned on who was 'westernising' whom.[36] Whatever the qualifications, of course, if you were at the receiving end you would no doubt have found it very hard to appreciate nice distinctions. 'In the physiology of colonialism it is results not motives that matter,' it has been well said.[37] Always, some submitted to the processes at work, some resisted. Many, had we their testimony, would no doubt have endorsed what was said in 1911, by a Nyasalander, Charles Domingo, who summed things up well in language all the more poignant because it was not his own:

> the three combined bodies — Missionaries, Government and Companies or gainers of money — do form the same rule to look upon the native with mockery eyes. It sometimes startles us to see that the three combined bodies are from Europe, and along with them is a title Christendom ... If we had power enough to communicate ourselves to Europe, we would advise them not to call themselves Christendom, but Europeandom ... The life of the three combined bodies is altogether too cheaty, too thefty, too mockery.[38]

XI
RESPONSES AND
REPERCUSSIONS

Europeans easily forgot, or perhaps never really knew, how vastly those who underwent their impact differed among themselves. Behind the simple and disparaging labels ('Moors', 'natives', 'niggers', *indigènes*) were hundreds of particular cultures. The cultural 'mix' which was the final product of the encounters of the rest of the world with the West never had a typical nature, flavour or strength. It could vary much within the same zone of civilisation. 'Islam' is an abstraction; it masks different realities in Arabia, Malaysia, Africa and China. Sunnite Turkey and Shi'ite Iran responded differently to western influences (and the differences are still making themselves felt today). In every non-western colony, too, there were competitions and struggles for status in the eye of the western ruler, for the patronage he could bestow, for the *douceurs* with which he could reward allies. There was bound to be a huge diversity of outcome, even had there been one monolithic 'western' culture imposing itself — and there was not. This diversity of response to the West is most obvious in Asia; unlike Africa or Australia, it was the home of great and ancient civilisations. That meant very different, sometimes creative, responses to the western challenges. China is the outstanding example.

At the beginning of the nineteenth century the historical weight and prestige of Chinese civilisation was enormous. For centuries there had never been a centre of civilised power sufficiently within range to challenge its supremacy. For nearly two thousand years, safe behind the mountains and rain forests of the south and the deserts and the Great Wall in the north, a Chinese empire had ruled the Chinese peoples and exercised sway and prestige beyond — sometimes far beyond — those borders. For a shorter time — but for centuries, all the same — the élites running that empire had, thanks to a remarkable system of selection by examination, been indoctrinated in the same values and habits of mind, those of Confucianism. For all the diversity of ethnic origins, religions, landscape, and spoken language within her boundaries, China was unique, a successful and splendid civilisation virtually coterminous with a great empire, a cultural entity rooted in intensive agriculture, tightly-organised family life and a bureaucratic administration drawn mainly from its gentry class.[1]

In 1800 China was ruled by an emperor of the Ch'ing dynasty whose ancestors had been set on the throne by barbarian newcomers in the seventeenth century. They came from the north beyond the Wall, from Manchuria — aptly, then as today, a major source of the ginseng root eagerly sought by elderly Chinese of flagging powers. Internal weakness had often exposed the empire to invasion; that was how the Mongol dynasty had come to be ruling China when Marco Polo paid his famous visits. But even when barbarians crossed the Wall and overthrew a dynasty (as they very occasionally did), they had always succumbed in the end to the cultural superiority of the Chinese. The immense prestige and spectacular achievements of Chinese civilisation awed them. Like the Germanic peoples who inherited the European lands of the old Roman empire, they gave way to what they had overrun; they became civilised. They might found new barbarian dynasties, but those dynasties soon began to reign, like their predecessors, within the framework of Confucian ideas. The Manchu kingdom was already in fact Confucian and semi-sinicised before one of their leaders openly attacked Ming China in 1618. The Ch'ing were to be the last emperors of barbarian origins to rule China and, indeed, China's last imperial dynasty at all, but in 1800 that could not have been known, any more than it could have been known that they were about to face the worst and last barbarian challenge that China ever confronted, and that their empire would not survive it.

Even at the beginning of the nineteenth century the Ch'ing already had their troubles. Famines and floods, peasant rebellion and a century-long inflation were some of the main causes and symptoms. In themselves they might have been manageable.[2] But they had to be tackled with the traditional means just as Europeans were beginning to press harder for freedoms inside the empire which would weaken it still further. The first Portuguese galleons had arrived in 1514. Since then, Europeans had been trading with China for nearly three centuries. Macao (still held by the Portuguese today) was after 1557 the gateway to the north Chinese trade through the great city of Canton, from which the Portuguese had soon been expelled. There, year after year, Europeans (mainly British) busily bought Chinese goods for European and Asian markets and sold goods from other parts of Asia to the Chinese. Tea, porcelain, silks were all coveted in the West where, in the eighteenth century, there was for a time a craze for Chinese designs of which we are reminded by objects as different as the pagoda at Kew, Chippendale chairs and the tile-lined Chinese rooms of many European palaces. There was also a Russian-China trade overland, but this was concentrated at Kyakhta and Curhaitu. The imperial government was content to tolerate these controlled channels of foreign trade, regulated and understood as a system of 'tribute'.

There was one snag to the Canton trade. Chinese goods had to be paid for in silver. There were no European products which the Chinese really desired, none they needed. They were even somewhat contemptuous of what was offered to them, though they had liked the scientific instruments and technical skill which Jesuit missionaries brought with them to China in the seventeenth century. Nevertheless, the conscious superiority of Chinese civilisation came out commercially in a lack of demand for European goods. So China had to be paid with bullion. That, for a long time, was where much of the silver of the Americas went (and partly explains why the Mexican dollar was for a long time current coin in China). This situation only changed early in the nineteenth century, with the discovery by the West of something the Chinese wanted and their government did not wish them to have: opium.

Opium could be grown easily in India. The British East India Company seized upon it with relief as a product to sell to the Chinese. Demand soared as the supply became more plentiful. Disastrous effects followed. In the Chinese coastal provinces millions were estimated to be addicted. China's balance of trade with England, hitherto favourable, swung into deficit; silver flowed out of the country with disastrous effects on the taxes assessed in it as inflation was suddenly reversed. The imperial government prohibited and tried to prevent the trade, but the British and American pushers were adamant. They were skilled in their handling of public opinion; the English press presented them not merely as seekers after profit, but as the bearers of a civilisation (as they indeed were). For some time, British governments had been trying to get other ports opened in China as ways in to what they believed were great potential markets for manufactures. The right to trade became a moral question, an issue in a dispute between two cultures. There may not now seem to have been much to respect in the self-interest of the merchants who wanted to push the drug into China, but it was of vital importance that the general sense of being in the right, of being on the side of Progress and History, of striving to break down barbarism, was available to ease the consciences of their supporters at home. Furthermore, the government of India itself had a secondary interest in the trade, for the opium tax became a major source of its revenue, amounting in the early 1830s to more than a tenth of the total.

When a Chinese official seized and destroyed some smuggled cargoes of opium at Canton, British arrogance and precipitateness led to the declaration by the Chinese government of the first of what have been called the 'Opium Wars' — among the most squalid episodes in the history of western imperialism, which contains a good many. The war of 1840–2 marks for today's Chinese orthodoxy 'the beginning of modern Chinese history',[3] but the British won it, and that was a nasty shock to the prestige of the Manchu regime, though not yet to its self-confidence. Defeat in itself was in any case less damaging than what followed. Permission to import opium was only a part of what the Chinese government had to concede. Within a few years a number of western powers imposed treaties on the Chinese which gave them privileged access to the imperial territory. France and the United States quickly followed the British lead. Diplomatic and commercial rivalry always gave any imperialist intervention in the nineteenth century a multiplier effect, and the British, dogmatically sure of the merits of Free Trade, did not try to prevent rivals following them. Within twenty years or so, the Chinese had to allow the establishment of foreign settlements and courts on Chinese soil, the rights of foreigners to own property and to preach Christianity, and had opened many more ports to trade (by the end of the century there were to be about ninety such). From these 'unequal' treaties (as they were to be called) grew eighty years of western interference and corrosion of Chinese ways by western ideas and institutions. Two civilisations were suddenly in competition within China itself.

At first, the Chinese government did not even show much concern over what had happened. The Treaty Port system was at first only seen as an extension of existing practice such as tolerated the Portuguese presence at Macao. Yet it was soon to be demonstrated that a clash of civilisations was being carried forward to new stages of intensity and in many forms; it was not just a matter of the irritated exchanges of diplomacy. Changes in Chinese society were under way: one example was the growth over the twenty or thirty years which followed the Treaty of Nanking with the British of a Sino-foreign trading community deeply committed to the maintenance of good commercial relations with Europe and the United States. Another was the expansion of Christian China, which had especially corrosive implications for the Manchu empire. Even in the seventeeth century, when Jesuits had enjoyed considerable influence and prestige at the imperial court, the conversion of members of the Chinese ruling class had never prospered, though some Jesuits had strongly advised that clergy should be sought among the gentry and literate. One Jesuit father drew telling parallels with the church in the Roman empire where it had first ordained indigenous priests; the appearance of a Chinese Constantine would follow, he was sure.[4] Then, in 1724, conversion had been forbidden and two savage persecutions in the 1740s and 1780s reduced the European missionary effort in China: there were only thirty-five European priests in China in 1810.[5] After the lifting of the prohibition in 1841, though, Christian missionaries began to act more vigorously and on a quite new scale. At first still mainly Catholic and few, but later Protestant and many, they soon awoke hostility among the Chinese Confucian gentry by their success in making converts among the poor and ignorant. This was subversive of China's social order, disrupting as it did traditional notions of duty, property, and filial obligation. The Protestants, most of them from the United States and Great Britain, were especially blatant in challenging the traditional order of Chinese society, bringing with them as they often did their families and more of the material culture of the West, and numbering in their ranks a growing cohort of women.[6]

Attacks on missionaries became more frequent as the century went on. Superstitious distrust among the populace, who believed tales about Christian cannibalism (the 'rescue' of Chinese orphans and abandoned children encouraged this slander), was exploited by the Chinese gentry and officials. But the mobbing, or even the murder, of missionaries was bad for Chinese government; it was likely to provoke threats by western governments, demands for retribution, and sometimes even punitive action. Whatever happened, the authority of the imperial Chinese government among its subjects was likely to be visibly damaged. So it was, too, when Chinese Christian converts — or nominal Christians — took shelter with the missionaries on their property and defied, from sanctuary, the police of the empire. Some of them were merely criminals (as were some of those who similarly established themselves within the comparative safety of the foreign Concessions in the Treaty Ports).[7]

One very visible record of the mutual incomprehension of China and the West can still be seen just outside Peking, where a complex of residences had been built by and added to by emperor after emperor across the centuries as a refuge from the July and August heat of the capital. These residences were what is still generally known as the 'Summer Palace'. The Mongol emperors had been the first to build them and their successors went on adding to their buildings. Some put up in the eighteenth century were even in a European style: the fragments that are all that is now left of them are one of the earlier visible effects of the West on China, a passing taste of the eighteenth-century imperial court, which led one emperor to ask some of the Jesuits to design and build him baroque palaces like those of Europe. They did, and we know what the result looked like because we also have some engravings of this cultural transfer from the West to Asia.

The Baroque fashion in China did not go deep. It did not spread so broadly through society as did the contemporary European craze for chinoiserie. But the palaces which reflected it remained like their predecessors, monuments to the emperors' pleasures until, in 1860, they and several others were destroyed. Their destroyers, like their architects, were Europeans — to be precise, British soldiers under the command of a British envoy, Lord Elgin, who had been sent to China to make the Chinese comply properly with a treaty they had signed two years before. His order to his soldiers to burn the Summer Palace (they and their French comrades-in-arms had already looted it), was by no means a simple act of vandalism. Elgin had no desire for aimless destruction. What lay behind his order was the murder by Chinese officials of some European hostages. Some of them, it appeared, had been killed at the express command of the emperor. So, the emperor's own property was deliberately chosen for reprisal. The destruction of the palace was to demonstrate the implacability and power of western justice. All Chinese, it was thought, would see that even the emperor himself would not escape punishment if he had done wrong.

Today, the murder of the hostages and the burning of the Summer Palace seems only a supreme expression of the gulf of non-comprehension which lay between China and the West. Chinese civilisation had remained immensely self-assured and self-confident even amid mounting troubles. The men who ruled it and constituted its cultural élite saw for a long time what was happening as only an accidental and temporary disturbance of the way the world usually ran. In the end, they were sure, things would settle down again as they had always done in the past. Behind this lay centuries of conviction of the superiority, and therefore the authority, of Chinese civilisation over all mankind. It was an outlook formed by the long, astonishingly successful continuity of China's institutions and the myth of social and cultural homogeneity taken for granted by the ruling élite. China's political norms were grounded in the belief that the rule of the emperor, the 'Son of Heaven', was a universal rule of virtue, in which the performance of duty took precedence over material interest. Its claims on the respect of mankind were — thought the Chinese — as self-evident as the claims to obedience and deference of the Confucian head of the family or household. Here lay the roots of the Chinese response to the non-Chinese world and therefore of the Chinese attitude to what we should call 'foreign affairs'. Interestingly, the empire did not have a ministry to deal with them; from the Chinese point of view, there were no independent foreign nations, but only non-Chinese peoples in greater or lesser degrees of dependence on the emperor. All people were seen as in some degree subject to the Son of Heaven and from Peking the world could best be visualised as a series of concentric circles. China and its people lay at their centre, the 'Middle' or 'Centre' Kingdom, directly subject to the imperial rule. Round them lay zones in which direct Chinese influence gradually faded away as you moved outwards. Nonetheless, all the peoples in those zones, too, owed respect to the imperial throne and might be expected, at appropriate times, to show this by bringing tribute. There was a long tradition of successful management, containment, reduction and finally absorption of barbarians which makes the absence of concern over external relations easy to understand.

Since Han times, the Chinese had seen the world in this Sinocentric way. To symbolise it, foreigners were expected to go through certain ritual forms.

One which was very important was the kowtow, or formal obeisance. The Dutch had made no difficulty over this in the eighteenth century. The Chinese therefore found it hard to see what prevented later western emissaries (such as Lord Macartney, the emissary of George III of England, on whose behalf he led a mission to China in 1793) from behaving in the same civilised way. In the nineteenth century, Europeans and Americans were as shocked by the suggestion that they should perform the kowtow as had been ancient Greeks who saw subjects of the great Persian emperor prostrate themselves before him. But, for all their confidence, the Chinese did not really know very much about most of the world outside China and were not likely to understand this. In 1800 the Court of Colonial Affairs which had responsibility for Tibet was not aware that the western visitors active to the south of that country were employed by the same East India Company whose ships came to Canton. And even when better information was available, it affected attitudes only very slowly. In 1860 the old world view persisted among most educated Chinese.

It could hardly have been more violently irreconcilable with the world view of the nineteenth-century western barbarians. Even in these enlightened days, a government based on virtue is not a concept which easily awakes a response among their descendants. Those in western countries who thought at all about such things tended to be sure that their own civilisation was far superior to that of China. They believed they were on the side of the angels — or of progress — and that they had a duty, not merely an interest, to propagate that message. Of course, plenty of them wanted rapid material reward, too. But that is far from being a satisfactory explanation of nearly a century of conflict. Elgin was not seeking to colonise China or bring it under the Union Jack. What he (and those who thought like him) wanted was to make China take its proper place in the world — and that meant coming within the ambit of western civilisation and accepting its assumptions. China should behave as a nation-state among others, an equal among equals, should recognise the rule of law and extend it to the protection of individual rights, instead of seeing law primarily as an instrument for the imposition of order and subordinate to the principles of moral conduct,[8] and it should also allow the spread of Christianity, the only true religion. And, of course, many in the western world believed that they were justified in resorting to force when the Chinese did not conform to such a programme.

This was both asking much too much, and asking it much too fast. Each side thought of the other as 'barbarian'. The West had power — though it was not limitless — but some Chinese long thought that western technical tricks could be learnt and its guns and steam ships bought and hired without any changes being needed in the far superior Chinese ways. 'Self-strengthening' was a phrase which began to be heard in the 1860s. Wealth and power, some began to argue, were not incompatible with the Confucian ideal of the state as the guardian and expression of morality.[9] The first contingent of Chinese students to go abroad for study left for North America in 1872. A need for new policies was not adequately met, though, by such a self-flattering approach. Broadly speaking, for the rest of the empire's history — and it lasted until 1911, when military revolution led at last to the inauguration of a Chinese Republic, even if that was not to prove the transformation it was sometimes imagined to be[10] — the story of Chinese government is one of conservative responses to the West only occasionally and briefly influenced by the realisation that China might have to make more radical changes if she was to resist the West successfully. Even the Chinese who saw this often recognised that this might cost too much in the eyes of their countrymen. It would, in fact, have meant moral surrender to the West, an admission of its superiority. And the rulers of China were not for a long time ready for that.

The difficulties of discerning China's true interests at a moment when the world was changing more rapidly than ever before can be seen in the empire's confrontation with one of the most serious internal threats ever posed to it, the 'Taiping rebellion'. This colossal upheaval, potentially a revolution, lasted fifteen years. It cost more lives than did the First World War. It started with peasant revolts against hunger, taxes and the Manchu, all familiar causes of disturbance,[11] but its leader, a young man called Hung Hsiu-ch'uan, who had failed in the imperial examinations for admission to the civil service, added something else to popular rebellion. From American Protestant missionaries he had picked up a smattering of Christian ideas. Inspired by them, he denounced idolatry, the Confucian tradition of worship given to ancestors, and talked of establishing an egalitarian kingdom of God on earth. From 1850 the Taiping army which he led threatened to revolutionise China on this basis. By the mid-1850s, Hung was established at Nanking at the head of a new court as 'Heavenly King'. Taiping social arrangements seem to have awoken welcoming responses among the masses; in theory at least, there was no private property, and general provision was to be made for communal needs. More startlingly still, the Taipings prohibited the binding of women's feet, extended social and educational equality to women and advocated a high degree of austerity in sexual relations — though the conduct of the Heavenly King himself perhaps paid less than full respect to this side of his teaching.

Foreign governments were for some time not quite sure what to make of the Taipings. The success of the movement, though, drove the imperial government at Peking into more concessions to the western powers; distracted by rebellion, it could resist them much less easily. One result was that the Russian government was able to exact greater territorial concessions from China than any other western power was ever to do.[12] Perhaps it is not surprising, too, that in 1861, overwhelmed by difficulties, the imperial government decided for the first time to set up a specialist department of foreign affairs. The old myth that all the world recognised the Mandate of Heaven was dead.

In the end, the West came round to helping Peking against its rebels. With western firearms and under the leadership of 'Chinese Gordon', an 'ever-victorious army' mastered Taiping bows and arrows. Cynics might find European help understandable; after all, the Taipings were against opium. There were signs, though, that the Taiping movement was failing internally even before its leader died in 1864. From Peking it looked as if, once more, traditional ways had prevailed; the defeat of rebellion was celebrated by scholars as a Ch'ing 'restoration'.[13] The bureaucratic ruling class of China had survived one more challenge from below.

That may have prolonged conservative resistance to self-adaptation, but the western ideas embedded (and distorted) in the Taiping movement were a warning portent; they had awoken responses among many Chinese. In any case, after this success the empire continued to drift from weakness to weakness. A society and polity which had for centuries been immensely successful was slowly crumbling. It is hard to believe it could have been otherwise, given the firmly-set Confucian traditions whose absorption and internalisation was so important in the formation of the official class. Nonetheless, two other oriental monarchies, Japan, and to a more qualified extent, Siam, succeeded in avoiding this fate. What is more, China in the past had shown huge powers of resistance, recovery and absorption. Buddhism and Islam had been swallowed without compromising the empire. And efforts were made: arsenals and shipyards were built, and more students were sent abroad. China's fate must surely be more than just an awful warning of what happens to a society which allows itself to be run by humane and well-educated civil servants. Some have blamed the influence of the dowager empress Tzu Hsi who dominated the court and was the real power behind the throne in the last decades of the nineteenth century, but that is not a sufficient explanation; her own priorities may have been expressed in spending money on new summer palaces instead of on a modern navy, but that was not all that stood in the way of real change and adaptive reform. China had to do much more than merely buy steamships and cannon if she was to survive the western challenge.

To many of her rulers, the real extent of China's danger probably only began to become apparent in the 1890s. In 1894 a war broke out with Japan over rivalries long-smouldering in Korea, nominally a Chinese dependency. China was soundly defeated, and not at the hands of the West, but at the hands of an Asian state armed and operating in western ways. The failure of 'self-strengthening' was patent. A ferocious dictated peace was imposed.[14] It was set aside only at a cost of further humiliation when Russia, Germany and France, fearing Japan's new vigour, made her accept less than she had originally exacted from the Chinese. This was something of a milestone in Japan's growing disillusionment with the West; after applying the western rules of the game — by bullying the Chinese — they were being told that these would not be allowed to work in their favour, but only in that of the European. And the protectors claimed their price from China in a spate of new concessions and leases. The Manchu empire seemed doomed; like the Ottoman in Europe, China was the Sick Man of Asia.

For a moment, though, it seemed that humiliation might stimulate a real change in China. A 'Reform Movement' came to a climax in the 'Hundred Days' of 1898, when a torrent of edicts set in hand changes in almost every aspect of government and administration. The shock of the Japanese victory had stimulated a fierce and radical wave of self-scrutiny among some Chinese intellectuals, and was the catalyst which led one of them to assert that the real secret of western wealth and power was to be sought not in technology but in ideas and values.[15] China had not merely to acquire the impedimenta of western power, but something of the energy which drove western civilisation irresistibly forward. They sought keys to understanding that energy in western texts, overwhelmingly those of enlightened, liberal, industrial, scientific Europe — Montesquieu, Mill, Huxley, Spencer. Some of them also began to advocate reforms of institutions which connoted backwardness in western eyes.

Yet conservatism remained in the saddle at Peking, a *coup d'état* restoring power to the dowager empress. She and some of her advisers were ready to encourage and use long-apparent popular reaction against the 'hairy barbarians' and their Christian convert protégés. This was the essence of the so-called 'Boxer' movement, a wave of attacks on Chinese Christians and western missionaries (30,000 of the former and over 200 of the latter perished) which, in the end, culminated in a dramatic siege of the European legation at Peking,[16] a declaration of war by the Chinese government on all foreigners, and the dispatch of an international army (which, significantly, included a Japanese contingent) to lift the siege. A heavy fine was then imposed upon the Chinese government and, it seemed, western domination of the empire was even more firmly assured by foreign garrisons in the legation quarter at Peking and along the lines of communication between there and the sea. Popular reaction had proved a dead end, and an expensive one. The compromised independence of China was more and more harshly apparent. Forms were still observed and after the Boxer episode the emperor still ruled in Peking. But the reality of that rule was sadly narrowed by comparison with the glorious days of the past.

China was one special case. The Indian sub-continent was another. It had been the seat of flourishing civilisations and complex religions. 'There is not and never was an India', said one British civil servant, 'possessing . . . any sort of unity, physical, political, social or religious.' So the West never had a single impact on India; it was always a case of many impacts on many Indias. Starkly contrasted geographical regions, a multitude of languages,[17] deeply antithetical religions gave shape to communities tightly bound together in differing and exclusive systems of customs and manners. There are still many Indians who believe that even the shadow of a fellow human being of a different caste can pollute their food. Abysses of poverty and fabulous wealth exist side by side and have long done so. We have to ask specific questions about what happened to communities and races — Pathans, Tamils, Bengalis — to different occupations — artisans, traders, soldiers — or in different places — Darjeeling, Goa, Calcutta. A gulf greater than any imaginable in European society separated the Parsi baronet, say, from the Sikh warrior. Until the late British era, the sub-continent never had a governing or cultural élite united by literacy in one language and a universally understood calligraphy such as that of China. Literature and art in India reflect layer upon layer of cultural influence from the outside, from China, Persia, Central Asia, the Arab world and, finally, the West.

This diversity was more continuously exposed to European influences than any part of Asia further east, and most of it finished by being ruled by the British Crown for a century. The British succeeded in squeezing out all except tiny enclaves of other Europeans. British India became the biggest single agglomeration of peoples ever ruled by a European state, as well as the only framework which ever — albeit briefly — held virtually all the peoples of the sub-continent together in one political matrix. At its height, the British Raj was a splendid spectacle, its majesty caught in the Coronation Durbar of 1911, when King George V received, together with his queen, the homage of India and her princes. The ceremony was a magnificent blend of East and West — crowns and monarchical robes from medieval Europe, and little Indian princes clustered as pages round the throne as they would have done about the feet of a Mogul emperor. It was a conscious use of imperial mythology and symbolism for purposes of government, like a medieval English king's solemn crown-wearing. The landaus of the royal procession and the sovereign's escort of lifeguards, no doubt sweating in buckskins and breastplates, even though it was December, were from Europe; around them were thousands of Indian sepoys, turbaned and putteed. Yet they, too, swaggered through their British-taught arms drill, slapping the stocks of their rifles as they came up to the 'present', the outcome of a long evolution of European military ceremonial.

Even at its height, though, the reality of imperial power, so much to be execrated by Indian patriots and so much idealised by British policy-makers, was very different from its appearance. It depended greatly on local conditions, local agencies, local allies. It had always to seek effective political support in the Indian communities; the British never sustained their rule by arms alone. Nor could they easily change things. The foundations of the tax system, for example, lay in the land revenue inherited from the Mogul government which the British continued to depend on, largely because they had to. You cannot do much to tax income or services in any economy which depends so little on money as did India until this century, where wealth that was not invested in land was held in jewellery or bullion, trade was still mainly local and most agriculture provided only for subsistence. No more than their predecessors, did the British have the machinery and personnel to investigate and measure other fiscal possibilities. So, like the Mogul emperors, they taxed land: it was the easiest thing to get at.

Yet to do that was not just to keep things as they were. One great paradox of imperialism is that even decisions to preserve bring change. Taxing land required the identification of those who in return for payment of revenue were recognised as the rightful occupants of the land, whether they were individuals or groups. But a 'settlement', as such a distribution of rights was called, meant altering the distribution of power in local society.[18] It meant choices among competitors. It meant, too, a blurring of institutions: the British idea of legal rights in land, going back through the centuries to roots in common and Roman law, had somehow to be brought into play in a society where no such idea existed. This was a fruitful source of unexpected consequences.

So was the rich and changing fund of ideas upon which British administrators drew. At the beginning of the nineteenth century, they usually were what we might call Whig ideas: let government do as little as possible, securing only the order necessary to protect persons and property, and social and individual well-being would follow as the day the night. In Bengal, for instance, the centre of British power from the later eighteenth century, they looked round, like good Whigs, for local men of property and substance — a gentry class, as it were — and 'settled' the land tax accordingly. British officials always tended to believe that if you gave a man a title to land which could not be questioned and assured him of a limited tax burden, he would be encouraged to improve his estate; that is, to behave like an English capitalist landlord. So, according to the economic ideas of the age, as the tax burden was intended to remain constant, there would follow falling costs, higher production, more capital for investment and all the benefits of the market economy according to Adam Smith. Yet things did not turn out like this. Bengal was Bengal, not East Anglia. Those who had been cast for the role of improving landlords turned out instead to be speculators in revenue-paying rights. In the south, the British took a different tack. In Madras they tried a tax settlement which interfered as little as possible with Indian society, and did not seek to force 'improvement' upon it, but emphasised the small landowner as a source of stability. The peasant ideal appealed also to the administrative ideologists who came to India from the Company's college at Haileybury, where the doctrines of utilitarianism were taught. Economic ideas evolved in the West with reference to western data and observations were thus released upon Indian society. Yet the result was not an enlightened absolutism rooted in doctrinaire and abstract ideas and steadily transforming India on standardised lines. The Raj was no more able to bring about an agrarian transformation of India than has been independent India, possessed of infinitely superior resources of experience, economic ideas, planning skills, and techniques of government. Local conditions almost always made nonsense of abstract theory.

'Utilitarianism' had its paradoxes, too. Its aim was happiness, but in India, that had to be sought through the state machine: a curious conclusion for many who saw utilitarian principles in England as essentially conducive to the reduction of the power of the state, though not one which would have startled eighteenth-century believers in 'enlightened despotism'. Improvement could be advanced through authority. So could salvation, thought many evangelicals: another paradox, given their Protestant origins. They often took the view that obstacles to salvation through Christ — pagan practice, idolatry, vicious social and personal habits — could be removed by state authority and should be. So, in spite of tensions, utilitarian and evangelical courses tended to converge. Both knew what was best for India and believed it could be advanced through the use of state power.

Some administrators applied their ideas crudely and simply; some managed to do so more moderately and humanely. One of the most striking of all records of British rule in India is an inscription on the base of a statue in Calcutta which now stands in the gardens of the Victoria Monument, a resting-place for several such proconsular relics. It reads, in the original layout of the lines:

To
William Cavendish Bentinck,
Who, during seven years, ruled India with eminent
Prudence, Integrity and Benevolence;
Who, placed at the head of a great
Empire, never laid aside
The simplicity and moderation of a private citizen:
Who infused into Oriental despotism the spirit of
British Freedom:
Who never forgot that the end of Government is

The Happiness of the Governed:
Who abolished cruel rites:
Who effaced humiliating distinctions:
Who gave liberty to the expression of public opinion:
Whose constant study it was, to elevate the intellectual
And moral character of
The Nation committed to his charge:
This Monument
Was erected by men,
Who, differing in Race, in
Manners, in Language, and in Religion
Cherish, with equal veneration and gratitude,
The memory of his wise, upright, and Paternal Administration.

That now seems somewhat grandiose. Such inscriptions are not to the twentieth-century taste. Nonetheless, as a catalogue of what an enlightened Englishman of the day could admire as imperial goals, Bentinck's monument is worth reflexion. It also shows the gap between the aspirations the seemingly despotic powers of Indian government could excite and what it could actually do.

Bentinck had been in India first as a young man, but his statue commemorates his service there from 1828 to 1835 as governor-general of Bengal and then as first governor-general, from 1834, of India. It has been said of him that he was the first British statesman to govern India to whom the interests of Indians were paramount. Though, by and large, he failed, he made determined efforts to advance Indians to levels of authority in the administration from which they had previously been excluded. He wanted Indians to sit on his legislative Council (though he did not get that either) and succeeded in suppressing the practice of *sutte* — the burning of Hindu widows — a greater interference with Indian custom than anything attempted by his predecessors.[19] Revealingly, he justified this by claiming it would be a step towards the improvement of the future lot of the Hindu peoples, by the 'establishment of a purer morality'. 'When they shall have been convinced of the error of this first and most capital of their customs', he wrote 'may it not be hoped that others which stand in the way of their improvement may likewise pass away, and that, thus emancipated from those chains and shackles upon their minds, they may no longer continue, as they have done, the slaves of every foreign conqueror, but that they may assume the first places among the great families of mankind?'[20] The way to nationality, evidently, was to lie through reform on European lines, such as was in the air in England, too, during the 1830s.

Bentinck's limited successes, vigorous and perceptive as he was, help to show that the achievements of reformers and conservatives in India do not now always seem very different. Perhaps that is most clearly shown in the educational efforts from which so many Englishmen hoped so much. The first allocation of public funds for Indian education in 1813 was trivial in amount but it had crystallised a debate on a pedagogic principle: should Indians be taught in the language and about the culture of England, or in the vernaculars about the cultures of India? 'Orientalisers' contested the issue with 'Anglicists'. In 1800, a governor-general had founded Fort William College at Calcutta, in which instruction was given in Urdu, and the writing of Urdu prose encouraged. Another governor-general helped to found Hindu College at Benares in 1816. Such developments fitted the view that Persian or Sanskrit should be the Latin and Greek of the Indian intelligentsia. Yet this was by no means what many Indians wanted. When the Company agreed, in 1823, to set up a college to teach traditional Indian studies, it was Bengalis who urged that European science and the English language should be taught there.[21] Englishmen who agreed with them believed that to encourage the traditional learning of India was 'to perpetuate the degradation and misery of the people'. The man who said that also argued that 'our duty is not to teach, but to unteach them — not to rivet the shackles which have for ages bound down the minds of our subjects, but to allow them to drop off by the lapse of time and the progress of events.'[22] It was a point of view well expressed, too, by the first general history of India available to the British public, published in 1818, that by James Mill, the utilitarian philosopher who largely owed to it his appointment to the India Office in London of which he became the head. He had never been to India, but had no doubts about the justification for the contempt he expressed in his book both towards Hindus and Muslims.

The decisive moment in the debate on Indian education came in 1835, thanks to the historian Thomas Macaulay, a former member of Bentinck's council (and, incidentally, the author of the inscription on his memorial) and at that moment president of the Indian Committee of Public Instruction. It had to settle the best means of spending money voted by parliament for the promotion of literature and science in India. Macaulay wrote a minute to the Governor-General's Council which is not only one of the most famous state papers of the Raj but also one of the most brilliant, unfair and cocksure expressions of the confidence with which western men faced alien societies. The argument is essentially simple. As Macaulay put it, the central question was 'simply whether ... we shall teach languages in which, by universal confession, there are no books on any subject to be compared with our own; whether, when we can teach European science, we shall teach systems which, by universal confession, whenever they differ from those of Europe, differ for the worse; and whether, when we can patronise sound Philosophy and true History, we shall countenance, at the public expense, medical doctrines which would disgrace an English Farrier — Astronomy, which would move laughter in girls at an English boarding school — History, abounding with kings thirty feet high, and reigns thirty thousand years long, — and Geography, made up of seas of treacle and seas of butter.' Traditional Indian learning which he condemned by the standards of the culture of which he was so confident a master, was, Macaulay argued, totally unfitted to achieve what should be achieved by public educational expenditure in India, the formation of 'a class who may be interpreters between us and the millions whom we govern; a class of persons, Indians in blood and colour, but English in taste, in opinions, in morals, and in intellect'.[23]

It could not turn out like that. In the first place, not all Indians responded in the same way. Brahmins often jumped at the chance of education in the European mode. It was, after all, a way to preferment, influence and status. Conversely, Muslims tended not to seek the new learning with much enthusiasm. They held their ground in posts of responsibility so long as Persian and Urdu continued to be the language of British administration. Once English predominated, they dropped behind because of their relative slowness in taking up new educational opportunities. At the other end of the spectrum and even more strikingly, the Parsis of the Bombay Presidency, a minority of only one in 250 of its population in 1881, nevertheless filled in the same year a fifth of the Presidency's places for college students.[24] Bengal, too, was to loom large in the regional recruitment of schools and India's new universities (in the very year of the Mutiny, the first three, Madras, Calcutta and Bombay, were founded with public funds). So, educational change meant different things to different communities.

Shortage of money, in any case, meant that educational effort by government could not for a long time amount to much. Yet confidence in western education was in India, as in many other parts of the world, never to disappear. 'The fresh air of European civilisation circulates freely through every pore of this vast community' rhapsodised one young commentator thirty years after Macaulay — a comment as exaggerated as was his hope that 'a Brahmin who travels from Burdwan to Calcutta cheek by jowl with a butcher, in order to see his son go up to receive a prize at the Presidency College in company with the offspring of a sweeper, is likely to go home with some new ideas on the question of caste'.[25] Macaulay's goal of a culturally Anglicised class of 'interpreters', apparently so clear and simple an idea, somehow aborted.

Not all Englishmen, of course, believed that education for Indians was a good thing. Once British distrust of the 'native' had been aroused by the shock of the 1857 Mutiny, ignorance, fear and prejudice made educated Indians unpopular with the Anglo-Indian community (as white society was then called). They were not welcomed into posts of responsibility. The occasional sympathetic official or viceroy hardly offset this. They began to feel cheated of status and rewards to which they felt entitled. More educated persons were being produced than could be absorbed, because of distrust of the Indian intelligentsia British education had created. In the 1880s, only a dozen or so Indians entered the I.C.S. through the open examinations which were formally open to them; there were many practical and psychological obstacles in their way. Lord Salisbury, while Secretary of State for India, termed the 'literary class' of India an 'opposition in quiet times, rebels in time of trouble'. The 'Babu', or educated Bengali, became a figure of fun — or suspicion — to Englishmen in India, though Kipling (in *Kim*) drew a kindly and appreciative portrait of him. By 1900 the partnership in carrying Indians to a higher degree of civilisation which Macaulay had envisaged was further than ever from realisation.

If too much had been expected from public policy, it is understandable. Although the Raj never brought the whole sub-continent under unified administration, it was a governmental machine of awesome aspect, operating throughout India as none of its predecessors had ever done. In its origins and its nature, it for a long time powerfully impressed the imaginations of its subjects; and, like the Spanish Empire in the Americas it was, as one of its outstanding apologists put it, essentially an absolute government founded on conquest.[26] But what government could actually *do* in India was another matter. Its communications tied different regions more closely together than ever before and so suggested new ties of interest between Indians. Its educational measures created new divisions in Indian society, but mass education was beyond its means. Economic developments encouraged by its provision of law and order changed relationships between town and country, region and region, sometimes transforming for the better life over large areas. Railway-building was the one major investment of European capital in India which had official support, and on that investment India is still drawing a dividend, though a declining one. Yet a lack of means and the sheer scale of its task gave the Raj little power to act as the modernisers and would-be enlightened despots wished. Its mode of rule has been called 'subtle and conditional'.[27] This did not mean that it did not stimulate change. Its role in political development was critical. Wherever administration intervened in Indian life, it provoked political response. Even when it tried merely to play the role of honest broker, it was an irritant, whatever policy-makers intended.

The Indian army, even the sepoy himself, with his respected communal and caste distinction from others who served beside him, but his standardised European discipline and drill, vividly and long embodied the ambiguities and ironies of British India. In the blend and interplay of cultures lies the continuing fascination of Indian history. Indians and Englishmen could never get one another quite right, tied together as they were. Nowhere do the difficulties of the relationship appear more clearly than among Indian patriots who struggled to wield dissatisfactions with British rule into a national movement on western lines. Nationalism in the way it was usually seen in this century and the last, is of course historical nonsense in India. Unconsciously, or consciously, most people have in mind models of nations like Spain, France or England, where some degree of cultural or other homogeneity exists (though often it is exaggerated; we need to remember, for instance, that among European nations only Portugal and Iceland are truly monoglot). Consciously, leaders of 'new nations' have usually tried to rewrite their own history in such modes, because that seemed to be the suasive course. In fact most modern nationalisms came to birth because of the experience and resentment of a common domination by groups otherwise differentiated from one another. The state-forms evolved in the struggle to break free then led to attempts to establish a new uniformity in the name of nationalism.

Indian nationalism reflects this. As there was no Indian nation with an objective geographical, linguistic or religious foundation, let alone one covering the whole area governed by the British, All-India nationalism could rest only on conscious politics. The nationalist movement was a response to the operation of western ideas, to the consequences of western administrative decisions and technology, to the role of the Raj as a common focus of discontents for those who sought power and status, and to the experience of shared political activity. Some Indians were clear about the decisive role of the British in this.[28] Once more, though, that is not the whole story. The West contributed to Indian self-consciousness in other, more indirect, ways, too. It was Warren Hastings, greatest of eighteenth-century British rulers of Bengal, who encouraged the introduction of the first printing-press in India, and thus, in 1778, the casting of the first Bengali typeface, an interestingly symbolic act. There is even an indirect western contribution to the thought of one outstanding Indian politician: Gandhi.

He was a very unorthodox Hindu, if the label fits him at all. His pacifism and advocacy of non-violence were as much indications of his wish to change much of traditional Indian life, soaked as it is in violence, as of his wish to preserve it. Though he described himself as 'grown disillusioned with Western civilisation', his first thinking on politics was drawn from the West, he exploited national feeling as a positive force and he employed the language of western liberalism and of Christianity. 'Is this Christian-like, is this fair play, is this justice, is this civilisation?' he once asked South Africans who had passed discriminatory legislation against Indian immigrants.[29] Of course, he was far from being a nationalist as many of those who looked to his leadership understood the term and he is especially remembered for a political tactic of passive resistance which may owe something to Hindu tradition;[30] it would be misleading, therefore, to seek in his teaching for systematic political thought on western lines, but equally misleading to try to give an account of his views which left out, say, Ruskin, or the Sermon on the Mount, although he rejected western civilisation in the end and once said that 'India is being ground down not under the British heel, but that of modern civilisation.'[31]

In India, as in other Asian countries, it has usually been those consciously or unconsciously touched by western ideas who have been most effective in mobilising feeling against western government. The story goes back a long way. In the 1820s, bright young former students of the recently-founded Hindu College at Benares idolised the *philosophes,* read Paine's *Age of Reason* and scandalised the orthodox by their behaviour.[32] Ram Mohan Roy, the first ambassador of the Mogul emperor to the Court of St James, was a Bengali Brahmin who, while remaining loyal to Hinduism, yet said (in words many Englishmen would have endorsed) that he found the 'doctrines of Christ more conducive to moral principles, and better adapted for the use of rational beings than any others which have come to my knowledge'.[33] He also upheld the benefits of Free Trade to India, and argued that 'the greater our intercourse with European gentlemen, the greater will be our improvement in literary, social and political affairs'.[34] At one moment, Roy even looked forward to the day when an India which had undergone the benefits of European settlement might have the status of a Canada (as it was in 1832) within the British Empire — one, that is to say, of practical internal self-government.[35] Given such views, it is less surprising that he should have been a leader in the campaign against *suttee.* Later, the campaigns against child-marriage and for the raising of the legal age of consent to twelve were to unite reformers across sectarian boundaries. All such campaigns were rooted in the critical attitude stimulated by the impact of such general western ideas as the fundamental equality of all men.

Western education, whether in India or Great Britain, presented to Indians not only moral and religious but also political lessons. Western political ideas had been forged in a European and English history which Indians were now taught to see as part of a general movement of material and moral progress, rather than as the peculiar products of the north-western peninsula of the Eurasian land mass. Liberty and equality, the struggle of church and state, the legalism of the Middle Ages, parliamentary practice, the American and French revolutions, helped to awaken many Indians to new visions of the future. 'The study of European history', said one, 'and particularly of the history of England and of English political institutions, is not calculated to deaden, but on the contrary to rouse and fire those instincts of patriotism, which have slumbered in the national breast of India for centuries.'[36] Taught that the nation was the proper expression of political authority, it is hardly surprising that Indians began to look round for a sense of nationhood of their own.

For the first time, the educated everywhere in the sub-continent had a new common language, English. It gave a wider circulation to ideas — often thanks to another western import, the newspaper press. Newspapers assisted the mutual discovery and the coming together of those frustrated by what they took to be unfair handicaps in public life and government service. They encouraged the educated to try to transcend the barriers within and between different Indian communities.[37] The vernacular press spread ideas, too. In the 1880s the British gave up censoring it in normal conditions (though they sometimes later did so during emergencies).

So Indians took their first steps towards modern politics. There began to emerge a national élite where none had existed; though this took time, differences were helpfully blurred by the existence of a common opponent. The 1870s and 1880s have been identified as the start of a mutation in Indian politics which turned many of the westernised from collaborators to critics. Institutional opportunities helped. In 1882 local government at the level of what would in England have been called county or municipal ad-ministration was opened to Indians. By then, too, Indians had begun to rise to judgeships and a few had senior posts in the administration. Soon, an outlet appeared for the expression of the wishes of the growing numbers of westernised Indians. The first Indian political association was formed, and the modern political style of agitation and publicity came to India when the Indian National Congress was set up in 1885. A former British civil servant, A. O. Hume, a Haileyburian who won a CB for dash and courage in the Mutiny, was its ideological godfather. Some believed that the Viceroy approved, too. The proceedings of Congress were, of course, in English, and for a long time its administrative staff was British; Hume was the dom-inant figure among them. Many of its first members shied away even from asking for Home Rule under the British crown. Meanwhile, in the 1890s two Indians were elected to the House of Commons.[38]

Increasingly, the westernised élite had some education in England. In 1845 the first four Indian students arrived; in the 1890s there were over three hundred of them there, in 1907 there were 780.[39] Harrow and Cam-bridge provided the educational background of Jawaharlal Nehru, for sev-enteen years to be prime minister of an independent India. His education led him to a very vocal advocacy of progressive ideas in Indian politics. 'I am convinced', he said in 1936, 'that the only key . . . to India's problems lies in socialism . . . not in a vague, humanitarian way, but in the scientific, economic sense.'[40] Such a coupling of socialism and science was an invocation of the very shibboleths of bien-pensant western progressive culture of the age. But westernisation could express itself less obviously, too. Cornelia Sorabji, the daughter of an Indian Christian minister of religion, after being the first woman student at her college in Poona was probably the first Indian woman to study at Oxford. She was admitted to Somerville Hall, a foundation sheltering studious young women whose formal admission the University of Oxford still resisted. Special permission was given to her in 1892 to sit the BCL examination (she got a third), but not for another thirty years was she called to the Bar (only in 1919 was it open to women). In spite of the obstacles to her career which she shared with her English sisters she retained a deep admiration for their country and its institutions. Showing no sympathy for the Indian independence movement, she threw herself into work for Indian women, and became an officially recognised adviser in the courts to women in purdah. In that role and by her example she must have disturbed traditional Indian views of women.

Western ideas came by many channels and in many forms. If you arrive at the Howrah station at Calcutta by an early morning train and walk across the bridge over the Hooghly, you can look down on the pilgrim boats loading to go upstream to Benares, and see beside them men wielding immense clubs and carrying out traditional gymnastics on exercise floors by the river. Not many do this, though. Go on walking — not very far — and you will come to the *maidan*, a vast stretch of ground separating the city of Calcutta from Fort William, the historic centre of British power in India. On a Sunday — the Christian sabbath which is now India's weekly holiday — it is covered with Indians playing cricket. In Fort William there are teams of soldiers playing soccer; 'Keeps their minds off the girls' said an Indian officer — an Eighth Army veteran — who showed me round. English sport has left its mark everywhere in the sub-continent, not least through the Indian army.

In Europe, sport and gymnastics have often been associated with patriotism and nationalism. Nationalists in other lands have followed suit. It would be going too far to see the Boxers as muscular progressives (though their name had its origin in the traditional Chinese martial arts) but Mao's first published essay was a plea for physical training as a way to greater fitness and martial skill.[41] In nineteenth-century Bengal, the connexion can be seen very clearly. English-educated, many young and not-so-young Bengalis readily accepted their rulers' view that they were physically degenerate. Not for them (or their masters) dietary explanations; impressed with the obvious disparity between their stature and strength and that of the British who stalked proudly among them, they accepted the western view that this was the result of the neglect of physical culture. So, extraordinarily, we find Bengalis accepting the advice of the Viceroy and missionaries to go in for manly sports and body-building, and from the 1880s onwards turning to gymnastics and western games. The relics are to be seen in any Indian gymnasium: parallel bars, horse, trapeze, rings — all promoted, originally,

by an enthusiastic British Lieutenent-Governor of Bengal, Sir George Camp-
bell. The story runs as far as a Boy Scout movement for Bengalis — the
Bratachari movement of the 1930s — launched by a Bengali member of the
ICS who recommended 'Tipperary' to his lads as a marching song.[42]

The institutional evolution of the Raj itself was the most positive force
shaping Indian nationalism. Government in India had to operate always
against the background of British politics. In the twentieth century the British will to resist Indian demands was increasingly sapped by a steady stream
of news from India about terrorist outrages, imprisonments for sedition,
police action against political demonstrators and the like. The spectacular
Durbar of 1911 had been followed even in the next year by an attempt —
nearly fatal — to kill the Viceroy with a bomb. Many Englishmen, too, wanted
to promote Indian self-government, a goal which seemed to them as appropriate as in other parts of the Empire. Some came to feel the Indians
deserved it because of the help they gave the allies during the Great War,
though reaction appeared to triumph in 1919, when wartime repressive
measures were re-imposed. Significantly, they were denounced by Gandhi
as 'unjust, subversive of the principle of liberty and destructive of the elementary rights of individuals on which the safety of the community as a
whole and of the State itself is based' — a model statement of western
liberalism.[43] In 1919 came the worst, least defensible, single incident in the
whole history of the Raj, at Amritsar, when a foolish officer ordered a crowd
to be fired upon and killed hundreds of Indians. By then, though, the
difficulty of maintaining British rule indefinitely was vividly apparent to
thoughtful administrators and statesmen. However noisy the protests of
colleagues and companions who disagreed, official opinion increasingly came
to favour Indian participation in government and administration.

In 1919 the provinces had been granted representative government. Large
electorates brought new possibilities to rulers and ruled alike.[44] Although
central government remained in British hands, the management of provincial matters and the patronage that went with it now passed into those of
Indians. Elections to municipal and provincial councils created new arenas
for political conflict. This both gave a new purpose to the Indian National
Congress, and promoted a new style of politics. Congress might be a loose,
ramshackle structure of factions and interest groups (as it has, in large
measure, remained) but it stepped forward with remarkable alacrity to work
the machinery which offered so many advantages. In so doing, though western clothes were seen less and less at Congress meetings, more than ever
was heard of western assumptions about political legitimacy. So unrolled the
political education of the Indian middle classes — and even of the masses
— in western liberal democracy and nationalism. So also began a notable

new stage in the politicisation of the service class, the westernised élite called into existence, educated, and formed by the Raj itself.

Representative government suited Congress for reasons other than the purely political — not that politics is ever pure. Because, through election, Congress increasingly provided access to political office, it found it easier to recruit supporters. More and more people were thus drawn almost incidentally into the national movement for political emancipation. Rivalries for power and patronage had to be fought out within the ranks of Congress, within the ranks of a movement whose original *raison d etre* had been the assertion of an Indian voice, as opposed to Indian voices. At first this was largely a matter of élites. Then, as the disasters of the world economic depression of the 1930s blighted India, the rural masses became increasingly susceptible to agitation against British rule. Mass participation strengthened the claims of Congress to be a nationalist movement.

By the end of the 1930s, it dominated provincial politics. By then, in 1935, the British parliament had set out arrangements for the participation of Indian politicians in the central government of India through a representative structure. There were now more than thirty million voters to compete for. Then came the Second World War, the anger of Congress leaders at India's commitment to it without any consultation, the threat of Japanese invasion and the mastery of the crisis of the 'Quit India' movement by the time-honoured methods of arrests, police action and detention. The Raj seemed still astonishingly strong; the Indian army recruited itself to a larger size than ever before, entirely from volunteers. But the tide was turning and the essential decisions in London were not long delayed. In 1947 the British Labour government led by a Haileyburian prime minister, Clement Attlee, handed over power to Jawaharlal Nehru, the first prime minister of India — a Harrovian.

At Independence, Congress appeared almost without question to opt for continuity rather than revolution — continuity with the institutions of government, participation and consultation set up by the Raj in its last decades. After all, Congress had been the agency by which these institutions had taken root in wide tracts of Indian society and, if its major historical role has to be specified, it seems likely that later generations will say it lies here. Congress showed that such fundamentally alien devices could be made to work usefully in Indian society. The tragic murder a few months after Independence of Mahatma Gandhi, the Indian who, more than any other, stood for the reconciliation of all Indians of all creeds and castes in one community, was symbolically terribly appropriate. His day was done. He had already failed to maintain India's unity, or to bring about the dismantling either of Congress or of the state structure inherited from the Raj which he had sought. A nationalist extremist murdered Gandhi, but partition and the new republican order had already disillusioned him. 'Today I am a back number,' he had written in his diary. The future of India was to be disputed by the élite the Raj had created. Of all sections of the population, it was the one most influenced by western ideas. Jinnah, the founder of Pakistan, habitually spoke in English — even when informing Bengali-speaking students from Bangladesh (to their chagrin) that the official language of Pakistan had to be Urdu. Partition confirmed the artificiality of the brief union imposed by British arms and diplomacy. It also exposed the fragile nature of the anti-British coalition which had monopolised thinking about nationhood. Pakistan's inability to retain Muslim Bangladesh within itself a quarter-century later underlines the lesson. So, though less blatantly, do India's wars with Pakistan and China, the second a struggle for the preservation by a new nation of a territorial integrity only defined by its former colonial status.[45]

Pakistan may be thought to show how transient were some western influences and institutions. An independent Pakistan had only become a likely outcome at a very late date; it had as little historic root in any idea of nationhood as did Indian nationalism. Pakistan was based on fear, a fear that Islam would dissolve or deteriorate in an independent India; an Islamic polity was therefore necessary. This obscured the important fact that there was no more one Muslim community in India under the Raj than there was one Indian. From the start, too, the new nation had a built-in paradox: its basic form of government was to be provided by Westminster parliamentarianism, but it was to be a confessional state. To Islamic Pakistan moved some of the most conservative Muslims of other parts of India. Yet its tiny political class (Pakistan took over only 83 of the 550 or so native-born Indian Civil Service officers in the administrative class at the moment of independence) was westernised and had taken up the communal politics of the Moslem League in a far from devout spirit. The outcome was the rapid stultification of any effort by the westernised élite to bring about progressive change and the disintegration of the League. Pakistan's constitution bears witness to the ideological success of orthodox Muslim thinkers.

The Indian republic, in contrast, has remained much more overtly shaped by western influences. In part this was a matter of direct inheritance — the bulk of an apolitical army and civil service, for example, a head of state in the British tradition of limited power, an independent judiciary, the emergency powers of the government. As late as 1970 the new state would still be served by some of the civil servants and soldiers recruited by the British. Something like two hundred and fifty articles of the Government of India Act of 1935 passed unchanged into the new state's constitutional legislation. And there were also the progressively inclined, democratic, vaguely socialist politicians who had such weight in the new state; above all, Nehru. Perhaps it is not surprising that a country where religion visibly has more influence than in most others on social behaviour should nonetheless firmly define itself as a secular state. Of course, such apparent western influence has to be understood in a qualified sense; simple prudence about public order ensured that constitutional law should also urge the special protection of cows and later concessions to Hindu extremists further weakened the proclaimed secularism of the state. Linguistic minorities won concessions which weakened the national state structure, while the practical importance of caste and community continues to determine the working of many of the formal protestations of equality. For all the Constitution might say, too, Untouchables were firmly kept in their place. The dilemma was very personal for many Indians. It was Nehru who said 'I have become a queer mixture of East and West, out of place everywhere, at home nowhere. Perhaps my thoughts and approach to life are more akin to what is called Western than Eastern, but India clings to me; . . . behind me lie, somewhere in the subconscious, racial memories of a hundred . . . generations of Brahmins.'[46] He spoke, perhaps, for more Indians than himself alone.

Nevertheless, the Indian republic remains a carrier of western ideas. Fragile as it sometimes looks, Indian democracy is all the more important and exemplary because elsewhere in Asia constitutional government and liberal values had far shallower roots, so that their frequent failures to survive do not surprise us. By comparison with most other nations in the world, India can be called a democracy, just as, long before the French Revolution, eighteenth-century England can be reasonably called a liberal polity if compared with any other major state.[47] That is not something that 'just happened'; it is the product of a very special experience of the West. It is an outcome quite unlike that in other Asian societies which — in the Chinese tradition — respect authority, giving it a moral endorsement never unquestioned in the West since the Dark Ages. Such societies sometimes actually appear to find the whole notion of principled opposition distasteful, because it appears to disrupt society itself; in India, at least, its constitutional entrenchment is one of the most telling evidences of the positive response of so many among her élites to the experience of western domination.

XII
A SENSE OF DECLINE

Since 1900, a great dream has faded. To many in the West, their civilisation appears to have gone wrong. Much that is unique about it has seemed to turn out to be weakness, or worse. Cultural self-criticism and self-questioning have seemed to lead to cultural self-destruction. From the mid-nineteenth century onwards, growing numbers of the educated in Europe and the West were not only abandoning particular creeds, but faith in absolute values of any kind. Although this for a long time affected only a few (and, at the same time, the ideas which rested on absolutes and universals no longer esteemed in the West were being taken up elsewhere in the world) the trend was clear. The founder of psycho-analysis, Sigmund Freud, was a product of Europe's high culture at its peak; though his greatest impact was made in the twentieth century, and even after 1918, his was a nineteenth-century mind. What precisely he taught or revealed though is less in point than the broad tendency of what he said (or was thought to have said) to throw doubt on the power of reason and traditional western values. The arts, too, provide instances of the same undermining of certainty about traditional standards. In politics, the decline of confidence in the absolute values of liberalism was rapid and spectacular. It ran away at best into an easy pragmatism and at worst into the outright irrationality which fed Fascism. Appropriately, the Nazis consciously adopted the symbols of a pre-Christian and therefore a pre-western, pagan past.

There seems to be little left for the educated to believe in. Christianity's decay as a persuasive intellectual system has been followed by that of its rival, Marxism. Both still have their churches of believers, sure of their ritual and dogma. But the hungry sheep look up, and more and more they are not fed. The uncertainty shown by Christian clergymen when they try to talk about belief is equalled by the disorder among Marxists and the ignorance of so many who claim that title. It is not hard to imagine what his own comments would have been had Marx been told that less than a century after his death there would be people claiming to be 'Christian' Marxists. As intellectual creeds winning conscious assent, Christianity and Marxism are now only minority concerns, even if their positive power is a very different matter. It remains colossal. History, custom and inertia can still win the Pope a warm response from millions and can give Communist parties in western democracies millions of votes.

Because men are more easily swayed by imagination and emotion than by reasoned argument, though, it is surely plausible to give as much weight to Europe's appalling civil wars of 1914–18 and 1939–45 as to intellectual disintegration in explaining what went wrong. Though Europe's struggles twice became mixed up inextricably with quite different wars,[1] these great conflicts were about a European question: the control of Germany. In Europe, they rolled up wars both between states and within them. In some countries, class struggled with class, in others, national aspirations and grievances which the old fabric of Europe had been able to contain so long as it was unshaken were unleashed. The effects spread outwards far beyond Europe to end an era of general peacefulness unparalleled in modern times. An international political and economic system which had on the whole worked effectively, was swept away. Instead, there opened an era of instability and unresolved conflict, unprecedented because it was global.

The political destruction wrought by those wars was spectacular. In the first, three great European empires collapsed: the German, the Habsburg and the Russian. With them disappeared the old framework of central and eastern Europe. Briefly revived under Hitler — and, indeed, expanded further than before — the German Reich was again shattered in 1945. The result was a division of Germany which went far deeper than any existing before the creation of a united Germany for the first time in 1871. The Habsburg empire, meanwhile, had vanished in 1918. Revolution after revolution threw up new states in its former territories. Some had no previous history as independent units. Poland re-emerged after a century and a quarter of subjugation to Prussia, the Habsburgs and Russia. The Tsar's empire, in fact, had been the first to crumble away after revolution in 1917. That had brought down the dynasty and the Tsarist autocracy. Then, a new sort of state, self-designated as the property of the workers of Russia, atheistical and materialist in philosophy, and committed to furthering the cause of revolution everywhere, emerged from the second, Bolshevik, revolution of 1917. Ever since there have been 'socialist' states in existence somewhere in the world. This awoke fears in some non-socialist countries that their own peoples might turn to Bolshevism, though the comparison of ideals with reality which the establishment of a communist regime has made possible has led to much disenchantment with socialist universalism, and much greater realism about it. It is only in 'socialist' states in recent years that the industrial masses have broken out in revolt against their governments.[2] There was better reason to fear the new Russian state, and its deliberate promotion by propaganda, diplomacy and military power of a new Russian

empire whose interests were proclaimed identical with those of the 'international working class'.

By the end of 1939 the new Russian autocracy had actually restored much
of the old Tsarist empire. Russia by then again ruled half Poland. She had
swallowed the Baltic states which had briefly emerged from the wreckage of
the old Russia to a fleeting independence between the two wars. She was
engaged in fighting the Finns (formerly subjects of the Tsars), and took
territory from them a few months later. Then came the war with Germany.
By the end of the war in Europe, the power the new Russia already showed,
and her expressed intentions, troubled many observers as never before.

After 1945, their alarm increased. Communist satellite governments were
installed over most of eastern Europe. In the Far East, too, Russian forces
had occupied south Sakhalin and stayed in Port Arthur until 1948. It now
looked as if Stalin was bent on rebuilding the former empire of the Tsars
in Asia, too. Once more, the old question was raised: were the Russians really
part of the West? As the 'Cold War' began to frighten people, many of them
were even less inclined to think she (or, for that matter, any other part of
communist Europe) was.

In these great political changes it was easy to lose sight of certain important
facts. Russian power was inevitable once the processes of modernisation were
released in her, and they were released well before 1914. It is likely that
Russia would have become as strong under the Tsars as under Stalin in the
1930s had not the Great War shattered the autocracy. She might well have
then expressed a grave threat to peace. But the ideological hostility of the
new Russian empire to every other government in the West was something
new, and a profound shock to western confidence. Its proclaimedly revolutionary orientation was one of the most profoundly disruptive forces
threatening international order and made a restoration of the old politics
of balancing power very hard to envisage.

Not only Europe lost in the Great War the stability given by old empires.
Once the first two centuries of the Ottoman hegemony were past, the Near
East had slowly reverted to being a disputed zone. From the seventeenth
century onwards there were signs that the Franks would before long again
be disputing it with one another — and with the Russians. Ottoman Europe
had virtually gone by 1914; in the next few years, Ottoman Asia followed.
Greeks and Italians were soon arguing about Turkey itself, the French and
British about formerly Turkish Mesopotamia, Syria and Palestine. The
French and British empires, indeed, had their last, brief surge of expansion
in 1919 in former Ottoman territory, but it was a flash in the pan. When
those empires in their turn collapsed after the Second World War, the Near
East faced political chaos made worse by new irritants: oil, intransigent Jewish
and Arab Nationalism, and Cold War.

The other big and obvious change which followed Europe's civil wars was the replacement of the old European world leadership by American. This can hardly be termed 'destabilising', but it was psychologically unsettling. Nor did it start with the Great War, in fact. It was a dimly-conceived threat even at the start of the century; it was in 1901 that a British journalist published a book with the title *The Americanization of the World*.[3] What was uneasily sensed behind this was as much a matter of modernisation as of specific Americanisation, but there was something in the view that an epoch had been reached in a nation's history at about that time.

In the 1890s the United States Department of the Interior announced that a 'frontier' no longer existed — the continuous line of settlement beyond which lay wilderness had disappeared. Symbolically, the United States was filled up. Of course, there were (and still are) huge empty spaces within the Republic and much of its territory was not yet organised into states with regular government. The transcontinental railroads had long been completed, though, and the days of the cowboy and trapper were numbered. Soon, the completion and consolidation of the map at home was followed by territorial imperialism overseas. Hawaii, the Philippines and Puerto Rico were all acquired in the 1890s; by 1914 the Americans had a lease of the Panama Canal Zone, the canal itself was nearly complete, and 'dollar diplomacy' and the 'Roosevelt corollary' to the Monroe doctrine were making it clear that they would be willing to intervene in the affairs of her neighbours by armed force if their interests appeared to demand it.

By then, though, something still more important for the world's future had come into existence — the greatest concentration ever of economic power under one government: the American industrial economy. It brought wealth — and therefore power — on an unimagined scale, and we have been living in its shadow and sunshine ever since. As a re-distributor of wealth, mass production was to leave socialism far behind, and as an extension of personal opportunity, the American economy remains unmatched.

Such power was hesitant to show itself politically outside the western hemisphere. It only gradually spread across the Pacific and hardly at all towards Europe before 1914. There at last came a time when Europeans cried for its deployment. After two years of war, the political and military dead-lock in the old heartland of the West could be broken only by the greatest democracy on earth. For three long years the British and French bought and borrowed America's help before, in 1917, the United States finally entered the war against Germany. It was an event as destructive of the old European order as the Bolshevik success, perhaps more so. For the first time since the sixteenth century, the fate of Europe was to be settled by outsiders. President Wilson's famous 'Fourteen Points' showed the weight now to be put behind self-determination and democratic nationalism in the reconstruction of Europe and much of its colonial heritage. Yet, though geographically outsiders, the Americans were born of and belonged to Europe's civilisation. There was, therefore, a displacement of power within western civilisation rather than a supersession of it.

For another twenty-odd years this was not very obvious. President Wilson's wish to use American power to create a new world order was frustrated by other politicians who responded to and helped to deepen a mood of isolationism in the United States. It seemed a safe, prosperous country and so Americans in the 1920s turned their backs on the world. Yet they could not avoid having a huge impact on it simply by not being there. If German power was one day to be rebuilt, that of England and France without America or some other powerful ally at their side (and Russia was not available) would not be enough to balance it. American decisions, even decisions to stay aloof, were bound to sway the fate of western civilisation without anyone deliberately intending it should do so. Economics alone made this certain. American industrial might had grown even more as a result of the First World War. American prosperity in the 1920s helped Europe to recover. When American loans began to be called in at the end of the decade, though, shocks ran through the whole European financial and business system. When 1929 brought bankruptcies and the collapse of credit in the United States, there followed financial disaster in Europe. As business stagnation in the United States deepened into a slump, the world slid into the first truly global economic depression. A dramatic demonstration of the irresistible weight of the American economy came when primary producers in Nigeria, Malaya, and the Argentine found themselves unable to sell food and raw materials to the penniless cities and silent factories of Europe.

In the Second World War, the United States at last consciously accepted the role thrust upon her by history and her own puissance. Her president took the political and military leadership within the West which had long been hers for the asking. Nor could there be any going back after 1945; too many of the conditions of the old world order had gone. Europe was so shattered physically and economically that some thought that it could never recover. But American support, in the form of the Marshall Plan, and American military protection, through the airpower which could deliver nuclear weapons, made that recovery possible after all. Furthermore, there was an American garrison in Europe, where the United States was formally installed as one of the four occupying powers in Germany. The coup in Prague, the Berlin blockade, and the creation of NATO followed. And so it became clear that the old order really had changed, giving place to new. This was not always something western Europeans found easy to accept and the psychological adjustments it calls for still cause difficulties.

Meanwhile, a whole civilisation had been shaken by psychological trauma.

The two great German wars left Europe stunned and dazed. Appalling destruction had been done; famine and disease came back to civilised Europe after decades. When they began to recover from the immediate shock of 1914–18 many Europeans looked round and felt that nothing they had believed in before could ever be believed in again in quite the same way. The unprecedented slaughter and physical violence of the First World War — the 'Great War', as it was revealingly called — was psychologically decisive, as that of the second was not, although it was even bloodier and physically more destructive. It ended an age of innocence about war in a democratic era. The toll of lives was inconceivably greater than had been expected. For four and a half years, a man was killed or died in Europe every twelve or fifteen seconds. Man-killing had never been so efficient. It was the first war in the history of mankind in which we know that weapons killed more men than died of disease. Millions who did not die were maimed, blinded, gassed; they were living reminders of the enormity of what had happened.

Demographers have tried to compute Europe's exact population loss but measurable genetic and economic consequences, great as they were, were surely not crucial. What mattered even more was the horror and terror such losses inspired. They were, in a deep sense of an old word, judgements. They seemed, without more ado, to condemn outright all the assumptions, beliefs, practices, institutions which had made them possible. They blighted western Europe's belief in itself. So, they released the demons of uncertainty, lack of confidence and scepticism which were so often to paralyse effective response to the problems left behind by the Great War.

The post-war world was bound to be depressing. The economic structures of the old confident days before 1914 were smashed or gravely damaged. Production had collapsed in much of Europe. New political boundaries made nonsense of old marketing patterns. The overturning of the old political structures spread uncertainty and disorder in countries previously thought law-abiding and liberal. Old hatreds like anti-semitism blossomed anew amid the ruins as economic privation gave people new grounds for struggle. Social tensions sharpened. Revolutionary forces — some of them supported by a temporarily prostrate, but soon resurgent, Russia — appeared which were dedicated to turning back the clock on liberal democracy. Significantly, it was the President of the United States, not the rulers of the victorious or defeated great powers of Europe, who had, in 1918, greatest confidence in the powers of democracy and nationalism, the old liberal shibboleths, to build a newer and healthier European order. Recovery of a sort there was, though. For a time, if you did not peer too deeply, it looked as if the old civilised order of the West had been put together again. Then, in the 1930s, the illusion fell apart.

The first shock was the onset of the economic slump which dramatically lowered production and earnings all round the world. Though it seems likely that the primary producers in countries where farms, ranches, plantations or mines were the backbone of the economy suffered most, the most dramatic and obvious effects were to be seen in the silent mills and factories of the industrial nations and the swelling numbers of their urban unemployed. Confidence in the 'natural' working of the self-adjusting capitalist system, in the mutual dependence of producers and consumers who providentially had compatible needs, in the automatic tendency of the self-interest of competing individuals to produce social harmony, was given a mortal wound. And with belief in *laissez-faire* went, increasingly, belief in liberal values.

The demons were clearly coming back, more menacing than ever as Europe began to edge down the road to a new war. International economic competition was only one reason. In one country after another, the belief that liberal values were still able to stand up to nihilism and barbarism crumbled. By 1939, Europe contained fewer constitutional states with liberal institutions working in a decent way than in 1914. Horrifyingly, Nazi Germany explicitly renounced all moral restraints except those derived from a mad racialism. So, Europe came to face the worst threat it has ever had to face.

When war came in 1939, it blew away the last of the hopes left of 1918. The only great European nation-states to survive its tests were Great Britain, protected by her moat, and Russia, saved by her continental mass. Outside their boundaries and those of the handful of neutral states, Europe in 1945 was prostrate, to all intents and purposes divided between victorious Russian and American armies. No revival of the old structures of power and stability was conceivable. The war had made clear the emergence of the two superpowers which Tocqueville had discerned over a century before as the dominating states of the future. Both had been brought out of isolation by the war, both had great Asian and Pacific concerns, both were truly world powers. Europeans seemed at last to have handed on their role as the pacemakers of modern history.

The world wars also dealt fatal blows to European empire overseas. Its moral basis had been eroded even before 1914 by liberal political criticism and the decline of confidence in Christianity — without which it was less easy to be sure that non-Christians were inferior. The First World War added enormously to that damage. Not only did subject-peoples see their overlords at one another's throats, but much else that exposed the hollowness of those overlords' claims to cultural and moral superiority.[4] President Wilson damaged imperialism, too, by strengthening the belief in self-determination as a principle. Though, in a last burst of expansion, both France and Great Britain actually acquired yet more overseas territory in 1919, it was mainly on a new basis: a 'mandate' from the League of Nations, by which an administering power for former subject territories of the defeated states was made responsible to the League for their management. Among the other mandated powers were the white British Dominions and Japan. Husbanded from dissipation in Europe's quarrels, Japan's strength was available for deployment in the Far East.

For all the glamour and excitement of the Wembley Exhibition of 1924 in London and the French *Exposition coloniale* in Paris six years later, the challengers were beginning to appear. Self-styled 'representatives of the negro world' turned up at the Paris peace conference. In the following year, at Baku on the Caspian, there took place a 'congress of peoples of the East'. Here were new actors — or would-be actors — thinking to push aside those who had dominated the world stage for so long. Ominously, they met under the wing of the new Russia; the patron of revolution did not confine its assistance to communists and Marxists, but gave it to nationalists as well. In 1919 the Communist International (the Comintern) was set up as a tactical device at a moment when the Soviet Union appeared gravely threatened, but it became a vehicle for the integration of revolutionary and anti-colonial movements with Soviet interests right round the world. In 1920 and 1921 special congresses of the Comintern were devoted exclusively to the problems of the Far East.

Ostrich-like ignorance of such changes in the once-secure world of empire was, of course, still evident in the 1920s and 1930s. Even if metropolitan governments recognised — and in some respects approved — the way things were going, Europeans and descendants of Europeans on the spot sometimes behaved as if nothing had changed. After the Second World War, though, the illusions of empire were almost impossible to maintain. The French, Belgian, Dutch and Italians had all undergone defeat and the occupation of their homelands, which compromised their imperial role. Far more grievous defeats than in the Great War, moreover, had been undergone by Europeans in Asia at the hands of the Japanese. The fall of Singapore, where 80,000 British Commonwealth prisoners were taken by them in February 1942, was the most resounding disaster to British arms since Yorktown. Nor was it only the British, driven from Hong Kong, Malaya and Burma, who were humiliated. French Indo-China passed effectively into Japanese control. The Dutch lost Indonesia. The United States was driven from the Philippines. Asians saw too many Europeans and Americans being defeated ever to forget it. Moreover, the Japanese and the anti-colonialists appeared in a sense to face a common enemy. Many of the local politicians in Japanese-occupied colonial territories were pleased to be patronised by the new masters, Asian like themselves. In this way, many post-war nationalist leaders first stepped forward onto the political stage. The Japanese deliberately chose coadjutors who had not served the former colonial regimes.

When their forces at last returned victorious to their former possessions, the imperial powers were hobbled by their own rhetoric. As early as 1941, a document called the Atlantic Charter was the first sign that at least the British recognised that the mobilisation of world opinion implied ideological and political concession. The Charter spoke of the 'rights of all peoples to choose the form of government under which they will live', and there can be little doubt that whatever careful drafters of such formulae intended, such words reflected the real aspirations of many Englishmen and Americans. They stood in the self-critical traditions of their own cultures. The German attack on Russia associated in some measure the Soviet Union's publicly anti-colonial stance with allied war aims, too, and it was a necessary fiction that the Nationalist Government of China, an Asian nation which had long suffered from western imperialism, was an equal of the other major combatant powers. In 1944, when the new United Nations Organisation made its appearance, China was given one of the four permanent seats on the Security Council. The thrust of American policy, too, opposed the restoration of imperial authority to former possessions and entangled the path of western statesmen by seeking to satisfy liberal sentiment and American business interest at the same time. Great Britain was terribly weakened and could not enforce her will where it was expensive to do so. There was little choice in the long run but, willingly or not, to dismantle the empire, especially when it seemed only a logical development of earlier British policy. Whatever the misgivings about timing and circumstance, India was abandoned in 1947. The implications for other empires were huge.

Dismantling empires took far less time than building them. By 1970 Africa was rid of all formal subjection to western colonial powers except in the Portuguese colonies. The nation which had begun the colonial era in Africa was to be the last to call its forces home, but even they had gone a few years later. The process was very uneven. The British managed to leave their colonies with little bloodshed; unlike the French in Algeria, they did not have to fight for their settlers. Algerians, of course, were technically citizens of metropolitan France, and so French settlers there exercised a political pressure at home which British residents in Africa could never achieve. In Asia the story was over even more quickly, partly because a Dutch attempt to recover Indonesia failed at an early date, partly because of the unbearable cost to the French of resistance to Indo-Chinese nationalism (and the dramatic defeat of French arms at Dien-Bien-Phu, though smaller in scale, had a moral effect like that of the Singapore surrender) and partly because of the potential danger of international questions aroused by Asian issues. So, a military and political tide which had flowed more or less unchecked for a couple of centuries had turned. 'Decolonisation' was the last, dramatic phase.

In a longer perspective, though, 1905 is a better marker of change than

1941. Japan's conscious modernisation had made it possible by then for her to be acknowledged by at least one western power to be part of the 'civilised world' of nations which had to be taken seriously: she had become an ally of Great Britain in 1902 (the Japanese were the only people with whom the British had a formal treaty of alliance in peacetime before 1914). Then in 1904, fearing the consolidation of Russia's grip on Manchuria and her pos- sible expansion into Korea, the Japanese attacked the Russian naval base at Port Arthur. In the following year, stretched to breaking-point, they yet forced their opponents to accept a peace treaty.[5] For the first time an Asiatic nation had defeated a European power in a full-scale war. Port Arthur was the real beginning of the road which was to wind through Kut, Singapore and Dien-Bien-Phu to Saigon and the final collapse of western power in Asia.[6] This is why 1905 is a landmark in the twentieth century.

The Japanese had already before that embarked on overseas aggression against fellow-Asians with the weapons and techniques of the West. Their first success had been the imposition in 1876 of an 'unequal' treaty of their own on Korea, a Chinese satellite kingdom. Soon attacks on China itself followed, but the humiliation of the victorious Japanese in 1895 by Russia, Germany and France went deep.[7] It helps to explain why the slogan 'Asia for the Asians' came from Japan. The next important milestone was the First World War. Japan's rulers used its opportunities shrewdly. Although they took part in operations against German stations in the Far East and the Pacific, they steadfastly declined to send an army to Europe to help the Allies, but benefited from the economic demands of the war. These were the real key to the achievement of an industrial economy. Meanwhile, the Japanese used the freedom from British and French restraint which the war gave them to bully the new Chinese republic. They had been nibbling away at the old empire for decades, seizing Formosa in 1895 and Korea in 1910 as well as assuring their own predominance in Manchuria after the Russian defeat. The possibility of a resurgent China, rejuvenated by the republic, was not welcome to them.

After 1918, too, Japan was alienated from her former allies in Europe by their refusal to embody the principle of racial equality in the Covenant of the new League of Nations. American opposition to claims on former Ger- man territory in China was a further irritant. Yet the current seemed set in Japan's favour long-term. Every European great power formerly interested in Asia was now hobbled or crippled. Renewed western expansion in the Far East was inconceivable. Germany had been stripped of her Asian pos- sessions. Russia, shattered by defeat and revolution, could for a long time do little except strive to hang on to the old monarchy's Far East provinces. The French sought to do little more than to dig their heels in over their own possessions. The British decision to build a naval base at Singapore showed that they thought at best in terms of defending India: economically and militarily weak, facing increasing provocation in western Europe and with rising misgivings over her imperial role, Great Britain had not since signing the Anglo-Japanese alliance believed she could single-handedly preserve the old western ascendancy in the Far East. To make matters worse, she scrapped her alliance with Japan in the face of pressure from the Canadians and Australians. As for the USA, sympathetic rhetoric did not mean she would ever go so far as to defend China with arms against Japanese aggression. So, in the 1930s, Japan proceeded first to the seizure of Manchuria and then, in 1937, to full-scale war with China. Looking back, that seems the beginning of a Far Eastern and Pacific War which was to merge in 1941 with European struggles in the Second World War. In 1937 Japanese aircraft sank an American gunboat, the *Panay*, and Japanese guns shelled a British, the *Ladybird*, without any redress except the compensation Japan offered.

For the quarter-century before 1941, then, during which western supremacy in Asia had been waning, only Japan was free to act in the Far East. Her vigour was based, though, on her earlier success in being the first non-western country successfully to take up the dangerous gifts of the West and follow its example. Predatory western powers had led the Japanese to decide that they were not going to be left behind in any 'scramble' for spoils in China: even Japan's imperialist justifications — in terms of economic needs — had much that was western about them. Moreover, Japan exploited the opportunities presented by subject colonial peoples who were beginning to question their western rulers.[8] More significantly, though, she had learnt the military lessons of the West. Both technologically, with her new battle-fleet and, later, air forces, and organisationally, through her new foreign-trained general staffs, Japan succeeded because she had modernised and westernised herself as China had been unable to do.

Yet when Japan again engaged in outright conflict with western nations, she was, for all her spectacular early triumphs, overthrown. She was already beaten by conventional weapons when given a final blow in August 1945 by the superior science which produced the first nuclear bombs — a strikingly symbolic event. She then underwent another one-sided 'westernising' experience at the hands of General MacArthur. A new, democratic constitution was imposed. Once more deliberate revolution from above sought to make Japan more 'western'. It was enthusiastically welcomed. The United States became the authoritative source of wisdom in every sphere. The first revolution had tried to modernise while making few moral and ideological concessions: the second sought the reverse — to turn the Japanese into western democrats. The monuments of the first were the conservation of the ethic of *bushido* and the devotion of the *kamikaze* pilot. The second is commemorated by a free press, a new constitution and — perhaps best of all — by the odd shape which rises over so many Japanese towns and cities, the bulbous form of the giant skittle which marks a bowling alley, just as a spire identified the parish church in a medieval European town.

The redirection of Japan was nevertheless only possible because of the strength of old ways. Unquestioning obedience to the emperor made possible the startling about-turn of surrender in 1945; the Japanese obeyed the highest law of their culture even in defeat. And this also made possible the surprising co-operation with the victor which followed. Deliberate democratising policy was, though, not the only force at work on Japan in the post-war years. MacArthur probably shaped Japanese minds less than did the sheer momentum of Japanese industrial development. It was only in 1951 that Japan launched the first ship ever built in her yards for export; twenty years later she was the largest shipbuilding country in the world. Her absorption of raw materials and energy shot up, and her domestic market flowered. Whole new industrial sectors appeared; in some of them Japan led the world. The roots of this economic transformation certainly lie far back in national attitudes favouring the emergence of a disciplined, skilled industrial workforce. Yet economic growth also owed much to chance and circumstance — to the emergence of a Communist regime in China which for a long time made Japan a favoured recipient of investment aid; and to the Korean war and the boom in supplies for the American armies which followed. The outcome was an industrial structure often seen in western countries as a threat.

There was much else in the East Asia of the post-1945 period to sap western confidence. Other Asian countries have sought to follow Japan's path to national independence and prosperity and they, too, have come to be seen as threats in their turn. Yet understandable as this is it is somewhat paradoxical, for the new nations which are the successor states to western empires seem often or always to turn to the West in their values, goals and methods. Very few of them are overtly conservative. Their traditional cultures have seemingly been preserved only as picturesque tourist attractions. Only recently, in Islamic countries, have there been grounds for thinking that a plausible alternative to westernisation by self-renewal and a return to tradition might be available.

Iran was the most striking case, at first sight, of an Islamic country rebelling against its rulers' attempt to take it down the road of westernising modernisation along which, in different ways, many rulers of Muslim peoples had tried to precede them. She has had, of course, a long history of civilisation. Though much decayed since her great age, Iranian vigour seemed to reassert itself under the last Shah, after a period of forced-draft westernisation whose roots lay in the opportunities of the Cold War and oil revenue. Western technology made Iran the strongest power in the Gulf area. But soon two things surprised western observers. In the first place, dramatic economic progress (measured by a growth rate of some 10 per cent a year) turned out to be not a stabilising, but a de-stabilising force. Secondly, in the Islamic revolution which overthrew the Shah, religious leadership was paramount.[9] Iranian society seemed to have taken to westernisation less than had been thought. The Shah was opposed because he affronted Islamic tradition: his acts promoted the liberation of women and the secularisation of society. But that is not quite the whole story, either. Iran had not simply turned to her past. Though part of the coalition which overthrew the Shah was based on an old and proud people's sense of long humiliation, another part of it was mobilised by an outraged liberalism. The Shah's secret police, his restraints on the press, the harshness of the judicial apparatus and the arbitrariness with which power was exercised turned many westernised Iranians against him. Iranian upholders of western standards associated with progress were affronted by oppression; it was in the name of western values, which they called universal, that they struggled. In the really important things, evidently, the Shah was not western enough.

The seemingly anti-western Islamic revival in Iran thus has a much more complicated relation to western civilisation than appears at first sight. History gives us one perspective. Islamic history has been punctuated by revivals. Usually, they had a conservative colour; they were responses to what was seen as failure by Islamic regimes to live up to the teachings of the Prophet.[10] As guidance on every aspect of life and society can be found in the Prophet's teaching it has never been hard for the believer to find evidence of such failure. Revivalism may call in question the legitimacy of any society in which the ulema, the Muslim learned men and clergy, do not play a dominant role — or, at least, are not satisfied with the regime. There is also always a potential challenge from Islam to any non-Muslim ruler claiming absolute authority, and it arises from the universalism of Islam itself, as the Ch'ing emperors found in Sinkiang in the nineteenth century and, perhaps, Soviet government is discovering today.[11] We should remember, too, that although we carelessly speak of Islam as a 'religion', that word carries many overtones of the special history of western Europe; the Muslim is primarily a member of a community, the follower of a certain way, an adherent to a system of law, rather than someone holding particular theological views.

Seen in this light, the present Islamic revival has been simmering for a long time. But the role of the West was crucial. It bred the long frustration and anger felt by many in the central, historical Islamic lands of the Near and Middle East, during the era when western power was at its height. To take the example of Persia alone, Russian victory over her was followed in 1828 by a treaty which forbade the Persians to impose a duty of more than

5 per cent on all imports; the collapse of their industries followed as imports from western countries shot up. 'Capitulations', or extra-territorial privileges, were granted to over a dozen European countries and a Persian constitutional revolution in 1906 was overthrown by Russian intervention. In the following year, the British and Russians divided the country between them into zones of influence. After the Great War, the British sought to protect the country from Bolshevism by putting on the throne a tractable soldier (he did not turn out to be easy to manage, but that is another story). And that was the experience of only one Islamic country. Meanwhile within a hundred years, the Mogul and Ottoman empires — two of the greatest structures of Islamic history — had collapsed before western imperialism. So did scores of lesser, but still significant, Islamic polities from the Sudan to Central Asia, and from the Gulf to Indonesia.

But impotence and frustration may not have been the most important source of the anger and violence which we see in the Islamic world today. That source has also to be sought in the way some rulers of Islamic peoples responded to western dynamism and power by seeking to tap it for themselves. Men like Mehemet Ali of Egypt, Kemal Atatürk of Turkey, Reza Shah of Iran, chose to westernise not only to increase their own power but as a way of holding the West at bay. Mehemet Ali sent to Europe for schoolteachers and engineers and had French taught in Egyptian schools. He gave the Egyptian state a brief, but important 'developmental' role in industrial innovation. Atatürk forbade polygamy, latinised the Turkish script, secularised the law, gave women the vote, and abolished the Muslim calendar. 'To be European is our ideal' wrote one of his followers, and Kemal himself spoke of European civilisation (in terms which recall Marx's paean of praise to the *bourgeoisie*) as one which 'pierces the mountains, flies across the heavens, sees everything, even to stars that are invisible to the naked eye . . . to whose seething torrent it is vain to offer resistance.'[12] Reza Shah, unbalanced and despotic though he became, abolished women's veils (his own wife went unveiled for the first time in 1937) and religious schools. Syed Ahmed Khan, the first Indian Muslim leader to send his son to Cambridge, saw education as the panacea for his co-religionists in India. 'All good things, spiritual and worldly', he once wrote, '. . . have been bestowed by the Almighty on Europe, and especially on England,' and he urged his co-religionists to seek them through education.[13] All such men, seeking to westernise and modernise, built with varying degrees of success new nations, predominantly Muslim but with a weaker commitment to Islam than before.

The most successful of them was Turkey's Atatürk. His achievement followed a long maturing of new forces within the Ottoman empire, the greatest non-European threat with which the West had to deal before the twentieth century and one of the largest states built up from contiguous territories that has ever existed. From the fifteenth century to the nineteenth, its Sultans ruled, at least in name, a huge arc of Islamic lands, stretching at its greatest from Morocco to Mesopotamia, as well as the Balkans and much of central and south-eastern Christian Europe. In the seventeenth century you could have gone from Budapest to the Yemen without leaving Ottoman territory except to take a ferry across the Bosphorus. Even by then, though, the zenith of Ottoman power was already past, and by 1900, the glory was long departed. Much of the empire had gone, sliced off by predatory European states or national risings. Some Ottoman subjects, far-sighted about the problems which would arise if ever the empire broke up and the spoils had to be divided, urged their rulers to put their house in order. Others wanted the dynasty to find the strength to win back freedom from foreign (which meant European) intervention. Some looked further and wanted liberalism and reform for their own sake: they were influenced by the spirit of the age, by the ideas of the French Revolution, by what they heard of western science and rationalism. And there were those who simply thought that too much money was going to the western *entrepreneurs* who did well out of their specially negotiated commercial and fiscal privileges.

As the nineteenth century closed against a background of renewed despotism and abortive reform, the regime sought to silence discussion. The question of modernisation and westernisation could not be openly debated, so opponents of the regime turned to plotting and subversion. Among them were young army officers, many of them, ironically, trained in new secondary and military schools which the regime had set up. Some of them organised themselves, within the empire and in exile, as the 'Ottoman Society of Union and Progress' — soon called, by foreigners, the 'Young Turks'. As one of its leaders put it, 'one of our chief desires is to see European civilisation spread in our country . . . we follow the path traced by Europe', adding significantly, 'even in our refusal to accept foreign intervention.'

Much of the army had already been won over to the cause of nationalism and reform when, in 1908, a new diplomatic humiliation detonated the explosion. Units stationed in Macedonia began a revolt. Within a few weeks the sultan gave in; a constitution suspended thirty years before was restored and a parliament met. Briefly, divisions between nationalities and communities seemed at an end: Turks, Greeks, Jews, Armenians hugged one another in the delirious streets of Constantinople. By 1914, though, the empire was again ruled autocratically — but by the sultan's Young Turk ministers this time. For them, 'Union' meant Ottomanisation: a strong, centralised, powerful government was to keep the minorities in line. As one Young Turk ominously put it, 'there are no longer Bulgars, Greeks, Romanians, Jews, Muslims . . . we are all equal, we glory in being Ottoman.' Political societies of a nationalist character were banned. New drains, a better fire brigade for Constantinople, and the extension of education to girls hardly seemed sufficient compensation.

Up to this point, the story of the patriotic reform movement in Turkey seems an uncanny prefiguring of what was to happen later in many other countries. The mixed sources of reform, the use of conspiracy and violence to achieve power, the key role of soldiers, the sacrifice of principles to nationalism, the disillusionment of liberals and minorities — this is a dismally familiar story. But in the Ottoman empire it did not end with the installation of the Young Turks in power, because there followed a much more revolutionary event — the outbreak of the Great War. Though it survived defeat longer than its allies, Germany and Austria-Hungary, and its old enemy, imperial Russia, the Ottoman empire was one of the losers in that conflict. True, the Sultan outlasted Tsar, Emperor and Kaiser; he was still on his throne and able to sign a humiliating surrender to the Allies in 1918. But by then Ottoman rule had been swept away in Arabia, and Palestine, Syria and Mesopotamia had been overrun by British armies. An 'Arab awakening' which had begun in the nineteenth century made it hard to believe that the Sultan would ever again rule the Arab lands. As for what had been Ottoman Europe, little more than Istanbul itself was left — and soon a British garrison was installed there. Meanwhile, immediately after the armistice, Italian, Greek and French forces had occupied parts of Asia Minor and some of the former Ottoman islands in the Aegean. What was left was little more than Anatolia, the old heartland of the empire, where the Turks themselves had settled when they arrived from the east five or six centuries before. Over that poverty-stricken, disheartened land presided the defeated, discredited and semi-captive government of the Sultan, lacking any ideological direction or idealism, wrapped only in the dwindling authority of what had once been the greatest Islamic empire.

From this wreckage there emerged, suddenly and dramatically, the man who was to build a new Turkish nation, succeeding where the Young Turks had failed. Mustafa Kemal had much in common with them. He was a professional soldier, made famous by a great exploit at Gallipoli, which perhaps diverted the course of history: had the Allies won at the Dardanelles, the Russian Revolution of 1917 might not have taken place. Already before 1914 he had been dabbling in the underworld of secret political societies; after the outbreak of war, he was among those disillusioned officers who feebly conspired against the Young Turk leaders of the government. Always a man of burning ambition, he had become, also, a Turkish nationalist. He believed the future lay not in continued Ottoman rule over non-Turks, but in the formation of a true Turk-based national state. With formidable abilities, demonstrated both as a battlefield commander and a staff officer, and an imposing presence (he stood six foot, was fair-haired and blue-eyed), he was a dominating, as well as domineering, figure. His combination of energy and will stamped him as a leader — as well as, it seems, making him almost irresistible to women.[14] When, therefore, in May 1919, he threw off the pretence of loyalty to the Sultan, his decision to do so was not altogether unexpected.

Kemal was sent by the government to Anatolia to inspect what remained of the Turkish army on the Black Sea coast. He recognised that the posting opened the way to winning control of Anatolia; when ordered to return by the alarmed authorities, he replied that there was no fuel for the steamboat in which he had come and set off inland with a few trusted cronies. Local resistance groups had already begun to form (largely because of the Greek invasion); by appealing to their anger and hatred of the foreigner Kemal slowly forged a national movement. In 1920 the first Turkish national assembly met in Ankara, which became the seat of a new government aiming at the overthrow of the Sultan, who had made a costly peace, and the liberation of Turkish territory from the foreigner. It was really an officers' government; in Turkey, as in South America in the previous century, and as in many African and Asian countries after 1945, circumstances and opportunity favoured the building of national movements around soldiers.

Civil war and war against Greek invaders of mainland Turkey went hand in hand and culminated in victory in 1922. Turks called Kemal by an ancient title: *Ghazi*, or 'champion of the Faith'. This was a misnomer. Although he had been brought up a Muslim, he was soon to show he saw Islam as little more than a political and military factor. He was, in fact, to reveal himself as a progressive, a secular moderniser, taking as his model the West whose ideas and skills he had admired long before 1914.

In 1922 the Kemalist forces entered Istanbul. The Sultan fled to a British battleship and a new peace settlement was negotiated with the Allies. It was — and has remained — unique, the only peace treaty after the First World War not to have been imposed on a defeated power, and the only one whose terms are, to all intents and purposes, still intact and respected today. Among other things, it swept away the 'Capitulations'. In 1923 a Turkish republic was proclaimed; although some of his supporters suggested he become Sultan, Kemal took office as President. A two-party system soon gave way to a more authoritarian regime. In spite of constitutional forms, power lay with the president and his entourage. Nonetheless, the forms were not unimportant. Peter the Great, in his westernising just over two centuries earlier, called on traditional respect for autocratic authority in Russia; with such respect dissipated in Turkey, Kemal had to dress dictatorship in democratic garb. He saw his task as one of national education, and the operation of a representative assembly and respect (normally) for the law had parts to play in that, even if the new Turkey was in fact a one-party state.

Although Kemal had found support among the Muslim religious leaders, any modernising regime would be likely, sooner or later, to confront Islam. From the nineteenth century, Ottoman sultans had been caliphs, claiming authority to interpret Muslim teaching which went back to the Prophet himself. The caliphate had even survived the end of the monarchy and the new Constitution said that 'the religion of the Turkish state is Islam'. Kemal, though, was anxious that, as one of his followers put it, 'the bridges joining Turkey to the Middle Ages were to be blown up' — and Islam was one of them. The first step was the expulsion of the caliph. Awoken one night, he was told to be gone by 5 a.m. and that was the end of the caliphate, too. On the following Friday, for the first time since 1453, the prayers in the great mosque of Istanbul, the old church of St Sophia, made no mention of the caliph. There followed the closing of religious courts, the introduction of a new code of civil law based on the Swiss model and, at last in 1928, the formal secularisation of the Turkish state and the striking from the Constitution of the reference to its religion. 'Islam, this theology of an immoral Arab', said Kemal, 'is a dead thing'.[15]

It was another symbol of movement away from Islamic roots that the Gregorian calendar was adopted officially in 1925. Such decisions identified the new Turkey with the West, with the ideas of a civilisation which Kemal wanted his own countrymen to adopt. Some went very deep, above all, a revolution in the legal and social status of women. New legal rights, the vote, and entry to the professions were given to them, but just as significant was the abolition of the veil and the spread of western dress, a process much accelerated by the example of the president's wife, in this respect thoroughly westernised. Symbols counted for much. It was in 1925, at Smyrna, that the first formal ball ever to be held in Turkey, where women and men had previously danced together in western fashion only in a few private (or disreputable) places, was opened by the president himself stepping onto the floor to foxtrot with the begowned daughter of the city's governor.

That was characteristic. Kemal was a born pedagogue. He knew, as does any good teacher, the value of the dramatic personal gesture. When the adoption of a new script based on the western alphabet severed another link with the Arabic-dominated culture of the past, Kemal himself went about the country giving lessons in it to the people, lecturing visitors to his palace with the help of the blackboards which were to be found scattered through the rooms. He would even get up between courses at dinner and address his guests, chalk in hand. More dramatic still was his attack on traditional Turkish costume. 'A civilised, international dress is worthy and appropriate for our nation,' he said, 'and we will wear it.' This meant abandoning the fez. Kemal deliberately chose one day to appear in a little Anatolian town, announcing that his unusual headgear was called a 'hat', that it was characterised by having a brim, and that other people should wear the same.

The most telling expression of Kemal's confidence that western ideas were the master-ideas of the age was his promotion of the concept of Turkish nationality. The collapse of the Ottoman empire left behind thirty or so successor states, many of them lacking any cohesive ideological principle. Ethnic or territorial nationhood was a latecomer to the Islamic world; it made its appearance there only as the ideas of the French Revolution penetrated the Near East in the nineteenth century. Kemal wanted nationalism to fill the ideological vacuum left among his own countrymen by the removal of Ottoman rule, which had aspired to religious legitimacy and had in practice depended largely upon the favouring of one ethnic or religious group against another and the selection of officials without regard to ethnic origin.[16] The name 'Turkey' had been unknown in the country to which the West applied it: it was simply taken over from European languages and adopted by the new republic in 1923. A cult of the Anatolian Turk then began. The man in the street learnt that Adam had been a Turk; for those requiring a more specious basis for their political loyalty, it was claimed that modern Turks were genetically pure descendants of a white Aryan people from Central Asia. The connexion of the leader with the nationalist cult was manifest in the new name Kemal was given by his countrymen: Atatürk — 'Father Turk'.

By the time he died, in 1938, the Turkish national revolution had been sufficiently digested for Kemal to consider his essential work done. Many other would-be nation-makers and reformers have since tried to emulate him. Often they failed because they were neither so single-minded as he, nor so clear-sighted in perceiving the implications of what they sought and that there might be opposition to paying the high sentimental and cultural costs involved. The chequered record of some who, without much regard for widespread and deeply felt attitudes, sought to industrialise Islamic countries shows this. Industrialising meant imitating the West. As one Egyptian put it in the 1920s, 'We merely desire a place in the sun, to live like other people, producing and increasing our production.' And went on, directly addressing himself to the West, 'we are working in accordance with your example. And we are grateful to you for having shown us this path.' Sometimes, economic development and industrialisation paid off.

By 1939, several Islamic nations appeared to be going down Kemal's road of national self-assertion. Reza Shah was the first non-European ruler to cancel a foreign oil concession and win (after taking his case to that shrine of western liberal idealism, the League of Nations). British governments were happy to placate Egyptian nationalism whenever strategy permitted. But things did not go smoothly in the Islamic lands. The concept of the territorial state did not make sufficiently rapid headway among them to contain the destabilisations caused by economic growth, urbanisation and detribalisation. These demanded new foci of loyalties, but such were not always easily to be found, even after 1945. Nor did older ones always meet the bill. Pakistan was startlingly unusual in emerging in the post-colonial world as a new nation defined by religion but, as the eventual breakaway of Bangladesh was to show, Islam was not a strong enough tie to hold it together. Nor did nationalism seem so successful in meeting popular needs and aspirations in the Arab Islamic lands as it had been in Europe. In the eyes of many Muslims, it failed to deliver what it had promised to nineteenth-century enthusiasts. Often it only multiplied quarrels between the Arab peoples. Perhaps no one should have been surprised by this. Save that it is Islamic, the Islamic world is emphatically not a unity. Yet after the collapse of the multi-ethnic empires of the Ottoman and Persian empires, there was no alternative to national states if the ruins were to be reorganised.

Fundamentalists were ready with an explanation: nationalism was bound to fail because it was alien, western. Their answer was to go back to Islamic teaching and turn on the would-be modernisers and westernisers.[17] As one of the Iranian reactionaries has put it, was it not 'the very humanist conception of man that has dragged him to the infra-human'? So the memory of the reforming dictators was turned upon. Atatürk was especially reviled. Had he not once called the Prophet 'immoral' and abolished the veil? It was a grievance against Reza Khan that he had taken the 'un-Islamic' name of Pahlavi. Jinnah, founder of Pakistan, was seen as a man who had put nationalism before the Faith.[18] Even the anti-Israeli Palestinians were criticised by some Muslim fundamentalists, for they were engaged in a struggle of nationalisms, not a struggle for Islam. To a fundamentalist like Maulana Mawdudi, an Islamic ideologist from Pakistan, capitalism, communism, and, for that matter, fascism, are all products of the same western decadence.

Revulsion against the West took a long time to come to a climax, but was bound to be sweeping and far-reaching when it did. Islam could mobilise huge forces of emotion and will for the moment of release, and had a doctrine at hand to canalise them; severely orthodox Islamic lawyers taught that there always had been and always would be a state of war between Islam and 'the House of War' (the non-Muslim world) and that it would cease only when all the world was Muslim. A step such as the foundation in 1973 of an Islamic Council of Europe for the evangelising of this continent has to be seen against both an ancient conceptual background, and a modern history of pure resentment of western power.

The explosion, when it came in the 1970s, was, as so many things in history are, a matter of circumstance. As membership of the United Nations Organisation soared upwards towards 150 states, majorities began steadily to go against the old western powers and their satellites. In the Middle East itself, Cold War had partly paralysed the rival imperialisms of the non-communist and communist West. The existence of Israel was a continuing focus of instability and frustration to Muslim rulers. Conservative Arab states feared the social consequences of technological change. Dissatisfaction with modernisation was specially acute in Iran, where the Shah was hated by westernised liberals as well as by the orthodox. Above all, in 1974, came the discovery of the magic power of the new sword of Allah: oil. Its diplomacy forced the great powers, Japan now among them, to take Muslims seriously as an international force for the first time since Ottoman times. What is more, Islamic brotherhood cast long shadows. The Russian and Chinese communist empires were both multi-national and multi-religious, and millions of their subjects belonged, through Islam, to a community with centres of gravity outside their borders.

The first results were notable triumphs for Islamic fundamentalism, especially in Iran and Libya. Western, industrial, liberal society was rejected and reviled. The government of Pakistan introduced the Koranic punishments of amputation for theft and whipping for drinking alcohol, made it a criminal offence for anyone to be seen eating or drinking during the fasting hours of Ramadan (foreigners lunched behind blacked-out windows in their hotels), and forbade women's hockey teams to compete in international matches if men would be watching. The deep changes really going on beneath the surface of events in societies so varied as those of the Islamic world, though, are hard to read. The Shah has gone, but Suni and Sufi still contend and Iraq and Iran are at war. In Wahabist Saudi Arabia, concessions had to be made long ago to telegraph, telephone and broadcasting; western oil companies operating there employ thousands of Arabians and teach them western ways. Saudi laws prohibit the taking of interest on money, yet practice allows it.

Education is a force particularly hard to assess. Oil money has poured into colleges and universities with predominantly technological, scientific and medical emphases, a major new departure. Until the middle of the last century, Muslim higher education had an almost exclusively theological and legal focus. It extended little beyond the reading and memorising of the Koran and Sunnah, and the study of commentary upon them. The next stage had been the attendance of Muslim students at western universities in Europe or the United States, and the foundation of colleges and universities on western lines in Islamic lands (notably the American University of Beirut). Many of these developments brought about further cultural contamination of Islamic society by the West. New universities now attempt to obtain the advantages of western knowledge without incurring such dangers. In many of them, new curricula and textbooks grapple with the problem of reclassifying knowledge in accordance with Islamic categories and criteria. Attempts have been made to formulate new Islamic concepts in order to restructure and reinterpret the natural sciences. Whether such withdrawal into cultural isolation is actually conceivable in the long run is another matter. The heirs of Mehemet Ali (so to speak), the young men seeking material advancement for themselves and their peoples, still go if they can to MIT or Imperial College to learn how to westernise and modernise — or, in some cases, flirt with Marxism, a western creed still able to express itself in militant, proselytising forms which not only challenge Islam but provide revolutionary force inside it. The young women at medical school in Cairo who, in 1978, refused to dissect male corpses, took to veil and *chador*, and demanded academic segregation from men and dual curricula, contrast with thousands of other Muslim girls who glimpse a different kind of life in the university education now being made available to them for the first time. Successful resistance to westernisation in Islamic countries may therefore well turn out to be less easy than appeared at first sight. A thousand years ago, in Sicily and Al-Andalus, the self-confidence of Christian culture was corroded by the seductive superiority of Islam. Now, the reverse is true.

One sensitive observer detects a lie in the soul of the Islamic reaction, in the unexpressed but crucial belief that whatever the changes Islam needs to make in order to ensure purification, they will never cut her off from the enjoyment of the fruits of modern science and technology; he identifies an 'expectation — of others continuing to create, of the alien, necessary civilisation going on' which he sees as 'implicit in the act of renunciation, and its great flaw'.[19] This is to see Islam as parasitic upon a western civilisation which it rejects emotionally, but which it cannot do without. The death of the unflinching Pakistani ideologist Maulana Mawdudi in a hospital in Boston, where he had gone for medical treatment, makes the point; the remittances from emigrant guest-workers in Europe, the students at western universities make it in other ways. It must be conceded that Islamic experience so far at least does not disprove the view that the best defence against western power has always turned out to be not rejection but acceptance of western ideas. It may be that Islam will yet reveal a capacity to accept and internalise them; after all, Islam's own roots lie in the same semitic and monotheistic tradition as those of Christianity. At least some Islamic fundamentalists concede that Christianity was *once* a healthy, undebased creed. Whether there is some rediscovery to be awaited here or not, though, the best means of successful ethical and political resistance to western power have so far proved to be western. Around the world, men and women still turn to the great European writers and thinkers for guidance and insight in striking out for themselves, even while others desperately try to revive their native traditions. Newton, Darwin, Marx, Mazzini, Tolstoy, Rousseau

— all these and many more, whatever we may now think of them, have deeply marked the non-western world. Their ideas are still at work there. The West, on the other hand, owes nothing comparable to any non-western figure since Jesus Christ — and when he died, of course, the West did not exist.

XIII

A POST-WESTERN WORLD?

A famous photograph from the last world war shows a couple of Indian soldiers with a machine-gun, in position near a Burmese pagoda. They were Asians fighting other Asians, but wearing the uniform of western armies. The machine-gun in the photograph is American; no doubt the Japanese at whom they were shooting were using similar weapons, evolved originally for western armies by western technology. In other ways, too, the photograph mirrors our multifarious, complicated theme. The pagoda in the photograph turns out on inspection to be built of corrugated iron, one of the convenience materials of the industrial West's building technology. The soldiers themselves were mercenaries. Among the things they were all fighting about were very clear western interests; was Great Britain to hang on to Burma and India? They were fighting for an alien ruler, as Indians had fought ever since, in the eighteenth century, the British East India Company launched the era of European-officered armies of natives. The practice spread. In the 1790s both the French and British raised black regiments in the West Indies; from that came the West India Regiment, the first to be raised from colonial subjects and kept up in peacetime. The Indian army was the greatest of all such forces, but all the nineteenth-century imperial powers enlisted native troops; askaris, goumiers, zouaves, sepoys, spahis. Even the United States raised the Philippine Scouts. The French envisaged a major strategic role in Europe for their large African armies. So millions of fighting men were enmeshed in a web of circumstance determined by the West.

Superficially, much of the case for the view that the day of the West is done is simply that the empires which could raise such forces are gone, and gone for good. Besides our civilisation's internal troubles and loss of self-confidence, there have been huge changes in the outside world. It is full of young nations which did not exist in 1939 and the present international system gives unrealistic weight to them. China has emerged as a super-power. All this makes nonsense of any idea of reviving the old direct political control of the globe by the West. As for the western economies, they have looked shakier since the oil crisis. And finally there are those signs in recent years which are taken by some to reveal that a deeper, cultural rejection of the

West is under way in countries which once seemed to welcome it. Is this once supremely effective civilisation now no longer able to offer leadership to the world it transformed? May there be further decline in store — or even worse? After all, entire cultures have disappeared before now — some at the hands of the West itself. Or does the West still possess reserves of power and intellectual and spiritual resources which can yet be tapped?

Historians must stay out of the business of prediction. On the basis of the world as it is, though, the more cool-headed — or perhaps more cynical — among them might observe that although much has changed in the last two decades, the power and the wealth of the West are still overwhelming. The United States, Europe and Soviet Russia are still industrial giants. The Second World War, though it weakened western power and wealth in so many ways, reinforced them in others — by, for example, leading to new economic developments in colonial territories so as to integrate them with western needs. Some African countries are still grappling with the consequences of the strategical planning which tied them to the growing of cash crops for export rather than of food for their own peoples. From similar necessity there flowed industrial and urban development, which now attracts hostile criticism.[1] Paradoxically, a state like Zambia now has to import food, and this locks it into the mechanism of world food prices as well as those of the minerals it exports.

Another great western civil war — perhaps between communist and non-communist — could compromise or even shatter forever the huge economic advantage still enjoyed by western countries, but we are still a long way from that point. Moreover, either directly or indirectly, through investment abroad or in multinational companies, the non-communist West still has a big voice in the management and exploitation of most of the world's raw materials. At the beginning of the 1970s, European or United States governments and companies were said to control between them 70 per cent of the world's copper production, three-quarters of its nickel, four-fifths of its aluminium refining.[2] True, many western countries depend upon non-western countries for oil, but Europe at least can now draw on the North Sea. Nor is it by any means certain that oil producers could hold the West to ransom indefinitely, for in extremity military power could secure it adequate supplies. This would, of course, be repugnant to many people. It would confirm what some of them already believe, namely, that the story of western civilisation in world history is essentially a matter of superior force.

The argument of power should, in my view, be disregarded for a better reason; there are stronger arguments for believing western civilisation's future to be less menacing than we sometimes think. That is suggested by the very violence of anti-western reaction by traditionalists within other cultures — a testimony, presumably, not to weakness but to a continuing effectiveness.

Here is another paradox. Western civilisation has always been terribly handicapped in trying to build a stable world order by its tendency to destabilise anything it touched. At times it seems almost to infect other cultures with madness, even if only in the pursuit of pleasure: Arabian princes flock to the fleshpots of the western world under influences as powerful as those which drew to Rome the barbarian warlords who admired and envied its achievement and luxuries. So the West unwittingly accelerates the corrosion of established structures in the old Islamic world and perhaps makes more likely the onset of crises which could threaten us with world war. But it is not just a matter of the attractiveness of the West's grosser temptations to some Muslims. Much more profoundly seismic is the slow alienation of whole generations of well-to-do youngsters from the ways of their parents the world round. Sometimes exposed also to formal education which insinuates western assumptions, they are everywhere slowly absorbing western tastes and fashions simply because of western-dominated styles of communication and consumption.

In West Africa, it is said, a western emphasis on the profit motive has led to a decline in traditional regard for the needs of the extended family — or those of society as a whole — as opposed to those of the individual. Changes follow a new emphasis on the individual in many ways, too — new assumptions are formed, about (for example) marriage as a matter of mutual attraction rather than dynastic strategy, about income as a means to immediate satisfactions, rather than as a means of accumulating status and power by deferring them. Monogamy, new in much of Africa, is said to reflect a new and disruptively individualist culture. No doubt, it will be a long time before Chinese or Indian families lose their strength and cohesiveness. Yet even among Hong Kong or Singapore Chinese a few cracks are beginning to show. Some Chinese parents in those communities are already dismayed by the weakening of those old, prudent, economic habits which built up the networks of security and investment which dominate the great Chinese communities abroad. Indian parents in England do their best to resist the erosion of old ideas about family loyalty and discipline which have served them so well. Not dissimilar assumptions were once strong in western society, though, and are now visibly crumbled. As for Japan, surveys show the distaste of many young people for traditional attitudes to employment, family and society; care of the old can no longer rest safely upon the old Confucian sense of filial loyalty.[3]

Reaction to destabilising contact with the West can nevertheless take many different forms. Some will still wish to embrace western civilisation as vigorously as they can — because they believe it to be the best. They are happy to buy the entire package: not just the technology, but the optimism, rationalism and individualism, too — an ideological Trinity of the civilisation from which the technology emerged. Others would like to pick and choose among the dangerous gifts of the West. Even hostility to western influence comes in different shapes. There are those in the modern Islamic world who violently and anachronistically reject anything which smacks of the West, but other Muslims commit themselves all the more strongly to the adoption of *some* western ways in order to gain or regain control of their own heritages. Both groups want the same thing — the dignity of emancipation from western power and the preservation of something they can feel is uniquely their own. Much of the world is like that today, but often the western challenge has broken down views of history and human destiny which animated old cultures; they have ceased to be adequate guides about the way society is going. People find themselves in a frightening, shifting landscape, and lose their security and understanding of where they are. Western knowledge has often been sought in order to retain the essence of an old society under strain, but usually with results which turn out to make that more difficult to achieve. One temptation in those circumstances is to take up someone else's views, other myths which seem to provide better guidance. And such alternative myths, for a long time now, have tended to be drawn from the mythologies of the West, whether Christian, Marxist, or merely vaguely and materially progressive. To seek from the West the intellectual means of grappling with the damage it has done is surely its most ironical triumph.

Even the greatest traditions reflect this. For more than a century now China has been redefining her relationships with the West. The story could not end with the burning of the Summer Palace, or the Boxer Rebellion. In the late nineteenth century many educated Chinese came at last to see that western power could not be contained within the framework provided by traditional ideas. The old Chinese world picture of the West as an inferior culture whose inhabitants should be confined to a subject and tributary status, and the psychological stance which went with this, received another grave blow in 1911, when a revolution abolished the Chinese empire, and a republic on western lines was set up. Two thousand years of tradition were formally set aside; it was the end of a state and society based on Confucianism. The Gregorian calendar was adopted in 1912, a good symbol of co-ordination with western standards. Centrifugal forces barely contained in the previous quarter-century could not but assert themselves. Some of them — indeed, the revolutionary leader Sun-Yat-sen himself — owed much to Japanese encouragement and example; Japan had been a refuge and a source of practical and monetary support for Chinese exiles under the Ch'ing.

Yet 1911 was not quite the end of Chinese traditionalism. Some held on to Confucian attitudes, with occasional encouragement from the government, during the Kuomintang era, when China was ruled by the successors of those who had made the revolution. The solidity and strength of the

Chinese family, the integument of Chinese civilisation, was hardly affected. Nonetheless, the formal change was immensely significant. Two thousand years of imperial history had evidently come to an end.[4] The Chinese who had wanted to embrace much of what the West had to offer had won, at least in form, and form counts for a great deal in China. The debate could move into a new phase, one about the pace and tactics of modernisation, that is, about how to imitate the West, which western model to choose — not about the principle. Or so it seemed; unfortunately, we all have to settle with a past at the same time as we grapple with a future.

For most of the period between the two world wars, the issues were made even more obscure by political confusion. The Chinese empire's disappearance was followed not by a clear transfer of power to the new republic, but by its near evaporation. The state went into eclipse. The abandonment of the old examination system in 1904 had already opened the way to the dissolution of the hegemony of the old gentry class which had held the empire together for centuries. Now it was to crumble further in the turmoil of civil war. This explains why the state could for some years do little but react defensively. Political disintegration went along with ideological. Central authority faded away as huge areas fell under the sway of 'warlords'. The revenues of the Republic dried up, tapped at their sources by strong men in the provinces. This delayed modernisation still further. Central government has usually been one of its most effective agencies and it did not operate over much of China between 1911 and 1949.

Yet during those years direct aggression against China by western imperialist states virtually came to an end. Military preoccupations after 1914 almost entirely finished off western diplomatic interest in China except in one respect: the British and French strove to get Chinese soliders to fight in the western front. They were unsuccessful, though China went to war against Germany in 1917. Apart from labour battalions, though, no Chinese military forces turned up in Europe. Still, many Chinese felt they should be rewarded for joining the winning side. That they were disappointed was largely because the Allies wanted to remain on good terms with the Japanese, potentially a much more powerful ally during the war which had been their opportunity. They, more clearly than ever, were the worst threat to the new China.

The knowledge that the European powers themselves were unlikely to encroach further upon China, and the opportunity to seize former German territories in China and the Pacific were the first advantages enjoyed by the Japanese. They encouraged China's internal divisions, too; Sun-Yat-sen himself asked for Japanese help in overthrowing the government of his main rival in the new republic. Then, the Japanese revealed their intentions in 1915 by presenting it with a list of 'Twenty-One Demands'. Acceptance of them all would have made China almost a Japanese protectorate. Chinese diplomacy averted the worst dangers but what had to be conceded was grave enough. Distrust of Japan's intentions was thereafter too firmly entrenched ever to be eradicated. Following the Russian collapse in 1917, Japan's old rival in Far Eastern aggression would clearly now be out of business for some time to come, paralysed by civil war and internal economic troubles. The wish to constitute a Siberian front against the Soviet Union during a brief but crucial period of western intervention in her affairs in 1918–19 further handicapped the Allies from doing much to restrain the Japanese — though they did insist that the Japanese forces withdrew from that theatre when the Americans and British left it.

Against this background, it may seem hardly surprising that the Chinese government found the peace terms of 1919 hard to bear. They revealed that the victorious Allies would not act to prevent Japanese influence in China replacing that of Germany. The Chinese delegates would not sign the treaty[5] and a great outburst of outraged Chinese national feeling followed; these were the riots which began what was soon known as the 'May 4th Movement'. Disillusionment with their own ineffectual government as well as with Great Britain, France and the Untied States turned many Chinese intellectuals towards communism. The Soviet Union had the great advantage of not being associated in their minds with the imperialism of old Russia and was hostile to China's other former oppressors. Moreover, like China, Russia had been a great backward empire which had cast off its dynasty in revolution, and was seeking to modernise.

The entry on stage of a Chinese communist party then completed the cast of Chinese politics down to 1949. Soon, communists and Kuomintang — the party founded by Sun-Yat-sen — were the main rivals for the support of the Chinese people. Sometimes they fought one another; sometimes they co-operated. Always, they acted in the presence of the third force, Japan, obstinately pressing her interests, despoiling China first of Manchuria in 1931, then after 1937, of her capital, her main coastal regions, ports and much of her interior. In invading China, the Japanese said they were saving the Chinese from communism. When Japan entered a wider struggle after 1941 and it became realistic to envisage the liberation of Chinese soil from foreign intervention, the final stage of the struggle of communists and Kuomintang could begin.

In the end, there were many reasons for the failure of the Kuomintang. Its efforts to maintain the governmental unity of the country in the 1920s and 1930s had led to neglect of social reform. It failed to crush its communist rivals during their Long March (1934–5) and then had to treat them as partners in the fight with Japan. It was associated with a long period of hardship and falling standards of living. It had a narrow social basis. During the war years it slid into corruption. Perhaps a successful completion of the Chinese revolution would always have eluded the Kuomintang, though it had its diplomatic successes — notably, obtaining the formal abrogation of the 'unequal' treaties, and gaining accreditation as a major power and so a permanent seat on the Security Council of the United Nations. The communists, meanwhile, had done better at home. They had won the loyalty of the peasants in many of the areas they controlled. Their land reforms held out the promise of real social advance. Geographically, they were well placed to seize quantities of Japanese arms and important strategical areas when the invader finally collapsed, and at that moment they benefited from Russian assistance. No more than the Kuomintang, though, did the Chinese communists defeat the Japanese.

China, instead, was given victory by the Pacific war. By 1945, American power had wiped out Japan's maritime communications, had shattered her industry by bombing, and had destroyed her armies and fleets in the south Pacific. The British had annihilated the Japanese army in Burma. The first two atomic bombs then precipitated Japanese surrender. So opened the last phase of the long-drawn-out Chinese revolution, a soon-acknowledged civil war between Kuomintang Nationalists and communists. It ended, formally, on 1 October 1949, with the proclamation in Peking of the Chinese People's Republic. The world's largest communist state had come into existence.

At last the debate on China's modernisation was to be settled. Ideological and institutional cohesion could be re-established. Yet there are few sharp breaks in history. During the inter-war years, many voices had been heard debating China's future, some still in traditional terms. The Chinese had not ceased to be Chinese in 1911. At a deep level, even revolutionary change was bound to be shaped by tradition, as perhaps Mao's efforts to wean his party from the orthodox Marxism of the day, with its emphasis on unavoidable historical stages of revolution and an industrial proletariat, to a recognition of the immense potential of China's rural misery, showed. Exasperated innovators sometimes railed against the handicaps tradition laid on them. One example was the old language; to abandon it would have something of the effect — though in much greater degree — of the abandonment of Latin as the medium of intellectual discourse in the West, and so there was an enthusiastic search by some for a new vernacular in which writers could express themselves and open official culture to new forces. Reformers were always liable to disagree over how far such changes should go, though, and this no doubt helps to explain why very revolutionary changes have often turned out to look very distinctively Chinese. Yet in the creation of the new China one obeisance to western civilisation was formally complete. With the approval and encouragement of Soviet Russia, the new

275

regime formally based itself on principles declared to be those of Marx and Lenin — western intellectuals who had never visited an oriental country in their lives. Their portraits, together with those of Engels and Stalin, are still ritually carried in procession and displayed on hoardings in demonstrations which recall the traditional respect shown to the great Chinese sages (no non-Chinese since the Buddha has received such official acclaim — unless, of course, he was, like the Mongol emperors, a conqueror). The new state religion of China comes from the West.

Time has shown that China's course was not made easier to predict. Her government did not, for instance, seem to show the missionary zeal often by Soviet communism in nearby countries. Perhaps the contrast says as much about the historical matrix provided by the Russian past and the myth of the 'Third Rome' as it does about China. Yet a crusade to establish a universal ideological domination had never been the aim of China's leaders in imperial times, and that may be relevant, too. On the other hand, there have also been extraordinary bursts of violent reaction against much of the Chinese past. In particular, in the 'Cultural Revolution', once-respected scholars were derided, and a deliberate attempt was made to undermine the family, bed-rock of the old China. A quarter of mankind hurled itself (or was hurled) into the assault on tradition. The memorial stele of Confucius at Qufu still reveals on close inspection the mass of repaired cracks which record its deliberate shattering during the Cultural Revolution. This might be taken as an extreme symptom of the westernising ethos, a brutal expression of the enthusiasm for modernisation which many radicals felt. Religion was attacked whatever its origin, and so in China the militant secularism of nineteenth-century Europe won some of its last victories; Buddhist and Christian places of worship alike were closed, while in Kashgar (where the veil was still worn by Muslim women), piles of Islamic books were fed to bonfires in front of the mosque. Nevertheless, there are difficulties in interpreting such events. Much of the Cultural Revolution, like the earlier displacement of the landlords, seems to have been merely a boiling-over of long-cherished dislikes.

It is difficult, too, to interpret the role of Mao, who presided more or less continuously over the foundation era of communist China. For all his lip service to Marxism and Leninism, from the 1920s onwards he advocated views about Chinese revolution which seem solidly grounded in a recognition of Chinese tradition and reality, rather that in the Marxist orthodoxy of those days. He spoke, in 1938, of the need for the 'Sinification of Marxism', as the huge role given to the peasantry in his rhetoric, doctrinal writings, tactical practice and strategy exemplifies. At least by implication, this was a rejection both of the orthodox Marxist and the market models of modernisation. What is more, Mao the ruler had much about him — including ruthlessness — to suggest the traditional great Chinese emperor. He spoke of (and used) his power specifically with reference to the moral betterment of his subjects, giving them doctrinal guidance as well as government; but ethical superiority had long been the justification of empire in China, hardly challenged as a political doctrine. Mao even wrote poems and practised calligraphy; his achievements in these arts were much advertised. In this, too, there was something of a spurning of the West, and Mao attacked 'comprador' culture in terms which suggest a more personal commitment to Chinese tradition than that of, say, Chou-en-lai. Such facts make it less surprising that one sometimes encounters a picture of Mao in an honoured place in Chinese households in the non-communist world, even though his policies are increasingly criticised by his successors.

China's debate has gone on since Mao died. In the last few years, political distrust and rejection of the West seem somewhat tempered, while the urgency felt by the Chinese to achieve technological modernisation seems stronger than ever. Circumstance and scale have once more begun to operate in China's favour. She has always been lucky in that the full force of western imperialism in its heyday could never be brought to bear on her; she had never had to surrender so completely as, say, India. Even the overt military threat from the West when the bankruptcy of the old empire had been shown by its impotence in the face of western aggression, and when its destroyers (Sun-Yat-sen, above all) owed much to western support, could not be brought to bear long or powerfully enough quite to take China's fate out of her own hands. The empire was in the end finished off by the Chinese themselves. After the Great War, the European nations in the Far East were unequivocally in retreat and China could debate westernisation and modernisation against the background of an actually ebbing western power. Within the limits set by history she could in the end choose her own path, having just managed to retain the possibility of self-change until the worst dangers were past. This makes it easier to see why so much of the Chinese past, in particular its ancient readiness to subordinate the individual to social disciplines which would be thought intolerable in the West, lives on. It is one reason why it is so difficult to judge what is really happening to China, although it was in the name of western values — both liberal and Marxist — that she was eventually forced into her era of modernisation.

In spite of Japan's early cultural debts to her great neighbour, her story had been very different. The continuity of her history was ruptured by contact with the West, but Japan embarked upon change much sooner than China and has been more obviously transformed as a result. Moreover, her people seemed to respond more readily and positively to western ideas: translations of J.S. Mill's *On Liberty* and Samuel Smiles' *Self-Help* were best-sellers in the 1870s. Yet Japan managed to hold on to much of her inherited structure. In spite of huge shocks on the way, change in Japan has been consciously regulated as China's could not be until very recently. Nonetheless, though the result now looks very 'western', native and western cultural strands are now so intertwined in Japan that any value there was in the old and misleadingly simple dichotomy has now disappeared. The speed with which nineteenth-century Japan moved down the road to modernisation, of course, quickly relieved her of the threat of western bullying such as China suffered. This was not merely because Japan soon acquired the military and technical power to stand up to the West. It was also important that her 'progressiveness' robbed western powers of moral grounds for interference. The British and Americans found it difficult in Japan (as elsewhere later) not to concede implicity that modernisation must connote liberalisation. Well before the Capitulations with Turkey, or the unequal treaties imposed on China, their Japanese equivalents had disappeared.

Just how deeply, or in what sense, the cultural mixture which is modern Japan can be termed 'westernised' is still debatable. The assumptions of the Meiji era had been summed up in slogans which implied discrimination and selection: 'Eastern morality, Western technology', or 'Japanese spirit, Western expertise'. If that no longer makes sense of the choices facing Japan today, it is because much has happened in a century.[7] What cannot be disputed is that, for all the huge differences between them, China and Japan have both striven to find protection against western civilisation in a measure of westernisation.

Here lies the deepest irony of post-western history: it is so often in the name of western values that the West is rejected and it is always with its skills and tools that its grasp is shaken off. Western values and assumptions have been internalised to a remarkable degree in almost every other major culture. The United Nations Organisation is built on the legal fiction that nation states are equal, sovereign individuals. That is a western concept, fully comprehensible only within the history of western legal and political thinking, but the world takes it for granted. Or take equality, the dominant social ideal of the age, and a western one; it is in the West that the historical debate about its means and realisation, about whether it can or should be satisfied externally or internally, objectively or subjectively, has taken place. Nor are such paradoxes confined to politics. When an Indian or Japanese intellectual looks today for guidance about where the avant-garde is to be found, he looks as did his predecessors fifty years ago, to the West, even if that means following the self-destructive trends of western culture. Even the western cult of the artist as not a craftsman, but someone whose characteristic activity is the creation of inspired expressions of subjective experience, whose lifestyle is unconventional, and whose claim to respect rests on his possession of a talent vouched for by the display of originality, is spreading to other cultures. The transformation of a European view of the artist which began (perhaps) with Beethoven can now be sensed world-wide.

It would be wrong, and perhaps dangerous, to exaggerate. Hundreds of millions live virtually untouched by such facts. Yet politicians, journalists, intellectuals increasingly take them for granted. Once a non-western society gets on the move, its élites seem drawn irresistibly in directions already pointed out by the West — towards the search for greater material well-being, towards the establishment of the formal values of democracy and nationalism; towards a commitment to progress; towards the corrosive ideas of personal accountability and choice, individualism and the right to a private life. The replacement in many Japanese homes of the traditional sliding screens with doors which close and lock like those of the West makes possible a definition of private space within the family dwelling which was traditionally unknown: a Japanese, too, can now aspire to a room of his own, private space in a once very collective society. Such tiny signs are the indicators of the power of the first civilisation to come within sight of spreading its universal ethical aspirations universally. The acceptability of such ideas and standards outside the old West seems ever growing.

This does not imply any intrinsic merit, even if that seems likely to some to be part of the story. A huge improvement in communications may matter more. Mainly in the last thirty years or so, objects, people and information have come to move about as never before. Travel and transmission over long distances is easier and faster than ever before. Whether the traffic goes one way or the other, it seems never to weaken or diminish the attractive power of western ways. Indeed, the opposite is the effect. The hundreds of thousands of travellers from western countries who go to Asia or Africa every year lead to the creation of more services on western lines to cater for them; very few of them 'go native' themselves. In the opposite direction, conflicts and cultural shocks are manifest. Indians and Pakistanis in Great Britain are often unhappy and ill at ease, and so are Algerians in France, Turks in Germany and Italy. Older, more conservative members of immigrant or recently-immigrant communities feel threats to their cherished traditions which are all the worse because so informal and all-pervasive. They fear cultural contamination. If you manage to keep your daughters out of mixed schools, you nonetheless find it almost impossible to control the play upon them of the most powerful engine of mass education the West has yet produced, commercial advertising. The other side of the coin is the positive demand of the younger members of these communities that they shall, indeed, be immersed in western society in a complete and unqualified way. They want it shown that western talk of tolerance, equal treatment by the law, and equal access to economic opportunity are not shams but reality. That, of course, implies that they accept western civilisation in a very deep way indeed. They are (like nineteenth-century Europeans and North Americans) rejecting assumptions held by the overwhelming majority of the human race until now: that kin are to be preferred to friends, and friends and neighbours to strangers; that he that hath shall hold that he hath. They are rejecting the age-old fatalism which says things will stay as they are, a fatalism from which European civilisation was the first to escape.

Personal interaction is, nonetheless, only a part of the story of modern communications, and a very recent part at that. A growing flow of information has been subverting non-western cultures for much longer. There is a fascinating memorandum by a seventeenth-century Belgian Jesuit who was anxious to urge the ordination of a native Chinese clergy. He did not want them to be taught Latin — not merely because the Chinese authorities would distrust those who consorted with foreigners in a language unknown to their own magistrates, but because Latin would bring with it access to non-Roman Catholic writings — even to the works of heretics or of those who criticised the colonial claims of Spain and Portugal. Chinese priests using only their own language, he thought, would learn 'only those portions of the Old and New Testaments which can be taught them without fear of misunderstanding and scandal'.[8] Access to the common language of educated Europe would be much more dangerous. Father Rougemont's misgivings have been startlingly borne out in a far wider way than he would have thought possible. Particularly in the last thirty years there has been an unprecedented increase in the volume and speed of information diffusion from western sources.

Printing was only the first, most striking technical change in communications. In the nineteenth century, steamships and railroads first made regular mails possible and electric telegraphs created world markets. But the take-off into world-wide mass communication really began only after 1945. It is a vast topic, ranging from the presenting of hard news through machinery and agencies from or still based in the West (and therefore suspect in many parts of the non-western world) to flickering performances of Hollywood spectaculars in Indonesian villages with the incomprehensible soundtrack turned off and the schoolmaster interpreting what is shown on the screen. The crucial change, though, was the coming of radio and television. This still has a long way to go; television sets are still unusual objects over most of the world. But transistor radios are not, while satellites and direct video filming are now beginning to add a new rapidity and immediacy to reporting.

The new scale of mass communication is reflected in other ways, stretching from advertising which urges certain consumption patterns by reflecting canons of success and status modelled on western prototypes, to the diffusion of images of western leaders and gurus in photographs and prints.[11] Such messages as they carry overwhelmingly, if indirectly and implicitly, endorse western ideas and assumptions, western procedures and models of behaviour, even western art forms, distorted though they must be. Here can be found the explanation of what has sometimes been called an 'international' youth culture. It is certainly international in its social composition, but it is hardly intercultural. It rests on a diffusion of western style in dress, amusement, manners, personal relationships by the western advertising and communications industries. Fashion is what matters in such things; jeans, teeshirts and sneakers are the modern equivalents of the top-hats and morning coats to which some Asiatics took in the last century because they saw them as showing their integration with a culture of superior attractive power.

Some of the most powerful images of western cultural power are provided by its science. Of course it has long been steadily, remorselessly and effortlessly promoted in the non-western world by the appearance there of the first steamships, locomotives, motor-cars and aeroplanes. Technology and medicine have always been the best advertisements for what it could do. The steady and growing fall-out in prestige from their daily, incidental evidence of western civilisation's mastery of nature has been a social and political force the world round. For most people, no doubt, scientific progress means technology. Television provides new images of it every day, from space shuttles to oil refineries. In such images are concentrated easily understood expressions of human potential. They provide new thoughts about more than just the material world. They are reinforced as cultural factors by more indirect contributions of science to human welfare such as the diffusion of experimental techniques, the growth of systematic investigation, the coordination of knowledge drawn from many different fields.

The intellectual hegemony of western science has also been buttressed by its sheer size and scale. By 1970 more than 100,000 scientific journals were already being published and the rate of increase suggested the number would double every fifteen years. There are more scientists alive and working at this moment than have lived and died in the whole of human history. All this explains why science is now a major religion, perhaps *the* religion, of our civilisation, for most men and women one of the few remaining unquestioned verities. It is sometimes the only one to which a post-Christian European admits any allegiance. It commands the emotional support of large numbers of men. This non-rational status is established by its power as a certificating authority, by the often unquestioned assumption that its ends are good, however it is sometimes misused, and by the elaboration of a hierarchy and priesthood which stimulates envy and aspiration. Ever since Voltaire canonised Newton, scientists have been allowed to make public pronouncements about matters outside their own professional competence with a confidence which used to be shown only by bishops. What is more, they often get the respectful attention which would once have been given to ecclesiastical rhetoric; like the priests before them, scientists have benefited from mankind's wish to discern in some of its members a general competence in human affairs.

Of course, there are suspicions of the new priesthood. Sometimes it has made mistakes and sometimes it cannot control what it releases; we are now beginning to worry about the implications of the fertilisation of the human ovum in the laboratory, though the achievement seemed amazing only a decade ago. The conscious application of science to humanity, indeed, is now beginning to awake very deep concern. The vision some cherish of a totally predictable mankind horrifies most of us. It would be bitter to have to concede that the manipulation of man as a part of nature was the logical end of the western dream. What is more, history is disrespectful of authority; however impressive and seemingly durable, it tends to wane with the particular social forms which gave it birth. Such collapses of authority cannot easily be predicted, and may be surprising; even after the Reformation it would have been a far-sighted man indeed who could have discerned much before the nineteenth century the advent of our modern secular and de-sacramentalised culture. Other authorities besides churches have been challenged and have sometimes crumbled. The family, absolute property, kingship; in some societies, each has had its day. Nothing human is immutable. New needs and demands will arise and the present authority of science may prove to be a little more limited than we are now tempted to think. But that it can ever be reduced to insignificance is unbelievable and its abandonment by non-western societies is inconceivable. Science is our civilisation's highest and most concentrated expression of man's status as a being capable of rational thought and as a change-maker. Faith in it lies at the very heart of the optimism with which western men so long confronted the future, and which they have since spread round the world.

Most universities and institutions of higher education founded in the non-western world since 1945 have a scientific or technological bias. Having taken up the western conception of higher education and the western institution of the university, non-western societies are now anxious to use them to domesticate the western scientific culture. The Sorcerer's Apprentice, though, may release more forces than he intended. Off campus, even when practised unskilfully, science is a terribly and fundamentally transforming force. It redistributes status and prestige, giving new weight to those who possess certain kinds of knowledge. As the notions of empiricism and experiment soak down into crevices and cracks in assumptions and daily practice, they encourage growth which gradually prises apart old mental worlds as remorselessly as plants and trees in the end break up temples swallowed by rain forest. Conventional assumptions do not give way easily, it is true.

Many Indian scientists still show great respect for caste when it comes to marrying off their children, and practical pagans in Northern Ireland respect communal bigotries. But cultural inconsistency can be, and mercifully often is, diminished by education and time. Someone accustomed to thinking of his work in terms of western science should, in the end, help to spread a new sense of critical response, even if the outcome is either a kind of schizophrenia, an acceptance of incompatibles as a practical requirement which cannot be sustained on intellectual grounds, or cynicism. Neither is a stabilising force.[10]

In some areas of traditional practice the rational criteria of our science-based, individualistic culture are only slowly coming to bear. Family and sexual life are obvious examples. For all the new pressures which play upon non-western societies, the family can still act as a great conservative force, influencing the relations of individual men and women in a way no longer unquestioned in the West. The daughter of a highly-educated Indian barrister may still prefer to accept the family view that a husband should be sought for her not merely from the same Brahmin caste, but even from a very restricted sub-caste within it.[11] That such a choice can be welcome to the individuals concerned shows the strength of tradition. Sometimes starker and more tragic decisions are involved. The Chinese Communist Party has set its face against the once widespread practice of female infanticide. Yet official policy to restrict families, if possible, to only one child, has re-awoken the old prejudice that sons, not daughters, are desirable; if there is to be only one child, it should, many Chinese mothers believe, be male, and so there is now plentiful evidence that girl babies are often murdered at birth — a reversion to traditional practice. As a Chinese communist magazine has observed, more than thirty years after the victory of the Chinese revolution, and 2300 years after his death, the ancient sage Mencius would today be happy; it is clear that many Chinese still fervently believe what he taught about male superiority and the essential worthlessness of women — and show it by infanticide.[12]

Such facts have to be taken into account in measuring 'westernisation'. The balance will vary not only from society to society, but from one institution to another in the same society. Evident as the weight and complexity of the past is, though, it is reasonable to ask whether a trend can be seen. Traditional behaviour may seem untouched by such changes as we have been thinking about only if we take a somewhat abstract and formal view of the way a science-based culture operates, or a somewhat superficial and short-term one. After all, it is not rationalism or scientific ideas which 'explain' the accelerating change in the role of women in western societies over the last two centuries. There was from the start an irreducible residue of Christian respect for women which made it awkward in the last and most vital respect

— capacity for salvation — to distinguish them from men, try as theologians might. Weaker vessels, daughters of Eve who led Adam astray, temptations to sin they might be, but the church had to teach that their souls were of infinite value in the eyes of God.

For hundreds of years this did little to change most women's lives. It safeguarded their status, though, and in some European countries that status improved. It was, significantly, the regions of Europe most influenced by Islam which remained most restrictive in their attitude to women. Later came the great secularisation of western civilisation from the eighteenth century onwards; that gave increasing weight to rationalising and individualist arguments for extending to women legal privileges more widely diffused among men. Finally, what really 'emancipated' women (to use the odd terminology of the classical women's movements) was not doctrine or politics, but technology and capitalism. The first gave most women more time. In industrial societies it relieved virtually all women (and not merely the rich) of some kinds of work, and that meant time for education for a few and time for earning for many more. No technological miracles are involved; the simple provision of a direct household supply of piped water or gas makes the point. In the end, technology even gave women reliable and safe means of avoiding child-bearing except when they wished. As for the new jobs which industrial capitalism offered them, they were better paid than the centuries-old drudgeries and hard labour of peasant life which is still the lot of many women in non-western countries. Education followed because women had to be mobilised for these jobs. Finally (an under-rated factor) commercial capitalism submitted them to an enormous and continuing stimulation and education by advertisement.[13]

Such forces have come now to bear on women almost world-wide, even if not evenly or with equal intensity. What has been described as the reciprocal sexual monopoly of two individuals has been identified by one African sociologist as the central institution conveyed by Christianity to the cultures of Africa.[14] Over much of Africa monogamy now successfully competes with polygamy (at least formally). The abandonment of foot-binding by itself was long ago rightly reckoned a landmark in the history of China. Some Arab states have built university buildings which segregate men and women studying the same subjects and following the same courses; it is hardly likely that those partition walls will seem economic or sensible when another decade or two has gone by. India's programmes of contraceptive propaganda may not make as much impact on the peasant masses as those of China on hers, but her middle-class families are now beginning to get smaller — a change which was the major indicator of different rates of adoption of contraceptive practice by European nations from the nineteenth century onwards. Of course, if the actual and legal treatment of women is the test, then the majority of women all over the world have still to experience the full benefits of westernisation (if benefits they are). But of the direction of the tide there can hardly be much doubt.[15]

Obviously, the psychological interaction of western civilisation with other parts of the world is huge and complex; it derives from the vast positive changes we have looked at, but ramifies far beyond them. The West has worked upon men's minds in a multitude of ways, not merely as an active shaping force (let alone solely as a self-conscious one), but just by being there. It has been both a signpost of something to be achieved (and, occasionally, of something to be avoided) and an exemplary object, by its very existence seducing or challenging other civilisations and their set ways, forcing them to self-examination and calling them in question.

This helps to illuminate the curious paradox that economic development is so often a destabilising process. Not only does it call into question traditional ways and values, but it can show up the inadequacy of other western imports — representative democracy, for example. Old loyalties are eroded just as new shibboleths turn out to be inefficacious. Even the knowledge of the West's abundance can be profoundly troubling. Goods which were luxuries only a few years ago are now much more widely known than hitherto, and their possession is often taken to be something all men should aspire to. Of course, this is not universally or uniformly true. Millions of people do not have a clean and sufficient water supply. Yet millions more people than even a few years ago now take it for granted that clean water, transport, electric light and food will normally be available and are usually fairly cheap. Many millions living above the starvation levels of India's poorest already take for granted clothes made from artificial fibres, ball-point pens, motor-scooters. Furthermore, there seems to many of them to be no reason why such goods, once luxuries, should not become cheaper still and even more available. Rising expectations have become normal for more people than ever before in the last twenty years, and these people are no longer to be found only in developed countries. Industrialisation in South Korea, Taiwan and Brazil is now having many of the effects it had long ago in Europe and North America.

A growing flow of consumer goods shatters important ties with the past, because it shatters the universe of stable expectations in which most men and women have lived and died throughout history. Only recently have many people lived without such stability. The effect can be seen most clearly in poor countries, where the import of cheap consumer goods — transistor radios, for example — can touch off rapid social changes. They provide powerful incentives for men and women to seek work where they can get higher wages to buy these goods. This means, at least, leaving the villages in which the majority of mankind still lives.

Here, surely, is a clue to the deepest, most irresistible changes in modern society. Hidden, awaiting discovery, in material abundance lies the old western and enlightenment idea that all problems are soluble. Another way to put it is that the eighteenth-century idea that happiness *should* be pursued as a moral goal is now beginning to be acted on the world round.[16] True, millions of Asians, Africans and Amerindians still accept, more or less passively, that their lives are determined by forces far beyond their control; to do so, for most of them, is only to recognise the truth. As did most medieval Europeans, they live fatalistically resigned to the idea that the world will always be as it is. Yet even this is changing. Forty or fifty years ago, most Chinese may have thought like this. It seems very unlikely that quite so many do any longer. Largely thanks to the European ideologies —nationalism, Marxism, faith in natural science — spawned in the wake of the Enlightenment, China's leaders now assume that her destiny is in her own hands. Problems will be solved, if sufficient thought and resources can be brought to bear. Such an attitude is strikingly optimistic; Man can and will be Master in his own house. This is perhaps the most important gift the West has offered: the belief that humanity might control its own fate.

This myth has persisted in the West even when so much else has crumbled. Freud, though a great destroyer of certainty, hoped to give men through self-knowledge a control of their lives which they had never had before. As the biologically-based, evolutionary models of nineteenth-century thought gave way to more analytical approaches in the twentieth century, fundamental concepts about progress and goals were often pushed out of the front door only to reappear in due course by the back. A teleology of the self-governing (because at last truly self-knowing) mind replaced an earlier, more determinist, view of progress, but still left intact an idea of what progress was and how it could be achieved. One idol was often replaced by another, even when changes once envisaged as solutions turned out to throw up new problems, or when people found it hard to cope with the strain of living in societies in which the stability drawn from a static view of history has disappeared. Strong though the influence of religion still is in many societies, it is still losing the enormous advantage it once enjoyed as the only source of consolation, explanation and hope to men who felt trapped in an unchanging order. Now the order is seen not merely to change but, in increasing degree, to be changeable at will. The disappointments which that awakes have not yet been strong enough to make the pendulum swing off in another, more pessimistic, direction. This western faith is blighting the tragic sense of life.

It is perhaps the final paradox of the paradoxical age in which we live that while no other has been so marked by personal suffering on such a vast scale, yet also in no other have so many agreed that violence and atrocity are controllable in principle. True, most of the appalling bloodshed of our century can be explained as a side-effect or function of the technological intensification of modern war rather than as evidence of increasing wickedness or cynical unwillingness to seek peaceful solutions. Nonetheless, the western world seems perversely to remain optimistic on one subject on which there may be less ground for optimism than any other: the innate improvability of man. Similarly, our belief that a benevolent world order is obtainable seems strangely undisturbed by the colossal spectres looming on the horizon as a result of what has been done so far. We cannot satisfy even basic expectations rapidly enough. There is just not enough power, food and basic medicine to go round without redistribution of so dramatic and radical a kind that it cannot be envisaged and would be practically impossible on a reasonable time-scale. Yet desire and envy are outrunning satisfaction.

An even more frightening spectre looms behind that one, too. May not the West have in fact communicated to the rest of the world expectations which are not merely unsatisfiable in the short run of a couple of decades, but unsatisfiable in principle, because limitlessly expanding beyond our power to meet them? It is not just the colossal demands of the burgeoning populations of poor countries for fuel, food, even water, that are so frightening (though there may be actual finite limits to our material resources). What is worse is that the faith that history is progressive may already have led us to set ourselves goals which are psychologically unattainable. Many people seem already to think that any physical or mental pain ought somehow to be removable. Such assurance is a terrible and burdensome legacy of our utopianism and our confidence in the rational manipulation of nature. Perhaps it is the same thing which has been identified by some as the 'Faustian' urge of western man, his relentless striving for power after power to open the way to felicity. If the West's ambiguous gifts to mankind include this, then along with our confidence and self-centredness we shall have passed to the rest of the world a bias towards self-destruction.

It is time to pick up the threads of a ragged conclusion. It seems reasonable to expect agreement that the course of 'modern' history (however defined in time but certainly from 1700 or so onwards) has been increasingly dominated by first the European and then the western civilisation which was its successor. By 'dominated', I mean that two things were going on. One was that the history of the rest of the globe was then changed for ever and irreversibly by the actions of the men of the West. The other was that it changed in a particular direction; it was overwhelmingly a matter of other cultures taking up western ideas, goals and values, not the reverse. Coupled with the spread of a western technology and the sheer momentum of economic and communication evolution, this made the human race for the first time truly a single entity — one world. We can agree, too, I hope, that at some time in the twentieth century the West ceased to be top dog in some very specific senses. To put it another way, from many points of view, the western group of nations is visibly no longer the same sort of determining historical force it once was. Whatever real power they retain, the wishes and authority of western men are less effective in many areas than they were in 1900, say. The most striking sign has been the ebbing of colonial empire. Whether we think that 1905, or 1918, or 1941 or any other date is the best landmark of that is not so very important; the change is easy to sense.

A new world political structure is visibly now in the making. Its shape is far from clear. We can sense it from the way we still flounder over terminology; talk of the 'Third World', 'uncommitted' nations, east and west, has been overtaken by 'rich and poor', 'developed' and 'less developed', 'north and south', terms which, like their predecessors, will endure so long as the particular problems for which they provide shorthand expressions. Whatever emerges, though, the old international system of formal equality between a small group of western nations which ran the world with as little friction between themselves as they could manage is now gone. No vocabulary or conceptual scheme has yet been found to do justice to the fluidity of the situation which has replaced this.

Pace our French friends (who prefer 1789 as a marker) this twentieth-century change can be labelled, for convenience, as the ending of 'modern' and the beginning of 'contemporary' history — the period during which we can see the outlines of our own world already in being. In that sense at least, contemporary history looks not only post-European, but post-western. The burden of this book, though, is that western civilisation has not lost its world dominance, whatever the political story, because political power was only one part of it. True, the once and briefly irresistible masterfulness of American power is not what it was. Nor can the Russians, it seems, still promote their interests so easily as they once did in many parts of the world. What is more, the assurance of an economic system based on the industrial strength of a few countries has been tempered by revelations of its vulnerability. Nor is industrial and economic power so narrowly shared as was formerly the case; India is now a steel exporter, the Chinese build railways for Africa, Volkswagen Beetles are made in Nigeria and South Korea's industrial prowess frightens even the Japanese, who now discuss the need to wind down their motor-car industry while there is still time to do so in a controlled way. More profoundly, too, there are the psychological challenges to the West implicit in its own cultural changes. Most of the fundamental ideas of the European tradition have been brought under question, many with irreparable consequences. Even in Europe itself, some have lost their old, firm grip — the rational intelligence; Christian religion; national independence; the idea of the sovereign state.

So much, then, is gone. Yet when we ask why it has gone, we must recognise, surely, that it is largely because of forces generated within the West and shaped by the western tradition, because of that tradition's own dynamism and self-critical power. If this is true, then the day of its creative role can hardly be thought to be over; western civilisation has evidently not lost a shaping power. Paradoxically, we may now be entering the era of its greatest triumph, one not over state structures and economic relationships, but over the minds and hearts of all men. Perhaps they are all westerners now.

'Is the triumph over?' 'Has the parade gone by?' Some of my colleagues will say that historians should not try to answer such questions. They know that they may look like historical enquiries, but are really questions about the future — what is going to happen next? Will the great forces we have considered go on having effects as great as they have had in the past? I do not dissent from my colleagues' scepticism; a historian has no claim to any special qualification to answer such questions. To look at the past is relevant to the future, but not because it makes predictions possible. Such questions, nevertheless, will quite reasonably occur to any reflective person; someone must try to answer them, if only with judgements in default of verifiable truths. Men need hypotheses for action. A historian has a particular background and perspective, that is all. No one can do more than guess, but guesses should have some reasoned perspective; history appears to me to provide the best.

The historian is paid to think about the past. It is, though, in a different sense, the most valuable thing he can do. It is valuable not because we ought to have a picture of the past (we are going to have one whether we know it or not) but because we need a pondered, critical picture of it. General historical ideas haunt the intellectual darkness around us. A very familiar one is that 'there is nothing to be learnt from history'. Here are some others: 'history is the story of progress and liberty'; 'history is the story of human arrogance'; 'history shows that the few always exploit the many'; 'history shows that the many always oppress the few.' The list could be very long. Recognised or unrecognised, such ideas are, all the time, influencing our behaviour. We had better be aware of them. Human beings are the only animals with histories; the study and narration of them needs no defence. History is a necessary pursuit if we are to master the chaos of unexamined assumption, fear, arrogance and stark irrationality which will otherwise master us. It can give us an articulate, conscious reading of the past against which other visions of that past can be tested. It is a matter of intellectual hygiene.

I have tried here to sketch a few of the myths and stereotypes clustered in one important area of modern history which brought about a great change in the relations of civilisations. It is for others to try to assess that change for themselves. The result is not a set of conclusions for experimental testing: history is not yet like that. It is essentially a speculative and critical activity, like reading great literature, or perhaps like psycho-analysis; its function is direct and illuminating, not instrumental or utilitarian. It is collective autobiography. We are looking at ourselves. In that light, some may question whether, looking back, we can say anything useful and truthful about the meaning of western history, and its interplay with that of the rest of the world? Can something so complicated be summed up at all?

In coming to terms with such questions at least there is nothing to be lost by stating once more the obvious and incontrovertible: what the West has done to the rest of the world has been done indelibly. Nothing can be the same again. History has been changed by the West, which has made the world One World. The sheer energy and dynamism it showed in doing this have never been equalled. Though individuals were often its beneficiaries, it also served collective ends — sometimes by remoulding the world in its own image. Some will want to strike a moral balance about this, awarding praise and blame. Scepticism holds me back. I neither believe it logically possible to draw up indictments against large abstractions and categories — such as civilisations, nations, peoples, classes — nor that it is easy to sort out most historical actions in moral terms. If we wish to reassure ourselves about our own moral sensibility, we need only to recognise that the bearers of western civilisation have often behaved with deliberate cruelty and ruthlessness towards other peoples, that some of them plundered their victims of wealth and their environment of resources, and that still others, even when more scrupulous or well-meaning, casually released shattering side-effects on societies and cultures they neither understood nor tried to understand. For centuries, many Europeans and many European peoples outside Europe showed astonishing cultural arrogance towards the rest of humanity. In doing so, they behaved much as men of power have always behaved in any vigorous civilisation. What was different was just that they had so much more power than any earlier conquerors, and even more convincing grounds for feeling they were entitled to use it.

All that said, if we are seriously concerned about our own sensitivity to ethical nuance, we ought also to recognise that administrators, missionaries, teachers were often right in thinking that they brought valuable gifts to non-Europeans. Those gifts included gentler standards of behaviour towards the weak, the ideal of a more objective justice, the intellectual rigour of science, its fruits in better health and technology, and many other good things. They spread progressive, humane aspirations about the world. In some places, the mere bringing of settled order was by itself an unquestionable good. They could also point, as time went by, to economic changes which brought new opportunities, longer lives, more comfort. And if they were very thoughtful, they might claim that the most valuable gift they brought was the implanting of the idea that willed change was possible.

It is this last which seems to me the essence of what was done by western civilisation. In principle, it brought into question everything that already existed on the spot — it forced people to think about their set ways and consider whether those ways could endure. Of course, it did not do so always and everywhere in the same way. Faiths and ideologies are changed by the world even as they change it. Nevertheless, western civilisation has been humanity's great champion; it is the greatest claim ever made for men's unique status among living creatures as a change-making animal. This is why, however we choose to draw our balance sheets about the value of the civilisation which dominates our world, its vigour is still so evident. When the first men on the moon stepped out to look about them and at the planet earth they had left not long before, they not only showed (simply by being there) the astonishing capacity of their civilisation to manipulate nature, but also the colossal promise it can still hold out. There is no unquestionable ground for thinking that mankind is in a dead-end, or that the creativity it has derived from western civilisation has been eclipsed. Both may be confronting no more than the end of their beginnings. What seems to be clear is that the story of western civilisation is now the story of mankind, its influence so diffused that old oppositions and antitheses are now meaningless. 'The West' is hardly now a meaningful term, except to historians.

NOTES

I ONE WORLD

1 In Japanese, 'Sabiro'.

2 Already in the 1820s, an English bishop noted the unsatisfactory appearance of the Europeanised equipage of an Indian prince's 'injudicious and imperfect adoption of European fashion. The Eastern courtier with his turban and flowing robes, is a striking object; and an eastern prince on horseback, and attended by his usual train of white-starred and high-capped janizaries, a still more noble one; but an eastern prince in a shabby carriage, guarded by men dressed like an equestrian troop at a fair, is nothing more than ridiculous and melancholy. It is, however, but natural that these unforunate sovereigns should imitate, as far as they can, those costumes which the example of their conquerors has associated with their most recent ideas of power and splendour.' *Bishop Heber in Northern India. Selections from Heber's Journal,* ed. M. A. Laird (Cambridge, 1971), p. 83.

3 Aizawa Seishisai, q. R. N. Bellah, 'Japan's cultural identity', *Journal of Asian Studies,* xxiv, 1965, p. 574.

4 See J. K. Fairbank, E. O. Reischauer, A. M. Craig, *East Asia. Tradition and Transformation* (London, 1973), p. 486. Interestingly, the latter slogan seems to have been coined by a Japanese gunner.

5 For information on China's fate in the 1840s, see below, ch. XI.

6 q. Fairbank *et al.,* pp. 503–4.

7 *The Autobiography of Yukichi Fukuzawa* (Tokyo, 1934), p. 113.

8 A German doctor protested: 'Hygiene apart, I said, from the cultural and aesthetic standpoint the proposed change was simply impossible. Ho (the Japanese Prime Minister) smiled and replied: "My dear Baelz, you don't in the least understand the requirements of high politics. All that you say may be perfectly sound, but as long as our ladies continue to appear in Japanese dress they will be regarded as mere dolls or bric-à-brac." ' From E. Baelz, *Awakening Japan: the Diary of a German Doctor* (Bloomington, Ind., 1974), p. 239.

9 q. J. P. Lehmann, *Image of Japan: From Feudal Isolation to World Power, 1850–1905* (London, 1978), p. 34.

10 When, in 1979, there was a parliamentary debate in Kenya on whether polygamy should be abolished or even somewhat regulated, the 'militant machismo of Kenyan parliamentarians was staggeringly clear' says one (African) observer: A. Mazuri, *The Listener,* 22 November 1979.

11 Nor does it, of course, say anything about explanation, and it carries no implication that the abilities of individual non-Europeans are inferior to those of Europeans. What might be more interesting to explore would be those effects of circumstance and environment which explain why other parts of the world did not come to dominate Europe.

II A Sense of Direction

1 In which they appear to have been successful, though one member of the Women's Battalion protecting the Provisional Government at the Palace is said to have committed suicide (there were three cases of rape, too). See M. Liebman, *The Russian Revolution* (London, 1970), p. 269. The pages in which this author describes the whole episode are well worth reading.

2 E. R. Dodds, *The Greeks and the Irrational* (Cambridge, 1951).

3 q. D. Bullough, 'The Ostrogothic and Lombard Kingdoms', in *The Dark Ages,* ed. D. Talbot Rice (London, 1965), p. 168.

4 As were also those of two other Apostles, St Philip and St James the Lesser. Such holy relics (and there were many others) were enormously important in drawing to Rome the pilgrims whose offerings did so much to fill Papal coffers as the centuries went by.

5 Peter Brown, *St. Augustine* (London, 1967), p. 81.

6 In fairness and to be exact, it must be allowed that much use was to be made (especially in the seventeenth and eighteenth centuries) by Christian writers of the curse Noah placed on the descendants of Ham (Gen. IX, 25–27), who were usually supposed to be the settlers of Africa; this has a place in the tragic story of black slavery. Nonetheless, the Old Testament assertion was never, I believe, acknowledged by the church to override the importance attached to the salvation of the individual soul.

7 See M. J. Lasky, *Utopia and Revolution* (London, 1977), pp. 102–3, where Marx is quoted to this effect from an article of 1847. Lasky also quotes another revealing sentence by Marx: 'an end that requires unjust means is not a just end.' This seems *à propos* to our argument, too. Many self-identified Marxists, of course, have argued otherwise, or that *no* means are 'objectively' unjust, if directed towards achieving the goal of the classless society.

III The Birth of The West

1 Apart from the major Celtic monastic movements already under way by St Benedict's day, other monastic developments of the Middle Ages which should, perhaps, be mentioned in order to give perspective, were (i) The Cluniac Reform — a very influential attempt to return to the simplicity of the original Benedictine ways which had a great impact throughout the western church in the eleventh and twelfth centuries; (ii) The Cistercian Order — another, mainly twelfth-century, attempt to return to primitive Benedictine ways with an emphasis on seclusion and manual labour leading, fortuitously, to many Cistercian houses playing a pioneer role in agricultural improvement; (iii) The Mendicant Orders of Friars (of whom the first were the thirteenth-century Franciscans and Dominicans) who, property-

less and not bound to live in communities, preached and taught in the lay world, relying upon alms for their maintenance. From their day there began, and has continued, a proliferation of other religious orders, including many which were or are monastic.

2 q. D. A. Bullough, *The Age of Charlemagne* (London, 1980), p.115.

3 *The Times Atlas of World History*, ed. G. Barraclough (London, 1978), has some interesting comparative plans, pp. 108–9.

4 664 is the traditional marker date; the Synod of Whitby then united the English church in obedience to Rome.

5 For a succinct summary of the case for 1100 or thereabouts, see the comments of Joan Evans in her admirable preface to *The Flowering of the Middle Ages* (London, 1966), p. 9.

6 *The Canterbury Tales* were completed in the 1390s.

7 Printing appeared first in China. What Gutenberg did was to devise cast-metal movable type, and to use it with a press derived from the wine-press, oil-based ink and paper (another invention originally from China). A good marker date is his printing of the Bible in 1456.

8 It is worth remarking, too, that not long after Luther, some writers who accepted the theological leadership of another great Reformation figure, Calvin, were led to stress the importance of certain kinds of liberty and certain individual rights, so reinforcing the long-range current towards individualism and secularism which Calvin himself would have abominated.

9 The American theologian Reinhold Niebuhr was by no means an unqualified admirer of liberal individualism. In *Reflections on the End of an Era* (London, 1934) he praised (p. 108) an earlier writer, Kidd, for rightly attributing to Christians 'the primary cause of the achievement of western civilisation in freeing the individual from the tyranny of the political group and giving his life a centre of reference by virtue of which he is able to defy the dictates of governments.' Niebuhr's own adverse criticism of later individualism was directed against its optimism, not against this dissenting emphasis.

10 Whether such a bias is objectively 'better' or 'worse' is, in my view, an historically unanswerable and (I incline to think) meaningless question. Raised in the western tradition, I favour the bias (but that answers a different question). What is hardly to be doubted is the objective historical impact of such ideas.

11 C. McEvedy and R. Jones, *Atlas of World Population History* (Harmondsworth, 1978), p. 18.

12 But cause-effect relationships in early advances in agricultural technology are not easy to establish; see E. L. Jones, *The European Miracle* (Cambridge, 1981), pp. 48–9.

13 A. E. J. Morris, *History of Urban Form* (London, 1972), p. 179; J. D. Port, *The Last Great Subsistence Crisis in the Western World* (Baltimore, 1977), pp. 1937–8.

14 Shakespeare, of course, often remarks that he thought kingly power an almost priceless public benefit. R. Bean, 'War and the birth of the nation state' (*Journal of Economic History*, 1973, p. 205) is interesting on the connexion of military change with state-building, a subject which deserves more than this passing reference.

15 This is literally true; it was time and again to help to preserve dissent and critical thought in Europe that those accused of them could move across borders from one sovereign jurisdiction to another.

16 The absence until very recent times of a state structure focused on nationality is one of the interesting contrasts between Europe and the Islamic world.

IV The World's Debate

1 See Ch. V.

2 'Such pairs of words as religious and secular, spiritual and temporal, clergy and laity, even sacred and profane, had no real equivalent in Islamic usage until much later times,' (B. Lewis, in *The Legacy of Islam*, ed. J. Schachs and C. G. Bosworth (Oxford, 1974), p. 158).

3 Before 1100, says Professor R. Southern, 'there is no sign that anyone in northern Europe had even heard the name of Mahomet.' *Western Views of Islam* (Cambridge, Mass., 1962), p. 15. He also says (p. 28) that he has found only one reference to the name in Christian Europe outside Spain or southern Italy before that date. No translation of the Koran into Latin was available until the middle of the twelfth century.

4 Though the same poem also has Charlemagne serving a Muslim king of Toledo and marrying a Moorish princess.

5 For further instances of crusader brutality, besides the sack and massacre at Jerusalem, taken in 1099, there are at the other end of the crusading cycle those at Alexandria (1365).

6 See the concluding comments of S. Runciman, *History of the Crusades* (Cambridge, 1954), iii, p. 492.

7 *Inferno*, xx, 115–117.

8 Dr Needham, though, speaks (*Science and Civilization in China* (Cambridge, 1954), I, p. 222) of 'a slow but massive infiltration from east to west throughout the first fourteen centuries of the Christian era'; this may imply merely that Islam's rise did not check a current already flowing. He specifically notes that the same does not apply to Chinese science and stresses 'a dividing line running north and south through Bactria and the opening of the Persian Gulf' (*ibid.*, p. 220).

9 *Inferno*, Jv, 143, 144. Dante puts Saladin there, too; iv, 129.

10 G. Mandisi, *The Rise of Colleges: Institutions of Learning in Islam and the West* (Edinburgh, 1982).

11 e.g. in Spanish, *aceituna, aduana;* in French, *douane;* in English, alembic, algebra, cipher.

12 F. Braudel, *The Mediterranean and the Mediterranean World in the Age of Philip II* (London, 1975), I, p. 118.

V Defining a World

1 e.g. *esclave* (Fr.) and *Sklave* (German), both derive from the Greek *Slobenoi*, used in the sixth century to denote the Slavs; no connotation of servile status appears to be traceable before the ninth century, when the word *sklabos*, a derivative from the ethnic label, meant either a slave or a foreigner. By then the Frankish *Drang nach Osten* had already begun to supply Slav prisoners to the slave markets of Venice and elsewhere. Muslim merchants were good customers for them.

2 The Tatar influence may have influenced this tendency in more direct ways, too. Russians already in the thirteenth century translated the Mongol-Tatar title of 'Khan' by the word 'Tsar' — 'Caesar' — signifying a perception of a ruler over many peoples. What that might mean helped to shape the evolving Russian notion of what ruler and subject should be to one another. In Muscovy, the highest official was the *Kholop*, a word which might mean 'slave'. That such a title was borne by a man from the Muscovite nobility surely hints at a striking ideological trend. See *The Mutual Effects of the Islamic and Judeo-Christian Worlds: the East European Pattern*, ed. A. A. Ascher *et al.* (New York, 1979).

3 The Russian army entered Poland the day after a cease-fire agreement with the Japanese came into effect. A. Resis, 'Spheres of Influence in Soviet Wartime Diplomacy', *The Journal of Modern History*, vol. 53, 1981, p. 421.

4 q. J. Stoye, *The Siege of Vienna* (London, 1964), p. 32, from E. Browne, *A brief account of some travels* (1685). The idea of a homogeneous Asia had a temporal dimension, too. See the passage from Chardin quoted by P. J. Marshall and G. Williams, *The Great Map of Mankind* (London, 1982), p. 128.

5 The monk Philotheus' letter to the Tsar Vasil III. See the longer quotation (with slightly different words) in G. Vernadsky *et al., A Source Book for Russian History from Early Times to 1917* (New Haven, 1972), I, p. 156.

6 Kuropatkin, later commander of the Russian army there during the Russo-Japanese war 1904–5.

7 q. M. Cunliffe, *The Age of Expansion 1848–1917* (London, 1974), p. 176.

8 As Professor Obolensky points out (*The Byzantine Commonwealth* (London, 1971), p. 364), the two-headed eagle was not the official coat of arms of the Byzantine empire, but appears from the end of the thirteenth century, during the early years of the Palaeologus dynasty, as a symbol of sovereignty. It was used in other Orthodox lands, too, as a sign of sovereignty in the thirteenth and fourteenth centuries.

VI An Exploring Civilisation

1 Ma Huan, *The Overall Survey of the Ocean's Shore*, trans. and ed. J. V. G. Mills (The Hakluyt Society, Extra Series, xlii, 1970).

2 One indicator of growing confidence is falling insurance rates. See J. Bernard in *The Fontana Economic History of Europe: the Middle Ages,* ed. C. Cipolla (London, 1972), p. 318.

3 C. R. Beazley, *Prince Henry the Navigator* (London, 1901), p. 122.

4 Beazley is still well worth reading but must be supplemented. An excellent introduction to later views is a lecture by P. E. Russell, *Prince Henry the Navigator* (Canning House Seventh Annual lecture; London, 1960). Professor Russell's emphasis on the complexities of Henry's motivation is convincing.

5 C. R. Boxer, *The Portuguese Seaborne Empire 1415–1825* (London, 1969), pp. 21–3.

6 Madeira had, in fact, been 'discovered' a few decades earlier by Robert Machin, a Bristol man who was shipwrecked (and died) there. In 1416, a report of this reached Henry, when a survivor of the wreck who had fallen into Muslim hands was ransomed, and then captured by a Portuguese ship while on his way home to Spain.

7 'Something like 150,000' is Professor Boxer's estimate of the number of black slaves taken by the Portuguese between 1450 and 1500 (*The Portuguese Seaborne Empire*, p. 31).

8 Boxer, p. 37.

9 By then, the Japanese had already shown a first instance of their keenness for western technology: they acquired their first firearms from the Portuguese and by the end of the 1570s the fire of musketeers had become the key to victory on the battlefields where Japan's over-mighty subjects fought out their clan and personal rivalries (Fairbank, Reischauer and Craig, p. 394). Gunpowder as a content for missiles they had known of since the thirteenth century, but not guns.

10 S. E. Morrison, *Christopher Columbus, Admiral of the Ocean Sea* (London, 1979).

11 A debate in the General Assembly of the United Nations in late 1982 on the means of celebrating the fifth centenary of Columbus' voyage suggests that there is ample room for disagreement about Columbus' priority on other grounds, though. The Icelandic representative sought historical justice for Leif Ericsson, supposedly the Viking discoverer of 'Vinland', c. 1000 AD, while the Irish representative plumped for the sixth-century St Brendan. Several African states appear to have taken the more radical (but hardly convincing) line that no arrival of white Europeans should constitute 'discovery' — even by Europeans, it would seem.

12 See L. Bagrow, *History of Cartography*, rev. and ed. R. A. Skelton (London, 1964), p. 109. For an alternative suggestion about the naming of America, see A. E. Hudd, 'Richard Ameryk and the name America', in *Gloucestershire Studies*, ed. H. P. R. Finberg (Leicester, 1957).

13 To distinguish: John Cabot (?1450–1499) was a Genoese who settled in London in 1484. His son, Sebastian, (?1476–1557) may have been born in Bristol, was cartographer to Henry VIII, served in the Spanish navy, was Pilot-Major (examiner of pilots and inspector of all charts and instruments) for the Spanish Council of the Indies, was pensioned by Edward VI and made a governor of the Merchant Adventurers and, through unsuccessful attempts to find a Northeast passage to Asia, helped to open up trade by sea with Russia.

14 It was in fact a renegotiation of the line — much further east — beyond which the Pope had given exclusive rights to the Catholic Monarchs the previous year.

15 *The New Cambridge Modern History:* vol. xiv, Atlas, ed. H. C. Darby and H. Fullard (Cambridge, 1970), pp. 6–7, shows maps entitled 'Expanding Knowledge of the World'. Presumably neither the distinguished editors nor the Syndics who ran the Press thought that those who lived outside the zone of European civilisation had *no* knowledge of the world, though that is what their failure to say 'European Knowledge' implies.

16 D. Hay, *Europe* (Edinburgh, 1957), p. 58.

17 *Idem*, p. 61.

18 The last major incorporation was that of the pagan Lithuanian Kingdom into the new Polish-Lithuanian state in 1386.

19 Hay (pp. 73–82) deals with the special significance of the Council of Constance and the debates connected with it.

20 Hay, *Europe* (p. 110) quotes *Purchas His Pilgrimages* (Hakluyt Society, Extra Series, i, 1905), p. 251. Samuel Purchas was a compiler of travel books.

21 H. D. Schmidt ('The establishment of Europe as a political expression', *Historical Journal*, 1966, p. 172) says that he finds the association of the concept 'Europe' with

the ideas of expanding liberty, commerce and a balance of power in a pamphlet of 1667. 'Christendom' had by then become a suspect word in England because its French equivalent was used by Louis XIV.

22 Bossuet, *Discours sur l'histoire universelle* (Paris, 1691), p. 4.

23 *Essays*, trans. F. Florio, Bk III, ch. vi (ed. Saintsbury, 1893, p. 141).

VII NEW WORLDS

1 D. W. Lomax, *The Reconquest of Spain* (London, 1978), p. 178. Another scholar (R. Ricard, *The Spiritual Conquest of Mexico* (Berkeley, 1966), p. 308) remarks that 'Because of her long contact with the Moslem world, Spain was perhaps the European nation best prepared for a great missionary enterprise.'

2 The Spanish laws of the Indies required that cities in the New World should 'evoke wonder' among the Indians for precisely this reason. See M. Picón-Salas, *A Cultural History of Spanish America* (Berkeley, 1962), p. 44.

3 Bernal Diaz, Hakluyt edn., I. p. 266 (*Amadis de Gaula* was the title of the most famous of Spain's medieval romances of chivalry, the tales and books later satirised in *Don Quixote*).

4 L. Hanke, *The First Social Experiments in America* (Cambridge, Mass, 1935), p. 60, quotes words of Peter Martyr, who was a member of the Council of the Indies, which have a resonance which echoes down the next three centuries of colonisation: 'when our compatriots reach that remote world, so far away and so removed from us, beyond the ocean whose courses imitate the changing heavens, they find themselves distant from any judge. Carried away by love of gold, they become ravenous wolves instead of gentle lambs, and heedless of royal instructions . . .'.

5 Quotation from the Bull *Inter Caetera*, 1493, q. by Hanke, *ibid.*

6 L. Hanke (ed.), *History of Latin American Civilization. Sources and Interpretations* (London, 1969), I, p. 122.

7 For this debate, see A. Pagden, *The Fall of Natural Man: the American Indian and the Origins of Comparative Ethnology* (Cambridge, 1982), p. 42.

8 q. L. Hanke, *The First Social Experiments in America*, p. 20.

9 This must surely be one of the earliest references by a European to the 'monetising' of the economies of other peoples, a process often revolutionary in its effects. The most striking thing about the remark is the obliviousness it shows to the possibility that the introduction of money could be anything but a boon.

10 Pagden, p. 96.

11 Ricard, p. 146 and refs. pp. 347–8.

12 I. Clendinnen, 'Missionary violence in Yucatán', *Past and Present*, 1982.

13 In the following year, by an interesting near-coincidence, the flag of the French King was raised at Quebec.

14 *Of Plymouth Plantation 1620–1647 by William Bradford sometime Governor thereof*, ed. S. E. Morison (New York, 1953), p. 236.

15 F. Jennings, *The Invasion of America: Indians, Colonialism, and the Cant of Conquest* (New York, 1976).

16 q. G. Mattingly, *Renaissance Diplomacy* (Boston, 1955), p. 290. His language is cautious and he gives no specific source. Tradition attributes this to the town of Milford, Connecticut.

17 q. L. Hanke, *Aristotle and the American Indians*, (Chicago, 1959), p. 100 (from Archdale). This was by no means an eccentrically complacent view. From New York in 1670 comes the reflexion that 'where the English come to settle, a Divine Hand makes way for them by removing or cutting off the Indians, either by wars one with the other, or by some raging mortal disease,' (q. P. J. Marshall and Glyndwr Williams, *The Great Map of Mankind* (London, 1982), p. 29).

VIII A New Age

1 M. Bloch, *The Royal Touch: Sacred Monarchy in England and France* (London, 1973), pp. 224–6.

2 q. Hugh Honour, *The New Golden Land: European Images of America* (New York, 1975), p. 84. One obvious problem was posed by the existence of human beings in the Americas: how, given the Biblical history, could they have got there?

3 N. Hampson, *The Enlightenment* (Harmondsworth, 1968), p. 146. This book is still the best short introduction to the subject.

4 See, for instance, what is said about him in the great *Encyclopédie*, s.v. *Expérimental* — an article which can be found reprinted in the helpful anthology edited by J. Lough, *The Encyclopédie of Diderot and d' Alembert* (Cambridge, 1969).

5 q. C. M. Cipolla, *European Culture and Overseas Expansion* (Harmondsworth, 1970), p. 26, who refers the reader to R. F. Jones, *Ancients and Moderns* (St Louis, 1936), p. 204.

6 If we reckon it in the number of passenger-miles travelled, then surely space travel must be one of the safest forms of travel known to man.

7 Voltaire, *The Age of Louis XIV* (trans. Pollack; London, Everyman, n.d.), p. 2. He distinguished four such 'happy' ages: those of classical Greece, of Caesar and Augustus, of Renaissance Europe, and that of Louis XIV.

8 The title by which it is usually known, though the one under which it was first published was *Du Contract Social; ou, Principes du Droit Politique*.

9 'L'homme est né libre, et partout il est dans les fers' (Edn. Bibl. de la Pléiade, *Oeuvres complètes*, III, p. 351).

10 I, Edward VI, c. 3; the Vagrancy Act of 1547.

11 I, xv, ch. 5.

12 Much of the book was by Diderot, in fact.

13 See E. L. Jones, *The European Miracle*, pp. 140–4 and 181–3. The whole topic has economic implications, and the importance of such a success on the eve of a huge nineteenth-century growth of European towns and cities is obvious. It is its interest as a symptom and stimulant of mental change which matters here, though.

14 Reinhold Niebuhr has made a shrewd association bearing on this point. 'Both the bourgeois idea of progress', he writes, 'and the Marxian idea of salvation through catastrophe express a faith in the character of life which is religious rather than scientific because the mechanisms of history are subsumed under a purpose of history' (*Reflections on the End of an Era*, p. 195).

15 Antoine-Nicolas de Condorcet, *Sketch for a Historical Picture of the Progress of the Human Mind* (London, 1955), p. 4.

IX HISTORY SPEEDS UP

1 He used it in two of his most famous poems, 'Locksley Hall' (which contains the often-quoted line about Cathay), and the 'Ode on the Death of the Duke of Wellington'.

2 In 500 years after the year 1000, Europe's population slightly more than doubled; it took about 250 years to double again; just over 150 more to double again — a good instance of accelerating change.

3 *Vide supra*, ch. III.

4 E. L. Jones, *The European Miracle*, pp. 81–2.

5 *Idem*, p. 56 'The [medieval technological] history of Europe does begin to look like a persistent drifting advance in which, compared with the sluggish nature of other civilizations, the lags seem relatively minor.'

6 q. J. Rosselli, *Lord William Bentinck: the Making of a Liberal Imperialist 1774–1839* (London, 1974), p. 285.

7 C. Torr, *Small Talk at Wreyland* (Cambridge, 1921), II, p. 1.

8 See A. Willis, *Crime and Punishment in Revolutionary Paris* (London, 1981).

9 F. Furet, in *Annales*, 1974, p. 3. For the general point, see also J. M. Roberts, *The French Revolution* (Oxford, 1974), *passim*.

10 H. Morse Stephens, *Orators of the French Revolution* (Oxford, 1892), II, p. 420.

11 Shortly before his death, Garibaldi wrote of 'a very different Italy which I have spent my life dreaming of, not the impoverished and humiliated country . . . now . . . ruled by the dregs of the nation'.

12 'All over the world, nationalist leaders have been formed out of government subordinates, men who put their working hours to good use in studying the mechanics of power and devoted their leisure to studying the obstacles barring their own promotion'. A. Seal, *The Emergence of Indian Nationalism* (Cambridge, 1970), p. 116.

13 There is a remarkable memorial in Kuala Lumpur to the successful conquest of threats to the new nation of Malaysia, which is a straight crib from a famous American patriotic group modelled on a photograph of American marines raising the flag on an island captured from the Japanese.

X THE CONFIDENT AGGRESSORS

1 Nepal might be argued to be in the same category, but it could never show even such independence of British policy as could Siam.

2 Nevertheless, death-rates from disease among European soldiers abroad were high. South Africa was by no means the most unhealthy place in the world to fight, but in the war of 1899–1902 only a quarter or so of the British dead died from Boer marksmanship and gunnery; dysentery, enteric fever and typhoid finished off three times as many. In Europe itself disease was always the greatest thinner of armies until the Great War.

3 It was Metcalfe who said, simply and splendidly, 'If India could only be preserved as part of the British empire, by keeping its inhabitants in a state of ignorance, our

domination would be a curse to the country, and ought to cease,' (q. P. Mudford, *Birds of a Different Plumage* (London, 1974), p. 126).

4 q. S. Gopal, *The Vice-royalty of Lord Ripon 1880–1884* (London, 1953), p. 116.

5 Distinctions between Europeans could be very important, as Bishop Heber noted in the 1820s, when he talked to Indians about the French. 'I was told that many people were accustomed to speak of them as often oppressive and avaricious, but as of more conciliatory and popular manners than the English Sahibs. Many of them . . . had completely adopted the Indian dress and customs, and most of them were free from that exclusive and intolerant spirit, which makes the English, wherever they go, a caste by themselves, disliking and disliked by all their neighbours . . . We are not guilty of injustice, wilful oppression, but we shut out the natives from our society, and a bullying, insolent manner is continually assumed in speaking to them.' *Bishop Heber in Northern India*, p. 249.

6 See P. J. Marshall and G. Williams, *The Great Map of Mankind*, pp. 24–5.

7 Admiration had, of course, hardly ever been extended to less civilised people — the indigenous Americans, for example. The best Red Indians could usually hope for was to be seen as 'noble savages'. The aborigines of Australia were not even to have *that* dubious accolade.

8 *Encyclopédie*, s.v. 'Bramines'.

9 'I am apt to suspect the Negroes and in general all other species of men (for there are four or five different kinds) to be naturally inferior to the whites. There never was a civilised nation of any other complexion than white, nor even any individual eminent in action or speculation. No ingenious manufacturing among them, no arts, no sciences'. From a note added to his 'Of National Characters', q. in Marshall and Williams, p. 246.

10 See Marshall and Williams, p. 98.

11 Though with a specific reference to nineteenth-century orientalism, a comment by the distinguished French scholar of Islam, Maxine Rodinson, is to the point here: 'In the Middle Ages, the Oriental had been regarded as a fierce enemy, but nevertheless on the same level as Western man; in the eighteenth-century enlightenment and the resulting ideology of the French Revolution the Oriental was, under his disguise, essentially a human being; now he became a creature apart . . .' (*The Legacy of Islam*, p. 48).

12 q. Marshall and Williams, p. 303.

13 See, e.g., his *Philosophy of History*.

14 P. Leroy-Beaulieu, *De la colonisation chez les peuples modernes* (Paris, 1891), p. 165. Salisbury uttered his words in a speech at the Albert Hall in May 1898.

15 The first African bishop has a slightly equivocal look; he was a Congolese prince consecrated at the insistence of the king of Portugal, but with the Pope's reluctant consent. The first Chinese bishop was Gregorio Lopez, or Lo Wentsao, a Dominican ordained at Manila in 1654. The ordination of Chinese clergy, nonetheless, was held up by disputes among the missionaries themselves about the advantages and disadvantages of such a strategy. See C. R. Boxer, 'European Missionaries and Chinese Clergy', in *The Age of Partnership*, ed. B. B. Kling (Hawaii, 1979), *passim*, for an illuminating account of this prolonged dispute and the changes in policy which followed it.

16 Though an attack by eighteenth-century governments on the Society of Jesus led to its dissolution in 1773.

17 Marshall and Williams, p. 122.

18 *Idem.*

19 C. R. Boxer, pp. 66–73.

20 A recent sympathetic, but somewhat disappointing, study is S. N. Mukherjee, *Sir William Jones: A Study of Eighteenth-Century British Attitudes to India* (Cambridge, 1968).

21 Charles Grant, q. Judith Brown, *Modern India: the Origin of an Asian Democracy* (Oxford, 1985). The same official marvellously sums up the arrogant distaste awoken in many earnest Christians by India in a description of the Hindus as 'a race' (sic) 'of men lamentably degenerate in their disregard of what they know to be right, governed by malevolent and licentious passions, strongly exemplifying the effects produced on society by great and general corruption of manners, and sunk in misery by their vices', (q. Mudford, 102).

22 See the Preface to *Hellas: A Lyrical Drama* (1822).

23 Elphinstone, I. Mudford, p. 124.

24 q. Brown, p. 140.

25 It should be noted that Stephen (and those of his mind) did not see their role as the upholding of *British* economic interests.

26 *Heart of Darkness* (1902). Penguin edition (Harmondsworth, 1973), p. 10.

27 'The inescapable reality is that English continues to be the only expedient language throughout India' said a speaker at a 1971 Congress of Indian Writers (q. Mudford, p. 16). Moreover, when Japanese nationalists sought to root out Anglo-Saxon elements from their own culture in the 1940s, they faced an additional difficulty in the fact that the English language was essential for government and communication over much of the Great East Asia Co-prosperity Sphere created by their conquests.

28 In other places similar linguistic adoptions did not occur, and that no doubt says something about the special history of Africa. In China, I am told, Europeans were called 'hairy ones', but the Chinese did not counter-define themselves as '*non-hairy ones*'.

29 B. Fredriksen (thesis), 'Slavery and its abolition in nineteenth-century Egypt' (Bergen, 1977), p. 53.

30 *Encycl. of Islam*, I. s.v., '*Abd*, p. 38.

31 It was only in 1843 that abolition came to India, though; it was not a Crown Colony. Other imperial powers followed suit, France in 1848, the Netherlands between 1854 and 1863, and the Russians (in their central Asian dependencies) in 1873.

32 See, particularly, the writings of the West Indians, C. L. R. James and Eric Williams.

33 E. L. Jones, p. 213.

34 A point well made by R. Rathbone in a lecture printed in *The Times Higher Education Supplement*, 24 October 1980; 'Birmingham-made steel machets were cheaper for cutting down bush than those made by the smith. Paraffin lamps were better for lighting huts in the long equatorial nights than rushlights . . . Holland's gin and sardines to some extent replaced distilled palm wine and tilapia.'

35 The point should not be enlarged into a generally negative judgement about British economic impact on India, a temptation to which some nationalist Indian

historians have readily succumbed. Even in the case of the textile industry the story seems to be first one of (local) stimulation, then of (local) devastation, and then, on a larger scale, of stimulation again.

36 A. Seal, *The Emergence of Indian Nationalism*, p. 9.

37 q. M. Cunliffe, *The Age of Expansion* (London, 1974), p. 177.

XI   RESPONSES AND REPERCUSSIONS

1 True, the nature of the last can be misconceived. The bureaucracy relied more upon codes of behaviour and cultural inertia than on substantive administration in the western sense. See *The Cambridge History of China* (hereafter *CHC*), Vol. X, part 1., pp. 2–6, for a good summary. E. L. Jones, *The European Miracle*, pp. 206–7, says that 'the Chinese system entangled society in a ball of string more than it hammered [it] with a mailed fist.'

2 Perhaps some additional perspective can be gained here from the comment that there was famine in at least one of China's provinces, whether as a result of flood or drought, in nearly every year from 108 BC to AD 1911 (W. H. Mallory, *China: Land of Famine* (New York, 1926), p. 1.

3 *The Opium War* (Peking, 1976), p. 1.

4 C. R. Boxer, 'European Missionaries and Chinese Clergy, 1654–1810', pp. 100–2.

5 Boxer, p. 114.

6 *CHC*, X, part 1, has some interesting data. Between 1845 and 1876, there were about 30 Roman Catholic missionaries in China (p. 229). Even by mid-century Protestant numbers were much larger, and grew much faster, ironically, after treaties between China and France in 1858 and 1860, which extended the privileges of the Roman clergy; most-favoured nation clauses followed in the treaties subsequently made by other western nations. 189 Protestant missionaries in 1864 became 3445 (one half of them women) in 1905 (p. 555). Most missionary schools were Protestant, and contained in 1877 6000 Chinese pupils, in 1906 more than 57,000 (p. 577). Protestant schools, colleges and hospitals encouraged the study of scientific subjects more than did the Roman institutions and by 1897, 300 Chinese physicians had graduated from medical schools attached to missionary hospitals (p. 575). In 1905 there were 300 qualified medical missionaries serving in China; in 1874 there had been 10 (p. 574).

7 The International Concession at Shanghai, run by the Americans and British, and the French Concession alongside it, were the outstanding examples.

8 Interestingly, it appears that no figure corresponding to the professional lawyer of western countries existed in imperial China, *CHC*, X, i. p. 24.

9 In 1864 a high official wrote to an imperial minister regretting the traditional literary emphasis in the training of officials, a telling straw in the wind. *CHC*, X, i., p. 498.

10 Even after that date, though, the last emperor had two further tastes of imperial status; he was again to be put on the throne of China in 1917, and then on that of the short-lived empire of Manchukuo, set up by the Japanese in 1931.

11 Their recrudescence in the first half of the nineteenth century must be functionally linked to the continued growth of population at a time when food production

was no longer rising (as it had for centuries) through internal colonisation of fresh land. See *CHC*, X, i. pp. 108–9.

12 The next major seizure of territory by a western power came when the French conquered a collection of Chinese tributaries in Indo-China, in 1884.

13 *CHC*, X, i. p. 477.

14 The treaty of Shimonoseki, April, 1895.

15 Yen Fu. See B. Schwartz, *In Search of Wealth and Power: Yen Fu and the West* (Cambridge, Mass., 1964).

16 During which the besieged had ample opportunity to note some of China's borrowings from the West down to that time. As an eyewitness noted at one point, 'the battery on the wall of the Imperial City began firing Krupp shells during the night . . . One of these fell in a dressing-room off Sir Claude's bedroom, and made a complete wreck of it.' A. H. Smith, *China in Convulsion* (London, 1901), II, p. 428.

17 'By the later nineteenth century', Dr Seal tells us, 'some 179 separate languages and 544 dialects had been identified, which were in turn grouped into fifteen main literary languages belonging to five or six distinct families, with differences in structure, vocabulary and script,' (*The Emergence of Indian Nationalism*, p. 30).

18 The famous settlement undertaken by Lord Cornwallis, for example, tended to reduce Muslim farmers to the level of agricultural labourers, while allowing Hindus to thrive at their expense.

19 A case was reported, though, as recently as 1980.

20 q. J. Rosselli, *Lord William Bentinck*, p. 211.

21 Seal, p. 17.

22 C. E. Trevelyan, q. Judith Brown, *Modern India*, p. 75. Brother-in-law of Macaulay and Governor of Madras, he was a deeply evangelical Christian, described by Bentinck as 'the ablest young man in the service and the most noble-minded man he had ever seen' (q. Rosselli, p. 188).

23 See G. O. Trevelyan, *Life and Letters of Macaulay* (London, 1876).

24 Dr Seal has some telling figures, pp. 85–6 and 302.

25 G. O. Trevelyan, nephew of Macaulay and himself later a distinguished historian, visited India in 1863, at the age of twenty-five, recording his impressions in a series of magazine articles, printed a year later as a book, *The Competition Wallah*, which made his name. The quotations are taken from a second edition of 1866, p. 311.

26 James Fitzjames Stephen, in a letter to *The Times*, 1 March 1883.

27 Seal, p. 3.

28 See, e.g. Surendranath Banerjee's autobiography *A Nation in the Making* (Oxford, 1925), a view of India through the filter of liberal ideas, as a nation to be made by working through British political principles.

29 q. Ved Mehta, *Mahatma Gandhi and his Apostles,* (London, 1977), p. 101.

30 See, e.g. Bishop Heber's note about a popular response at Benares to the disturbance by the British government of certain tax privileges in the 1820s. *Bishop Heber in Northern India*, p. 150.

31 q. Fischer, p. 59.

32 Seal, p. 196.

33 q. Brown, p. 76.

34 q. Rosselli, p. 194.

35 Seal, p. 196.

36 Lal Malam Ghose, q. Brown, p. 150.

37 Dr Seal prints (p. 147) a revealing remark by a British official in 1878: 'With the last . . . 20 years . . . a feeling of nationality, which formerly had no existence . . . has grown up, and the . . . Press can now, for the first time in the history of our rule, appeal to the *whole Native population* of India against their foreign rulers. Twenty years ago . . . we had to take account of local nationalities and particular races . . . *Now* . . . we have changed all that. . . .'

38 Both were Parsees educated at Elphinstone College, Bombay. The first was Dabadhai Naoroji, elected as Liberal Member for Central Finsbury in 1892. In 1895 Mancherjee Bhownaggree became Conservative Member for Bethnal Green, N.E. He was also the translator into Gujarati of the Queen's book, *Our Life in the Highlands*.

39 Seal, p. 246.

40 Presidential address at Lucknow Congress Session, April 1936; q. D. Norman (ed.), *Nehru: The First Sixty Years* (London, 1965), I, p. 433.

41 J. D. Spence, *The Gate of Heavenly Peace* (1980), p. 131, says that Mao's essay appeared in 1917 in the journal *New Growth*.

42 In this paragraph I have drawn on the excellent article by Dr J. Rosselli, 'Physical education and nationalism in nineteenth-century Bengal', *Past and Present*, 1980, which contains much other interesting information. The fascinating chapter in the history of the influence of the West which is provided by the Boy Scout movement still awaits its historians, it can be further remarked.

43 q. Fischer, p. 225.

44 As Dr Seal so stimulatingly puts it, 'Like a croupier, the Raj made contracts with one player after another; but as the one turned aside, the next always made his way to the table,' p. 349.

45 See A. Lamb, *Asian Frontiers* (London, 1968), pp. 110–17.

46 Jawaharlal Nehru, *Toward Freedom*, q. Norman, I, p. 351. The signs were there a long time before. Congress in the 1890s had overwhelmingly reflected the views of westernised Indians, but when the Indian government put forward an Age of Consent Bill in 1891, with the aim of preventing child marriage, Congress opposed it; its members could not cut themselves off from their orthodox Hindu origins.

47 The parallels, in fact, go deeper. The politics of modern India are just as focused on place, profit and persons as were those of Walpole's England. 'All these men have their price' must surely have been a thought that often recurred to Mrs Gandhi. Indian newspapers are filled with reports of elections and ministerial changes, but singularly lack statements of policy. Even the plea for local autonomy, too, was represented by Mrs Gandhi as the treason of those who desire to break up the Union — just as eighteenth-century Whigs succeeded in tarring Tories with the Jacobite brush.

XII A Sense of Decline

1 The wars of the Ottoman Succession (1911–22), the Sino-Japanese War of 1937–45, the Pacific War of 1941–45.

2 East Germany 1953, Hungary 1956, Czechoslovakia 1968, Poland 1982. In Paris in 1968, on the other hand, the workers stood aside.

3 W. T. Stead.

4 See Sarraut q. in Christopher M. Andrew and A. S. Kanya-Forstner, *France Overseas: The Great War and the Climax of French Imperial Expansion* (London, 1981), p. 242.

5 The Treaty of Portsmouth (New Hampshire) which, incidentally, ignored the fact that the Russians and Japanese had done all their land fighting on Chinese territory.

6 And elsewhere: Storry points out (pp. 84–5) that Sun-Yat-sen was impressed by the joy Egyptians showed over the Japanese victory and the French Governor-General of Madagascar thought a revolt there was in part the effect of Japan's example.

7 See the comments by a junior minister, Hayashi Tadasu, quoted by R. Storry, *Japan and the Decline of the West in Asia 1894–1943* (London, 1979), p. 30.

8 The importance of the moral element in Japan's strategy appears in the official commentary on the Imperial Declaration of War in 1941. 'The various races of Asia', it stated, 'look upon the British and Americans as superior to the Nippon race . . . We must show our real strength before all our fellow-races of East Asia. We must show them an object lesson. It is not a lesson in words. It should be a lesson in facts. In other words, before we can expel the Anglo-Saxons . . . from East Asia, we must annihilate them.' q. E. Wilkinson, *Japan versus Europe: A History of Misunderstanding* (Harmondsworth, 1983), p. 122.

9 As E. Abrahamian points out in his *Iran between Two Revolutions* (Princeton, 1982), p. 536, the Shah's land reform drove peasants into urban slums where the mosque and mullah were eagerly accepted as substitutes for the old community sense of the villages as a focus and reassurance.

10 e.g. the puritan Wahabist movement of eighteenth-century Arabia, from which is descended the official ideology of modern Saudi Arabia, itself under challenge from more vigorous schools.

11 See, e.g. *CHC*, X, 1, p. 407.

12 q. M. Rodinson, *Islam and Capitalism* (Harmondsworth, 1977), p. 12. I have found this book of great help and suggestiveness.

13 Seal, p. 317. Founding the Anglo-Oriental college at Aligarh (it opened in 1875) was the first of Syed's efforts, teaching Muslim students in English.

14 It is said that when he was asked what he found most attractive about them, he replied 'Availability'.

15 q. H. C. Armstrong, *Grey Wolf* (London, 1937), p. 205.

16 'In 1878, Prince Otto von Bismarck, who shared the habit of most of his European contemporaries of thinking of the Ottomans as "Turks" and as Asiatic, Muslim and backward, was surprised to find that the Ottoman delegation to the Congress of Berlin was headed by Karatodori Pasha, an Orthodox Greek, and Mehemed Ali Pasha, a native of the city of Magdeburg, not far from Bismarck's own estate of Schönhausen' (*The Mutual Effects of the Islamic and Judeo-Christian Worlds: the East European Pattern*, ed. A. Ascher *et al.*, p. 65).

17 e.g. from a recent publication by a Tanzanian Muslim. 'With the emergence of Mustafa Kemal in the political arena in Turkey, a stage was set to fling overboard Islam and Islamic heritage and values and establish a secular state. Rezakhan Pahlavi, a soldier in the Iranian army, another imperialist puppet usurped power and followed suit. There followed a barrage of attack on Islamic values, from the western oriented elite decrying Islam as medieval, old-fashioned, anti-science and reactionary.' F. A.

Hamelt, 'Iranian Islamic Revolution from my viewpoint', in a collection of essays with the same title, published in 1982 by the International Educational Department, Isfahan University, Iran.

18 Though his reputation is undergoing rehabilitation in Pakistan where (according to the *International Herald Tribune*, 19 July 1982) a contest was held for an official portrait of Jinnah wearing Pakistani dress instead of the western clothes he preferred.

19 V. S. Naipaul, *Among the Believers* (London, 1981), p. 19. See also p. 158.

XIII A POST-WESTERN WORLD?

1 So easily is righteous indignation aroused on such matters that it is worthwhile pointing out that not only western forces have casually and unwittingly transformed the economies of other parts of the world in historical times, but that Islam revolutionised the economy of El-Andalus, and in East Africa the Arab introduction of cloves and bananas shares with the huge Arab-controlled slave trade the responsibility for a huge economic transformation.

2 J. Halliday and G. McCormack, *Japanese Imperialism Today* (Harmondsworth, 1973), p. 20.

3 See *The Economist*, 9–15 July 1983. For a further comment on Japanese youth, see Wilkinson, p. 138.

4 The three-month reappearance in 1916 of an 'emperor' who was the major military leader of the 1911 revolution, and had succeeded Sun-Yat-sen as President of the new republic in 1912, Yuan Shih-k'ai, hardly invalidates this summary statement.

5 The eventual rejection of the Treaty by the Americans also owed something to the terms affecting China.

6 Wilkinson, pp. 108–9, who also quotes a Japanese scholar of the early Meiji era: 'Magna Carta was circulated in facsimile reprints; the name of Rousseau was repeated as if it were [that of] a saviour; Patrick Henry was well known to many, and his words "Give me liberty, or give me death", became a slogan.' Samuel Smiles was to remain an important influence long after his vogue waned in the West.

7 See Seizaburo Sato, 'Japan's World Order', in *Modern Japan. An interpretive* (sic) *Anthology*, ed. I. Scheiner (New York, 1974).

8 C. R. Boxer, 'European Missionaries and Chinese Clergy', p. 103.

9 In 1964 I visited a temple in Bengal where pedlars at the gate sold little tin triptychs with pictures of Gandhi, Christ — and J. F. Kennedy.

' 10 For an interesting personal example, see the case of Yen Fu, whose entry to the School of Navigation in Foochow in the 1860s introduced him to the methods and data of the natural sciences, the cause of his later enthusiasm for Western science. See B. Schwartz, *In Search of Wealth and Power*, p. 27. Professor Schwartz has also some interesting remarks about the connexion of such 'practical' studies with the awakening of more general critical responses (p. 28).

11 Personal information.

12 See the report by Jonathan Mirsky, 'Infanticide in the one-child, one-party state', which contains other interesting facts, in *The Times*, March 1983, and a report of the Seventh Women's Congress of Beijing municipality in *China Daily*, 4 April 1983.

13 So far as the broader context of leisure is relevant, this, too, involves changes too often underrated. See, *passim*, H. Cunningham, *Leisure in the Industrial Revolution* (London, 1980).

14 A. Mazuri, in *The Listener*, 22 November 1979.

15 There is much to follow up here, not least in the standardisation of notions of sexual attractiveness the world round increasingly reflected in women's hairstyles, make-up, posture, clothes. Having made the point about Japan, the sociologist Hiroshi Wagatsuma comments ('The Social Perception of Skin Color in Japan', *Daedalus*, 1967) that 'physical attractiveness is gradually losing its unitary cultural or racial basis in most societies'. Any visitor can see this almost the world round by looking at advertisement hoardings or the windows of photographic studios (always a rich stimulus for speculation by social historians).

16 The eighteenth century, helped by Bentham, also invented the idea that happiness can be measured.

INDEX

newspapers, 237
Newton, Isaac (1642–
1727), British scientist,
161, 162
'New World': concept of,
126; discovery of, 126;
European settlement
of, 136–137
Nicaea, Council of (325),
45
nineteenth century: be-
lief in progress, 173,
200, 209, 287; indus-
trialisation, 177–178,
180; missionary activ-
ity, 205–206; technical
change, 280
Normans, 84; in Byzan-
tium, 90; in England,
84–85; in Sicily, 86–87,
88, 91–92
Norsemen, 84
North, Frederick, Lord
(1732–92), British
prime minister, 197
North Atlantic Treaty
Organization (NATO),
249
Novgorod, 107, 108, 112
nuclear power, 178
nuclear weapons, 249,
255

O

oil, importance to west-
ern economies, 152,
265, 269–270
Olga (d. c. 969), Kievan
princess, 105
opium, 'Opium Wars',
221–222, 227
Organisation of African
Unity, 28
Orthodox churches:
Greek, 86; relations
with state, 100–101;
schism with papacy,
102, 109
Ostrogoths, 47
Otto I 'the Saxon' (912–

973), Holy Roman
Emperor (936–973),
63
Ottoman empire: 'capitu-
lations' of, 195–196;
characteristics of, 202–
203; collapse of, 188,
247, 258–259, 260,
263; in First World
War, 263
Ottonians, 63
Outremer, 89, 90–91

P

Pacific War, 275
Pakistan: foundation of,
241–242; Islamic fun-
damentalism, 264
Palermo, 85–86, 91
Palestinians, 191
Pan-Africanism, 28
Panama, 137
Panama canal, 248
Pantheon, Rome, 46
Papacy: bureaucracy, 69;
in Dark Ages, 55; rela-
tions with Frankish
monarchs, 62–63;
struggle over Investi-
ture Contest, 67–68
Papal States, 62
Paris Commune (1871),
185
Paris Peace Conference
(1919), 188, 252
parliament: English
model, 77; in non-
western countries, 19,
187, 205
Paul, St (d. c. 67), Christian apostle: martyr-
dom in Rome, 48, 62;
teachings of, 42–43, 72
Peking, 227–228, 275;
Summer Palace, 223–
224, 272
Penn, William (1644–
1718), English quaker,
150
Perry, Matthew (1794–

1858), US naval offi-
cer, 16, 20–21
Persia: independence,
197; Sassanid rule, 81–
82; struggle with
Greeks, 38; war with
Russia, 257–258. See
also Iran
Peru, 138
Peter, St (d. c. 67), Christian apostle, 48, 62
Peter I 'the Great' (1672–
1725), tsar of Russia
(1682–1725), 99; mod-
ernises Russia, 25;
moves Russian capital
to St Petersburg, 115
Philip II (1527–98), king
of Spain (1556–98),
136
Philippines: acquired by
US, 199; independ-
ence, 252
Pilate, Pontius (1st cen-
tury), Roman procura-
tor of Judaea (26–36),
42
Pilgrim Fathers, 148
Pitt, William (1708–78),
earl of Chatham, Brit-
ish prime minister, 197
Pizarro, Francisco
(c. 1475–1541), Span-
ish conquistador, 138
Pizarro, Gonzalo (c.
1505–48), Spanish con-
quistador, 138
plagues, 74, 145, 170–171
Plassey, battle of (1757),
196
Plato (c. 428–c. 348 BC),
Greek philosopher, 39,
43
pluralism, 51, 69, 72
Plymouth Plantation, 148
Poitiers (Tours), battle of
(732), 83
Poland: conversion to
Christianity, 105; na-
tionalism, 188; after
First World War, 247

1945
BdS